Law School Admission Test

by ALFRED J. CANDRILLI, J.D., M.B.A.
and ALBERT A. SLAWSKY, J.D.

 arco 219 Park Avenue South
New York, N.Y. 10003

The authors would like to thank Vada Patterson, Ezra
Black, Joyce Obolsky, Gary Kleinman, and the staff and
students of Academic Review Center Limited.

First Edition B-3272
Second Printing, 1978

Published by ARCO PUBLISHING COMPANY, INC.
219 Park Avenue South, New York, N.Y. 10003

Library of Congress Cataloging in Publication Data

Candrilli, Alfred J
  LSAT : law school admission test.

  (Arco professional career examination series)
  1. Law schools—United States—Entrance examinations.
I. Slawsky, Albert A., joint author. II. Title.
III. Title: Law school admission test.
KF285.Z9C36   340'.076   78-4630
ISBN 0-668-03946-9

Printed in the United States of America

CONTENTS

HOW TO USE THIS INDEX
Slightly bend the right-hand edge of the book. This will expose the corresponding Parts which match the index, below.

PART

1

2

PART ONE
SUBJECTS ON WHICH YOU
ARE LIKELY TO BE TESTED

...continued on next page

CONTENTS continued

PART

1

2

PART TWO
FIVE SAMPLE EXAMS WITH COMPLETE EXPLANATIONS

ALL ABOUT THE TEST

A great deal depends on your examination score, as you know. And this book will help you achieve your highest possible score. You'll get plenty of practice with relevant test subjects and questions. But first we want you to pick up a few facts about the test which may make things easier for you. Forgive us if some of these facts seem self-evident. Our experience has shown that this kind of information is sometimes overlooked . . . to the candidate's detriment.

WHAT IS THE LSAT?

The Law School Admission Test is a standardized test administered to all law school candidates in an attempt to measure those mental capabilities which past experience has shown to be important to the study of law. The questions are designed to evaluate the candidate's ability to reason in verbal and quantitative terms, to use standard written English correctly and effectively, and to think logically.

IS THE LSAT REALLY NECESSARY?

Students often say that there is no need for a Law School Admission Test because the law schools can always look at the students' grade point average. True! But grade point averages can differ not only from school to school, but also from major to major within the same school. Because the LSAT presents every student with an equally difficult problem, it provides a common means for comparing students with widely varying academic backgrounds.

When considering candidates for acceptance, most law schools tend to put more weight on G.P.A.s than LSAT scores. However, the weight given to each of these indicators is up to the individual law school.

WHAT DO THE SCORES MEAN?

The LSAT is not an I.Q. test. It is a test which measures certain aptitudes which the Educational Testing Service claims reflect a person's ability to do well in law school.

It is the firm belief of the authors of this book that whatever aptitude the LSAT is supposed to be testing, no one can be measured properly on the first brush with this exam. There are many outside factors, such as unfamiliarity with the type of questions, anxiety, etc., which tend to lower that first test score.

CAN YOU RAISE YOUR LSAT SCORE?

We believe you certainly can. In fact, each time you take the LSAT your score should go up until you finally reach a leveling off point. When you reach this point, you will have achieved your *true test score,* which is the score that measures your natural ability when all possible distracting factors are removed.

Since law schools do not look favorably upon multiple LSAT scores, it is neither practical nor wise to take the LSAT time after time in order to achieve your true test score. That's where this book can help. It will provide all the practice and preparation you need to achieve the highest possible LSAT score.

To get the greatest help from this self-tutor, you must follow all instructions to the letter, adhere strictly to the time limits given, and take each Sample Test as though it were the actual LSAT.

Law School Admission Test

TEST TAKING TECHNIQUES

Although a thorough knowledge of the subject matter is the most important factor in succeeding on your exam, the following suggestions could raise your score substantially. These few pointers will give you the strategy employed on tests by those who are most successful in this not-so-mysterious art.

1. *Prepare Yourself Physically.* Chess masters often prepare for tournaments by doing roadwork or hitting punching bags. Why? Because they know that being in good physical condition is essential to doing well at mental tasks. So it goes for test-taking too.

The night before you take the LSAT, get about the same amount of sleep you usually get. Don't stay up too late partying or worrying, and don't try to put yourself to sleep with drugs or alcohol. Either approach will result in dulling your mental responses on test day.

If you wear glasses, make sure you have them with you when you go to the test center. If you have a physical problem that may keep you from doing your best on test day, consider postponing the test to a later date. Keep in mind, however, that each law school sets a deadline for the acceptance of completed applications and you must get your score in on time.

2. *Take Advantage of the "Testing Effect."* Studies prove that people who have been exposed to a particular type of test consistently score higher than people who are taking that type of test for the first time. This phenomenon is known as the "testing effect," and it can be used to your advantage. In fact, people who have taken the LSAT twice have shown an average rise of 42 points from the first to the second score. This rise in test scores is caused not by additional study, but merely by gaining familiarity with the types of questions and the way in which they are asked. By taking the tests in this book, you should be able to achieve a similar testing effect. Except in this case a low score on one of the tests cannot hurt you as a low score may on the actual LSAT. Look upon a low score as something to be learned from and improved upon, not as something to be worried about.

The LSAT should test your real ability, but it won't do so the first time you take it. The more often you take verisimilar LSATs, the more you will be able to eliminate outside influences and the higher your score will be.

3. *Follow Directions To The Letter.* Become familiar with the directions given in this book. They're probably quite like the ones you'll get on your exam. On the other hand, don't assume that you can skip over the directions on the LSAT just because you have seen this type of question before. There is always the chance that the directions may be different on the test you take.

Pay particularly close attention to the time allotments for each test. If you fall behind in time, you will not finish the test and the resulting increase in tension may affect your performance.

4. *Practice Using Answer Sheets.* Mark all your responses to the Sample Exams on the special tear-out answer sheets provided. This will give you valuable practice for the actual exam. Selecting the correct answer for each question is only the first step toward your goal of scoring high. The next step is recording that answer in the right spot on the answer sheet.

Check your answer sheet after every tenth response to make certain that you have not made a mistake in numbering. Going back to correct a string of misnumbered answers wastes time and heightens tension.

5. *Do Not Hesitate to Change An Answer If You Feel That You Should.* Many studies have shown that the percentage of changes from wrong answers to right answers far exceeds the number of changes from right answers to wrong answers. However, do not bother changing your answers more than once. If you have to change an answer more than once, you probably have no idea at all which answer is correct and you will be better off making the kind of educated guess described below.

6. *Choose Your Answers Strategically.* In answering multiple-choice questions, first read all the choices carefully. Then eliminate those choices which you know are incorrect and select your answer from the remaining alternatives. By eliminating the obviously wrong answers, the probability of your answering the question correctly increases greatly.

Sometimes certain options will imply the correctness of each other. In other words, if one option is correct, the other will also be correct and vice versa. In this case, neither one can be correct. Since there is only one answer for each question, both options can be eliminated.

You can also eliminate those options which would be true if something else which you are not told is also true. The LSAT does not expect you to use your outside knowledge, but merely to answer each question based on the information stated or implied.

It is usually best to select an option which resembles an aspect of the question such as a name or a phrase repeated in both question and answer. In any case, this strategy is an excellent means of guessing and usually results in correct answers. You should also look for correct alternatives which are longer and more specific than other possibly correct alternatives. In any one group of answers where more than one answer is correct, you must select the one that is most precise.

Sometimes a question has certain grammatical clues which are similar to the grammatical clues in the correct answer. Be aware of such clues and also of other questions in the exam that can suggest the answer to the question at hand. Incorrect items often tend to be more absolute than correct items. Be wary of choices which include the words, "all," "none," "everyone," "nobody," etc.

7. *Make Notes Effectively.* When you are reading a passage on which you will have to answer questions later, by all means take notes and underline. Although you are not allowed to bring scrap paper into the examination center with you when you take the LSAT, you are free to make notes in the test booklet itself.

There is a right way and a wrong way to take notes on what you read. The wrong way is to jot down a note in the margin everytime you see something you think might be of future interest. The right way to take notes is to make, in effect, a grocery list.

When you make a list of items to buy before going to a store, you are doing a certain type of organization. Often, when you are at the store, you can remember all the items on your list without having to refer to it. The reason for this is that the information has been imprinted not only on the paper, but also in your brain. Similarly, by taking notes on reading passages, you will find that you are better able to recall the facts than you would be if you had not made notes. This is especially true of the reading recall test where you must answer the questions without referring to the reading.

Remember that your "grocery list" should include major factors, topic sentences, key dates, important persons and other essential items. It should not include minor factors or details which will merely add to the complexity of your list without giving you any more useable information.

On the referrent reading section where you may look back at the passages to find the answers to the questions, your notes should be even more abbreviated. They should serve as an index to help you locate the appropriate portion of the reading passage quickly and easily. Here it will probably be most useful to merely underline main points. The key to both underlining and note taking is not to do too much of either.

8. *Keep Test Anxiety at Bay.* Before you answer a question, you should try to recall all the relevant information you have amassed. However, there comes a point when you are not recalling any more information and you seem to have done all the reasoning or pondering possible. Usually, at this point, one response seems to "make sense." At the least, one answer seems somewhat better than the others. It is very important to become aware of and learn to stop at this point when your own judgment tells you that a response makes sense, either because you recall the correct answer, or arrive at a conclusion, or perhaps because you have a strong feeling that one answer is right. At this point you are getting a type of feedback from your own thinking processes. Usually, this feedback is correct. Almost always (i.e., except in those situations that call for trained guessing), it is your best bet. Test anxiety can interfere with this process because it may force you to focus your attention on yourself rather than on the question at hand. It may also generate useless worries and doubts about your certainty or your ability to understand the question. Do not let these thoughts trouble you, but read instead the chapter dealing with test anxiety.

WHAT TO DO ABOUT TEST ANXIETY

Anxiety can be used to advantage in taking tests. All it takes is learning to channel the nervous energy produced outward toward the task at hand rather than inward where it results in tension, worry, and self-doubt. This chapter will show you how to recognize and deal with test anxiety.

Most people are nervous when they take tests. Indeed, a certain amount of tension is necessary to help you do your best. For nervousness is simply the physical manifestation of the process by which your body prepares to meet the challenge ahead of you. However, it is important not to let feelings of anxiety distract you from turning in the best possible performance on your test.

Test-anxious people tend to be self-oriented. They worry about how well (or poorly) they are doing, how tense they are, how quickly time is passing and similar non-productive things which hinder rather than help their test-taking. In fact, test-anxious people consistently perform less well on cognitive tasks under test conditions than do less anxious people.

While taking the Sample Exams in this book, try to keep your attention focused on what you are doing, not on yourself. Whenever you find you are thinking about yourself, stop work and relax until you can resume thinking solely about the test. In the beginning you may have to stop for long periods of time. However, as you progress you will be able to put your anxiety aside more and more quickly. Eventually, you should be able to stop momentarily, take a deep breath, and return to the test questions with all distractions put out of mind.

HOW TO AVOID ANXIETY AT THE EXAM

The best way to avoid test anxiety is to know what to expect. The five Sample Exams that follow will do much to familiarize you with the test and so keep anxiety to a minimum.

On the day of your test, be sure to allow ample time to get to the test center. Arrive early enough to look around and settle yourself comfortably before the test begins. Be sure to pick your test center wisely because they vary greatly. Some centers are as quiet as a library, while others echo with sounds from a nearby highway or football field.

Listen carefully to all directions given by the proctor and, if you have any questions, by all means ask them. It will not help to act competent if you are not.

Wear a watch and pace yourself so that you answer as many questions as possible on each section of the exam. Work as quickly and accurately as you can. Since all questions have the same weight, it is best to answer the ones which are easier for you first. Don't waste too much time on any one question, but rather go on to others which may be less difficult for you.

Do not answer a question if you have no idea of the right answer; leave it blank and come back to it if you have time at the end of the section. If at that time you can make an intelligent guess for any question, which means that you are able to eliminate some choices as definitely wrong, then do so. If, however, you still have no idea of the answers to the questions you skipped, then pick one letter, such as "B," and fill in all the blank spaces on your answer sheet with that letter. Remember to use only one letter, because depending on which section it is, you will still have a 20 to 25 percent chance of getting the answer correct.

ANXIETY CHECKLIST

The following checklist will help you recognize the signs of test anxiety. Rate yourself now, then track your progress in overcoming these distracting tendencies as you prepare to take the Law School Admission Test.

(Circle one)

	NONE	A LITTLE	A FAIR AMOUNT	MUCH	VERY MUCH
1. Feeling of physical or muscular tension during study or test periods.	1	2	(3)	4	5
2. Difficulty in remembering material on exams.	1	2	(3)	4	5
3. Difficulty in thinking during tests: organizing answers, reasoning, solving problems, etc.	1	2	(3)	4	5
4. Heavy sweating, for example, of the palms or face.	1	(2)	3	4	5
5. Difficulty comprehending fairly simple sentences or instructions.	(1)	2	3	4	5
6. Disturbing, panicky feeling of not having enough time to finish.	1	(2)	3	4	5
7. Thoughts of being inadequate, a poor student, stupid, "no good," etc.	(1)	2	3	4	5

	NONE	A LITTLE	A FAIR AMOUNT	MUCH	VERY MUCH
8. Rapid breathing or difficulty in breathing.	1	(2)	3	4	5
9. Rapid or pounding heartbeat.	1	(2)	3	4	5
10. Feelings of anxiety, fearfulness, or panic before or during tests.	1	(2)	3	4	5
11. Inability to select alternatives in a multiple-choice item.	1	(2)	3	4	5
12. Thinking processes that become very slow and labored.	1	(2)	3	4	5
13. Thinking processes that become more rapid but unclear or inaccurate.	1	(2)	3	4	5
14. Trembling during tests.	(1)	2	3	4	5
15. Thoughts or fantasies about disapproval, punishment, or humiliation that will follow if you do poorly on the test.	(1)	2	3	4	5
16. Self-critical and self-condemning thoughts during tests.	(1)	2	3	4	5
17. Disruption of patterns of eating or sleeping before exams.	1	(2)	3	4	5
18. Worrying about how well you are doing on the test.	1	(2)	3	4	5
19. Worrying about how well you are doing in relation to others on the test.	(1)	2	3	4	5
20. Headaches before or during tests.	(1)	2	3	4	5
21. Difficulty in focusing attention or concentrating on the test.	(1)	2	3	4	5
22. Feelings of pessimism, fatalism, or helplessness about the outcome of the test.	(1)	2	3	4	5

	NONE	A LITTLE	A FAIR AMOUNT	MUCH	VERY MUCH
23. Losing confidence in your ability or judgment in answering a question.	1	2	3	4	5
24. Being preoccupied with nervous bodily reactions (like sweating).	1	2	3	4	5
25. Difficulty in sleeping before exams.	1	2	3	4	5
26. Nausea before or during tests.	1	2	3	4	5
27. Making mistakes on very simple matters, e.g., adding 9 and 3 and getting 11.	1	2	3	4	5

Be assured that these symptoms of anxiety in testing situations are not abnormal or strange. They are the kinds of reactions most people experience when they are under stress. As you have probably noticed, these feelings (including the irrational thoughts) disappear when the test is over and the situation changes. It is possible to learn to control anxiety of this kind when you know how to go about it.

WHAT TO DO TO RELIEVE ANXIETY

In most study and test situations when you notice yourself becoming tense or anxious, you can effectively relax (and diminish tension) by taking a very deep breath, holding it for two or three seconds, and then letting it out very slowly. Usually it is best to repeat this deep-breathing exercise several times. There is good evidence that such deep-breathing has the effect of directly slowing down your heart rate and reducing accompanying anxiety. Here's how it's done:

1. *Take your attention completely away from the test (or studying) for 20 to 30 seconds.* The few seconds involved will cost you little and they may gain you much. It is important to forget the test for the moment.

2. *Settle back or slump into a comfortable and relaxing position and close your eyes.* Do not try to do this breathing exercise in anything but the most comfortable position you can quickly assume.

3. *Relax every muscle in your body.* Just let go and make yourself as floppy as a rag doll. Some people help this along by first tensing all their muscles in the comfortable position they have assumed, holding the tension for about five seconds, and then letting go and relaxing completely.

4. *This is the most important step of all.* After you have let go and relaxed completely, take a very deep breath, hold it for a few seconds, then very slowly let it out. Repeat this step two or three times, keeping your eyes closed.

5. *You can deepen the relaxation and help ease tension by repeating to yourself the words "calm" and "relax" as you slowly exhale.* Practice relaxing and deep-breathing while you study and before your test so that you become adept at the technique and can relax quickly and completely during the test.

Stated more briefly, the important steps are:

1. Forget about the test.
2. Get comfortable.
3. Relax all muscles.
4. Take slow, deep breaths.
5. Think "calm" and "relax."

The key to this procedure is to relax all over and take several slow, deep breaths. If it helps, you can adjust the rest of the procedure to make it work better for you. It is very important to practice this exercise while sitting at a table or desk because that is the way you will have to do it when you take your test.

One of the real problems with tension is that you are often unaware you are tense until it is too late to do anything about it. Knowing how to relax will greatly increase your awareness of what the states of tension and relaxation feel like and this, in turn, will make it possible for you to stop and loosen up before your tension gets too great.

An important advantage of this relaxation technique is that it gives you something to do when you feel tense. By intentionally doing something different, you take your mind off the tension and so reduce it automatically. Also, this relaxation process is directly incompatible with *increasing* tension and anxiety. To the degree that you can relax like this, anxiety and tension must decrease. It is like coming to a fork in the road—you can go one way or the other, but not both. By developing the skill of relaxing through slow, deep breathing you can choose the more desirable road (i.e., behavior route) and thus rule out traveling the other.

PART ONE

Subjects On Which You Are Likely To Be Tested

EXAM FORECAST

In writing this book, we examined all available announcements and official statements about the exam, and thus predict that this is what you may face. Since examiners like to experiment with various types of questions the subjects tested and times allotted may vary from test to test. However, we feel certain that if you have touched on each of the subjects covered here, you will be well on your way to scoring high

The LSAT is a three and one-half hour exam designed to measure your capacity to read, understand, reason and express yourself both verbally and quantitatively. These skills are rated by a variety of separately timed tests which cover a broad range of disciplines in order to afford equal opportunity to all candidates regardless of their individual areas of specialization.

Although the LSAT uses many different types of questions to assess your ability to do well in law school, any one form of the test will consist of some, but not all, of the following question categories.

1.   READING COMPREHENSION. A 30-minute test which includes four passages of 500 to 1000 words each and approximately 25 questions about the readings.

2.   READING RECALL. A 30-minute test in which you are given 15 minutes to read three or four passages, absorbing as much information as possible, and then 15 minutes to answer 25 to 30 questions about the readings without looking back at them.

3.   DATA INTERPRETATION. A 30-minute test of approximately 25 questions based upon the information presented in 4 or 5 graphs, charts or tables.

4.   QUANTITATIVE COMPARISON. A 15-minute test consisting of 25 mathematical comparisons in which you must determine the relationship that exists between two given quantities. Are they equal? Is one greater than the other? Or is the information given insufficient to establish any relationship?

5.   PRINCIPLES AND CASES. A 40 -minute test of about 30 questions which involve applying given principles to specific cases or determining the reasoning which underlies the decisions of the court as indicated for a variety of cases.

6.   LOGICAL REASONING. A 20-minute test of approximately 15 to 20 questions which require you to read brief passages and then analyze, interpret, criticize or draw conclusions from them.

7.   PRACTICAL JUDGMENT. A 45-minute test which presents two long and highly detailed case studies of practical business situations and then poses questions which require you to evaluate, classify and apply the data given.

8.   ERROR RECOGNITION. A 20-minute test of approximately 35 questions in which you must demonstrate your ability to distinguish between well- and poorly-written sentences and to recognize errors in diction, verbosity or grammar.

9.   SENTENCE CORRECTION. A 20-minute test of 25 questions which indicate your ability to recognize the most correct and effective way to express a particular thought.

On the pages that follow we provide explanations of the various question types which are likely to be new to you and helpful hints on handling each of them. Later on, in the Sample Exams, you will get plenty of practice with these and every other type of question commonly asked on the LSAT.

READING COMPREHENSION

It is essential that you read both quickly and carefully to do well on your test. For this reason, we suggest several different techniques to increase your reading speed and sharpen your ability to comprehend what you read. Try a variety of approaches during your practice sessions, then choose the one that is most comfortable for you when you actually take the exam.

The Reading Comprehension Test is designed to measure your ability to read and analyze difficult passages drawn from a variety of disciplines. The reading passages are chosen from the humanities, social science and science to ensure that all candidates have an equal opportunity to do well on the test regardless of their major field of study. The questions following each passage may ask you to demonstrate your comprehension of the sense of what you have read, they may require you to make a reasonable application of the principles or opinions stated, or they may test your ability to evaluate the strengths or weaknesses of the author's argument.

DOS AND DON'TS FOR SCORING HIGH ON READING TESTS

Do Read, Read, Read! The best way to increase your reading speed is to read. Read everything in sight between now and the test. Newspaper reading is an especially good way to improve your reading skills. Don't be satisfied with just the opening paragraph of each article. Push yourself to read the whole story and give it your full attention as you read. If your mind wanders, you will not comprehend what you read.

Don't Regress. The average college student regresses (i.e., rereads words) nine times out of every one hundred words. Since the average reading passage on the LSAT is 500 to 1000 words long, that means the average student will look over what he has already read 45 to 90 times during each reading passage! Just think of all that wasted time which could have been used to move ahead and get a higher score on the test.

Do Expand Your Peripheral Vision. You have probably heard about speed readers who can race down a page, consuming it almost instantaneously. Unfortunately, that technique works for very few people. To read with understanding your eyes must fixate (i.e., stop). Most people fixate on each word because that is the way reading is taught. However, this method wastes a great deal of time.

The key to increasing your reading speed is to take in more words each time your eyes stop. If a line has ten words in it and you are able to read the line by stopping only twice instead of ten times, you would be reading five times as fast as you do now. For example, if you are now reading at about 200 words per minute, by stopping only twice per line you would increase your speed to 1000 words per minute.

Don't Subvocalize. If you can hear every word you read, you are subvocalizing. No matter how fast you can talk, you can read faster if you stop subvocalizing. Reading teachers have employed many tricks to stop people from subvocalizing. They may ask students to put pebbles in their mouths or to chew on pencils. We ask only that you be aware that you may be subvocalizing. Reading is a very psychological thing; if you become aware of your bad habits, you may be able to correct them.

Do Become Aware of Words. You cannot build a good vocabulary in a day or even a week. However, you can increase your knowledge of words by stopping to look up each new word you run across and by systematic study of those prefixes, suffixes and roots which make up the greater part of the English language.

Do Keep Your Interest High. There are three types of reading passages on the LSAT: science, social science and humanities. You should be able to develop an interest in all three of these areas. The one factor that may lower more people's scores than anything else is boredom. Do not allow yourself to think, "I don't understand science," or "I don't like humanities." For the sake of getting into law school, for just three hours one Saturday morning, tell yourself that the LSAT is the most interesting and exciting test you have ever taken. If you are interested in something, you will read it faster and understand it better.

Do Use Your Hand. Here is a simple technique for you to try: when you read, move your hand or your pen underneath the line you are reading. Because your eyes tend to move as quickly as your pen, you will not stop on every word, you will not regress, and you probably will not subvocalize. However, what you may do is concentrate on your pen and not on the reading passage. That is why you must practice this technique before using it on your test.

Start your pen at the second or third word in the line and stop it before the last word in the line. Your peripheral vision will pick up the first and last words in the lines and you will save time by not having to focus on them.

Do Try the SQ2R Method. The SQ2R method of reading was developed by the government during World War II in an attempt to advance men to officer rank as quickly as possible. The method used may be helpful to you and so it is presented here.

1. Before you read, scan the material (S). On the LSAT scanning a typical reading passage should take about 30 seconds. Once you have scanned the passage, you should be aware of the type of passage you are about to read (Is it science, humanities, social science?) and the logical structure of the passage.

2.   Scanning the passage should bring questions to mind (Q).

3.   Now read the passage (R1), trying to answer your own questions. By using this question and answer method you will become involved in what you are reading and consequently you will remember more of it. As you read, stop briefly at the end of each paragraph and think about what you have read. If you cannot remember what you have read, reread the paragraph immediately. Don't wait until the end of the passage expecting that understanding will come later.

4.   After you have read the passage, reread it quickly (R2). In other words, scan it a second time. This second scanning should give you additional information and allow you to fill in gaps in your understanding of the passage.

Do Keep Track of Your Time. Timing is an essential element of this test. That is why it is important that you wear a watch while taking the exam. You may think the suggestions given here will slow you down. On the contrary, if you practice these techniques before taking the test, you will actually finish the readings faster and your score will be higher.

In order to finish the LSAT, you will have to read at approximately 400 words per minute. Here is a short test to judge how fast you are reading now.

SPEED READING TESTS

DIRECTIONS: Read the following passage as quickly as possible, timing yourself as you read. When you are finished, divide the number of minutes it took you to read the passage into the number of words in the passage (435). This will give you the number of words you are reading per minute. Next, answer the questions following the reading passage. Multiply the number of words you are reading per minute by the number of questions which you answered correctly and divide by the number of questions in the test (5). This will give you your Real Reading Speed. To illustrate, if you read 200 words per minute and answered three questions correctly, your Real Reading Speed would be:

$$\frac{200 \text{ words per minute} \times 3 \text{ correct answers}}{5 \text{ questions}} = 120 \text{ words per min.}$$

Remember you must read at the rate of 400 words per minute in order to complete the L.S.A.T.

Sample Reading Passage

The supernatural world was both real and awesome to early man, as it still is in primitive societies, and heavy dependency was put upon it in worshiping and propitiating the gods. It is more than likely the degree to which our ancestral homo sapiens relied upon telepathic communication instead of articulate speech would today fill us with both amazement and disbelief. Certainly human beings who populated the earth prior to the fourteenth century are well documented as having had a keen interest in the spirit world, thought transference, witches, premonitions and so forth.

In order to conjure up departed spirits, make predictions or go into a trance, a variety of drugs existing since antiquity (many of which are now classed as hallucinogens) were used by witch doctors, alchemists, shaman and cultist tribesmen throughout the world, and seemed to buttress natural powers. Yage, a drug related to LSD and known under several different names (including "telepathine"), is from a vine native to the Amazon Basin and is identical with harmine, an alkaloid from the seeds of wild rue. Both are reputed to aid in locating missing objects, in transporting users to distant lands and times, and in communicating with the dead. Greatly favored in Europe at witches' sabbaths are bufotenin (related to serotonin and first obtained from toad skins), scopolamine and henbane.

However, by Savonarola's time the church itself had declared magic and witchcraft evil. After the witch-hunts and witch burnings that continued for three centuries, the supernatural world with its ghosts, demons and human emissaries was in a state of subjugation. It was not until the nineteenth century that there was any open revival of interest in "seers" and "spooks" or acceptance of their possible validity.

Those who pioneered the re-exploration of what is now called "psi phenomena," or all things pertaining to the psychic world, were considered crazy, pathetic, eccentric and ridiculous. They were sneered at for their sacrilegious superstition and made to feel uncomfortable among their fellow men. Sir Oliver Lodge and a handful of others did succeed, however, in establishing the Society for Psychical Research in London in 1882, and gradually interest in spiritualism, clairvoyance and mental telepathy seeped out of its small confines and spread elsewhere. The American Society for Psychic Research was founded in 1906; however, the psi subject did not gain much public ground until the 1930s and it is still far from respected despite the efforts of such men as Drs. J.B. Rhine and Gardner Murphy, who have approached it scientifically and have been steadily working at it in conjunction with their European colleagues.   (431)

1. The author's attitude toward telepathic communication is one of

(A) disbelief
(B) skepticism
(C) acceptance
(D) inquisitiveness
(E) reserved judgment

2. All of the following groups were mentioned by the author as using drugs of ancient origin except

  I. witch doctors
 II. voodooists
III. alchemists
 IV. shamen
  V. cultist tribesmen

(A) I only
(B) I and II only
(C) II, III, and IV only
(D) II only
(E) IV only

3. Another name for the drug known as telepathine is

   (A) marijuana   (D) yage
   (B) LSD   (E) harmine
   (C) wild rice

4. Harmine is reputed to have the ability to

   (A) aid in locating missing objects
   (B) transport users to distant lands and aid in communication with the dead
   (C) enable one to communicate with spirits
   (D) help the user find his directions
   (E) transport the users to distant lands, aid in locating missing objects, and help the user communicate with the dead.

5. During what period of time, approximately, did the church declare magic and witchcraft evil?

   (A) 1400s   (B) 1500s   (C) 1600s   (D) 1900s   (E) 1500s

ANSWERS TO SPEED READING TEST

1. C   2. D   3. D   4. E   5. C

Another valuable technique for increasing reading speed is learning to pare a reading passage down to its essentials. To illustrate this technique, we have provided two similar reading passages. First read Passage A. It contains 204 words. Then read Passage B. You will notice that Passage B contains all the essential information in Passage A, but it eliminates every extraneous word. You lose nothing in terms of comprehension when you read Passage B, but you cut your reading time in half because Passage B contains only 98 words. Practice this technique as you take the Sample Exams later in the book. It's a valuable knack to acquire in preparation for the LSAT.

Passage A

Remarriage of a former spouse often evokes in the ex-partner envy and bitterness that had previously been kept under control by the rationalization that the other was in the same, if not a worse, predicament. "Suddenly the louse gets married again—the injustice of it all," moans the ex-wife, and then promptly demands more support for the children. The father may demand more liberal visitation rights. If, on the other hand, the remarried parent becomes overly guilty about his new found love, he will become overly compliant with his former partner's demands. As has been repeatedly emphasized, the way in which each parent meets a new situation involving the other depends on the extent to which he was clear in his desire for the divorce, made fair and just arrangements for it, and then concentrated on enhancing his freedom from the ex-partner. Some mixed feelings toward the former spouse are always likely to arise, and it is best not to deny these. But, it is also well not to act on them. Continuing to play out the role of the aggrieved one, or of the guilty one who must make up to the other for his better life, will make difficulties for all concerned.

Passage B

Remarriage . . . former spouse often evokes . . ex-partner envy . . bitterness . . . previously . . . under control . . . rationalization . . . other was . . . same, worse . . . predicament. "louse gets married again . . injustice" . . . moans ex-wife . . . demands more support. Father . . . demand . . . liberal visitation. If . . . remarried parent . . . overly guilty . . . newfound love, . . . become overly compliant . . . former partner's demands. Way . . . parent meets new situation involving . . . other depends . . . extent to which . . . clear in his desire . . . divorce . . . fair . . . just arrangements . . . then concentrated . . . enhancing . . . freedom . . . ex-partner. Mixed feelings toward . . . former spouse . . . always likely . . . best . . . deny these. Not . . . act on them. Continuing to play . . . aggrieved one, or . . . guilty one . . . for his better life . . . make difficulties for all.

THE LSAT READING TEST

The three types of reading passages you may expect on the LSAT are:

1. Humanities passages which may be concerned with art, music, literature or the analysis of an idea;

2. Social Science passages which may cover sociology, education, culture, history or politics;

3. Science passages which may present detailed discussions of a particular process or a generalized treatment of an idea.

The same reading techniques apply to all types of reading passages. However, due to the nature of the passage some may have to be read more slowly than others.

Humanities passages either discuss trends or literary personalities. For example, (A) Trend: Contrast between American and British Romantic literature. (B) Personality: The quality of Melville's writing or his work as illustrative of some trend or ethic.

Science and Social Science passages may be very general or they may be highly specific and full of detail. Some of these readings may be self-contained; that is, all the information on which you will be questioned is stated in the passage. Others are idea oriented and may require that you draw conclusions from the information given in order to answer the questions.

TYPES OF QUESTIONS YOU MAY BE ASKED

1. General Question. These questions are usually based on the main idea of the passage, its purpose or the best title for it. To answer this type of question, look for the choice which takes in the greatest amount of information. Wrong answers are usually too limited or too vague.

2. Inclusive Question. These questions often contain the phrase "all of the following EXCEPT" and are best answered by attempting to eliminate all the alternatives that do not fit first. This narrows the field considerably, increasing your chances for choosing the right answer.

3. Comparison Question. If the passage mentions both nineteenth- and twentieth-century authors, for example, you can expect to be quizzed on comparisons between the two. Try to spot these obvious sources of comparison as you read.

4. Detail Question. These questions refer to a fact or statistic given in the reading. Don't try to memorize these specifics. A glance back at the reading will enable you to answer this type of question.

DATA INTERPRETATION

The Data Interpretation questions on the Law School Admission Test are designed to test your ability to comprehend and make calculations from material presented in the form of graphs, charts or tables. Most of the questions involve some mathematics, but all can be answered on the basis of high school mathematics.

1. Get a grasp of the data before you start. Check dates, kinds of information supplied, units of measure, etc.

2. Do the easier questions first, those that can be answered by observation alone. Then turn to those questions that require calculating. There are usually some easy questions in each set and they count just as much as the more difficult ones in determining your score.

3. Visualize rather than calculate answers wherever possible. When dealing with averages, for example, imagine a line between the highest and lowest readings given in the particular graph or chart. Since the average of any group of numbers must fall somewhere between the highest and lowest points, establishing a visual midpoint can save valuable time.

4. Use the edge of your answer sheet or your pencil to help you read line and bar graphs or tables more accurately.

5. Rephrase questions that seem to stump you at first. Change verbal problems into mathematical ones or vice versa to see if you can get a better grasp of the situation.

6. Work with round numbers where possible. Often questions do not require exact answers and you can arrive at the correct answer faster and more easily by using approximate numbers.

7. Work with the smallest possible units. It is a waste of time to convert readings to fractional parts of a million and then try to work with the resulting huge numbers. If a table concerns population in millions, for example, calculate as follows:

    2 units + 1½ units = 3½ units.

    If each unit = 2 million, then 3½ × 2 million = 7 million

8. Do your figuring as neatly as possible so that you can refer to it if necessary. Calculations from a previous question in the set may save valuable time in answering subsequent questions on the same data.

9. Make certain that the answer you choose is in the same terms as the question; for example, dollars, millions, tons, miles. Pay particular attention to problems involving percentages. Remember that to change a number to a percentage you must multiply by 100. Thus, .049 × 100 = 4.9% while .49 × 100 = 49%.

10. Work only with the information stated or implied in the data presented. Attempting to bring outside knowledge to bear in answering a particular question may only lead you astray.

PRINCIPLES AND CASES

This chapter presents each of the five different types of Cases and Principles questions you may expect to face on the L.S.A.T. Following the description of each question type you will find sample questions and detailed explanations of the how and why of the correct answers. Study this section well, for it is sure to head you toward higher L.S.A.T. scores.

PRINCIPLES AND CASES TYPE A

(Case-Principle-Reason)

In this type of question you will be asked to apply several different—and possibly conflicting—principles of law to a single fact pattern or "Case". You will have to determine which of the four alternatives given best expresses both the proper result and the reasoning behind it under the particular principle stated.

It is important to remember that each question is completely independent of all other questions in the same set. Therefore, you must restrict your attention solely to the principle presented in the particular question you are attempting to answer without referring to any other principles relating to the same case. These questions require no actual legal knowledge. They do, however, expect you to bring into play your common sense notions of what reasonable people do.

SAMPLE QUESTIONS EXPLAINED

DIRECTIONS: Each law case described below is followed by several legal principles. These principles may be either real or imaginary, but for purposes of this test you are to assume them to be valid. Following each legal principle are four statements regarding the possible applicability of the principle to the law case. You are to select the one statement which most appropriately describes the applicability of the principle to the law case and blacken the space beneath the letter of the statement you select.
These questions do not presuppose any specific legal knowledge on your part; you are to arrive at your answers entirely by the ordinary processes of logical reasoning.

Case One

The Baker brothers owned a mill which made flour for their special cracked soybean bread. They hired the Build-em-Right Construction Company to build a reservoir on their land. During the construction, water broke through into the filled in shaft of an abandoned coal mine, and seeped along connecting passages into an adjoining mine operated by the Deep Shaft Engineering Company. The leakage into the Deep Shaft mine was slow and gradual.

The drilling in the mine shaft sent strong vibrations through the earth which weakened the structure of the Baker Brothers mill. Finally the mill collapsed from the vibrations and the mine caved in because of the seepage. George and Fred were hurt in the mill, and Mike and Roger were injured in the mine shaft.

On the land above the Deep Shaft mine was the farm of Jake McSeed. Due to the sudden crash of the mine shaft Jake's prize mare, Speedy, lost her foal. The McSeed farm was completely ravaged. The barn collapsed, the cows ran off and McSeed's silo crashed into the house of Pat Pending, McSeed's neighbor. Martha Pending came screaming from the house and ran into the road where she was run over by Bill Bumpem. Bumpem screeched to a halt and tried to give aid to Martha, but it was too late.

1. *Trespass is the voluntary movement by a person of some part of his body onto another's land, or the action of some force set in motion by such movement which results in an immediate intrusion on another's land without the owner's consent.*

   If Deep Shaft sues the Baker brothers, it will

   (A) win because the water flowed from the land of the Baker brothers into Deep Shaft's mine
   (B) win because the seepage into the Deep Shaft mine was gradual
   (C) lose because the Baker brothers did not know about the abandoned shaft under their property
   (D) lose because the Deep Shaft mine did not become waterlogged immediately

In this case no person intruded upon the Deep Shaft property, but rather water from the Baker brothers' reservoir flowed into the Deep Shaft Mine. Therefore, we are primarily concerned with the second part of the principle given which states that in order for liability to ensue, the intrusion must be the immediate result of a voluntary action. It is stated in the case that the flooding into the Deep Shaft mine was slow and gradual. Therefore, answer (D) is correct since it reflects this fact.

Alternative (A) does not take into account the speed with which the Deep Shaft mine became waterlogged and is therefore incorrect. Alternative (B) is wrong because it would give an improper holding and alternative (C) is irrelevant because the principle never mentions the idea of knowledge.

2. *The person who, for his own purposes, brings on his land and collects and keeps there anything likely to do mischief if it escapes, does so at his peril.*

If the Deep Shaft Engineering Company sues the Baker brothers under the above principle, Deep Shaft will

(A) win because the Baker brothers are absolutely liable under the above principle
(B) win because extensive damage was done to their mine
(C) lose because a reservoir is not likely to do mischief
(D) lose because the seepage into the mine shaft was gradual

The principle for this question states that liability ensues absolutely from anything which is likely to do damage if it escapes from a person's land. It does not say, as is the common misinterpretation, that liability ensues from anything brought onto a person's land which is likely to escape. Therefore (A) is correct because a large amount of water is likely to damage if it escapes from a person's land.

(B) is incorrect because the principle is not concerned with the degree of liability. Baker brothers, under the above principle, would be responsible for any amount of damage done to the Deep Shaft Mine. (C) shows the misunderstanding described above, since the water in a reservoir is likely to do mischief if it escapes. (D) is an attempt to confuse you by referring to the previous question. Remember questions of this type are not related.

3. *A motorist will only be liable for any injuries to a pedestrian if the pedestrian is acting under ordinary powers of reasoning at the time of an accident.*

If the estate of Martha Pending sues Bill Bumpem for damages, the estate will

(A) win because Martha was a pedestrian who was killed by Bill Bumpen
(B) win because Martha was emotionally disturbed at the time
(C) lose because Martha should have looked before running into the road
(D) lose because Martha was terrified at the time she ran into the road

Alternative (D) is correct because the principle requires that the pedestrian be acting under ordinary powers of reasoning at the time of injury and (D) correctly states that Martha was terrified, which would excuse Bill Bumpem from liability.

(A) is incorrect because it does not take into account Martha's state of mind. (B) is incorrect because in order to win Martha would have had to have been acting under ordinary power of reasoning. (C) is incorrect because looking onto the road for traffic is not required by the principle.

PRINCIPLES AND CASES TYPE B

(Principle-Case-Reason)

In this type of question you are given one principle of law followed by several different questions, each with its own set of facts. You are to apply the principle to each set of facts and decide:

1. which party will win or lose the decision and —
2. the reason for that result under the principle given.

The answer for each question in this section should be determined independently without referring to any other question in the set.

Key words in the principle such as *or, if, and, when,* and *unless* may be critical in reaching the proper decision for each case. Pay close attention to any relationships that these words may establish. Remember that if you can make the right choice as to who won or lost the case, you will have a 50% chance of answering the question correctly.

SAMPLE QUESTIONS EXPLAINED

DIRECTIONS: Each principle of law given below is followed by several law cases: These principles may be either real or imaginary, but for purposes of this test you are to assume them to be valid. Following each law case are four statements regarding the possible applicability of the principle to the law case. You are to select the one statement which most appropriately describes the applicability of the principle to the law case decision. Blacken the space beneath the letter of the statement you select. These questions do not presuppose any specific legal knowledge on your part; you are to arrive at your answers entirely by the ordinary processes of logical reasoning.

Principle Two

The crime of larceny is the wrongful taking and carrying away of the property of another with intent to deprive him permanently of the property. A wrongful taking is the acquiring of possession of the property without the consent of the owner. In order to be found guilty of larceny, the actor must have the necessary intent at the time he performs the wrongful taking.

4. One rainy day absent-minded Professor Fuddle takes the umbrella of his colleague, Professor Archie Bald by mistake. The next day Bald informs Fuddle of the mistake and Fuddle promises to return the umbrella. Bald has Fuddle arrested for larceny. Fuddle is

   (A) innocent because when he took the umbrella he intended to return it
   (B) innocent because he took the umbrella by mistake
   (C) guilty because he failed to return the umbrella
   (D) guilty because he took the umbrella without Bald's consent

In order to be guilty of larceny the actor must have the intent to deprive another of his property at the time the property is taken. Professor Fuddle did not have such an intent because he mistakenly thought the umbrella to be his own. Therefore the correct answer is (B).

Alternative (A) is incorrect because it is a misstatement of the facts. Alternatives (C) and (D) are wrong because they do not take into account Fuddle's lack of intent.

5. One day while shopping at the A & P, Softouch, a hungry student, pockets a candy bar, walks out without paying for it and immediately eats it. As soon as he finishes the candy, Softouch's conscience starts to bother him. He returns to the store, confesses to the manager, Mr. Scrooge, and offers to pay for the candy. Scrooge, wanting to make an example of a shoplifter, refuses to accept payment and has Softouch arrested for larceny. Softouch is

   (A) innocent because he offered to pay for the candy
   (B) innocent because Scrooge should have accepted payment
   (C) guilty because he did not return the candy
   (D) guilty because he originally intended not to pay for the candy

The principle deals with the intent to commit a crime at the time of the act. It does not take into account any later change of mind. Therefore alternative (D) is correct since at the time of Softouch's initial act all of the elements for larceny were present.

Alternatives (A) and (B) are both attempts to play on your sympathy. However, they are both incorrect.

Alternative (C) is not as precise as (D) and is therefore incorrect. Had Softouch intended to return the candy bar, he would have been innocent of the crime of larceny.

6. Payday at Scrooge and Marley is the 24th of the month. On Christmas Eve, Scrooge goes home early before he pays his clerk, Cratchit. In the past, Cratchit has waited until the 26th to be paid. However, this time he is fed up, so he walks over to the cash drawer and takes his pay. When Scrooge finds out, he has Cratchit prosecuted for larceny. Cratchit is found

   (A) innocent because the money was his property
   (B) innocent because the taking was not wrongful
   (C) guilty because he did not have Scrooge's consent to take the money
   (D) guilty because he intended to keep the money

The crime of larceny calls for the wrongful taking of the property of another. Cratchit has already performed the services required to earn the money which he took. Therefore, since the money was rightfully his, the correct answer is (A).

(B) is correct in stating that the taking was not wrongful. However, the reason that the taking was not wrongful was that the money rightfully belonged to Cratchit. Therefore (A) is a better answer. Alternative (C) is incorrect because the principle requires the owner's consent, but Scrooge is not the owner. Alternative (D) is incorrect because it is superseded by the fact that the money rightfully belonged to Cratchit.

PRINCIPLES AND CASES TYPE C

(Related Cases)

These questions are known as "group" or "string" questions because they come in sets of four or five and there is a relationship among the questions in a particular group. Each question presents a set of facts and a legal holding which you are to assume was handed down by the court. The words *Held for* mean that the party specified won.

Following each case are four legal principles. Your task is to select the one principle which meets all of the following conditions:
1. It reasonably explains the holding (i.e., it lets the proper party win).
2. It is the narrowest, in the sense that it comes closest to the facts in the case. The narrowest principle as used here does not mean the principle that has the fewest restrictions, but rather the one which is most relevant to the particular facts of the case given.
Hint: If two alternatives have an equal number of elements of equal significance to the case, pick the one which is worded most nearly the same as the fact pattern. However, if one particular alternative has more elements which relate to the fact pattern than any other alternative, pick it as the correct answer.
3. It does not contradict any earlier holding in the same group of questions. This means, the principle must be consistent with both the principle of law and the decision of the court for each preceding question in the group.

Hint: When you finish an entire group of questions, read through all of your answers. If all the answers together do not read like one consistent principle of law, you have probably made a mistake. Because of the relationship of these questions, it is important that you answer the first question in each set correctly.

SAMPLE QUESTIONS EXPLAINED

DIRECTIONS: In this section you will be given several groups of imaginary law cases. Each question will present a set of facts and a fictitious court holding, which you are to presume to be valid. Following each case are four legal principles, lettered (A), (B), (C), and (D). You are to choose the narrowest (most precise) principle which explains the court decision given. However, this principle may not conflict with the holdings given in any of the preceding cases in the same group. The correct answer to the first case in any group will always be the most precise principle which correctly explains the legal decision made. From the second question until the end of each group, you are to select the narrowest principle which does not conflict with any of the previous holdings.

These questions do not presuppose any specific legal knowledge on your part. They are to be answered entirely by the ordinary processes of logical reasoning. Indicate your choice by blackening the appropriate space on the answer sheet.

Group Three

7. J&L is a major steel manufacturer. It owns mines in four states, interstate rail lines which connect its plants, river and lake transportation facilities, and manufacturing plants in six states. It ships its products to warehouses in eighteen states. When labor problems arise in its Pennsylvania plants, the Federal National Labor Relations Board enters the case to prevent J&L from engaging in unfair labor practices. J&L brings a suit to prevent the NLRB from interfering in a labor dispute which is entirely within the boundaries of the state of Pennsylvania. *Held*, for NLRB.

The *narrowest principle* that reasonably explains this result is:

(A)   The NLRB has the authority to intervene in all labor disputes.

(B)   The NLRB has the authority to intervene in all labor disputes in Pennsylvania.

(C)   The NLRB has the authority to intervene in labor disputes involving a multistate company, even if the actual dispute is entirely in one state.

(D)   The NLRB has the authority to intervene in any labor dispute involving a steel company.

Alternative (C) is the correct answer since it allows the NLRB to win; it takes into account that J&L is a multistate company and that this particular labor dispute is entirely in one state. In other words it specifically covers more elements of the case than any other alternative.

While (A), (B) and (D) would all give the correct holding, they are not as narrow as alternative (C) and thus they are incorrect.

8. The Koka Coal Co. has one mine in West Virginia. Although it sells coal in twelve states, it does not buy anything from any state but West Virginia. When a strike is threatened, the NLRB intervenes and establishes a minimum wage and minimum working conditions at the mine. Koka Coal sues to overturn the NLRB ruling. *Held,* for Koka Coal.

The *narrowest principle* that explains this result and is *not inconsistent* with the ruling given in the previous case is:

(A) The NLRB has no authority to intervene in labor disputes involving mining companies which have one mine.

(B) The NLRB has no authority to intervene in labor disputes involving a company which sells its goods out of state.

(C) The NLRB has no authority to establish a minimum wage for workers of a company which does not buy goods from outside its home state.

(D) The NLRB has no authority to set minimum wages or minimum working conditions.

Alternative (C) is correct because it allows Koka Coal to win, and since it mentions the idea of a minimum wage and the fact that Koka Coal does not buy goods from outside the state, it is narrower than (A). It also does not contradict the previous principle since the facts may be distinguished on the grounds that J&L Steel both bought goods from outside its home state and sold goods in interstate commerce.

Alternative (B) does not mention the idea of a minimum wage and therefore is not as narrow as (C). Alternative (D) does not deal with the idea of interstate commerce and is therefore not as narrow as (C).

9. Esso Bee is a New York oil refining company that buys all of its raw materials from other states and sells all of its output in New York. Esso Bee's drivers go on strike because the trucks are unsafe. The NLRB steps in and orders Esso Bee to fix its trucks. Esso Bee sues to overturn this ruling. *Held,* for Esso Bee.

The *narrowest principle* which reasonably explains the result and is *not inconsistent* with the previous cases in this group is:

(A) The NLRB has no authority to regulate working conditions of a company which either buys most of its raw materials or sells most of its output outside its home state.

(B) The NLRB has no authority to regulate any labor dispute involving working conditions.

(C) The NLRB has no authority to intervene in a labor dispute if the employer does not sell his goods in interstate commerce.

(D) The NLRB has no authority to regulate the working conditions of a manufacturer who does not sell his output in interstate commerce.

Alternative (D) is correct. It correctly states the fact pattern and, since Esso Bee sells all of its output in New York, it does not contradict the ruling in question 7 (J&L sold its goods in interstate commerce). Nor does it contradict the ruling in question 8, since that question dealt with buying, not selling, goods.

Choice (A) is incorrect because it deals with both the buying and selling of goods outside of the home state. This opens up the possibility of conflict with the holding in question 7. Also, because it deals with both buying and selling it is not as narrow as (D). Choice (B) would contradict the holding in question 7 and (C) is not as precise as (D) since it does not deal specifically with working conditions.

PRINCIPLES AND CASES TYPE D

(Major Factor-Case)

In this type of question you are presented with a particular set of facts (the Case), which applies for each question in the group. Each question then describes a legal action taken by one of the participants mentioned in the case, gives the decision rendered by the court and the principle of law on which the decision was based. You are to pick the one alternative which was the major factor in the disposition of each action based upon the facts given in the case and the principle stated in the question.

The questions in this section are entirely independent of each other and the reasonsing used for any particular question may actually contradict the reasoning used for another question in the same set.

SAMPLE QUESTIONS EXPLAINED

DIRECTIONS: In this test you are given a set of facts followed by several questions relating to them. Each question presents a different legal principle to be applied to the set of facts. All principles given are to be assumed to be valid even though they may be either real or imaginary. You are to apply the principle to the given statement of facts and then pick the one of the four alternatives which is the MAJOR FACTOR in the legal decision. Blacken the space on the answer sheet corresponding to the alternative of your choice. These questions do not relate to one another. You are to answer each one solely on the basis of the material given for that specific question. Arrive at your answers by ordinary logical reasoning alone. Do not be influenced by any outside legal knowledge that you may possess.

Case Four

Dodo Segetti worked for the Raymond Noxon campaign for President. Noxon had the nomination of his party, but there were certain candidates in the other party whom Noxon did not want to run against. Noxon told Segetti to take care of his opponents. Segetti took to the task with a vengeance.

He had leaflets prepared saying that Humbert Humbert, a strong political contender, liked to pursue twelve-year old girls. The leaflets were stamped "Moe Muskrat," another opposition candidate. Using this tactic, Segetti hoped to end the political chances of Humbert Humbert and Moe Muskrat at the same time and insure that Georgy Porgy would win his party's nomination.

Dodo Segetti continued to hound Georgy Porgy even after he won the nomination. He'd wade into the crowd at political rallies and yell, "Georgy Porgy has acne!" In response the crowd would move away from Georgy Porgy and the rally would be ruined. However, one day at a rally in a supermarket parking lot, Georgy's security men spotted Segetti just as he was about to utter his famous yell and spirited him away before he could say a word. Dodo Segetti, Lance Lurk, a security man, and Lily Pasadena, a little old lady who was minding her own business, were all hurt in the ensuing scuffle. Lance Lurk apologized to Segetti after the scuffle but Lily Pasadena kicked him in the leg repeatedly until Segetti got so angry that he punched her in the jaw. Lance Lurk intervened at this point, handcuffed Segetti and turned him over to the local police.

10. A suit for defamation brought by Humbert Humbert against Dodo Segetti is held for Humbert on the following principle:

Defamation is constituted by a publication, understood as referring to the person claiming injury, which maligns that person's character and does him actual harm.

Which of the following was the major factor in the disposition of this case?

(A) The pamphlet said that Humbert Humbert pursued twelve-year old girls.
(B) Dodo Segetti purposely wanted to malign Humbert Humbert.
(C) The pamphlets maligned Humbert Humbert and he lost the nomination.
(D) The pamphlets maligned Humbert Humbert and they had Moe Muskrat's name on them.

The crime of defamation requires that actual harm be done to the person maligned and since (C) states how this condition was met, it is the correct answer. By this reasoning (A), (B) and (D) are incorrect since they do not show any actual harm.

11. A suit for damages brought by Lily Pasadena against Lance Lurk is held for Lance Lurk on the following principle:

   A security guard is only responsible for injuries he causes when not in pursuit of his duty.

   Which of the following was the major factor in the disposition of this case?

   (A) Lance Lurk was in the crowd waiting to catch Dodo Segetti.
   (B) Lance Lurk was in pursuit of his duty when he apprehended Segetti.
   (C) Lily Pasadena was accidentally hurt while Lance Lurk was in pursuit of his duty.
   (D) Dodo Segetti was standing next to Lily Pasadena at the time of the scuffle.

Lance Lurk was in the process of hauling away Dodo Segetti when the scuffle occurred which injured Lily Pasadena. The principle in this case says that a security man is not responsible for injuries that he causes while in the pursuit of his duty. Since Lance won the case and he was in the pursuit of his duty, alternative (C) must be correct. Choice (A) does not mention either Lance's duty or Lily's injury. (B) does not deal with when Lily was hurt and (D) does not show us Lance's relationship to Lily's injury.

12. A suit for damages brought by Lily Pasadena against Dodo Segetti is held for Lily Pasadena on the following principle:

   When a party is threatened with force that party may only use means which in themselves are reasonable and which appear reasonably necessary to avoid or prevent the threatened contact.

   Which of the following was the major factor in the disposition of this case?

   (A) Lily Pasadena attacked Dodo Segetti first.
   (B) Lily Pasadena was a helpless little old lady.
   (C) Dodo Segetti overreacted to Lily's attack.
   (D) Dodo seriously injured Lily.

The key element in this case is the reasonableness of the force that one uses to protect himself. In other words a person is only allowed, under the principle, to use only as much force as is necessary to protect himself. We may reasonably assume from the passage that Segetti is a relatively young man and that he could have fended off Lily Pasadena without punching her in the jaw. Therefore (C) is correct since it applies this reasoning.

None of the other alternatives focuses on the reasonableness of the use of force which the principle requires.

PRINCIPLES AND CASES TYPE E

(Major Factor-Principle)

The format of these questions is almost the same as the Major Factor - Case questions (Type D) just described. The difference is that in Major Factor - Principle questions a single principle is given first which applies for the entire set of questions. In each question, one case is given along with the result reached by applying the principle to that particular case. You are to decide which alternative was the major factor in determining why the case was decided as it was.

FACTS TO REMEMBER ABOUT CASES AND PRINCIPLES

1. Never assume that a thought or emotion is in any character's mind. If a man is fearful the case will tell you that he is fearful. If the case does not tell you that a character is fearful, you are not to assume that he is without strong evidence of that fact. When a statement is made about someone's mental state, you must assume that it is proven, regardless of the difficulty of presenting evidence about it in court.

2. The principles of law given may be either "and principles", or "or principles."

And Principle

"In order to be guilty of the crime of burglary a man must break into a dwelling place at night *and* there must be a human being inside."

If, in the particular case you are dealing with, a man breaks into a house at night but there is no human being inside, the fact that there was no one home *supercedes* the fact of the breaking in, and no burglary has been committed according to this principle.

Or Principle

"In order to be guilty of the crime of burglary a man must break into a house at night *or* there must be a human being inside at the time of the initial entering."

Under this principle a man could be guilty of burglary even if he broke into a house in broad daylight as long as there was a human being inside.

3. Read all cases and principles questions literally. More can be gained from critical reading than from logical analysis, even though the importance of logical analysis should not be minimized.

LOGICAL REASONING

The ability to reason clearly and logically is essential to the study of law. This ability is measured not by testing your knowledge of the formal rules of logic, but rather by testing your basic common sense and judgment. The sample questions and explanatory answers that follow will be an invaluable aid to understanding how to attack this type of question.

Each question in the Logical Reasoning section of your test consists of a brief reading passage from natural science, social science or the humanities, plus one or more questions about the reading. The questions do not test your knowledge of the subject matter, but rather your ability to understand, analyze, use and/or criticize the arguments presented in the reading. While some of the topics covered may be controversial, the questions do not require that you take a stand on the issues, only that you examine the evidence and evaluate all claims critically.

The correct answer to a logical reasoning question will always be that alternative which most closely duplicates the reading passage in both structure and content, or which may most reasonably be derived from the facts presented in the passage.

SAMPLE QUESTIONS EXPLAINED

This is a test of your ability to evaluate the reasoning contained in a statement or reading passage. Each statement or passage is followed by one or more questions. Answer each question solely on the basis of information stated or implied in the reading. If more than one choice seems possible, then you must select the one answer that does not require making implausible or superfluous assumptions. Blacken the space on the answer sheet that corresponds to the letter of your choice.

1. The difficulty is somewhere else. It is in that strange territory that is so all important now—the distinction between science which is knowing, and technology which is application. To put it in a simple phrase, I would say my own position is "Know all you can, but do only that which is socially useful to do."

    It may be reasonably inferred from the above passage that the author would be in favor of

    (A) increased technological applications of science
    (B) a decrease in the number of research chemists and an increase in the number of chemical engineers

(C)   extensive research in scientific fields but only carefully selected applications of such research

(D)   the search for knowledge for knowledge's sake

(E)   the funding of more schools for technical education.

The reasoning involved in this argument is rather straightforward. The author is saying that science and, by implication, scientific research represents knowledge. Therefore when he says "Know all you can, . . ." he is saying that he is in favor of extensive scientific research, thus when he says ". . . do only that which is socially useful to do" he is saying that not all research should be carried through to technology. We can now make the reasonable leap to the conclusion that the author would be in favor of only well chosen applications of scientific knowledge to technological development. Therefore the correct answer is (C).

We are not given enough information in the passage to know whether the author would be in favor of (A), (B), or (E). (D) might be true but since it doesn't deal with the technological part of the author's argument (C) is the better answer.

2.   Civil defense authorities recognize that in a national disaster, safe, potable water supplies will be vital for the survival of the population. Civil authorities of areas designed as reception centers in the event of major disaster, especially in southern California where water transportation lines may be easily disrupted, are concerned with the necessity to provide alternative sources of potable, emergency water. The problem has already been revealed during the course of a test exercise.

The above article seems to be primarily concerned with which of the following?

(A)   The threat of a nuclear disaster in southern California.

(B)   The danger of saboteurs disrupting existing water supplies.

(C)   What can be learned from test exercises concerning the existing water supply.

(D)   The need for new techniques to supplement existing water supplies in certain areas.

(E)   What the Civil defense authorities are doing to provide safe, potable water supplies.

The key to answering this question is in the word 'primarily'. Alternatives (A) and (B) give specific emergency situations. However, no specific emergency was mentioned in the passage. The term 'disaster' is only referred to in a general sense. Therefore neither (A) nor (B) can be correct. (C) is only mentioned in passing and (E) is not mentioned at all. The entire passage deals with the severe consequences of not having a potable water supply, thus (D) must be the correct answer.

3. It has not yet been possible to extract for chemical analysis myelin that is undergoing destruction in the M 5 brain tissue. However, intact myelin from 'normal appearing' white matter and from M 5 patients has been shown to have the same total protein content and the same percentage composition of the different amino acids as normal human myelin.

The reader may logically conclude from the above passage that

(A) the myelin of M 5 patients may be inherently different from that of normal persons

(B) it will soon be possible to extract myelin that is undergoing destruction from the M 5 brain tissue

(C) the protein content of myelin is not an important determinant when investigating the myelin tissue

(D) amino acids are the part of the myelin tissue that undergo destruction

(E) the intact myelin of M 5 patients may not be inherently different from that of normal persons.

It is stated in the passage that there is no real difference in the protein content of intact myelin in the M 5 patient and normal human myelin. Therefore, based on the evidence given, we have no way of distinguishing between the two types of myelin; thus alternative (E) is correct. Note that alternative (A) is the exact opposite of (E). This is done to mislead you. This trap also comes in another variety where neither of the two opposites is correct. It is natural to assume that if something is bad its opposite is good, and testmakers often use this tactic when writing questions. There is no information given in the passage to support alternatives (B), (C), or (D).

4. The alcoholic's psychological deviations are in the areas of dependency, egocentricity, depression, and hostility. Dependency although seemingly the least provocative of these traits, is the most difficult to handle. Initially the patient's dependency will probably increase or remain static. Therapists with unresolved dependency needs of their own may give in to anger quickly, but persistent pressure is frustrating for any therapist. Such patients arouse doubts in the psychotherapist about his abilities. Many alcoholics are extremely selfish and it is only human for a therapist to feel anger toward his patient and sympathy for the patient's victims.

The author of this article most probably believes that which of the following is true?

(A) The personality of the alcoholic is an impediment to psychotherapy.

(B) Often the main reason for the failure of therapy is the psychotherapist's own dependency needs.

(C) Psychotherapists use the dependency needs of the patients as a tool.
(D) Psychotherapy is almost always doomed to failure in cases of alcoholism.
(E) Therapists need specific training in order to treat the alcoholic.

After reading the passage many applicants will mistakenly pick (B) as the right answer. This alternative is mentioned in the passage; however, the word "often" which gives undue weight to the statement, is not used. The main thrust of this passage is made clear in the statement, which immediately follows the statement dealt with in (B), "but persistent pressure is frustrating for any therapist." The author goes on to state that, "it is only human for a therapist to feel anger toward his patient . . ." Therefore the correct answer is (A). In order to pick the correct answer in a case like this the applicant must keep in his mind the whole passage. Alternatives (C), (D), and (E) are never directly dealt with in the passage. You might be tempted to pick (D) as the right answer but remember that the author has only dealt with the frustrations connected with treating the alcoholic, not with the treatment itself.

5. Since all of the red cars that I have seen have been very fast, all red cars must be very fast.

Which of the following most closely resembles the reasoning used in the sentence above?

(A) The pinto pony is faster than any other horse on the range.
(B) That red Maserati has won all of the major races.
(C) All of the Irishmen I have met have been very bright therefore all Irishmen must be very bright.
(D) Since all of the yellow cabs that I've seen have been speeding, it can be assumed that most cab drivers drive fast.
(E) Since everything that I've heard about Foley Square has been strange, Foley Square must be a strange place.

Remember what was said in the introduction to this section—a correct answer is often similar in structure to the question. In this case, the correct answer (C) almost duplicates the structure of the question. Notice how both the question and the answer deal in absolutes, "all . . . red cars" and "all . . . Irishmen" and how the reference group at the beginning and end of each sentence remains the same, "red cars" and "Irishmen." Also, both are invalid generalizations.

Choice (A) does not make any assumption and the reference group changes from "pony" to "horse." Choice (B) gives no comparison and no alternative reference group. Choice (D) does not deal entirely in absolutes, "most cab drivers," when making its assumption. Choice (E) has a similar structure to the question, but it does not deal in plural terms and the question does. Therefore (C) is the best answer.

6. Judging from the tone of the following sentences and the sources from which they come, which is the most believable? .

   (A) Transit Worker: "The New York city subways are the safest mass transportation system in the country."
   (B) Contractor: "I have never built a building which does not meet the city's code specifications."
   (C) Ladies Shop Owner: "This year's fashions have a much fresher look about them than last year's."
   (D) Radar Operator: "At 12:00 three blips suddenly appeared on the radar screen and then disappeared."
   (E) Accountant: "These books which I have prepared meet with generally accepted accounting principles."

This question is very easy, as are practically all questions of this type. The correct answer is usually the one in which the speaker has no personal stake in being correct, has no personal bias as to the interpretation of facts dealt with in the statement and is in a position to know that the facts in the statement are true.

Therefore (D) is the correct answer because a radar operator is rewarded for accurately reporting what he has seen. (A), (B), (C), and (E) are all incorrect since in each case the speaker will benefit if the facts are interpreted in the way he wishes to interpret them.

PRACTICAL BUSINESS JUDGMENT

This is a test of your ability to evaluate and apply data presented in the form of actual case studies of practical situations. After reading each situation, you will be required to pinpoint the problem, identify the options available, determine the goal sought, and make judgments based upon your assessment of the information presented.

In this type of question you are presented with a reading passage which outlines a specific business situation. Following the reading you will be required to answer two types of questions:

Data Evaluation Questions in which you are to classify certain facts on the basis of their importance to the decision to be made and

Data Application Questions in which you will have to apply the information you have read to indicate your understanding of the situation.

In tackling Data Evaluation Questions, there are four essential questions you must ask yourself before you begin. These questions will provide the framework for analyzing the passage and will permit you to organize the information given into a comprehensible pattern.

1. Who is the decision maker? This may seem to be a foolish question, but since a decision may affect more than one individual or organization, it is necessary to determine whose values are to be considered in reaching the decision.

2. What is the decision being made? The answer to this question will help you pinpoint the Major Objective of the decision maker and the alternative means which might be employed to reach the desired end.

3. Why is one alternative more desirable than another? Answering this question will bring to light the Major Factors involved in making the decision.

4. On what basis was the decision made? The answer to this question will point to the Major Assumptions underlying the decision.

In Data Application Questions you may refer back to the reading to find the answers. For this reason, it is helpful to underline or make brief notes in the margin as you read each business situation so that you can locate the essential points more quickly when attempting to answer these questions.

SAMPLE QUESTIONS EXPLAINED

DIRECTIONS: In this test you will be presented with a detailed case study of a practical business situation. Read the study carefully. Then answer the two sets of questions based upon the reading. In the Data Evaluation questions, you will be asked to classify certain facts on the basis of their importance to the case presented. In the Data Application questions you will be asked to make judgments based upon your comprehension of the information.

Sample Business Situation. To Buy or Not to Buy?

The Widget Division of the Relsat Company, a profitable, diversified manufacturing firm, purchased a machine five years ago at a cost of $7,500. The machine had an expected life of 15 years at time of purchase and a zero estimated salvage value at the end of the 15 years. It is being depreciated on a straight line basis and has a book value of $5,000 at present. The division manager reports that he can buy a new machine for $10,000 (including installation) which, over its 10-year life, will expand sales from $10,000 to $11,000. Further, it should reduce labor and raw materials usage sufficiently to cut operating costs from $7,000 to $5,000. The old machine's current market value is $1,000. Taxes are at a rate of 50 percent and are paid quarterly, and the firm's cost of capital is 10 percent. Should Relsat buy the new machine?

DATA EVALUATION

DIRECTIONS: Based on your analysis of the Situation, classify each of the following items in one of five categories. On your answer sheet blacken the space under:
(A) if the item is a MAJOR OBJECTIVE in making the decision; that is, one of the outcomes or results sought by the decision-maker.
(B) if the item is a MAJOR FACTOR in arriving at the decision; that is, a consideration explicitly mentioned in the passage that is basic in determining the decision.
(C) if the item is a MINOR FACTOR in making the decision; that is, a secondary consideration that affects the criteria tangentially, relating to a Major Factor rather than to an Objective.
(D) if the item is a MAJOR ASSUMPTION made in deliberating; that is, a supposition or projection made by the decision-maker before weighing the variables.
(E) if the item is an UNIMPORTANT ISSUE in getting to the point; that is, a factor that is insignificant or not immediately relevant to the situation.

1. Expansion of sales

2. Reduction of operating costs

3. Taxes and the cost of capital

4. Current market value of the old machine

5. Installation cost of the new machine

The Major Objective (A) is the goal sought by the decision maker. It is obvious from the reading that expansion of sales (question 1) is a Major Objective of the Widget Division. This is a Major Objective rather than a Major Factor because expansion of sales is a sought-after goal of the division and because it is a goal that can be brought about by the manipulation of certain elements (such as purchasing the new machine).

Major Factors (B) are elements already in existence over which a company probably does not have a great degree of control but which are, nevertheless, of great importance in making key decisions. Taxes and the cost of capital (question 3) are Major Factors. While Widget has no control over either one, these elements will play an important part in the financing of a new machine should Widget decide to buy it.

Minor Factors (C) are usually related to Major Factors. In many cases a group of Minor Factors will form one Major Factor. Current market value of the old machine (question 4) is a Minor Factor. The salvage value of the old machine is only one of the ways in which the company will raise money to purchase a new machine. Because current market value does not have a cumulative nature, as taxes and the cost of capital do, it cannot be considered a Major Factor. Also, in relation to the total cost of the new machine, the salvage value is insignificant.

Major Assumptions (D) are beliefs by the participants in the case study that certain events, over which these participants have no control, will happen in the future and will affect the decision being made in an important way. Since there is no category called Minor Assumption, if an assumption is not of major importance to the decision, you must relegate it to the category of Minor Factor (C) or Unimportant Issue (E).

Reduction of operating costs (question 2) is a Major Assumption. Operating costs are cumulative costs and a reduction of $2000 in a cumulative cost will be significant in relation to the other revenues and costs mentioned in the passage. However, this reduction in costs, while hoped for, is not definite, and therefore it is a Major Assumption.

Unimportant Issues (E) are never given any serious consideration by the decision makers in a passage. Installation charges (question 5) are an Unimportant Issue. Installation charges are never given in the passage and, on this basis alone, should be considered an Unimportant Issue. However, even if they had been mentioned, if the charges seemed to be relatively insignificant in relation to other costs, they would remain an Unimportant Issue. The best way in which to separate an Unimportant Issue from a Minor Factor is to determine whether the decision maker will pay any attention to it.

DATA APPLICATION

DIRECTIONS: Based on your understanding of the Business Situation, answer the following questions testing your comprehension of the information supplied in the passage. For each question, select the choice which best answers the question or completes the statement.

6. Which of the following are benefits Relsat expects to derive from purchasing a new machine?

    I. Decrease labor usage
    II. Decrease raw material usage
    III. Increase production

    (A) I only
    (B) III only
    (C) I and II only

    (D) II and III only
    (E) I, II and III only

The correct answer is (C). Remember that the best way to answer this type of question is to eliminate the wrong alternatives first. For instance, if you know that III is definitely wrong you can eliminate (B), (D), and (E) immediately.

7. The new operating costs are expected to be

    (A) $7,000
    (B) $1,000
    (C) $5,000

    (D) $10,000
    (E) $11,000

The correct answer is (C) $5000. This is a detail question. Obviously you can't remember all of the details in a passage, but if you outline the passage in the margin while you are reading it, you will be able to refer back quickly to the portion of the passage where the detail is mentioned.

Note that all of the other wrong answers are numbers which are mentioned in the passage.

2

PART TWO

Five Sample Exams With Complete Explanations

Law School Admission Test

FIRST VERISIMILAR EXAM

The Sample Test which follows is patterned after the actual test. In all fairness, we emphasize that this Sample Test is not an actual test. The Law School Admission Test is a secure test which cannot be duplicated. The actual test which you are going to take may, in some areas, have more difficult questions than you will encounter in this Sample Test. On the other hand, the questions may be less difficult, but don't bank on this. We trust that in your use of this book, you will gain confidence—not overconfidence. Use the special Answer Sheet to record your answers.

Allow about 3½ hours for this Examination.

That's approximately how much time you'll have on the actual exam. Keep a record of your time, especially if you want to break up this practice into several convenient sessions. Then you'll be able to simulate actual exam conditions.

In constructing this Examination we tried to visualize the questions you are *likely* to face on your actual exam. We included those subjects on which they are *probably* going to test you.

Although copies of past exams are not released, we were able to piece together a fairly complete picture of the forthcoming exam.

A principal source of information was our analysis of official announcements going back several years.

Critical comparison of these announcements, particularly the sample questions, revealed the testing trend; foretold the important subjects, and those that are likely to recur.

In making up the Tests we predict for your exam, great care was exercised to prepare questions having just the difficulty level you'll encounter on your exam. Not easier; not harder, but just what you may expect.

The various subjects expected on your exam are represented by separate Tests. Each Test has just about the number of questions you may find on the actual exam. And each Test is timed accordingly.

The questions on each Test are represented exactly on the special Answer Sheet provided. Mark your answers on this sheet. It's just about the way you'll have to do it on the real exam.

As a result you have an Examination which simulates the real one closely enough to provide you with important training.

Correct answers for all the questions in all the Tests of this Exam appear at the end of the Exam.

ANALYSIS AND TIMETABLE: VERISIMILAR EXAMINATION I.		
This table is both an analysis of the exam that follows and a priceless preview of the actual test. Look it over carefully and use it well.		
SUBJECT TESTED	*Time Allowed*	*Questions*
LOGICAL REASONING	20 minutes	15
PRINCIPLES AND CASES	55 minutes	40
PRACTICAL JUDGMENT	40 minutes	40
DATA INTERPRETATION	30 minutes	25
ERROR RECOGNITION	20 minutes	35
SENTENCE CORRECTION	20 minutes	25
QUANTITATIVE COMPARISON	15 minutes	25
TOTALS EXAM I	200 minutes	205

ANSWER SHEET FOR VERISIMILAR EXAMINATION I.

Consolidate your key answers here just as you would do on the actual exam. Using this type of Answer Sheet will provide valuable practice. Tear it out along the indicated lines and mark it up correctly. Use a No. 2 (medium) pencil. Make only ONE mark for each answer. Additional and stray marks may be counted as mistakes. In making corrections erase errors COMPLETELY. Make glossy black marks.

TEST I. LOGICAL REASONING

TEST II. PRINCIPLES AND CASES

TEST III. PRACTICAL JUDGMENT

TEST IV. DATA INTERPRETATION

TEST V. ERROR RECOGNITION

A B C D E (answer grid for questions 1–40)

TEST VI. SENTENCE CORRECTION

A B C D E (answer grid for questions 1–32)

TEST VII. QUANTITATIVE COMPARISON

A B C D E (answer grid for questions 1–32)

TEST I. LOGICAL REASONING

TIME: 20 Minutes. 15 Questions.

This is a test of your ability to evaluate the reasoning contained in a statement or reading passage. Each statement or passage is followed by one or more questions. Answer each question solely on the basis of information stated or implied in the reading. If more than one choice seems possible, then you must select the one answer that does not require making implausible or superfluous assumptions. Blacken the space on the answer sheet that corresponds to the letter of your choice.

Correct and explanatory answers are provided at the end of the exam. After you have completed the entire exam, read the explanations carefully. They'll reinforce your strengths and pinpoint your weaknesses so that you know just what to study to raise your score.

1. Mary: All the boys at the Ramsey Prep School are students.
    John: That's not true. I know some very bright people at the Ramsey School who are good basketball players.

    John's response shows that he believes that

    (A) not all the people at the Ramsey Prep School are intelligent
    (B) someone who is studious has no athletic interests
    (C) people who are studious are not very bright
    (D) someone who is a good basketball player cannot be intelligent
    (E) people in prep schools are not as studious as they appear to the rest of the world.

2. Poe conceived of art, you see, not as a means of giving imaginative order to earthly experience, but as a stimulus to unearthly visions. The work of literary art does not, in Poe's view, present the reader with a provisional arrangement of reality; instead, it seeks to disengage the reader's mind from reality and propel it toward the ideal.

    It may be inferred from the author's comments about Poe's art that such art is

    (A) not really art
    (B) inspired by unearthly forces affecting Poe
    (C) beyond the comprehension of any reader
    (D) outside the realm of life's normal experiences
    (E) due to Poe's unequalled creative imagination in perceiving the ideal

3. When one says, "I don't know," whether one is speaking of one's state of being or one is speaking of the state of Poetry, the answer possesses a genuine accuracy.

   Which of the following statements can most reasonably be made concerning the attitude expressed above?

   (A) The author will prove that modern poetry is barren as compared to the great poetry of the past.
   (B) If a man were to reply, "I don't know," upon being asked, "How do you feel?" the author would take issue with the response.
   (C) Uncertainty is inexcusable when evidence is available.
   (D) An answer is wrong if it cannot encompass the entire meaning of the question.
   (E) Ambiguity is a finer quality than continual accuracy.

Questions 4 and 5

The universe may be conceived as divided into two parts. There is the outer objective universe of so-called reality, the quantitative, measurable complex of mass energy in space-time; and there is the equally real inner, subjective universe, the qualitative, undimensional complex of spirit, of feeling, of experience, which is the image of the objective universe as it is reflected in every consciousness. The inner universe is a part of, and is contained within, the outer structural universe, which, so to speak, overarches it and is mirrored in it, as the sky, with its stars, is mirrored in a lake.

But here the analogy ends.

Mirrored in consciousness, in the world of spirit, the objective universe is as by creative fusion transfigured.

4. With which one of the following statements is the author most likely to agree?

   (A) Beauty is in the eyes of the beholder.
   (B) A rose by any other name would smell as sweet.
   (C) Make hay while the sun shines.
   (D) What profit it a man if he gains the whole world but suffers the loss of his soul?
   (E) All that glitters is not gold.

5. Which of the following are parts of the author's arguments concerning the inner and outer universe?

   I. The image of the objective universe is reflected in the same manner in every consciousness.
   II. The outer universe is a mirror image of the inner subjective universe.
   III. The subjective universe is encompassed by the objective universe.

   (A) II only
   (B) III only
   (C) I and II only
   (D) II and III only
   (E) I, II, and III only

6. Poetry is an advanced pattern of public behavior in the hierarchy of patterns. I should imagine that this is quite according to the understanding of the anthropologist. The anthropologist is the analyst and historian who identifies the essential cultural forms of a society on the assumption that man is a measure of all things.

   (A) Poetry is a reflection of the desire of man to escape the borders of objectivity.
   (B) Poetry is the reflection of man's most primitive rhythmical nature.
   (C) As a mode of the mind, poetry is one of the divisions of man's experience.
   (D) The anthropologists' objective analysis of poetry is fruitless unless he also considers the nature of the poetry.
   (E) A society can be measured by its poetry.

7. Alice: Democracy means equality for all men.
   Ted: Then you'll have to show me a democracy because all I see are the rich, poor and the middle class.

   Alice's reply to Ted's remark will most likely be

   (A) Democracy does not mean economic equality.
   (B) Democracy was only meant for the rich.
   (C) Democracy is spreading rapidly throughout the world.
   (D) Democracy means equality of opportunity.
   (E) Democracy is a new institution and needs time to grow.

8. If Tolstoi could begin a great novel by saying that all happy marriages were the same, all unhappy ones different, we can say that every age has a new way of finding human relations difficult or impossible: the very hardships and the very joy of life which we cannot and would not escape and with which we must deal.

   Which of the following best expresses the author's attitude toward life's problems?

   (A) All men try to escape their pains in much the same way.
   (B) Pathos is part of life's exciting experience but different generations of men have different ways of expressing their troubles.
   (C) Tolstoi thought that men expressed and suffered their problems differently.
   (D) Mankind's basic desires are masochistic since men love to revel in sorrow.
   (E) Pain is a tactic used to gain power by making others feel sorry for you.

9. Judging from the tenor of the following statements and the apparent authoritativeness of their sources, which is the most reasonable and trustworthy?

    (A) Insurance agent: "Life insurance is the best means for protecting your family after you die."
    (B) Skin diver: "The ski slopes of Vermont are the best in the eastern United States."
    (C) Traffic patrolman: "We observed a horse loose on Eastern Parkway at approximately 4:45."
    (D) Daughter: "My father has always been a perfect gentleman with everyone with whom I've seen him deal."
    (E) Soldier: "Even though today's battle was indecisive we delivered the enemy twice as much punishment as he delivered us."

10. It has always been difficult to find a pure or satisfactory audience for the living artist; and this has become increasingly difficult in societies like our own where education has become both universal and largely technical—at any rate, less generally literate—and which has at the same time, enormously multiplied the number of its artists.

    An underlying assumption in the author's argument is that

    (A) there are more artists in today's society than society needs
    (B) in order for a society as a whole to appreciate its artists its members must have a broad formal education
    (C) the reason for so many artists today is a cultural climate that encourages them to proliferate
    (D) no matter how hard a society tries it cannot destroy its artistic population
    (E) the artist is the antenna of his society warning it of what is to come

11. Employer: All of the men in my company are happy.
    Job applicant: I'm sorry to hear that. I've just been divorced so I suppose you won't hire me.

    The job applicant's response shows that he interpreted the employer's remark to mean that

    (A) the employer will not be able to make him happy
    (B) the employer is a kind employer
    (C) the employer only hires happy people
    (D) the applicant will not be happy in the job being discussed
    (E) the employer has filled the job already

12. We are torpid only because we are glutted with energy and feel it only as trouble. The strains are out of phase with each other and we have techniques only for troubles.

    What may we reasonably assume the author feels about our energy glut?

    (A) Our energy glut means more than trouble and misery.

(B)   The energy glut represents a positive good which we must seek to channel.

(C)   Our energy glut must be something that we learn to live with even though it will always cause us misery.

(D)   We should not suffer strain because of our torpid nature but rather we should be languid.

(E)   Our energy glut can and should be done away with.

13.   The typical is already the mythical, insofar as it is pristine pattern and pristine form of life, timeless model and formula of old, into which life enters by reproducing its traits out of the unconscious.

It may logically be assumed that the author believes that man does most things because

(A)   he is predestined by certain archetypal traits existing in him as a biological pattern

(B)   the spirit of man is fluid and changes with time

(C)   he is molded by his environs

(D)   he is happiest when exercising his free will

(E)   the profit motive is one of man's greatest incentives

14.   The civil law, as well as nature herself, has always recognized a wide difference in the respective spheres and destinies of man and woman. Man is, or should be, woman's protector and defender. The natural and proper timidity and delicacy which belong to the female sex evidently unfit it for the occupation of civil life.

The above speech was probably given for the purpose of

(A)   granting women the right to vote

(B)   preventing women from becoming lawyers

(C)   praising motherhood

(D)   honoring a heroic woman

(E)   thanking a woman who had given the writer aid and comfort

15.   Women's liberation is: a slogan—a challenge—a movement—a threat—a cliché—an enigma—or something else, depending on who you are. It is not surprising that Women's Lib connotes different things to different people; their perceptions of it reflect differing social and cultural backgrounds and varying levels of sensitivity to the disadvantages inflicted on some members of society solely for being female.

It may be most safely inferred that the writer of the above passage is:

(A)   a woman

(B)   a man

(C)   a politician

(D)   a supporter of the Women's Liberation movement

(E)   an organizer of women's groups

END OF TEST

TEST II. PRINCIPLES AND CASES

TIME: 55 Minutes. 40 Questions.

Correct and explanatory answers are provided at the end of the exam. After you have completed the entire exam, read the explanations carefully. They'll reinforce your strengths and pinpoint your weaknesses so that you know just what to study to raise your score.

PART A. APPLYING SEVERAL PRINCIPLES TO A CASE

DIRECTIONS: Each law case described below is followed by several legal principles. These principles may be either real or imaginary, but for purposes of this test you are to assume them to be valid. Following each legal principle are four statements regarding the possible applicability of the principle to the law case. You are to select the one statement which most appropriately describes the applicability of the principle to the law case and blacken the space beneath the letter of the statement you select.
These questions do not presuppose any specific legal knowledge on your part; you are to arrive at your answers entirely by the ordinary processes of logical reasoning.

Case One

Federal agents Brown and Collins obtained an arrest warrant for Erwin, charging him with "transportation of obscene matter for sale or distribution" under 18 U.S.C. 1465. The agents went to Erwin's apartment, knocked, and were admitted. When the agents entered, Erwin and a Mr. Roche were seated on a couch in the living room watching television. Erwin was placed under arrest and Collins made a cursory inspection of the three-room apartment to see if anyone else was present. He found no one and, since neither agent felt any particular threat, neither Erwin nor Roche were handcuffed or in any other way restrained. When Erwin went into the bedroom to get a shirt and shoes, Brown accompanied him and confiscated a pistol from a drawer in the night table which was some six feet from Erwin's closet.

Brown accompanied Erwin to the living room and told Collins about the pistol. Agent Collins then returned to the bedroom and discovered a box of shotgun shells and a shotgun on a shelf in the open closet. These were confiscated by Collins. Collins continued to look around the bedroom and, upon opening a trunk at the foot of the bed, discovered hundreds of photographs depicting, as Collins said, "every sexual perversion known to man or beast."

The pictures were taken along with the weapons in order to be used as evidence in a trial involving the original obscenity charges as well as a charge of illegal possession of unregistered firearms.

1. *An officer of the law may search an area in the immediate vicinity of a suspect after the suspect has been arrested.*

   When Erwin moves to have the pistol excluded from evidence, Erwin will

   (A) win because the Federal agents allowed him to move freely so that they could search the areas in his immediate vicinity
   (B) win because the Federal agents had an arrest warrant not a search warrant
   (C) lose because the gun was found in his immediate vicinity
   (D) lose because an arrest warrant gives a law officer a right to search anywhere in a suspect's apartment

2. *An officer of the law is only allowed to make a search for weapons in a suspect's immediate vicinity if the officer fears for his own or for others' safety.*

   When Erwin moves to have the pistol removed from evidence, Erwin will

   (A) win because the pistol was not in his immediate vicinity
   (B) win because the agents did not fear for their own or others' safety
   (C) lose because the number of guns present in the apartment would indicate that there was real danger present
   (D) lose because he was in fact guilty of the obscenity charge

3. *If an officer of the law is in the same room as a suspect and objects of evidentiary value are in plain view, the officer may seize these objects even if he does not have a search warrant naming them specifically.*

   When Erwin moves to have the obscene material excluded from evidence, Erwin will

   (A) win because the agents had an arrest warrant not a search warrant
   (B) win because the agents had entered his apartment unlawfully
   (C) lose because the obscene material was in plain sight of Officer Collins
   (D) lose because the obscene matter directly related to the obscenity charge on the arrest warrant

4. *An officer of the law may not seize evidence even if it is directly related to the crime in question unless he has a search warrant to seize that evidence.*

When Erwin moves to have the obscene material excluded from evidence, Erwin will

(A) win because the agents had an arrest warrant not a search warrant
(B) win because the agents had entered his apartment unlawfully
(C) lose because the obscene material was in plain view of Officer Collins
(D) lose because the obscene material directly related to the obscenity charge on the arrest warrant

5. *An officer of the law will be guilty of violating a suspect's civil rights if the suspect's personal belongings are searched without the suspect's permission.*

If Collins is charged with violating Erwin's civil rights by his confiscation of the obscene material, Collins will

(A) win because all of his actions were taken in the pursuit of his duty
(B) win because he was carrying out a general search for his own self protection
(C) lose because Erwin was not in the same room as he
(D) lose because Erwin did not give Collins permission to open his trunk

Case Two

Tom Testator was fifty-six years old and he decided that it was time for him to write a will. He had believed for years, entirely without evidence, that his wife Mary was unfaithful to him. Tom normally would have left his wife the house and the car but he decided under these circumstances to leave her only the house.

Bob Bumble, Tom's friend, told Tom that Lotta Luck, Tom's niece who had been living in a Hippie commune in Greenwich Village, was dead. Bob really did believe that Lotta was dead. Tom would have given Lotta his summer house, but since he believed Bob, Tom gave the summer house to him. Tom had never particularly liked his nephew Harry but Tom still intended to give Harry part of his business. Burton, one of Tom's employees, wanted this part of Tom's business for himself, so he went to Tom and told him that Harry was a frequent cocaine user. Burton knew that this was untrue and that Harry did not use drugs at all, but he hoped that Tom would be influenced by this lie. Tom in reaction to these accusations by Burton, excluded the gift to Harry from his will and instead gave this part of his business to his wife Mary.

Tom wanted to give $10,000 to his half-brother Lenny. However, since Lenny had not been seen for 20 years, Tom presumed Lenny was dead. Nevertheless, Tom included these words in his will: "I give $10,000 to my employee Burton; this gift would have gone to my half-brother Lenny but, since he is dead, Burton shall be my beneficiary."

Tom died shortly after including all of the above elements in his will.

6. *If a delusion is a motivating factor for the making or not making of any disposition under a will, and the delusion has no rational basis, the will will be revised to what it would have been if the testator had not been suffering from the delusion.*

    If Mary brings an action for the rights to Tom's car, Mary will

    (A) win because Tom didn't give the car to any other beneficiary
    (B) win because Tom's delusion was the reason why Mary did not receive the car
    (C) lose because Tom had reason to believe Mary was unfaithful
    (D) lose because she did not prove that she was not unfaithful

7. *A gift is void due to undue influence if the testator is in a state of mind to be influenced and the person exerting the influence is guilty of deceit.*

    If an action is brought against Mary to declare the gift to her of part of the business void, Mary will

    (A) win because she did not try to influence Tom concerning the business
    (B) win because Harry was not a frequent cocaine user
    (C) lose because Tom did not like Harry and Harry was not a drug user
    (D) lose because Burton lied to Tom

8. *A gift will not be void due to mistake unless a testator states in his will what he would have done if the mistake had not been made.*

    If Lenny brings an action against Burton in order to void Burton's gift, Lenny will

    (A) win because he was in fact alive
    (B) win because Tom stated in his will what he would have done if Lenny was alive
    (C) lose because Burton did not practice deceit in acquiring this gift
    (D) lose because Tom sincerely believed that he was dead

9. *A gift is void due to fraud if the person so charged purposefully lied to the testator and benefitted under the testator's will.*

If Lotta brings action to have gifts to Bob Bumble declared void due to fraud, Lotta will

(A) win because she was alive and well and living in Greenwich Village
(B) win because Bob had no right to tell Tom that she was dead
(C) lose because Bob had not influenced Tom
(D) lose because Bob did not know that Lotta was alive

10. *A person is liable for punitive damages if due to his own deceit he benefits under the will of another.*

If Harry brings an action against Burton for punitive damages, Harry will

(A) win because Tom would have given him part of his business if Burton had not lied
(B) win because he was not a frequent cocaine user
(C) lose because Burton was not mentioned in the will
(D) lose because Burton really did believe that Harry was a frequent cocaine user

Proceed directly to the next Part.

PART B   APPLYING ONE PRINCIPLE TO SEVERAL CASES

DIRECTIONS: Each principle of law given below is followed by several law cases: These principles may be either real or imaginary, but for purposes of this test you are to assume them to be valid. Following each law case are four statements regarding the possible applicability of the principle to the law case. You are to select the one statement which most appropriately describes the applicability of the principle to the law case decision. Blacken the space beneath the letter of the statement you select. These questions do not presuppose any specific legal knowledge on your part; you are to arrive at your answers entirely by the ordinary processes of logical reasoning.

Principle One

An employer must bargain with the representative of a union if the union can demonstrate that it represents a majority of the company's employees. The union's proof need not be entirely accurate, but it must be of the type which would normally be the basis of a belief by a reasonable man. Temporary employees are not to be considered when determining if there is majority support for union status.

11.   Mike Muscles, the representative of Trucker's Union Local 105, walks into the office of Fred Friendly, the owner of Travel Trucking, Inc., and demands that Fred talk with him concerning the wages, hours, and conditions of employment of Fred's employees. Travel Trucking is not a unionized business, but Fred pays his employees the same wages as employees who work for unionized businesses. Travel has one hundred and sixty workers. Mike shows Fred union recognition cards signed by seventy-nine of them, and points to the forty pickets outside of Fred's office window. Fred refuses to talk to Mike or recognize Mike's union.

In the Union's suit against Fred, Fred will

(A)   win because he is already paying union scale wages
(B)   win because the Union has not clearly demonstrated that it represents a majority of Fred's workers
(C)   lose because 119 of his employees support Local 105
(D)   lose because all that Mike wanted to talk about was wages, hours, and conditions of employment

12.   Roger Rumple is the owner of a small toy manufacturing concern which employs forty workers. At 11 o'clock one morning the representative of Union Blue walks into Roger's office and shows him

twenty-three union recognition cards signed by Roger's employees. At 11:30 the representative of Union Red walks into Roger's office and shows Roger twenty-five recognition cards also signed by Roger's workers. Roger refuses to recognize either union until this apparent inconsistency is explained.

In the suit by Union Red and Union Blue against Roger, Roger will

(A) win because neither union clearly demonstrated a majority
(B) win because in this case he could pick the union he wished to bargain with
(C) lose to Union Red because they had more authorization cards than Union Blue
(D) lose to Union Blue because they did have a majority of authorization cards and they came to see Roger before Union Red

13. While driving up to the main gate of his plant, Egor Ignats, the owner of Egor's Wonderful Wickets, Inc., is forced to bring his car to a halt because twelve of his twenty workers are picketing at the gate. The men are carrying signs which say, "Egor must bargain with Union X!" and "Egor's plant has Rats inside who do not support Unionization!" Egor normally would have recognized the union's bargaining agent, but since he felt personally insulted by many of the signs, he refused to negotiate.

In a suit by Union X against Egor, Egor will

(A) win because picketing for union recognition must at all times stay within the bounds of courtesy and fair play
(B) win because by blocking the main entrance of his plant the work of Wonderful Wickets, Inc. has been interfered with
(C) lose because a majority of his workers have demonstrated their support for Union X
(D) lose because his plant really does have Rats inside who do not support unionization

14. Carla Cola owns a moderate-sized dress shop. She employs one full-time clerk and fifteen part-time seamstresses. All fifteen seamstresses sign union recognition cards but Carla refuses to recognize the union representative. All of her employees, including the clerk, go out on strike in protest over Carla's refusal to bargain.

In the suit by the Union against Carla, Carla will

(A) win because only the part-time employees signed union recognition cards
(B) win because the clerk was not allowed to strike because she had not signed a union recognition card
(C) lose because a majority of her full-time employees went out on strike
(D) lose because all her employees went out on strike

15. Hold the Road Tires, Inc., is a small tire manufacturing plant. Generally, the employer and the employees had a very good working relationship. The company normally pays for Saturday night bowling for the men, and Terry Tread, the employer, usually joins his men. One Saturday, a majority of Terry's men happen to mention while bowling that they would like a union in the plant, and they ask Terry to talk to the union representative sometime. The next Monday when the union representative comes to see Terry, Terry refuses to see him.

In an action by the union against Terry, Terry will

(A) win because his employees did not make a formal request that Terry receive the union representative
(B) win because the men in Terry's plant had no real grievances
(C) lose because a majority of Terry's employees were unhappy with their working conditions
(D) lose because a majority of Terry's employees wanted to be represented by a union

Principle Two

Where a police officer observes unusual conduct which leads him reasonably to conclude, in light of his experience, that criminal activity may be afoot, and that persons with whom he is dealing may be armed and presently dangerous; where in the course of investigating this behavior he identifies himself as a policeman and makes reasonable inquiries; and where nothing in the initial stages of the encounter serves to dispel his reasonable fear for his own or others' safety, he is entitled, for the protection of himself and others in the area, to conduct a carefully limited search of the outer clothing of such person in an attempt to discover weapons which might be used to assault him. An officer may put a hand beneath a suspect's clothes if he feels what appears to be a weapon.

16. Clancy O'Toole, a New York Policeman, while walking his beat in a bad neighborhood observed Polonius Punk, a known narcotics addict, consorting with three other men. All four men were standing in front of the First National Town Bank. During this period, Clancy observed that one of the men handed Punk an object of some sort which Punk put into his jacket pocket. When Clancy approached Punk and asked him what he was doing, Punk simply mumbled something unintelligible. At that point Clancy stuck his hand into Punk's pocket and pulled out a nonregistered gun.

When Punk moves to have a charge of possessing a nonregistered firearm dismissed, he will

(A) win because Clancy had no right to stick his hand into Punk's pocket, at that point
(B) win because Clancy did not know what the object was that Punk put into his pocket

    (C)   lose because Punk did have a gun and he was acting suspiciously in front of a bank

    (D)   lose because Punk was guilty of both conspiracy to rob a bank and attempt to rob a bank

17.   While on his way home from the station house, Burny Guardino, an off-duty police officer, spotted three men cruising in a car up and down in front of a jewelry store. When the men finally stopped in front of the store, Burny approached the driver, Kelly Klinker, and asked to see his license and registration; Kelly refused. Burny ordered the men out of the car and patted them down. Under Kelly's jacket he felt what appeared to be a crumpled ball of paper. When Burny stuck his hand into Kelly's pocket, he found a small package containing heroin. Kelly is arrested for possession of narcotics.

When Kelly moves to have the charges against him dismissed, he will

    (A)   win because he was not really trying to rob the jewelry store

    (B)   win because Burny did not feel what appeared to be a weapon beneath Kelly's clothes

    (C)   lose because Burny could really believe that criminal activity was afoot

    (D)   lose because Burny first made a limited search of Kelly's outer clothing

18.   Casey, an ex-convict, was employed as a handyman in a pawnshop. Officer Fogarty spotted Casey staring into the window of the pawnshop. Suspecting that Casey was about to rob the shop, Fogarty approached Casey and began to question him. Casey told Fogarty that he was the handyman and was about to wash the windows. The owner of the store corroborated Casey's story. Nevertheless, Fogarty patted Casey down and, upon feeling what appeared to be a gun, went inside Casey's clothing and did in fact find an unregistered firearm. Casey is charged with illegal possession of a weapon.

When Casey moves to have the charge against him dismissed, he will

    (A)   win because the owner corroborated Casey's story

    (B)   win because Fogarty should have first asked the shopkeeper if he knew Casey

    (C)   lose because Casey did in fact have an unregistered gun

    (D)   lose because it is reasonable to search an ex-convict under almost any circumstances

19.   Smith was locked out of his apartment one day and the superintendent, who had the only passkey, was nowhere to be found. Realizing that his window was unlocked Smith went to the roof of the building, climbed

down the fire escape, and entered his apartment through the open window. Officer Jones saw Smith climb in the window and decided to investigate. Jones knocked on Smith's door and when Smith answered, Jones identified himself as a policeman and asked Smith why he was on the fire escape. Smith refused to answer so Jones searched his outer clothes and, upon feeling what appeared to be an ice pick, Jones went into Smith's pocket and removed an ice pick and a small quantity of marijuana. Smith is charged with the possession of marijuana.

When Smith moves to have the charges dismissed, he will

(A) win because it was his own apartment that he entered
(B) win because he had a right to remain silent
(C) lose because Jones' suspicions were reasonable in the light of the facts available to him
(D) lose because it is unlawful to be on a fire escape except in an emergency

20. Roger, a plainclothes policeman, saw Lefty keeping a close watch on the activity of the store clerk in Julius' Diamond Exchange. Roger approached Lefty and asked him to state the nature of his business but Lefty merely sneered at him. Roger searched Lefty's outer clothing and felt what appeared to be a sharp object. Upon reaching into Lefty's trouser pockets, Roger found a glass cutter. Lefty is charged with attempted robbery.

When Lefty moves to have the charge against him dismissed, he will

(A) win because Roger did not identify himself as a policeman
(B) win because he had a right to be where he was
(C) lose because all the elements of this particular case do appear to add up to an attempt to rob the store
(D) lose because all elements of the search were carried out properly

Proceed directly to the next Part.

PART C. CHOOSING THE NARROWEST JUSTIFYING PRINCIPLE

DIRECTIONS: In this section you will be given several groups of imaginary law cases. Each question will present a set of facts and a fictitious court holding, which you are to presume to be valid. Following each case are four legal principles, lettered (A), (B), (C), and (D). You are to choose the narrowest (most precise) principle which explains the court decision given. However, this principle may not conflict with the holdings given in any of the preceding cases in the same group. The correct answer to the first case in any group will always be the most precise principle which correctly explains the legal decision made. From the second question until the end of each group, you are to select the narrowest principle which does not conflict with any of the previous holdings.

These questions do not presuppose any specific legal knowledge on your part. They are to be answered entirely by the ordinary processes of logical reasoning. Indicate your choice by blackening the appropriate space on the answer sheet.

Group One

21. Jake was the owner of a small dairy farm. Jake's cattle had never strayed off his pasture so he was not accustomed to paying close attention to their movements. One day while Jake was in his house one of his cows strayed off his property and into McPherson's Country Store where it ate a large quantity of fruit and vegetables. McPherson brought an action against Jake for the cost of the produce. *Held*, for McPherson.

The *narrowest principle* that reasonably explains this result is:

(A) The possessor of any animal which goes onto the property of another is strictly liable for any damage done by the animal.

(B) The possessor of livestock which go onto the property of another is liable for any damage done by the livestock.

(C) The possessor of livestock which go onto the farm of another is strictly liable for any damage done to the farm.

(D) The possessor of any wild animal is strictly liable for any damage done by that animal.

22. Jack owned a dog which was known to bite people. One day Harry, the mailman, who knew that Jack's dog had bitten people in the past, went to Jack's house to deliver a package. Harry reached out to pat the dog on the head and the dog bit him. Harry brought a suit for damages against Jack. *Held*, for Jack.

The *narrowest principle* that reasonably explains this result and is *not inconsistent* with the ruling given in the preceding case is:

(A) The possessor of an animal with a known dangerous propensity is strictly liable for all injuries done as the result of that dangerous propensity.

(B)   The possessor of an animal with a known dangerous propensity is strictly liable for all injuries done as the result of that dangerous propensity except where such propensity was known to the injured person, or such person should have reasonably known of the danger.

(C)   The owner of a dog is strictly liable for any damage or injury done to a person by the dog while such person is on the owner's property.

(D)   The possessor of an animal is strictly liable for any injury caused by that animal except where the animal is aroused by the person it injures.

23.   Buster owned a junkyard in a bad neighborhood in the city. A high fence surrounded the yard and Buster kept two killer guard dogs on the inside for protection against intruders. A large sign outside the junkyard warned, "Beware of Vicious Dogs Inside!" Crafty, a petty thief, scaled the fence, ignoring the warning, and was badly mauled by the dogs. Crafty brought a suit against Buster for damages. *Held,* for Buster.

The *narrowest principle* that reasonably explains this result and is *not inconsistent* with the rulings given in the preceding cases is:

(A)   The owner of a dangerous animal is strictly liable for all injuries caused by that animal.

(B)   The owner of a dangerous animal is not responsible for injuries done to another by that animal while that other person is on the property of the owner.

(C)   The owner of a dangerous animal is strictly liable for injuries done to another by that animal except when that person is on the owner's property.

(D)   The owner of a dangerous animal is strictly liable for injuries done to another by that animal except where the owner has reason to believe that others will know of the present danger.

24.   Fearless owns a piece of property adjoining Lester's farm. Lester raises fighting bulls for the bullfights in Mexico. Fearless has always held a secret desire to become a bullfighter, so one day, while standing on his own property, Fearless began waving a red towel at a bull on Lester's land. The bull charged onto Fearless's property and, besides injuring Fearless, it did great damage to his garden furniture. Fearless brought an action against Lester for the damages. *Held,* for Lester.

The *narrowest principle* that reasonably explains this result and is *not inconsistent* with the rulings given in the preceding cases is:

(A)   The possessor of a wild animal is strictly liable for any harm done by the animal, provided that such harm was a result of the animal's normally dangerous propensities.

(B)   The possessor of livestock which trespasses onto the lands or other property of another incurs liability for the trespass itself and any harm done by the animal.

(C) The possessor of an animal that is not known to have dangerous propensities is not held to strict liability for the animal's acts.

(D) The possessor of a dangerous animal which trespasses onto the lands or properties of another incurs liability for the trespass itself and any harm done by the animal except where the animal has been provoked to make the trespass.

25. Wallet was an investment banker who raised alligators as a hobby. Having decided to increase his life insurance coverage, Wallet invited Jeff, an insurance agent, to come to his home and discuss Wallet's insurance needs. While Jeff was walking up the driveway, he saw a sign which read, "Danger! Alligator Crossing!" Jeff ignored the sign, continued toward Wallet's house, and enroute he was badly mauled by one of Wallet's pet alligators. Jeff brought suit against Wallet for damages. *Held,* for Jeff.

The *narrowest principle* that reasonably explains this result and is *not inconsistent* with the rulings given in the preceding cases is:

(A) If the party injured on the land of another is a constant trespasser upon a limited area, liability can be predicated only on negligence.

(B) The possessor of dangerous animals is strictly liable for any harm done by the animal.

(C) If the person who is injured by a dangerous animal on the land of another has been invited on the land of that person, the owner of the animal is liable for any harm done by it.

(D) A property owner has only the duty to warn other persons of any danger that may exist on his property.

Group Two

26. Seller wanted to make an offer to Buyer to buy Seller's horse for a thousand dollars. However, Buyer was out of town on vacation. Buyer's brother-in-law, who had never acted in Buyer's behalf before, thought that Seller had made a very good offer, and since he did not want Buyer to miss this opportunity, he accepted the offer in Buyer's name. A month later when Seller demanded a thousand dollars from Buyer, Buyer refused to pay. Seller brought an action against Buyer for the money. *Held,* for Buyer.

The *narrowest principle* that reasonably explains this result is:

(A) An offer made to the public may be accepted by anyone.

(B) An offer made to a specific person may not be transferred to a third party until the first person has come to a decision.

(C) An offer may be accepted only by the person to whom it is made or by a person acting on his behalf.

(D) An offer may be accepted only by the person to whom it is made or by a person authorized to act on his behalf.

27. Hank Rupt knew that Wealthy did not want to buy his worthless piece of farmland. However, Hank knew that Ed Agent was authorized to act on Wealthy's behalf. Hank convinced Ed to buy the farmland for Wealthy. Wealthy did not learn of the transaction until his bank sent him the cancelled check that had been paid over to Hank Rupt. Wealthy brought an action against Hank Rupt for return of the money. *Held,* for Wealthy.

The *narrowest principle* that reasonably explains this result and is *not inconsistent* with the ruling given in the preceding case is:

(A) Where a person with authority accepts an offer on the behalf of another whose identity is known to the person making the offer, both the person making the offer and the person in whose name it is accepted are bound.

(B) A seller cannot hold a buyer to his agent's acceptance of an offer if the seller knew that the buyer would not have accepted the offer in a direct negotiation.

(C) An offer may be accepted only by the person to whom it is made.

(D) In a transaction which involves land an authorized agent of the buyer may accept an offer from a seller on the buyer's behalf.

28. Baker is in the milling business and he employs Dealer to act as his purchasing agent. One day, while Baker is busy with other matters, Dealer discovers that Kane has put a large quantity of sugar on the market, and Dealer enters into a contract with Kane to buy it. When Baker discovers what Dealer has done, he is furious and refuses to go through with the contract. Kane brings a suit against Baker. *Held,* for Kane.

The *narrowest principle* that reasonably explains this result and is *not inconsistent* with the rulings given in the preceding cases is:

(A) Where a person with authority makes an offer to buy on behalf of another, and the seller has no reason to believe that the buyer disagrees with such offer, then such offer is binding.

(B) A contract made by the agent of a buyer, between a buyer and seller is valid, unless the buyer disagrees with the action of his agent.

(C) The authorized agent of a buyer can enter into a binding agreement with a seller as long as such agent acts within the scope of his authority.

(D) The principle party in an agreement will be bound by the actions of his agent when such agent contracts with a third party.

29. Broker owned a valuable piece of real estate which he wanted to sell to the mayor of the town, at a bargain price, for the purpose of establishing good will. When he called the mayor's office, Nightshade, the town clerk, answered the phone. Broker thought that he was talking to the mayor and he made his offer to sell the land to Nightshade. Nightshade recognized this offer as a bargain and immediately accepted. When Broker realized his mistake, he withdrew his offer to Nightshade. Nightshade brought suit to enforce the deal. *Held,* for Broker.

The *narrowest principle* that reasonably explains the result and is *not inconsistent* with the rulings given in the preceding cases is:

(A) Where the offerer and the propsective buyer are dealing face to face and the offerer mistakes its prospective buyer for someone else, the offer remains binding on the offerer.

(B) Only in cases where the offerer and the prospective buyer are dealing face to face and the offerer mistakes the buyer for someone else will the offer remain binding on the offerer.

(C) Where two parties are dealing by mail or telephone the court will not hold the offer binding if someone other than the intended party accepts the offer.

(D) Where the two parties are dealing at length, the court will not hold the offer binding if someone other than the interested party accepts the offer.

30. Parts, the owner of the Humdinger Garage, received an offer from Glick to buy one hundred gallons of oil at a good price. Parts tells his mechanic, Gears, to give Glick a call and to accept the offer. After Parts receives the oil, he decides that he has no real use for so much oil and tries to return it to Glick, but Glick refuses to accept it. Parts brings suit against Glick for the return of his money. *Held,* for Glick.

The *narrowest principle* that reasonably explains this result and is *not inconsistent* with the rulings given in the preceding cases is:

(A) There is no binding obligation where the offer was accepted by someone other than the intended party.

(B) A person acting at the direction of a buyer has the authority to enter into a binding obligation on the buyer's behalf.

(C) A person acting at the direction of a buyer may not enter into a binding obligation on the part of the buyer through the use of a telephone.

(D) Any employee of an owner may enter into a binding obligation on the behalf of the owner if he feels it is in the owner's best interest.

Proceed directly to the next Part.

PART D. CHOOSING THE MAJOR FACTOR (PRINCIPLE)

DIRECTIONS: In the following questions you are given a principle of law followed by several questions, each providing a new set of facts. All principles given are to be assumed to be valid even though they may be either real or imaginary. You are to apply the principle to the given statement of facts and then pick the one of the four alternatives which is the MAJOR FACTOR in the legal decision. Once you have decided upon the answer, blacken the space on the answer sheet corresponding to the letter of your choice.

These questions do not relate to one another. You are to answer each one solely on the basis of the material given for that specific question. Arrive at your answers by ordinary logical reasoning alone. Do not be influenced by any outside legal knowledge that you may possess.

Principle One

Any person unlawfully assaulted may stand his ground and resist force with force; and such person has the right to exercise and use such reasonable force as may reasonably appear to him in good faith to be necessary to protect himself from bodily harm even though he may not actually be in danger.

31. Arnie was rushing to catch the 5:15 train at Grand Central Station. As he was elbowing his way through the crowds, he happened to give a poke in the ribs to Cooper, who was irritated from a long, hard day at work. Cooper grabbed Arnie by the tie and hit him, breaking Arnie's jaw. A suit by Arnie against Cooper for damages to his jaw is decided for Arnie.

   Which one of the following choices was the major factor in the disposition of the case, considering the principle above?

   (A) Arnie was wrong in shoving Cooper, but Cooper had the right to protect himself in a reasonable way.
   (B) Cooper did not respond to Arnie's shove reasonably.
   (C) Cooper had a legal right to resist force with force.
   (D) Cooper had a good faith belief that he was in danger of bodily harm.

32. Mabel Blackjack had a friend, Roger, who was fond of practical jokes. One day Roger crept up behind Mabel, pushed a toy pistol against her back and said, "Your money or your life!" Mabel, not recognizing Roger's voice, swung around and sprayed him with mace. Roger, in agony, reeled backward and fell down a staircase knocking over Upton Descending. Descending, in ire, threw his briefcase at Roger. The

briefcase seriously injured Roger's back. A suit by Roger against Descending for damages to his back is decided for Roger.

Which one of the following choices was the major factor in the disposition of this case, considering the principle above?

(A) Mabel responded reasonably to the threatened assault by a mugger.
(B) Roger was foolish for playing such a practical joke.
(C) Descending did not act in order to defend himself from bodily harm.
(D) Descending should not have been where he was when Roger bumped into him.

33. Peter Print was the editor of *The Daily Bungle. The Bungle* ran a series of feature stories one week concerning the inept way in which the local garage mechanics serviced cars. Greasy McGuirk, a local garage mechanic, took the stories personally and decided to get even with Peter Print. McGuirk went to *The Bungle*'s offices, kicked open Peter's door, and stood over Peter menacingly with a knife. Peter ran into an adjoining bathroom and locked the metal door behind himself. McGuirk pounded futilely on the door but could not make it budge. Peter could have used the bathroom telephone to call the police, but instead he took a gun from the medicine cabinet, swung open the door, and shot McGuirk, severely injuring him. A suit by Greasy McGuirk against Peter Print for damages due to his wounding is decided for McGuirk.

Which one of the following choices was the major factor in the disposition of this case considering the principle above?

(A) Peter could not reasonably believe that he was in fear of bodily harm.
(B) It was not necessary for Peter to shoot McGuirk.
(C) McGuirk would not have hurt Peter; he only wanted to frighten him.
(D) Peter could have screamed for help.

34. Jolly was a member of the Bull Moose Lodge and a friendly fellow. Upon seeing his friend Ben approaching, Jolly rushed to greet him and slapped Ben on the back with all of his might. Ben became frightened that Jolly would hit him again, so in order to deter him, Ben slapped Jolly on the back. The force of the blow was so great that Ben knocked a cap off one of Jolly's front teeth. A suit by Jolly against Ben for damages to his tooth was held for Ben.

Which one of the following choices was the major factor in the disposition of this case, considering the principle above?

(A) Ben used reasonable force to protect himself.
(B) Jolly should have known that back slapping was unlawful.
(C) Ben could not be held responsible for a loose cap on Jolly's tooth.
(D) Ben had Jolly's implied consent to strike him on the back.

Principle Two

If the nature of a product is such that it is reasonably certain to place life and limb in peril when negligently made, it is then a thing of danger and the manufacturer will be liable for damages to the purchaser due to his negligence. If to the element of danger there is added knowledge that the product will be used by persons other than the purchaser without further testing, then irrespective of contract, the manufacturer is under a duty to make the product carefully, or the manufacturer will be responsible for all damages to any party that ensue from the manufacturer's negligence.

35. Piper was a manufacturer of small boats. He employed an inspection staff to check the boats for malfunction, and they usually did their job carefully. Ed, one of Piper's inspectors, was momentarily distracted by a pretty girl and he missed a minor flaw in the hull of one of the boats. Wilson loved boating and just happened to buy this particular boat. Lucky, Wilson's son, took the new boat out for a spin on the lake and, under pressure, the hull sprang a leak. Lucky was just barely able to swim to shore and had to spend several days in a hospital suffering from shock. A suit by Lucky against Piper for damages due to shock is decided for Lucky.

    Which one of the following choices was the major factor in the disposition of the case, considering the principle above?

    (A) Ed was responsible for the flaw in the boat.
    (B) An employee of Piper was responsible for the flaw in the boat slipping by.
    (C) Lucky was not the owner of the boat.
    (D) Wilson was the only person to whom the manufacturer owed a duty of due care.

36. Wally was a new and used car dealer. His repairman usually gave each car that was sold a complete inspection before it was delivered to the customer. However, one day, Benny, the chief mechanic, was out sick, and several cars with malfunctions dating from the time of manufacture were sold without inspection. Ted, who bought one of these cars, was seriously injured when a faulty suspension arm broke and the car veered into a highway guardrail. A suit by Ted against the manufacturer is decided for Ted.

    Which one of the following choices was the major factor in the disposition of the case, considering the principle above?

    (A) Wally should have made sure that all cars were inspected.
    (B) A car is a thing of danger when negligently made.
    (C) Benny was ultimately liable because it was his negligence that allowed the malfunction to slip by.
    (D) The manufacturer is always responsible for the action of any dealer.

37. Firefly, a manufacturer of small aircraft, guaranteed that it would pay for any damage to the purchaser which resulted from the operation of a Firefly aircraft, if the reason for the damage was the negligence of Firefly. Roger loaned his Firefly aircraft to his friend Skipper for the weekend. Skipper was normally a very careful pilot and had never been in an accident. While airborne, Skipper noticed that the plane's headlights were not working, and he decided to get them repaired before dark. However, as Skipper was approaching the runway, the plane got caught in a downdraft. The plane crashed, and Skipper broke his arm. A suit by Skipper against Firefly for the damage done to his arm is decided for Firefly.

Which of the following choices was the major factor in the disposition of the case, considering the principle above?

(A) Firefly did not guarantee to pay for damages to anyone but the purchaser.
(B) The faulty headlights were not the cause of the accident.
(C) Roger should have checked the headlights before he loaned the plane to Skipper.
(D) Skipper, being an experienced pilot, should have looked for malfunctions before starting.

Principle Three

Any person, firm, or corporation who brings, or permits to be brought, upon its premises that which is of an ultra-hazardous nature, and who knows, or in the exercise of reasonable care should have known, its ultra-hazardous nature, is liable for any injury proximately caused another by its miscarriage, unless the person so harmed knows, or in the exercise of reasonable care should have known of its ultra-hazardous nature and failed to exercise reasonable care for his own safety; or unless he knowingly and voluntarily invited the injury and brought it upon himself.

38. The Debuke Construction Company was blasting a roadway through the side of a mountain. Sparks was the chief blasting engineer. The Transport Freight Company was employed to carry the dynamite to the construction site but they did their job in a very careless manner. The dynamite was not tied down securely in the truck nor was the truck a specially-made vehicle for this type of work. Sparks had been around dynamite for years and was sure that he knew how to handle it; so sure in fact, that he often smoked while standing close to a full case of explosives. Sparks entered the Transport truck and lit a match, which caused the dynamite to explode, killing Sparks. A suit by the estate of Sparks for wrongful death against Transport Freight Co. is decided for Transport.

Which one of the following choices was the major factor in the disposition of the case, considering the principle above?

(A) The suit for damages should have been brought against the De-
buke Construction Co.
(B) The Transport Freight Co. is not responsible for the way its men
handle their work.
(C) The chief blasting engineer always assumes the risk of a mishap.
(D) Sparks did not exercise reasonable care for his own safety.

39. The Boxo Warehouse Company wanted to clean the outside walls of its
building. It contracted with the Clean Rite Maintenance Company to
do the job. Clean Rite brought a large vat of sulfuric acid onto the
premises of the Boxo Warehouse. Billy, one of Boxo's employees, was
carrying a large pile of cartons across the warehouse. One of the
cartons fell into the vat of acid causing some of the acid to splash up on
Barry burning him badly. A suit by Barry against Boxo for damages is
decided for Barry.

Which one of the following choices was the major factor in the disposition of the case, considering the principle above?

(A) It was a Boxo employee who caused the acid to splash onto Barry.
(B) Boxo was liable because sulfuric acid is of an ultra-hazardous na-
ture.
(C) Clean Rite was negligent in the storage of the sulfuric acid.
(D) Billy was carrying a pile of cartons which was too large.

40. Gaser was an exterminator contracted to get the bugs out of the Ace
Widget Factory. One morning, before any employee arrived, Gaser
went into the basement of the Ace Factory and sprayed a highly poi-
sonous gas. Before spraying, Gaser tried to seal off the basement so that
the gas would not escape into the factory itself; however, he was unsuccessful. During the normal work day much of the gas did escape into the
work area, and Spiro was overcome by the fumes. The Ace management had Spiro rushed to a hospital, but it was too late to prevent
permanent damage to his lungs. A suit by Spiro against the Ace Widget
Factory for damage to his lungs is decided for Spiro.

Which one of the following choices was the major factor in the disposition of the case, considering the principle above?

(A) Gaser was negligent in not sealing off the basement properly.
(B) The gas was dangerous to both bugs and human beings.
(C) The Ace Factory employed Gaser to exterminate the bugs.
(D) It was defects in the factory that allowed the gas to seep into the
work area.

END OF TEST

TEST III. PRACTICAL JUDGMENT

TIME: 40 Minutes. 40 Questions.

DIRECTIONS: In this test you will be presented with a detailed case study of a practical business situation. Read the study carefully. Then answer the two sets of questions based upon the reading. In the Data Evaluation questions, you will be asked to classify certain facts on the basis of their importance to the case presented. In the Data Application questions you will be asked to make judgments based upon your comprehension of the information.

Correct and explanatory answers are provided at the end of the exam. After you have completed the entire exam, read the explanations carefully. They'll reinforce your strengths and pinpoint your weaknesses so that you know just what to study to raise your score.

Business Situation I. Monitor Textile

In January, Mr. Norman Dixon, superintendent of the Monitor Textile Company, was considering replacing one of the two industrial forklift trucks operating in the plant. The two trucks in question are gasoline operated, and three and four years old, respectively. They can be used interchangeably. The maintenance expense for the older truck has been rising steadily, and currently amounts to about $20 per month in addition to normal servicing, gasoline, and oil. This truck is not dependable and is frequently out of service awaiting repairs.

One truck is used on the truck dock for loading and unloading packages of mohair wool and cloth from highway trucks. The "dock" truck is used only during the day shift when the company's two highway trucks are in operation. This "dock" truck must climb a ramp into the highway trucks.

The other truck is used inside the plant to move goods from machines to storage, from dyeing to finishing, and to take goods to the repair room. It is also used to carry drums of chemicals. When used to move pallets of goods from the pallet stacking machine, the "inside" truck must return promptly to pick up the next load. If the truck is delayed during this operation, the machine has to be shut down. For the most part, the "inside" truck operates on an intermittent schedule, not following any fixed pattern. During the day shift, there is one driver with the "inside" truck at all times. During the other two shifts, the "inside" truck is in use about half the time, or a total of about eight hours for these two shifts.

Mr. Dixon is undecided as to whether the company should buy an electric or a gasoline operated fork truck. The Stevens Industrial Truck Company, distributors of Columbia fork trucks, services the two Columbia trucks in the Monitor plant. If a new fork truck is bought, it will be bought through the

Stevens company. This company offers a service agreement which provides for a monthly visit by an experienced serviceman who lubricates and adjusts both gas and electric trucks. The rate is $15 per month for the first gas truck and $10 for each additional truck. A flat fee of $10 per month is charged for each electric truck. The difference between the charge for a gas and for an electric truck represents the cost of an oil filter cartridge that has to be replaced on gas trucks. If additional repairs for either type of truck are required, the owner is charged for the cost of parts and for the serviceman's time at the rate of $6 per hour.

The power supply for an electric truck of the type being considered by Mr. Dixon is an 18-cell, lead acid, 6.68 kilowatt-hour capacity battery. The cost of this battery is about $1,000. Mr. Suiter, the sales representative for the Stevens Company, says that this battery will provide sufficient power for the truck to travel continuously for eight hours over a level surface and still have the power needed to operate the lifting mechanism. This power supply would be adequate for the operation of the "inside" truck for the entire day shift. A second battery would be required if the truck were to be used in excess of one eight-hour shift. On this basis, Mr. Dixon anticipates that two batteries, each charged once a day, will provide sufficient power for the operation of the "inside" truck for all three shifts.

It is difficult to estimate how much of a power drain the ramp will cause if an electric truck were to be used on the dock. Although Mr. Suiter is confident that the regular charge is adequate for the "inside" truck, which operates without going up or down any inclines, he is uncertain whether this charge will suffice for ramp operation. The use of the ramp causes a heavy drain on the battery. A power failure on the ramp would delay all operations until the battery could be recharged and the truck put back to work.

The life expectancy of a battery is largely dependent on the number of times it is charged and discharged. A battery which is charged once a day can be expected to last approximately five years. When the output of a battery is less than 80 percent of its initial capacity, it is discarded. Mr. Suiter states that the Monitor Company can count on at least a $50 salvage value for the discarded battery.

If an electric truck is used inside, it will be necessary to charge the battery in the truck twice a day. To facilitate this operation, a heavy metal stand with rollers on its top, at the same level as the battery roll-out compartment, will have to be constructed. This will cost $170.

The installation of battery charging equipment is another cost incurred by electric trucks. A charger capable of charging one battery at a time costs $550. Mr. Suiter recommends purchasing independent chargers so that in the rare event of a breakdown of a charger, all batteries will not be disabled. A charger is expected to last as long as an electric truck. The installation of a charger necessitates bringing a 550-volt power line from another section of the plant which will cost $50. The cost of electricity required to charge the battery for eight hours of operation is about $0.20. Mr. Dixon understands that the charging operation requires about three hours.

The two gasoline operated trucks have been using a total of about five gallons of gasoline per day, at a cost of $0.50 per gallon. Mr. Suiter states that this rate of gasoline consumption is normal for these trucks. They are equipped with two-gallon gasoline tanks, which the manufacturer considers adequate for eight hours of operation.

The initial cost of a gas truck is $3,600. The cost of an electric truck without a battery is $4,700. It is expected that an electric truck will operate efficiently for at least ten years when operated eight hours a day. The life of a gas truck is expected to be six to eight years on the same basis, assuming a major ($200) engine overhaul sometime after the third year. If operated 16 hours a day, as is the case with the "inside" truck, the life expectancy of either an electric or a gas truck will be cut in half, and the overhaul of the gas engine will probably be required at the end of two years.

Mr. Suiter explains the longer life of the electric trucks by stating that there are a great many more moving parts in a gas truck than in an electric one. The gas trucks can be "pushed" to get a job done faster at the expense of increasing wear on the moving parts. Because of the power limitations of the electric trucks, excessive wear is largely eliminated.

Mr. Suiter estimates that for about $1,000 the service department of his company can overhaul the older gas truck. Because of the condition of this truck, however, the Stevens service manager recommends a "factory overhaul" that includes installation of a new engine and replacement of practically all moving parts in the truck. This will cost roughly 75 percent of the cost of a new gas truck. About a week will be required for either type of overhaul, and the Stevens Company will lend the Monitor Company a truck for that period. Mr. Hunt, the Stevens sales manager, has offered the Monitor Company a trade-in allowance of $750 for the four-year-old gas truck and $1,000 for the newer truck.

Mr. Hunt states that the Monitor Company can expect shipment of a gas truck late in February, or of an electric truck in March.

DATA EVALUATION

DIRECTIONS: Based on your analysis of the Situation, classify each of the following items in one of five categories. On your answer sheet blacken the space under:

(A) *if the item is a MAJOR OBJECTIVE in making the decision; that is, one of the outcomes or results sought by the decision-maker.*

(B) *if the item is a MAJOR FACTOR in arriving at the decision; that is, a consideration explicitly mentioned in the passage that is basic in determining the decision.*

(C) *if the item is a MINOR FACTOR in making the decision; that is, a secondary consideration that affects the criteria tangentially, relating to a Major Factor rather than to an Objective.*

(D) *if the item is a MAJOR ASSUMPTION made in deliberating; that is, a supposition or projection made by the decision-maker before weighing the variables.*

(E) *if the item is an UNIMPORTANT ISSUE in getting to the point; that is, a factor that is insignificant or not immediately relevant to the situation.*

1. Cost of an engine overhaul for a gas truck

2. Increased forklift reliability

3. Cost of bringing a 550-volt power line into the charging area

4. Initial cost of a gas truck

5. Number of batteries required for daily operation of the "inside" electric truck

6. Cost of a battery

7. Uses of "inside" truck

8. Cost of a battery charge

9. Amount of trade-in allowance for current trucks

10. Safety standards for operation of forklift trucks

11. Cost of serviceman's time in excess of normal maintenance

12. Size of gasoline tanks in the gas trucks

13. Cost of gasoline

14. Delivery dates for new trucks

DATA APPLICATION

DIRECTIONS: Based on your understanding of the Business Situation, answer the following questions testing your comprehension of the information supplied in the passage. For each question, select the choice which best answers the question or completes the statement.

15. The normal annual maintenance charge for the *second* gas forklift is

    (A) $180   (B) $10   (C) $3,600   (D) $120   (E) $200

16. It can be inferred that the major advantage of an electric forklift over one powered by gasoline is

    (A) lower initial cost
    (B) lower maintenance costs
    (C) greater reliability
    (D) lower operating costs
    (E) fewer moving parts

17. Which of the following is *not* included in the initial expenditures required for an electric forklift?

    (A) a battery
    (B) a battery charger
    (C) an oil filter cartridge
    (D) a 550-volt cable
    (E) a roller stand

18. Which of the following problems might result from the failure of one of the forklifts:

    I. Shutdown of the pallet-stacking machine
    II. Shutdown of the dying machinery
    III. Rising maintenance costs
    IV. Lost time for charging the battery

    (A) II and III only
    (B) I and IV only
    (C) I, II, and III only
    (D) II and IV only
    (E) I, II, III, and IV

19. Which of the following was mentioned as an advantage of gasoline forklifts over those powered by electricity?

    (A) longer useful life
    (B) less restrictive power limitations
    (C) lower maintenance costs
    (D) lower operating costs
    (E) greater reliability

20. The total annual cost of operation (normal annual maintenance costs plus the cost of the electricity required for 300 eight-hour shifts) of an electric forklift is

    (A) $180.00
    (B) $30.00
    (C) $4,700
    (D) $1,000
    (E) none of the above

Business Situation II. A. C. Chase, Ltd.

A. C. Chase, Ltd. is a manufacturer of canned goods located near Liverpool, England. It distributes its products to retailers, wholesalers, chain stores, co-operatives, hotels, and restaurants either directly from the factory or from several field warehouses. In recent years, sales have grown so enormously that some of the field warehouses have become too small. One of the warehouses is in Arlington, only 65 miles from the Liverpool plant. In October, the question arose as to whether the presently rented premises in Arlington should be replaced by a larger, company-owned warehouse, or whether the Arlington area should henceforth be supplied directly from the factory. In order to get a clearer picture of the financial consequences of both alternatives, Mr. Martin, Chase's sales manager, asked his assistant, Mr. Ellington, to gather together some preliminary data which could be used as a basis for further discussions.

Knowing that a new warehouse could not be completed for about two years, Mr. Ellington based his calculations on a projection of Chase's sales two years hence, namely: 8,400 tons, or 756,000 cases of canned goods. He then determined, after considering the size of the present facilities and discussing the proposal with a building contractor, that a new warehouse should contain at least 18,000 square feet of floor space and that building costs would approximate $8.40 per square foot. The additional warehouse equipment required could be purchased for around $7,000. Maintenance costs per annum as estimated by the technical department would be $8,400, excluding depreciation.

The company normally depreciates its buildings of similar construction at 2½ percent per annum. While this rate seems low in comparison with that applied to other fixed assets, Mr. Ellington realized that the proposed warehouse would be what is often called a multipurpose structure. The equipment, on the other hand, would be amortized over ten years.

Mr. Ellington next turned his attention to the transportation costs between the Liverpool plant and Arlington. Chase does not own a truck fleet of its own, but uses the services of Blackpool Truck Company, a Liverpool shipping firm. This firm, using 16-ton vehicles for supplying the Arlington warehouse, charges what is believed to be a favorable rate of $2.90 per ton for the trip of 65 miles. Blackpool can offer this rate only because it gets a substantial amount of freight from Arlington to Liverpool. Since Mr. Ellington does not have any idea what the rates will be in two years, he decides to use those currently in effect.

The cost of handling the goods at Arlington, that is, putting them into storage, taking them out, and assembling them for delivery to customers, is estimated at $0.70 per ton. Delivery from Arlington is by 7-ton trucks hired from Blackpool. Currently, the average size delivery is 29 cases (90 cases = one ton), but it is likely that this will decrease as chain stores asked for more and more deliveries to their branches rather than to their central warehouses.

The following list shows the proportion of the goods distributed from Arlington to different kinds of customers. If the trend of the last few years continues, within the next five years about 60 percent of the chain stores' deliveries will be to individual stores as against 30 percent at present.

PATTERN OF TRADE DELIVERIES
(Quantities for the Past Four Months)

Retail	29.0%
Wholesale	29.4
Chain Stores	29.9
Co-operatives	7.4
Hotel and Restaurant	4.3
	100.0%

The somewhat more than 2,000 customers that might be serviced from Arlington are located at distances from 47 to 110 miles (on the average 80 miles) from Liverpool. From Arlington the average distance is only 25 miles and the delivery cost per 25 miles is $0.061 per case, or $5.50 per ton. The total distribution cost per ton is therefore:

Liverpool plant to Arlington	$2.90
Warehouse handling	.70
Arlington to customers	5.50
Total	$9.10

If the new Arlington warehouse is not built, the customers will have to be supplied directly from the factory because it will not be feasible to continue to use the present facilities (which are rented from a railroad on the promise that it will handle a large amount of the in-freight from the Liverpool plant) for part of the volume and to ship the remainder directly from the Liverpool plant. If 7-ton trucks are used, Mr. Ellington estimates that the average delivery cost would be $0.14 per case, or $12.60 per ton. This rate was determined from the mileage and time consumption involved as well as costs obtained in connection with the first alternative. Instead of 7-ton trucks, Mr. Ellington thought of using 16-ton trucks for the second alternative until he noticed that the time per trip (it would take three days to distribute 16 tons) made this possibility completely unattractive. He therefore compared the distribution cost of alternative one with alternative two assuming the use of 7-ton trucks and arrived at a difference of $3.50 per ton, $29,400 for 8,400 tons.

If all shipments are to be made from the Liverpool plant, however, additional storage facilities of about 12,000 square feet will have to be provided, at a cost of about $5.60 per square foot. The extra equipment necessary will cost $2,800. Mr. Ellington estimates that the handling charges will be $0.56 per ton at the Liverpool plant and the additional maintenance charges will total $4,200 per year excluding depreciation.

Both alternatives call for capital expenditures and therefore the savings of each will have to be measured in some way against the necessary outlay. Intangible factors, such as the future of the senior employees at Arlington, the potential growth in the market area, and the likelihood of the demand for more direct shipments to individual stores will all have to be determined.

DATA EVALUATION

DIRECTIONS: Based on your analysis of the Situation, classify each of the following items in one of five categories. On your answer sheet blacken the space under:
(A) *if the item is a MAJOR OBJECTIVE in making the decision; that is, one of the outcomes or results sought by the decision-maker.*
(B) *if the item is a MAJOR FACTOR in arriving at the decision; that is, a consideration explicitly mentioned in the passage that is basic in determining the decision.*
(C) *if the item is a MINOR FACTOR in making the decision; that is, a secondary consideration that affects the criteria tangentially, relating to a Major Factor rather than to an Objective.*
(D) *if the item is a MAJOR ASSUMPTION made in deliberating; that is, a supposition or projection made by the decision-maker before weighing the variables.*
(E) *if the item is an UNIMPORTANT ISSUE in getting to the point; that is, a factor that is insignificant or not immediately relevant to the situation.*

21. Demand for direct shipments to chain stores

22. Blackpool's rates for shipping to Arlington in two years

23. Cost of renting new warehouse space in Arlington

24. Distance of customers from Liverpool factory

25. Maintenance costs of new warehouse

26. Transportation costs from Liverpool to Arlington

27. Delivery of products at lowest cost

28. Sales volume in two years

29. Impact of freeze-dried foods on the canned goods market

30. Distance of customers from Arlington warehouse

31. Volume of inbound freight for Liverpool plant two years hence

32. Transportation costs from plant to customers

33. Rate of fuel consumption of 16-ton trucks

34. Building costs of a new warehouse

DATA APPLICATION

DIRECTIONS: Based on your understanding of the Business Situation, answer the following questions testing your comprehension of the information supplied in the passage. For each question, select the choice which best answers the question or completes the statement.

35. Total construction costs of a new warehouse were estimated to be how much more than costs of additional storage space at the Liverpool plant?

(A) $2,800
(B) $6,000
(C) $4,200
(D) $84,000
(E) $29,400

36. It can be inferred that the importance of the projected increase in the number of deliveries to branches as a percentage of total deliveries to chain stores is that

(A) the company could not use 16-ton trucks for deliveries to branch stores
(B) it would require more shipments for the same level of sales
(C) it would permit a reduced rate for shipping
(D) it would make shipping direct from the factory more attractive than shipping from a new warehouse
(E) it would increase total sales

37. The level of freight traffic from Arlington to Liverpool is important because

(A) Blackpool does not have to charge for the cost of returning empty trucks to Liverpool
(B) it implies a uniform demand for Chase's product
(C) it implies a seasonal demand for Chase's product
(D) it permits Blackpool to use 16-ton trucks instead of 7-ton trucks
(E) it lowers handling costs at the Arlington warehouse

38. One may infer that one reason the costs of handling goods at the Arlington warehouse are higher than handling costs at the Liverpool plant is

(A) 16-ton trucks take longer to unload than 7-ton trucks
(B) maintenance charges are higher at the Arlington warehouse
(C) additional equipment is required at the Arlington warehouse
(D) Arlington is closer to the customers than Liverpool
(E) handling at the warehouse includes unloading trucks

39. All the following are intangible factors bearing on Mr. Ellington's decision except

(A) growth in the market area
(B) demand for direct shipments
(C) employee morale at the Arlington warehouse
(D) construction costs of a new warehouse
(E) demand for shipments to customers' central warehouses

40. The major disadvantage of making shipments direct from the factory instead of building a new warehouse is:

(A) the greater initial costs
(B) the unfeasibility of using 16-ton trucks
(C) higher transportation costs
(D) lower handling costs
(E) higher maintenance costs

END OF TEST

Go on to do the following Test in this Examination, just as you would be expected to do on the actual exam. You will find correct answers for the entire Examination following the last question. Check your answers carefully after you have completed the whole Examination.

TEST IV. DATA INTERPRETATION

TIME: 30 Minutes. 25 Questions.

*DIRECTIONS: This test consists of data presented in graphic form
followed by questions based on the information contained in the graph,
chart or table shown. After studying the data given, choose the best
answer for each question and blacken the corresponding space on the
answer sheet. Answer each group of questions solely on the basis of the
information given or implied in the data preceding it.*

*Correct and explanatory answers are provided at the end of the exam.
After you have completed the entire exam, read the explanations carefully. They'll reinforce your strengths and pinpoint your weaknesses so
that you know just what to study to raise your score.*

Questions 1 to 6

NET FUNDS RAISED

MAJOR NONFINANCIAL SECTORS

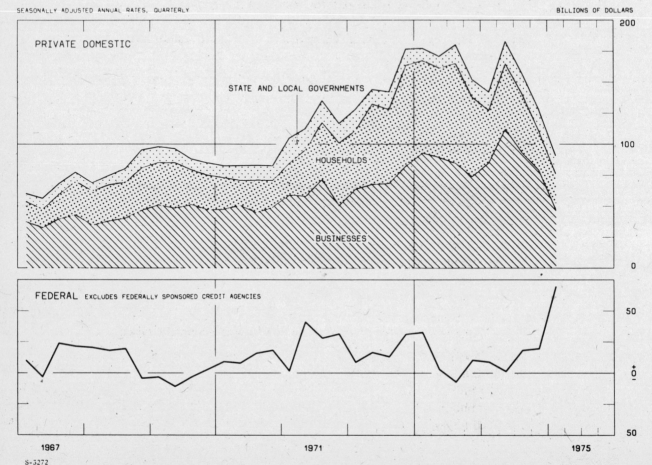

SEASONALLY ADJUSTED ANNUAL RATES, QUARTERLY

BILLIONS OF DOLLARS

PRIVATE DOMESTIC

STATE AND LOCAL GOVERNMENTS

HOUSEHOLDS

BUSINESSES

FEDERAL EXCLUDES FEDERALLY SPONSORED CREDIT AGENCIES

1967

1971

1975

S-3272

1. From the second quarter of 1974 through the first quarter of 1975 net funds raised by all private domestic financial institutions combined

   (A) increased by 27%
   (B) increased by 75%
   (C) declined by 50%
   (D) declined by 33%
   (E) remained approximately constant

2. In the first quarter of 1974, what percent of the net funds raised by the private domestic nonfinancial sector was raised by households?

   (A) 95%
   (B) 42%
   (C) 50%
   (D) 10%
   (E) 25%

3. One can infer that the sector whose fund requirements are most variable is

   (A) federal government
   (B) state and local governments
   (C) households
   (D) businesses
   (E) There is no difference among the sectors in this respect.

4. Between January 1, 1967 and December 31, 1972 net funds raised by households

   (A) increased 400%
   (B) increased 250%
   (C) increased 100%
   (D) increased 75%
   (E) increased 50%

5. Between January 1, 1970 and December 31, 1972 business's share of net funds raised by private domestic nonfinancial sectors

   (A) increased by 300%
   (B) increased by 100%
   (C) decreased by 50%
   (D) decreased by 75%
   (E) remained nearly constant

6. During the second quarter of 1974, state and local governments raised

   (A) $175 billion
   (B) $160 billion
   (C) $20 billion
   (D) $10 billion
   (E) $110 billion

Questions 7 to 12

Worldwide Military Expenditures

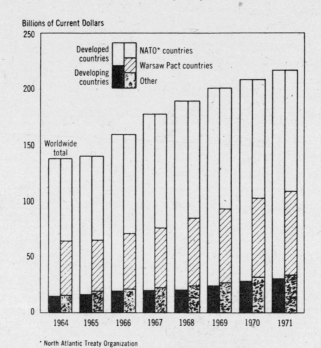

* North Atlantic Treaty Organization

7. In 1970, military expenditures by the developed countries were approximately

   (A) $25 billion   (B) $30 billion
   (C) $200 million   (D) $200 billion
   (E) $100 billion

8. Total worldwide military expenditures in 1966 were approximately

   (A) $160 million   (B) $200 million
   (C) $160 billion   (D) $200 billion
   (E) $320 billion

9. In 1971, military spending by NATO countries constituted what percentage of all worldwide military expenditures?

   (A) 15%   (B) 20%
   (C) 50%   (D) 75%
   (E) 90%

10. In 1971, developing countries' military expenditures were how many times as great as they were in 1964?

    (A) 1   (B) 2
    (C) 3   (D) 4
    (E) 5

11. The ratio between military expenditures of the NATO countries and the Warsaw Pact countries for the years shown

(A) was always greater than 2:1
(B) was always less than 1:1
(C) was approximately constant
(D) ranged from 1:1 to 3:1
(E) is none of the above

12. From 1964 through 1971, worldwide military expenditures

(A) increased by over 100%
(B) increased by $140 billion
(C) increased by more each year than in the previous year
(D) increased by less each year than in the previous year
(E) increased by about 50%

Questions 13 to 18

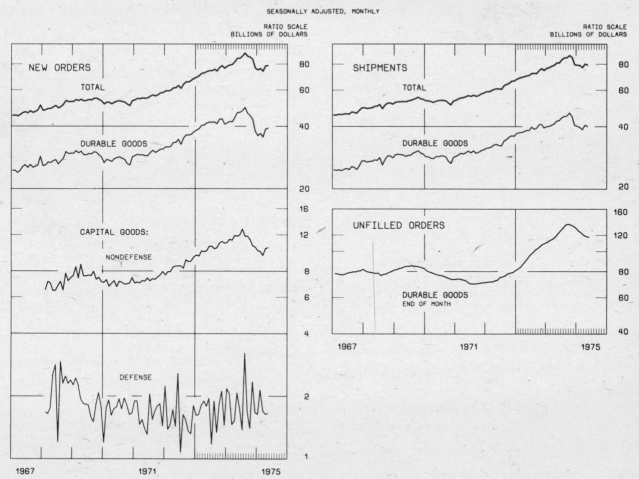

MANUFACTURERS' ORDERS AND SHIPMENTS

SEASONALLY ADJUSTED, MONTHLY

13. On January 1, 1975 new orders for durable goods composed what percent of total new orders?

    (A) 33%   (B) 50%
    (C) 87%   (D) 80%
    (E) 95%

14. On December 31, 1973 unfilled orders for durable goods exceeded shipments of durable goods by

    (A) 93%
    (B) 100%
    (C) 175%
    (D) 283%
    (E) 45%

15. The greatest range in one year for new orders for capital goods for defense was

    (A) $1 billion
    (B) $1.4 billion
    (C) $1.9 billion
    (D) $2.4 billion
    (E) $3.5 billion

16. From January 1, 1973 through December 31, 1974 the ratio of unfilled orders for durable goods to new orders for durable goods

    (A) decreased by 60%
    (B) decreased by 16%
    (C) stayed the same
    (D) increased by 16%
    (E) increased by 60%

17. From January 1, 1973 until December 31, 1974 unfilled orders for durable goods

    (A) more than doubled
    (B) increased at a rate of 3% per month
    (C) were always three times the shipments of durable goods
    (D) were 25% of total new orders for all goods
    (E) were three times new orders for capital goods for defense

18. On January 1, 1970 new orders for non-defense capital goods were approximately

    (A) $7 billion
    (B) 50% of new orders for durable goods
    (C) equal to unfilled orders for durable goods
    (D) 25% of total new orders for all goods
    (E) three times new orders for capital goods for defense

Questions 19 to 25

Federal Budget , Annual Average: 1968-72

Percent Distribution by Function

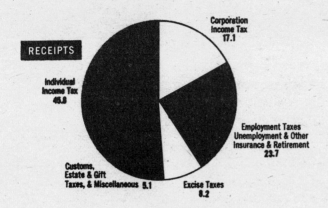

Federal Budget and Debt

In billions of dollars

Year	Receipts	Outlays		Surplus (+) or deficit (−)	
		Expend-itures	Net lending	Total	Percent of receipts
1968............	154	173	6.0	−25.2	16.4
1969............	188	183	1.5	+3.2	1.7
1970............	194	195	2.1	−2.8	1.4
1971............	188	210	1.1	−23.0	12.2
1972............	209	236	1.0	−23.2	11.1
1973 est........	225	246	−.2	−24.8	11.0

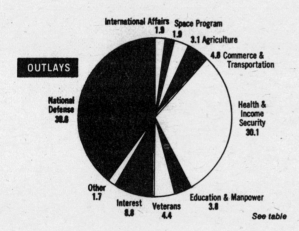

See table

19. The average annual customs, estate, gift & miscellaneous tax receipts from 1968 through 1972 were

(A) 5.1%

(B) $9.5 billion

(C) $47.5 billion

(D) $10.2 billion

(E) impossible to calculate from the information given

20. The total deficit for the period 1968-1972 was what percent of total expenses?

(A) 7.1%

(B) 7.3%

(C) 7.6%

(D) 7.9%

(E) 8.6%

21. If the budget were in balance, then what portion of health and income security expenditures could not be paid for by employment tax receipts.

(A) 6.4%
(B) 78.7%
(C) $12 billion
(D) 21.3%
(E) ½

22. Assuming that the distribution of receipts and expenditures in 1971 was the same as the five-year average, then by how much did the receipts from the individual income tax exceed the expenditures for national defense?

(A) 6.2%
(B) $11.6 billion
(C) $2.9 billion
(D) $13 billion
(E) $12.3 billion

23. How much interest did the United States pay during the period 1968-1972?

(A) $11.7 billion
(B) $17.5 billion
(C) $16.4 billion
(D) $82.1 billion
(E) $87.7 billion

24. Excise tax receipts were how many times customs, estate and gift tax and miscellaneous receipts?

(A) 0.62
(B) 1.61
(C) 16.1
(D) 6.2
(E) 3.1

25. Assuming that the distribution of expenditures was the same in 1968 and 1972 as the average for the 5-year period, what was the change in the expenditures for commerce and transportation between 1968 and 1972?

(A) 0
(B) $6.3 billion increase
(C) $3.0 billion increase
(D) $6.3 billion decrease
(E) $3.0 billion decrease

END OF TEST

TEST V. ERROR RECOGNITION

TIME: 20 Minutes. 35 Questions.

DIRECTIONS: This is a test of your ability to recognize standard written English. Some of the sentences presented are acceptable as written English. Others contain errors of diction, verbosity or grammar. No one sentence contains more than one kind of error. Read each sentence carefully, then classify each according to the categories that follow. Mark your answer sheet:

(A) if the sentence contains an error in DICTION; that is, the use of a word which is incorrect because its meaning does not fit the sentence, or because it is not acceptable in standard written English.

(B) if the sentence is VERBOSE; that is, wordy or repetitious without justification by the need for emphasis.

(C) if the sentence contains FAULTY GRAMMAR; that is, errors in parallelism, number, case, tense, etc.

(D) if the sentence contains none of these errors.

Correct and explanatory answers are provided at the end of the exam.

1. John, in an abstract mood, almost cut himself peeling an orange.

2. In those days, the most active, enthusiastic, and intelligent students were Joseph and me.

3. Any human group which exceeds in size that which can be held together by personal love and friendship, depends for its existence on certain culturally ritualized behavior patterns.

4. A New York City fireman has been accused with the abduction of Samuel Bronfman, heir to a great fortune.

5. At the time Lady Mary Wortley Montagu learned about the practice of smallpox inoculation, she was then living in Turkey with her husband.

6. Dioddorus was, as we know from a careful study of his works, not the most intelligent of men.

7. A comparatively few members of the council approved Mr. Smith's behavior.

8. There appear to be much unjustified criticism abroad of the manner in which our government officials are fulfilling their public obligations.

9. During the late nineteen-fifties and early nineteen-sixties a vast number of changes took place in America, not the least of which was a dramatic upsurge in civil rights activity.

10. The lawyer, speaking in measured tones, abjured his client to tell the truth.

11. I flunked the test because I had not studied my lesson.

12. When the ballots were counted, Lincoln had carried the state by only twenty thousand votes, and would have lost entirely but for the army.

13. There is no point in you saying your lines if we cannot hear you.

14. That suitcase was taken here from Europe.

15. Once one is sure that large enough vehicles are available, you can begin to operate an economically rewarding center.

16. Pasteur, in his studies of hydrophobia, could neither find nor discover an organism in the body that could reasonably be suspected of causing the disease.

17. Throughout his long political career, Disraeli was activated by his love of country and his fear of God.

18. It is generally to this part of the city that the heart of the exiled New Yorker usually turns.

19. The magazine you were reading was older than the other students.

20. The *New York Times* cautioned its readers and warned them concerning the poor food and high prices at Mr. Colatto's restaurant.

21. Our country home in Southwestern Connecticut is surrounded with verdant greenery.

22. In ancient Greece, only the aristocrats had enough money and liesure to undergo the strenuous discipline of the athlete for the reward of a crown of wild olives.

23. If the beverage industry would have acted upon its threat to produce carbonated beverages in plastic bottles, there would have been considerable protest on the part of environmentalists.

24. You should have became an engineer instead of a politician.

25. It is now generally recognized that cigarette smoking can seriously effect one's health.

26. The Beame administration is inflicted with fiscal troubles and internal dissention.

27. The three men who had taken the girl to the airport tried futilely to persuade her to take her seat on the plane.

28. Having just returned from a long vacation, the city seemed unbearably crowded to us both.

29. The table was beautifully arranged, laid with rare china and silver and supplied with both the luxuries of the fertile country and tropical delicacies.

30. Harvey is usually indolent, but when he gets into something, he becomes quite assiduous.

31. He turned to wait for his companion to join him.

32. John and Robert are totally disinterested in geology.

33. Realism, like nominalism, has undergone metamorphoses since Durkeim's time.

34. Darkness, rather than stormy conditions, mitigated against spotting the lifeboats.

35. Mount Vernon is neither the oldest, nor the most sumptuous, nor even the most ancient of the President's homes.

END OF TEST

Go on to do the following Test in this Examination, just as you would be expected to do on the actual exam. You will find correct answers for the entire Examination following the last question. Check your answers carefully after you have completed the whole Examination.

TEST VI. SENTENCE CORRECTION

TIME: 20 Minutes. 25 Questions.

DIRECTIONS: Some part of each of the following sentences is underlined. After each sentence are five ways of stating the underlined part. Choice A simply repeats the original sentence or phrase. If you think that the original sentence is more effective than any of the alternatives, pick Choice A. If you believe the underlined part is incorrect, select from the other choices (B, C, D, or E) the one you think is best and blacken the corresponding space on the answer sheet. In choosing the best alternative, consider grammar, sentence structure, punctuation and word usage. Do not choose an answer that changes the meaning of the original sentence.

Correct and explanatory answers are provided at the end of the exam.

1. Mr. George was as old, if not older, than any other man in the community.

   (A) was as old, if not older, than any other man in the community.
   (B) was older than any other man in the community.
   (C) was, if not older, at least as old as every other man in the community.
   (D) was, as old as any other man in the community, if not older.
   (E) was as old as any other man in the community, or older than him.

2. In accordance with the President's proclamation, a day is set aside for Thanksgiving every year in the United States.

   (A) In accordance with the President's proclamation, a day is set aside
   (B) In accordance to the President's proclamation a day is set aside
   (C) In accordance to the President's proclamation, a day is set off
   (D) In accordance, the President's proclamation, setting aside a day
   (E) In accordance with the President's proclamation, a day is set off

3. When a poor woman came to Jane Addams's Hull House, she always gave help.

   (A) she always gave help.
   (B) she always received help.
   (C) help was always given by her.
   (D) help was always received by her.
   (E) she was always given help by Jane Addams.

4. <u>You can own your own personal copy</u> of this record, if you wish.

    (A) You can own your own personal copy   (D) You can own a personal copy
    (B) You can own your own copy   (E) You can own a copy
    (C) You can own your personal copy

5. <u>Betsy was standing beside the horse wearing a white dress and red shoes.</u>

    (A) Betsy was standing beside the horse wearing a white dress and red shoes.
    (B) Betsy, wearing a white dress and red shoes, was standing beside the horse.
    (C) Betsy was standing beside the horse, wearing a white dress and red shoes.
    (D) Beside the horse, wearing a white dress and red shoes, Betsy was standing.
    (E) Beside the horse, Betsy was wearing a white dress and red shoes as she was standing there.

6. <u>His dog ran away while John was waiting for Adele.</u>

    (A) His dog ran away while John was waiting for Adele.
    (B) While waiting for Adele, John's dog ran away.
    (C) While John was waiting for Adele, John's dog ran away.
    (D) While John was waiting for Adele, his dog ran away.
    (E) John waiting for Adele his dog ran away.

7. We must consider the possibility <u>of him being barred</u> from the United States.

    (A) of him being barred   (D) of barring him
    (B) of he being barred   (E) of the barring of him
    (C) of his being barred

8. If a person wishes to succeed as a teacher, <u>you must have</u> patience and intelligence.

    (A) you must have   (D) one must have
    (B) that person must have   (E) every one of them must have
    (C) he must have

9. When a problem in chemistry arises, <u>or when we wish to calculate certain formulas, we find that a knowledge of mathematics is quite useful.</u>

    (A) or when we wish to calculate certain formulas, we find that a knowledge of mathematics is quite useful.
    (B) or we wish to calculate certain formulas, we find that a knowledge of mathematics is quite useful.

(C)   or when certain formulas require calculating, a knowledge of mathematics is quite useful.

(D)   or when we wish to calculate certain formulas—this is when a knowledge of mathematics is quite useful.

(E)   or when certain formulas require calculating, we find that a knowledge of mathematics is quite useful.

10.   The lead <u>laid</u> where it had fallen.

    (A)   laid   (B)   lain   (C)   lay   (D)   lied   (E)   lie

11.   <u>We could not hardly see through the mist.</u>

    (A)   We could not hardly see through the mist.
    (B)   We could hardly see through the mist.
    (C)   We could see through the mist, but hardly.
    (D)   We could see, through the mist, hardly.
    (E)   We could not see hardly through the mist.

12.   The election <u>affects both they and us.</u>

    (A)   affects both they and us.   (D)   effects both them and we.
    (B)   effects both them and us.   (E)   affects both them and us.
    (C)   affects both they and we.

13.   I feel tired this morning <u>on account of</u> I could not sleep last night.

    (A)   on account of   (D)   while
    (B)   due to   (E)   because
    (C)   owing to

14.   He is one of the most <u>skillful, if not the most skillful basketball players in the state.</u>

    (A)   skillful, if not the most skillful basketball players in the state.
    (B)   skillful, but not the most skillful, basketball player in the state.
    (C)   skillful basketball players in the state, if not the most skillful.
    (D)   skillful, yet still not the most skillful, basketball players in the state.
    (E)   skillful basketball players in the state, but not the most skillful.

15.   <u>The day, though quite cold, was windless.</u>

    (A)   The day, though quite cold, was windless.
    (B)   The day, though plenty cold, was windless.
    (C)   It was plenty cold, but the day was windless.
    (D)   It was plenty cold, but the wind had quit blowing.
    (E)   It was quite a cold day, but the wind had quit blowing.

16. The hammer strikes the bell, continuing as long as the button is pressed.

    (A) The hammer strikes the bell, continuing as long as the button is pressed.
    (B) The hammer strikes the bell, continuing this for as long as the bell is pressed.
    (C) The hammer strikes the bell, which continues as long as the button is pressed.
    (D) The hammer strikes the bell as long as the button is pressed.
    (E) The hammer's striking of the bell continues for as long as the button is pressed.

17. The crate suddenly fell apart; all the spikes having been removed.

    (A) The crate suddenly fell apart; all the spikes having been removed.
    (B) The crate, all the spikes having been removed, suddenly fell apart.
    (C) All the spikes having been removed, fell apart.
    (D) The crate suddenly fell apart, all the spikes having been removed.
    (E) All the spikes were removed from the crate which had suddenly fallen apart.

18. In the morning I found on the table a heap of snow which had drifted in through the window.

    (A) In the morning I found on the table a heap of snow which had drifted in through the window.
    (B) I found on the table a heap of snow in the morning which had drifted in through the window.
    (C) In the morning I found a heap of snow on the table which had drifted in through the window.
    (D) I found a heap of snow on the table in the morning which had drifted in through the window.
    (E) On the table in the morning I found a heap of snow which had drifted in through the window.

19. After my mother had awakened me, I laid in bed too long.

    (A) I laid in bed too long.
    (B) I lay in bed too long.
    (C) I lied in bed too long.
    (D) I have lain in bed too long.
    (E) I have laid in bed too long.

20. Many families are resettling in other slums, as bad or worse than those marked for obliteration in the current slum-clearance programs.

    (A) as bad or worse than those marked for obliteration in the current slum-clearance programs.
    (B) as bad as those marked for obliteration in the current slum-clearance programs.
    (C) worse than those marked for obliteration in the current slum-clearance programs.
    (D) as bad as those marked for obliteration in the current slum-clearance programs, or worse.
    (E) as bad as those marked for obliteration in the current slum-clearance programs, or worse than they.

21. Professor Hege rejects the pluralist concept of "rule by minorities," arguing instead that the American upper class occupies such a large proportion of leadership roles and has such high cohesion that it is actually a governing class.

    (A) that the American upper class occupies such a large proportion of leadership roles
    (B) that because the American upper class occupies such a large proportion of leadership roles
    (C) that the American upper class, because it occupies such a large proportion of the leadership roles
    (D) that the American upper class occupies a large proportion of leadership roles
    (E) that the American upper class, occupying such a large proportion of leadership roles

22. A careful driver can go thirty miles on a gallon of gasoline, and at the same time very little lubricating oil is used.

    (A) gasoline, and at the same time very little lubricating oil is used.
    (B) gasoline and at the same time use very little lubricating oil.
    (C) gasoline, his car requiring very little lubricating oil.
    (D) gasoline, with little use of lubricating oil.
    (E) gasoline and at the same time he can use very little lubricating oil.

23. Inspecting Robert's report card, his mother noted that he had received high ratings in Latin and history.

    (A) his mother noted
    (B) it was noted by his mother
    (C) his mother had noted
    (D) a notation was made by his mother
    (E) Robert's mother noted

24. I shall eat lunch now not because I am hungry, but it is being served.

    (A) not because I am hungry, but it is being served.
    (B) not because I am hungry, it is being served.
    (C) not because I am hungry but it is being served.
    (D) not because I am hungry, just because it is being served.
    (E) not because I am hungry but because it is being served.

25. No one raised their hand.

    (A) their   (B) his   (C) one's   (D) a   (E) they're

END OF TEST

Go on to do the following Test in this Examination, just as you would be expected to do on the actual exam.

TEST VII. QUANTITATIVE COMPARISON

TIME: 15 Minutes. 25 Questions.

DIRECTIONS: For each of the following questions two quantities are given . . . one in Column A; and one in Column B. Compare the two quantities and mark your answer sheet with the correct, lettered conclusion. These are your options:
A: if the quantity in Column A is the greater;
B: if the quantity in Column B is the greater;
C: if the two quantities are equal;
D: if the relationship cannot be determined from the information given.

COMMON INFORMATION: In each question, information concerning one or both of the quantities to be compared is given in the Common Information column. A symbol that appears in any column represents the same thing in Column A as in Column B.
NUMBERS: All numbers used are real numbers.
FIGURES: Assume that the position of points, angles, regions, and so forth, are in the order shown.
Assume that the lines shown as straight are indeed straight. Figures are assumed to lie in a plane unless otherwise indicated.
Figures accompanying questions are intended to provide information you can use in answering the questions. However, unless a note states that a figure is drawn to scale, you should solve the problems by using your knowledge of mathematics, and NOT by estimating sizes by sight or by measurement.

Correct answers for these questions appear at the end of this examination, together with the answers to all the other tests.

	Common Information	*Column A.*	*Column B.*
1.	$x > 0, \; y > 0$	$\dfrac{x+y}{2}$	$\sqrt{xy}$
2.		y	x
3.	$y = 3x + 7$	x	$\dfrac{1}{xy}$
4.	$y = 7$	$\dfrac{x}{y}$	$\dfrac{y}{x}$
5.		$x + y$	$x - y$

	Common Information	Column A.	Column B.

ABC is an equilateral triangle

6. | Area of inner circle | half area of outer circle

7. | Area of triangle ABC | $10\sqrt{3}$ square inches

8. | Area of outer circle | 2 times area of triangle

9. | $\dfrac{\text{Circumference of inner circle}}{r}$ | $\dfrac{\text{Circumference of outer circle}}{R}$

10. | Perimeter of triangle | $2\sqrt{3}\,R$

$\overline{AB}, \overline{CD},$ and $\overline{EF}$
are parallel
and equidistant

11. | $\dfrac{HI}{HG}$ | $\dfrac{HG}{HF}$

12. | IG | $1/2\,JF$

13. | HI | $1/2\,IG$

14. | Angle GHI | $2 \times$ angle HGI

15. | $\dfrac{10^4}{10^{-1}}$ | $10^6 \times 10^{-2}$

16. | $(82)^{-1/4}$ | $(27)^{-1/3}$

17. | $(0.003)(0.0021)$ | 60×10^{-7}

18. | $\dfrac{1}{5-3}$ | $\dfrac{1}{5 \times 3}$

19. | $\dfrac{\frac{1}{7-4}}{3}$ | $\dfrac{3}{2}$

20. | $\sqrt{9} - \sqrt{4}$ | $\sqrt{9-4}$

21. | $(.01)^2$ | $\sqrt{.01}$

22. | $\dfrac{0.1}{2}$ | $\dfrac{1}{0.2}$

23. | $\dfrac{0.7}{3}$ | $\dfrac{3}{.7}$

24. | $5\sqrt{33}$ | $3\sqrt{9}$

25. | $(2^3)^2$ | $(2^2)^3$

END OF EXAMINATION

CORRECT ANSWERS FOR VERISIMILAR EXAMINATION I.

Now compare your answers with these Correct Key Answers. If your answers differ from these, go back and study the Practice Questions to see where and how you made your mistakes. In doing this, the following Explanatory Answers should prove helpful. They provide concise clarifications of the basic points behind the Key Answers. Even where your Key Answers are the same as ours, go over the explanations carefully because they may be quite useful in helping you pick up extra points on the exam.

TEST I. LOGICAL REASONING

1.B	3.D	5.B	7.D	9.C	11.C	13.A	15.D
2.D	4.A	6.E	8.B	10.B	12.A	14.B	

TEST II. PRINCIPLES AND CASES

1.C	6.B	11.B	16.A	21.B	26.D	31.B	36.B
2.B	7.C	12.A	17.B	22.B	27.B	32.C	37.B
3.A	8.B	13.C	18.A	23.D	28.A	33.B	38.D
4.A	9.D	14.C	19.C	24.D	29.C	34.A	39.B
5.D	10.C	15.D	20.A	25.C	30.B	35.B	40.C

TEST III. PRACTICAL JUDGMENT

1.C	6.B	11.E	16.D	21.D	26.B	31.E	36.B
2.A	7.E	12.E	17.C	22.E	27.A	32.B	37.A
3.C	8.B	13.B	18.B	23.E	28.D	33.E	38.E
4.B	9.E	14.E	19.B	24.C	29.E	34.B	39.D
5.D	10.E	15.D	20.A	25.C	30.C	35.D	40.C

TEST IV. DATA INTERPRETATION

1.C	5.E	9.C	13.B	17.B	21.D	25.C
2.B	6.C	10.B	14.C	18.A	22.C	
3.A	7.D	11.C	15.C	19.B	23.E	
4.A	8.C	12.E	16.E	20.A	24.B	

TEST V. ERROR RECOGNITION

1.A	6.D	11.A	16.B	21.B	26.A	31.D
2.C	7.A	12.D	17.A	22.D	27.D	32.A
3.D	8.C	13.C	18.B	23.C	28.C	33.D
4.A	9.D	14.A	19.C	24.C	29.D	34.A
5.B	10.A	15.C	20.B	25.A	30.A	35.D

TEST VI. SENTENCE CORRECTION

1.D	5.B	9.C	13.E	17.D	21.A	25.B
2.A	6.D	10.C	14.C	18.A	22.B	
3.B	7.C	11.B	15.A	19.B	23.A	
4.E	8.C	12.E	16.D	20.D	24.E	

TEST VII. QUANTITATIVE COMPARISONS

1.D	5.A	9.C	13.D	17.A	21.B	25.C
2.A	6.B	10.A	14.D	18.A	22.B	
3.D	7.D	11.D	15.A	19.B	23.B	
4.D	8.A	12.C	16.B	20.B	24.B	

EXPLANATORY ANSWERS FOR VERISIMILAR EXAMINATION I.

Here you have the heart of the Question and Answer Method. . .getting help when and where you need it. Where one of your Key Answers differs from ours you have a problem which can easily be remedied by reading the explanation. Then, if you have time, you might be able to pick up points on the exam by reading the other explanations, even where you wrote the Key Answers correctly. These explanations stress fundamental facts, ideas, and principles which just might pop up as questions on future exams.

TEST I. LOGICAL REASONING

1. **(B)** is correct. Since both John and Mary appear to be referring to the students at the prep school, it would appear likely that the disagreement is over the characteristics of individual students. The thrust of this disagreement is that studious people are not athletic. (A) is incorrect because John admits that the students are bright. (C) is incorrect because John and Mary do not differ as to the students' intelligence. (D) is a contradiction of John's statement. (E) is completely irrelevant to either remark.

2. **(D)** is correct based on the thought of the passage especially the phrase "The work of literary art does not . . . present the reader with a provisional arrangement of reality." (A), (B), and (C) are incorrect because there is nothing in the passage to substantiate them. (E) is incorrect because although the passage makes us think of Poe's greatness in art, in no place does it state that his greatness was unparalleled.

3. **(D)** is correct because one cannot be positive of one's state of being, and the author makes this transition to poetry. (A) is incorrect because the passage does not support any value judgment about poetry. (B) is incorrect because it contradicts the passage. (C) and (E) are generalities which have no support in the passage.

4. **(A)** is correct. This statement implies taking in the objective world and transforming it in one's subjective consciousness which is the premise of the passage. (B), (C), (D), and (E) are incorrect because they do not relate objective reality to man's perception of it.

5. **(B)** is correct because (III) is the only statement which is not contradicted by the passage. (I) is wrong because the author implies that everyone has a different subjective consciousness. (II) is wrong because the passage states that the objective universe is mirrored in the subjective universe as the sky is mirrored in a lake. The lake is not mirrored in the sky.

6. **(E)** is correct because the passage is concerned with the "cultural forms of a society" and how they can be used as measures. (C) is incorrect because while the statement is true, it is not as precise as (E). (A), (B), and (D) are not substantiated by the passage.

7. **(D)** is correct. It is more reasonable for Alice to qualify her position as in (D) than to surrender it as in (A), or contradict it as in (B). (C) and (E) are *non sequiturs*.

8. **(B)** is correct because it incorporates the universality of pain with the different modes of expression found in every age. (A), (D), and (E) make flat statements about pain in a one-dimensional way and they do not follow the integrated pattern of the passage. (C) is incorrect because it only deals with Tolstoi and not the different ages.

9. **(C)** is correct because it is reasonable for a traffic patrolman to observe unusual occurrences and report them faithfully. (A) is incorrect because the agent has a vested interest in what he is saying. (B) is incorrect because a skin diver might not be expected to have great knowledge of ski slopes. (D) is incorrect because a daughter's love of her father will probably interfere with her judgment. (E) is incorrect because the soldier is too close to the situation to make an objective analysis of it.

10. **(B)** is correct because the author's assumption is that the artist's audience diminishes as our education becomes more largely technical. (A) is incorrect because saying that there are more artists than society needs is not saying there are more than society can appreciate. (C) is incorrect because it is a conclusion that may be derived rather than an assumption on which the argument is based. (D) is incorrect because no determined effort to destroy artists is stated. (E) is incorrect because no evidence of this is stated or implied in the passage.

11. **(C)** is correct. The job applicant has definitely interpreted the employer's remark to mean that happiness is a condition of employment and, therefore, the applicant's unhappiness will bar his employment. (A) and (D) deal with future states which are not covered in the dialogue. (B) is most likely what the employer meant to imply. (E) is incorrect since it is not indicated in the dialogue.

12. **(A)** is correct because the use of the phrase "only as trouble" implies that there are other ways to experience being glutted with energy. (B), (C), (D), and (E) all draw conclusions which cannot be supported solely by the content of the passage.

13. **(A)** is correct because the typical, according to the passage, is the "timeless model of old" implying what exists now has always existed. (B) and (C) are incorrect because they indicate change rather than stability as implied by the passage. (D) and (E) are incorrect because neither happiness nor monetary factors are dealt with in the passage.

14. **(B)** is correct. The key phrase is "evidently unfit it" which implies that the speaker wishes to deny women some right or privilege. Choice (B) is the only one that refers to such a denial.

15. **(D)** is correct because the use of the word "disadvantages" to describe the difference in treatment of men and women implies that the author disapproves of such differences and so would support a movement which is opposed to them. (A) and (B) can be ruled out since the sex of the author cannot be determined from the passage. While the passage is persuasive there is no indication that it was written by a politician as in (C) or an organizer of women's groups as in (E).

TEST II. PRINCIPLES AND CASES

1. **(C)** is correct because it most closely parallels the wording of the principle given. (A) is wrong because the principle says nothing about the motive of the agents. (B) and (D) are wrong because the principle says nothing about a warrant.

2. **(B)** is correct because it follows the case which states that the agents did not fear for their safety. (A) is trying to trick the examinee with the previous principle and this principle does not deal with location. (C) is completely erroneous. (D) is incorrect because this question is not dealing with the obscenity charge.

3. **(A)** is correct because the obscene material was not in plain view and the officers had only an arrest warrant. (B) is incorrect because the officers possessed an arrest warrant at the time of entry. (C) is incorrect because the objects were not in plain view. (D) is incorrect because it is covered by the principle.

4. **(A)** is correct because the agents had only an arrest warrant and the principle clearly states that a search warrant is required to seize evidence. (B) is incorrect because the matter of unlawful entry is not dealt with in this principle. (C) and (D) are incorrect because according to the principle a search warrant is required to gather evidence no matter how evident it may be or how directly related to the case.

5. **(D)** is correct because it deals with the issue of personal permission as in the principle. (A) is incorrect because permission of the suspect is required by the principle. (B) is incorrect because the principle does not deal with a self-protective search. (C) refers to a previous principle, not to the principle given here.

6. **(B)** is correct because it deals with the matter of delusion as stated in the principle. (A) is incorrect because the principle is not concerned with the fact of delivery. (C) is incorrect because it is contrary to the facts of the case. (D) is incorrect because the principle does not place any burden of proof on Mary.

7. **(C)** is correct because it gives the reason why Tom was susceptible to influence and deals with the actual deceit. (A) is incorrect because according to the principle it is not necessary for the beneficiary to exert the undue influence. (B) is incorrect because the falsity of Burton's statement relates to the proper beneficiary of the gift, and Mary is not the proper beneficiary. (D) is true but it is incorrect because it is not as inclusive as (C).

8. **(B)** is correct because it follows the principle and is true to the facts. (A) is incorrect because the key point on which the principle turns is that the testator must state his intended purpose if conditions were contrary to what he believed. (C) is incorrect because the principle concerns intention, not deceit. (D) is incorrect because Tom stated in the will what he would have done if Lenny were alive.

9. **(D)** is correct because Bob did not intentionally deceive Tom. (A) is incorrect because Bob truly believed her to be dead. (B) is incorrect because the principle does not deny a person the right to express his beliefs. (C) is incorrect because it is contrary to the facts of the case.

10. **(C)** is correct because the benefit went to Mary. (A) is incorrect because Burton did not benefit from his lie. This part of the business went to Mary. (B) is incorrect because the principle deals not with the lie itself, but with the ultimate result of the lie. (D) is incorrect because Burton knew that he was lying.

11. **(B)** is correct because majority support has not been clearly shown. The 40 pickets could have come from the ranks of those who signed the 79 cards. (A) is incorrect because the key point in this principle is majority support. (C) is incorrect because it is not clear that 119 of Fred's employees support the union. It is possible that only 79 of them support it. (D) is incorrect because the principle states that the basis of any bargaining is a demonstration of majority support of the union.

12. **(A)** is correct because the principle calls for proof of majority support that would be accepted by a reasonable man, and in this case neither union can prove a majority. (B) is incorrect because the principle does not provide for this alternative when an ambiguity is shown. (C) is incorrect because while it is true that Union Red had more authorization cards, it is not clear that they had the support of a majority of the employees. (D) is incorrect because the principle does not deal with the time at which an employer is approached by a union.

13. **(C)** is correct because in this case we do have a clear majority of employees supporting Union X. (A) is incorrect because the principle does not deal with courtesy. (B) is incorrect because the principle only calls for majority support, not peaceful majority support. (D) is incorrect because it is not covered by the principle.

14. **(C)** is correct because the one and only full-time employee did strike. (A) is incorrect. True, only the part-time employees signed the union recognition cards, but the full-time clerk showed support of the union by striking. (B) is incorrect because the privilege of striking is not covered by the principle. (D) is incorrect because the part-time employees are not to be considered in determining majority support; therefore, (C), which deals with the full-time employees, is more precise.

15. **(D)** is correct because it was reasonably clear to Terry that a majority of employees wanted representation. (A) is incorrect because according to the principle a formal request is not necessary. (B) is incorrect. It is majority support that is necessary for bargaining, not a real grievance. (C) is incorrect not only because the statement is untrue, but also because the state of employee satisfaction is not relevant to the principle.

16. **(A)** is correct because Clancy did not first make a search of Punk's outer clothing. (B) is incorrect because it is not knowledge of a weapon that is important, but rather the procedure that is followed. (C) is incorrect because it is not possession of a weapon which is important, but rather the procedure by which the search is carried out. (D) is incorrect because guilt is not relevant to the manner of searching the suspect.

17. **(B)** is correct because there was no real evidence of a weapon. (A) is incorrect because the principle stresses not the motive but the manner in which the search is carried out. (C) is incorrect. It is true but Burny did not feel what might be a weapon. (D) is incorrect because it ignores the requirement that the officer feel something that appears to be a weapon.

18. **(A)** is correct because the owner's statement made Fogarty's fear unreasonable. (B) is incorrect because it contradicts the facts. The owner did corroborate Casey's story. (C) is incorrect because it is the manner of the search, not the possession of a weapon, that is important. (D) is incorrect because the principle does not make a special exception for ex-convicts.

19. **(C)** is correct. There was suspicion which Smith did nothing to dispel, and a reasonable belief of a weapon on the part of Jones. (A) is incorrect because innocence alone will not dismiss suspicion of a crime. (B) is incorrect because the right to remain silent is not covered by the principle. (D) is incorrect and irrelevant to the principle.

20. **(A)** is correct. The principle calls for self-identification by the policeman. (B) is incorrect because a right alone will not quell suspicion. (C) is incorrect because while there appears to be an attempt, it was an improper search. (D) is incorrect because Roger did not identify himself as a policeman.

21. **(B)** is correct because it explains the court decision and fits the facts of the case. (A) is incorrect because it is too broad. (C) is incorrect because the cow went into a store, not a farm, and therefore (C) does not fit the case. (D) is incorrect because the principle is too broad and a cow is not a wild animal.

22. **(B)** is correct because it follows the facts of the case closely and justifies the decision in Jack's favor. (A) and (C) are incorrect because if either one were true, Jack would have lost. (D) is incorrect because it is too broad.

23. **(D)** is correct because it fits the facts presented. The sign should have warned Crafty of the present danger. (A) is incorrect because Buster would lose. (B) is incorrect because it is inconsistent with the principle stated in question 22. (C) is incorrect because it does not explain this result.

24. **(D)** is correct because it restates the fact pattern and takes into account Fearless' provocation of the bull. (A) and (B) are incorrect because either of these principles would cause Lester to lose. (C) is incorrect because Lester's bulls were known to have dangerous propensities.

25. **(C)** is correct because it takes into account that Wallet invited Jeff onto his land; that fact distinguishes this case from the previous ones. (A) is incorrect because there is no indication that Jeff constantly trespassed on Wallet's land. (B) is incorrect because the result would contradict the principle given in both 22 and 23, since the owner was not liable in either of these cases. (D) is incorrect because according to this principle Wallet would win.

26. **(D)** is correct because it is consistent with the facts of the case and explains why Buyer won. There is no proof of authorization for the brother-in-law to act on Buyer's behalf. (A) is incorrect because by using it Seller would win. (B) is incorrect because it does not fit the facts of the case; there was no attempt to change the offer of the sale of the horse to another buyer. (C) is incorrect because by using it Seller would win, since the brother-in-law acted on Buyer's behalf.

27. **(B)** is correct because it takes into account that Ed is the agent but it makes an exception since Hank knew that Wealthy would not buy Hank's land. (A) is incorrect because by it Wealthy would lose since Ed was his agent. (C) is incorrect because it does not provide for the actions of an authorized agent. (D) is incorrect because by using it Wealthy would lose.

28. **(A)** is correct because Dealer did have authority and Kane did not know that Baker would not buy. (B) is incorrect because by it Kane would lose since Baker did not approve of Dealer's action. (C) is incorrect even though it might give the proper result. It is not as narrow as (A) since it mentions a contract which binds the purchaser for more than one year. (D) is incorrect because it is much broader than (A).

29. **(C)** is correct because it mentions both the telephone and an intended party, and it allows Broker to win. (A) is incorrect because by this principle Broker would still be bound and Nightshade would win. (B) is incorrect, even though it will allow Broker to win, because it does not meet the facts as closely as (C). (D) is incorrect, even though it would allow Broker to win, because the term "at length" is not defined as precisely as in (C).

30. **(B)** is correct because Gears was acting at Parts' direction. (A) is incorrect because this case held that there was a binding obligation on Parts. (C) is incorrect because by this principle Parts would win. (D) is incorrect because it is too broad.

31. **(B)** is correct because a sock hard enough to break Arnie's jaw is an unreasonable reaction to a shove. (A) is incorrect because, while it is true, it would make Arnie lose. (C) is incorrect, even though it is true; there is only a legal right to resist with reasonable force. (D) is incorrect because the only physical harm to be expected by Cooper would appear to be inconsequential.

32. **(C)** is correct because the principle only allows the use of force in order to protect oneself from bodily harm. (A) is incorrect because the issue in question concerns only Roger and Descending. (B) is incorrect because Roger's initial motivation is not the immediate reason for the dispute with Descending. (D) is incorrect because Descending was justified in being on the staircase.

33. **(B)** is correct because McGuirk could not get at Peter in the bathroom, and Peter could have used the telephone to call the police. (A) is incorrect because McGuirk did act menacingly with a knife. (C) is incorrect because we are given every reason to believe that McGuirk wanted to harm Peter. (D) is incorrect. While it is a contributing factor to the court decision, it is not the major factor.

34. **(A)** is correct because according to the principle it is permissible to respond with equal force but not with greater force. (B) is incorrect because backslapping is not unlawful. (C) is incorrect because the law does not take into account the physical condition of the victim. (D) is incorrect because it is only a contributing factor.

35. **(B)** is correct because this choice lays the ultimate responsibility on the manufacturer. (A) is incorrect because it is not an employee but the manufacturer who is ultimately liable under the principle. (C) and (D) are incorrect because the principle covers any party who is likely to use the manufactured product.

36. **(B)** is correct because the car was negligently made by the manufacturer. (A) is incorrect because the manufacturer holds the ultimate liability in any case. (C) is incorrect because the principle only places liability on the manufacturer, not on the dealer. (D) is incorrect because the manufacturer is responsible for his own negligence according to the principle.

37. **(B)** is correct because the manufacturer's negligence was not the cause of the accident. (A) is incorrect because this is irrelevant since Firefly is liable for damages to any party who is injured due to its negligence. (C) is incorrect because the headlights did not play the major role in Skipper's injury. (D) is incorrect because even if he found the malfunction it would not have prevented the downdraft.

38. **(D)** is correct because Sparks foolishly lit a match in the dynamite truck. (A) is incorrect because it is overridden by Sparks' own negligence. (B) is incorrect because just as in (A) it is Sparks' negligence which is the key point. (C) is incorrect because it is not covered by the principle.

39. **(B)** is correct because Boxo took all responsibility for bringing the dangerous acid onto its property. (A) is incorrect because no matter how the accident occurred on Boxo property, Boxo would be liable. (C) is incorrect because Clean Rite is not liable under the principle. (D) is incorrect because we are dealing with strict liability which is not mitigated by comparative negligence.

40. **(C)** is correct since Ace ultimately caused the gas to be on its premises. (A) is incorrect because according to the principle the ultimate liability lies with Ace on whose premises the accident occurred. (B) and (D) are incorrect because they are only contributing factors not the major one.

TEST III. PRACTICAL JUDGMENT

DATA EVALUATION

(A) means that the Conclusion is a Major Objective;
(B) means that the Conclusion is a Major Factor;
(C) means that the Conclusion is a Minor Factor;
(D) means that the Conclusion is a Major Assumption;
(E) means that the Conclusion is an Unimportant Issue.

1. **(C)** The cost of an engine overhaul is a very small component of the operating cost of a gas truck.

2. **(A)** The passage states that the older truck was not dependable and was frequently out of service.

3. **(C)** The cost of bringing a 550-volt power line is $50 and the total initial capital investment for the electric truck is over $5,000. This is a minor factor affecting the total capital investment.

4. **(B)** The relative desirability of a gas truck depends primarily on its much lower initial cost.

5. **(D)** This is a major assumption because the number of batteries purchased determines the initial capital cost of the electric truck. Mr. Dixon assumes that two batteries are necessary.

6. **(B)** The cost of the battery is a major component of the initial cost of an electric truck.

7. **(E)** The uses of the inside truck are unimportant because they will be the same for an electric truck as for a gas truck.

8. **(B)** The cost of a battery charge is the effective daily operating cost of an electric truck. This lower cost is what makes the electric truck more attractive than the gas truck.

9. **(E)** Regardless of which truck is ultimately purchased, the trade-in allowance for the current trucks will be the same.

10. **(E)** There is no discussion of safety standards nor how they vary for electric trucks or for gas trucks.

11. **(E)** The passage does not specify which type of truck is more likely to require additional servicing, so the cost of this servicing is irrelevant to Mr. Dixon's decision.

12. **(E)** No mention is made of the effect of a smaller or larger gas tank.

13. **(B)** The cost of gasoline for daily operation of the truck is almost $1.00 as opposed to $0.20 a day for the electricity to operate an electric truck. The higher operating cost is the major disadvantage of the gas truck.

14. **(E)** The one month difference in delivery dates is irrelevant.

DATA APPLICATION

15. **(D)** The normal maintenance contract charge is given as $10 a month for each additional forklift; hence, $120 per year for the second gas forklift.

16. **(D)** The operating costs for the electric truck average approximately $2 less per day. It is also true that the electric truck is less costly to maintain, however this is not the major advantage because the difference in maintenance costs is only $5 per month.

17. **(C)** Replacement of the oil filter cartridge is what is responsible for the higher cost of maintenance for the gas forklift. All of the other choices are additional expenditures required for electric forklifts.

18. **(B)** Only shutdowns of the pallet-stacking machine and time lost in order to charge the battery might directly result from failure of one of the forklifts.

19. **(B)** The passage states that the gas truck can be pushed to get the job done faster.

20. **(A)** Maintenance costs are $10 per month or $120 annually plus electricity at $0.20 per shift or $60 annually for a total of $180.

DATA EVALUATION
(A) means that the Conclusion is a Major Objective;
(B) means that the Conclusion is a Major Factor;
(C) means that the Conclusion is a Minor Factor;
(D) means that the Conclusion is a Major Assumption;
(E) means that the Conclusion is an Unimportant Issue.

21. **(D)** Mr. Ellington assumed that the trend for increased direct shipments to chain stores will continue.

22. **(E)** Since Mr. Ellington's decision must be made now, Blackpool's actual rates in two years will not have any effect on that decision.

23. **(E)** Since Mr. Ellington has already decided that the two best alternatives are either building a new warehouse or shipping to Arlington directly from the factory, the cost of renting new warehouse space is unimportant.

24. **(C)** The distance of the customers from the Liverpool factory is a minor factor which affects the transportation costs from the plants to the customers.

25. **(C)** The maintenance cost of the new warehouse affects the major objective indirectly as one of the operating costs of the first alternative.

26. **(B)** Whether the first alternative achieves the objective depends directly on its operating cost.

27. **(A)** Since Mr. Martin and Mr. Ellington have accepted the necessity of altering their storage facilities, the objective is to do it at the lowest cost.

28. **(D)** Mr. Ellington based his cost estimates on assumptions he made about sales over the next two years.

29. **(E)** This is not mentioned in the passage and does not enter into Mr. Ellington's considerations.

30. **(C)** The distance from Arlington to the customers determines the transportation costs from Arlington to the customers.

31. **(E)** Inbound freight for Liverpool is neither mentioned nor considered. This is not to be confused with the volume of inbound freight for the Arlington warehouse *from* Liverpool.

32. **(B)** Whether the second alternative achieves the objective depends directly on its operating costs.

33. **(E)** Since the unloading time for 16-ton trucks of 3 days rendered them unusable, their rate of fuel consumption is unimportant.

34. **(B)** Whether the first alternative accomplishes the objective depends directly on its capital costs.

DATA APPLICATION

35. **(D)** The cost of a new warehouse is 18,000 square feet at $8.40 per square foot, for a total of $151,200. The cost of additional space in Liverpool would be 12,000 square feet at $5.60 per square foot, for a total of $67,200. The difference is $84,000.

36. **(B)** Shipping to branch stores rather than to a central warehouse would necessitate a larger number of shipments for the same volume of sales.

37. **(A)** Blackpool is able to offer Chase such a favorable rate because it gets a substantial amount of freight from Arlington. For this reason, the rate charged by Blackpool does not have to cover the cost of returning empty trucks to Liverpool.

38. **(E)** The major difference between the handling procedure at the warehouse and the plant is the extra step of unloading the trucks that deliver from the plant to the warehouse, and reloading the goods into the ultimate delivery vehicles. Unloading time (A) depends on the size of the load, not the size of the truck. Although (B) and (C) are true, these are not included in handling costs. The distance from Arlington to the customers (D) has no effect on the cost of an operation that takes place entirely within the warehouse or the plant.

39. **(D)** The cost of constructing a new warehouse is a tangible, not intangible, factor.

40. **(C)** It is stated that delivery costs will increase about $3.50 per ton (or $29,400 for 8,400 tons) if Arlington customers are supplied directly from the factory.

TEST IV. DATA INTERPRETATION

1. **(C)** Net funds raised in 1974 were $180 billion; in 1975 they were $90 billion.

   Percentage change $= \dfrac{180 - 90}{180} \times 100 = 50\%$ decline

2. **(B)** Funds raised by households = $170B − $90 B = 80 billion
   Total funds raised = $180 billion.

   Percentage $= \dfrac{80}{180} \times 100 = 44\%$

   Therefore the closest answer is (B).

3. **(A)** This answer can be inferred from the fact that funds raised by the Federal Government during the period show the greatest variation between a low of −$5 B to a high of +$70 B.

4. **(A)** Net funds raised in 1967: $52 B − $37 B = $15 B
   Net funds raised in 1972: $265 B − $190 B = $75 B

   Percentage increase $= \dfrac{75 - 15}{15} \times 100 = 400\%$

5. **(E)**   In 1970 business' share was $\dfrac{\$50 \text{ B}}{\$80 \text{ B}} = 62.5\%$

   In 1972 business' share was $\dfrac{\$90 \text{ B}}{\$175 \text{ B}} = 51\%$

Therefore the closest answer is (E).

6. **(C)**   Funds raised = $185 B − $165 B = $20 B

7. **(D)**   Military expenditures of the developed countries are represented by the unfilled-in portion of the first bar shown for 1970. By observation this bar indicates expenditures of approximately $200 billion.

8. **(C)**   This question can also be answered at a glance. The top of the bar for 1966 is slightly over $150 billion.

9. **(C)**   The answer to this question can be estimated quickly by noting that NATO expenditures were slightly over $100 billion out of a total of slightly over $200 billion, or about 50%.

10. **(B)**   The dark bar indicating military expenditures for developing countries in 1971 is approximately twice the length of the dark bar shown for 1964. Therefore the answer is 2.

11. **(C)**   By inspection of the graph it can be observed that the ratio of the length of the NATO bar to the Warsaw Pact bar is about the same for each year shown.

12. **(E)**   World wide expenditures went from $140 billion in 1964 to $220 billion in 1971. This is an increase of $80 billion which is an increase of approximately 50%.

13. **(B)**   When reading a ratio scale, such as this one, you must remember that the values are compressed toward the top end of the scale.

New orders for durable goods = $38 billion
New orders for all goods   = $75 billion
Percentage = $\dfrac{38}{75} \times 100 = 50\%$

14. **(C)**   Unfilled orders for durable goods were about $110 billion; shipments were $40 billion. The excess, $70 billion, is 175% of $40 billion.

15. **(C)**   The greatest spans in new orders for capital goods for defense occurred in the years 1968, 1972 and 1974. In each of these cases, the range can be observed as approximately $2 billion, making the closest possible answer choice $1.9 billion.

16. **(E)** Since new orders for durable goods were approximately the same (almost $40 billion) on the two dates given, the ratio can be determined solely on the basis of unfilled orders for those dates. This value went from $80 billion to about $130 billion or an increase of about 60%.

$$\frac{130 - 80}{80} \times 100 = 62\%$$

17. **(B)** This question can best be answered by elimination. From the previous question it is obvious that choice (A) must be wrong. Choice (C) can be eliminated because shipments of durable goods remained around $40 billion, which is only ½ of the $80 billion in unfilled orders on January 1, 1973. Total new orders ranged around $80 billion during the period in question, which is far more than 25% of the $80 to $120 billion range for unfilled orders, thus eliminating choice (D). Similarly, new orders for defense were at all times less than $40 billion and, therefore, much less than 1/3 of the unfilled orders. Thus, by process of elimination, (B) must be right.

18. **(A)** The answer to this question can be read directly from the graph. New orders for non-defense capital goods on January 1, 1970 were approximately $7 billion.

19. **(B)** The solution to this question is a two step process: first the total annual receipts must be averaged; and, second, we must take 5.1% of this total. Total receipts for the five years = 154 + 188 + 194 + 188 + 209 = $933 billion. Average annual receipts = 933 ÷ 5 = $186.6 billion. Since this is less than $200 billion, 5.1% of it must be less than 10.2 billion. There is only one such choice.

20. **(A)** The net deficit for the period was $71 billion, which is just a hair greater than 7.1% of the total expenditures of $997 billion.

21. **(D)** If the budget were in balance, then 30.1% − 23.7% = 6.4% of the *total budget* would not be covered by employment taxes. However, this 6.4% of the budget is $\frac{6.4}{30.1}$ = 21.3% of the health and income security expenditures.

22. **(C)** In 1971, receipts from the individual income tax were 45.8% of $188 billion or $86.1 billion. National defense expenditures were 39.6% of $210 billion or $83.2 billion. The difference was $2.9 billion.

23. **(E)** Interest was 8.8% of total expenditures, which we know from question 20 to be $997 billion. Rounding $997 to $1000 billion and multiplying by .088, we can estimate interest as almost $88 billion.

24. **(B)** This question merely asks for the ratio between 8.2% and 5.1%. This value must be between 1 and 2; therefore, the only possible choice is (B).

$$\frac{8.2}{5.1} = 1.607$$

25. **(C)** In 1968 commerce expenditures were 4.8% of $173 billion = $8.3 billion. In 1972 they were 4.8% of $236 billion = $11.3 billion. The difference between these two figures (11.3 − 8.3) = an increase of $3.0 billion.

TEST V. ERROR RECOGNITION

(A) means the sentence contains an error in DICTION;
(B) means the sentence is VERBOSE;
(C) means the sentence contains FAULTY GRAMMAR;
(D) means the sentence contains NO ERROR.

1. **(A)** "John, in an *abstracted* mood———." *Abstract* means theoretical, ideal. *Abstracted* means absent in mind.

2. **(C)** "———Joseph and *I*." *I*, not *me*, is the predicate nominative form.

3. **(D)** No errors.

4. **(A)** "———accused *of*———." One can be *accused of*, or *charged with,* a crime, but not vice versa.

5. **(B)** "At the time Lady Mary Wortley Montagu learned about the practice of smallpox inoculation, she was living———." *At the time* and *then* are synonyms.

6. **(D)** No errors.

7. **(A)** "Comparatively few———." *Comparatively few* should not be preceded by *a* or *the*.

8. **(C)** "There *appears* to be much unjustified criticism———." The subject, *criticism*, requires a singular verb.

9. **(D)** No errors.

10. **(A)** "———*adjured* his client———." *Abjure* means to renounce an oath. *Adjure* means to command solemnly.

11. **(A)** "I *failed*———" *Flunk* is out of place in standard written English.

12. **(D)** No errors.

13. **(C)** "There is no point in *your* saying *your* lines———." A pronoun preceding a gerund (an *-ing* form of a verb, used as a noun) takes the possessive case (*your* saying your lines).

14. **(A)** "That suitcase was *brought* here . . ." *Take* means to carry away from the speaker. *Bring* means to carry toward him.

15. **(C)** "Once one is sure that large enough vehicles are available, *one* can begin———." The pronoun must agree with its antecedent. *One*, not *you*, agrees with the antecedent *one*.

16. **(B)** "———could not *discover* an organism———." *Find* and *discover* are synonyms.

17. **(A)** "———Disraeli was *actuated*———." *Activate* is a scientific term meaning to make active. *Actuate* means to impel, act upon the will.

18. **(B)** "It is to this part———." *Generally* and *usually* are synonyms.

19. **(C)** "———than *those of* the other students." The magazine you were reading was older than the magazines the other students were reading, not older than the other students.

20. **(B)** "———cautioned its readers concerning———." *Cautioned* and *warned* are synonyms.

21. **(B)** "———surrounded with *greenery*." *Verdant* means covered with green vegetation.

22. **(D)** No errors.

23. **(C)** "If the beverage industry *had* acted———." The past perfect subjunctive form (*had acted*) belongs in the "if" clause in a past, contrary-to-fact, conditional construction.

24. **(C)** "———you should have *become*———." *Become*, not *became*, is the part participle.

25. **(A)** "———can seriously *affect* one's health———." *Affect* means have an influence on someone or something. *Effect* means result in or cause.

26. **(A)** "———is *afflicted* with———." *Afflict* means torment, torture. *Inflict* means impose (especially something unpleasant).

27. **(D)** No errors.

28. **(C)** "Having just returned from a long vacation, we found the city unbearably crowded." The city had not been on a vacation—we had. The participle (*having returned*) must be attached to the noun responsible for the action (*we,* not *the city*).

29. **(D)** No errors.

30. **(A)** "———but when *something interests him*———." *To get into something* is a colloquial expression meaning *to become interested in something.*

31. **(D)** No errors.

32. **(A)** "———are totally *uninterested* in geology." *Disinterested* means neutral, having no selfish interest. *Uninterested* means indifferent, not interested.

33. **(D)** No errors.

34. **(A)** "———*militated* against spotting the lifeboats." *To mitigate* is to moderate or to soften. *To militate* is to have effect, for or against.

35. **(D)** No errors.

TEST VI. SENTENCE CORRECTION

1. **(D)** is correct. In (A) both *as old* and *if not older* make use of the conjunction *than.* One of these uses, *as old than,* is ungrammatical. (B) changes the meaning of the original sentence, (C) is unclear, and (E) is ungrammatical.

2. **(A)** is correct. The idioms are *in accordance with* and *to set aside.* (D) is a sentence fragment.

3. **(B)** is correct. In this sentence, *poor woman* and *Hull House* are the emphatic expressions to which any pronoun used later must refer. Since the pronoun used is *She* (*her*), it must stand for *poor woman.* In (A) and (C) the pronoun incorrectly represents *Jane Addams.* (D) is awkward and (E) is repetitious.

4. **(E)** is correct. If you own something, it is necessarily *your own.* Therefore, (A), (B), (C), and (D) are all redundant.

5. **(B)** is correct. From (A), (C), and (D), it is not clear whether Betsy or the horse was wearing the dress and shoes. (E) suggests that Betsy was wearing the horse!

6. **(D)** is correct. In (A), it is not absolutely clear that the dog belongs to John. (B) suggests that John's dog, not John was awaiting Adele. (C) needlessly repeats *John.* (E) is not a complete sentence.

7. **(C)** is correct. A pronoun preceding a gerund (an *-ing* form of a verb, used as a noun) takes the possessive case. (A) and (B) disregard this rule. (E) is wordy; (D) changes the meaning of the original sentence.

8. **(C)** is correct. A pronoun must agree in number and gender with its antecedent. The antecedent, *person,* is singular and by convention is considered masculine. The appropriate pronoun therefore is *he. You* (Choice A), which is not singular, and *one* (Choice D), which is not masculine, are wrong. (E) incorrectly refers to the plural *them,* and (B) is unnecessarily repetitive.

9. **(C)** is correct. In all other choices, changes in subject unnecessarily alter the point of view from impersonal to personal.

10. **(C)** is correct. *Lay* is the past form of the intransitive verb *to lie* meaning to be in a horizontal position. *Lie* (E) is the present form, *lain* (B) is the past participle. *Laid* (A) is the past form of the transitive verb *to lay,* which means to put or set down. *Lied* is the past tense form of the verb *to lie,* which means to utter falsehood.

11. **(B)** is correct. (A) mixes two thoughts: *We could hardly see* and *We could not see well.* Choices (C), (D), and (E) are meaningless.

12. **(E)** is correct. *To affect* is to act upon; *to effect* is to bring to pass. The direct object of a verb must be in the objective case (*them, us*—not *they, we*).

13. **(E)** is correct. Choices (A), (B), and (C) require the insertion of the expression *the fact that* before *I could not sleep last night.* (D) makes no sense.

14. **(C)** is correct. (A), (B), and (D) make double use of *player;* in each case, one of the uses is ungrammatical (He is one of the most skillful *player,* He is the most skillful *players*). (B), (D), and (E) change the meaning of the original sentence. (D) is also redundant (*yet still*).

15. **(A)** is correct. Choices (B), (C), (D), and (E) contain colloquial expressions (*plenty cold, quit blowing*) which are not acceptable.

16. **(D)** is correct. It is unclear whether continuing refers to *hammer* or *bell* in (A) and (B). In (C), *which* refers to the entire preceding clause; this obscures the sentence's meaning. Choice (E) is awkward.

17. **(D)** is correct. (A) contains a sentence fragment. In (B) there is too great a distance between subject and verb. Choice (C) is not a sentence, and (E) changes the order in which the events occurred.

18. **(A)** is correct. (B) and (D) suggest that the morning had drifted in through the window. In (C) it is the table which has drifted in. In (E) I seem to have been on the table in the morning.

19. **(B)** is correct. *Lay* is the past form of the intransitive verb *to lie*, meaning to be in a horizontal position. *Laid* is the past form of the transitive verb *to lay*, meaning to put or set down. Choices (D) and (E) are in the present perfect tense (*have lain, have laid*), whereas the past tense (*lay*) must follow the past perfect tense (*had awakened*). *Lain* is the past participle of *to lie*, *laid* the past participle of *to lay*. I *lied* means I uttered a falsehood.

20. **(D)** is correct. In (A), *worse* is completed by *than*, but *as bad* is not completed by *as*. Choices (B) and (C) change the original meaning of the sentence, and (E) is awkward.

21. **(A)** is correct. (B) and (C) incorrectly substitute *because that* for *because*. (D) changes the meaning of the original sentence. (E) is a run-on sentence.

22. **(B)** is correct. (A), (C), and (D) unnecessarily shift the subject. In (A), there is also an awkward change from active to passive voice. Choice (E) is too wordy.

23. **(A)** is correct. (B), (C), (D), and (E) are awkward.

24. **(E)** is correct. The subordinating conjunction *because* is needed to make clear the relation between the two clauses of the sentence. (A), (B), and (C) omit this word. Choice (D) changes the meaning of the original sentence.

25. **(B)** is correct. Since *no one* is singular, the pronoun referring to it must also be singular; by convention such a pronoun is also masculine (*his*). (D) changes the meaning of the original sentence. (A) is not singular, and (C) not masculine. *They're* (E) means *they are*.

TEST VII. QUANTITATIVE COMPARISONS

1. **(D)** If $x = 1$ and $y = 4$, then $\frac{x + y}{2} = 2.5$ and $\sqrt{xy} = 2$

   If $x = 4$ and $y = 4$, then $\frac{x + y}{2} = 4$ and $\sqrt{xy} = 4$

   Therefore, the relationship cannot be determined from the information given.

2. **(A)** Since $y = 7$, $x = 0$.

3. **(D)** $\frac{1}{xy} = \frac{1}{0}$ and $\frac{1}{0}$ is an indeterminate quantity. The comparison cannot be determined.

4. **(D)** x/y is an indeterminate quantity.

5. **(A)** $x + y = 7$, $x - y = -7$.

6. **(B)** $r = 1/2R$, so $\pi r^2 = 1/4\,\pi R^2$.

7. **(D)** There are no dimensions given.

8. **(A)** Area of the outer circle is πR^2. Area of the triangle is $\dfrac{3\sqrt{3}}{4} R^2$. Twice the area of the triangle is $\dfrac{3\sqrt{3}}{2} R^2 < 3R^2$.

9. **(C)** These are both π by definition.

10. **(A)** One side of the triangle is $R\sqrt{3}$, so its perimeter is $3R\sqrt{3}$.

11. **(D)** Since HGI is similar to HFJ, $\dfrac{HI}{HG} = \dfrac{HJ}{HF}$.

   Whether $\overline{HG} = \overline{HJ}$ cannot be determined.

12. **(C)** Since the triangles are similar and the lines are equidistant, $IG = \dfrac{1}{2}JF$.

13. **(D)** No information is given about the ratios of the sides of HGI.

14. **(D)** No information is given about the angles of HGI.

15. **(A)** 10^5, 10^4.

16. **(B)** $(82)^{-1/4} = \dfrac{1}{(82)^{1/4}} < \dfrac{1}{(81)^{1/4}} = 1/3 = \dfrac{1}{(27)^{1/3}} = (27)^{-1/3}$.

17. **(A)** $0.0000063 > 60 \times 10^{-7}$.

18. **(A)** $1/2 > 1/15$.

19. **(B)** $1 < 3/2$.

20. **(B)** $1 < \sqrt{5}$.

21. **(B)** $.0001 < .1$.

22. **(B)** $.05 < 5$.

23. **(B)** $0.7/3 < 1 < 3/0.7$.

24. **(B)** $\sqrt[5]{33}$ is approximately 2.2, $\sqrt[3]{9}$ is approximately 2.5.

25. **(C)** $64 = 64$.

SCORE YOURSELF

Compare your answers to the Correct Key Answers at the end of the Examination. To determine your score, count the number of correct answers in each test. Then count the number of incorrect answers. Subtract ¼ of the number of incorrect answers from the number of correct answers. Plot the resulting figure on the graph below by blackening the bar under each test to the point of your score. Plan your study to strengthen the weaknesses indicated on your scoring graph.

EXAM I	Very Poor	Poor	Average	Good	Excellent
LOGICAL REASONING 15 Questions	1-2	3-6	7-10	11-13	14-15
PRINCIPLES AND CASES 40 Questions	1-7	8-17	18-28	29-35	36-40
PRACTICAL JUDGMENT 40 Questions	1-7	8-17	18-28	29-35	36-40
DATA INTERPRETATION 25 Questions	1-4	5-10	11-17	18-22	23-25
ERROR RECOGNITION 35 Questions	1-6	7-15	16-25	26-31	32-35
SENTENCE CORRECTION 25 Questions	1-4	5-10	11-17	18-22	23-25
QUANTITATIVE COMPARISON 25 Questions	1-4	5-10	11-17	18-22	23-25

EXAM II	Very Poor	Poor	Average	Good	Excellent
READING COMPREHENSION 25 Questions	1-4	5-10	11-17	18-22	23-25
PRINCIPLES AND CASES 40 Questions	1-7	8-17	18-28	29-35	36-40
PRACTICAL JUDGMENT 20 Questions	1-3	4-8	9-15	16-18	19-20
DATA INTERPRETATION 25 Questions	1-4	5-10	11-17	18-22	23-25
ERROR RECOGNITION 35 Questions	1-6	7-15	16-25	26-31	32-35
SENTENCE CORRECTION 25 Questions	1-4	5-10	11-17	18-22	23-25
LOGICAL REASONING 20 Questions	1-3	4-8	9-15	16-18	19-20

Law School Admission Test

SECOND VERISIMILAR EXAM

This Examination is very much like the one you'll take. It was constructed by professionals who utilized all the latest information available. They derived a series of Tests which neatly cover all the subjects you are likely to encounter on the actual examination. Stick to business, follow all instructions closely, and score yourself objectively. If you do poorly . . . review. If necessary, take this Examination again for comparison.

Allow about 3½ hours for this Examination.

In order to create the climate of the actual exam, that's exactly what you should allow yourself . . . no more, no less. Use a watch to keep a record of your time, since it might suit your convenience to try this practice exam in several short takes.

ANALYSIS AND TIMETABLE: VERISIMILAR EXAMINATION II.		
This table is both an analysis of the exam that follows and a priceless preview of the actual test. Look it over carefully and use it well.		
SUBJECT TESTED	*Time Allowed*	*Questions*
READING COMPREHENSION	30 minutes	25
PRINCIPLES AND CASES	55 minutes	40
PRACTICAL JUDGMENT	20 minutes	20
DATA INTERPRETATION	30 minutes	25
ERROR RECOGNITION	20 minutes	35
SENTENCE CORRECTION	20 minutes	25
LOGICAL REASONING	25 minutes	20
TOTALS EXAM II	200 minutes	190

ANSWER SHEET FOR VERISIMILAR EXAMINATION II.

Consolidate your key answers here just as you would do on the actual exam. Using this type of Answer Sheet will provide valuable practice. Tear it out along the indicated lines and mark it up correctly. Use a No. 2 (medium) pencil. Make only ONE mark for each answer. Additional and stray marks may be counted as mistakes. In making corrections erase errors COMPLETELY. Make glossy black marks.

TEST I. READING COMPREHENSION

TEST II. PRINCIPLES AND CASES

TEST III. PRACTICAL JUDGMENT

TEST IV. DATA INTERPRETATION

TEST V. ERROR RECOGNITION

TEST VI. SENTENCE CORRECTION

TEST VII. LOGICAL REASONING

TEST I. READING COMPREHENSION

TIME: 30 Minutes. 25 Questions.

DIRECTIONS: Below each of the following passages, you will find questions or incomplete statements about the passage. Each statement or question is followed by lettered words or expressions. Select the word or expression that most satisfactorily completes each statement or answers each question in accordance with the meaning of the passage. Write the letter of that word or expression on your answer paper.

Correct and explanatory answers are provided at the end of the exam.

Reading Passage I

The growth and change that our nation has experienced in the past have brought substantial benefits. Population growth has been accompanied by even more rapid economic expansion, enabling the United States to enjoy the highest standard of living ever achieved by a major nation. Generally, the patterns of migration from rural to urban areas and from one region of the country to another have brought population to those areas where employment opportunities are greatest. Urban development and suburban growth have given millions of American families better housing, facilities, and services. The automobile and the extensive highway system—probably the most important forces influencing the pattern of growth in the post-World War II period—have increased the mobility of American families and provided them with greater access to jobs, housing, recreation, and shopping. This growth, in the form of population changes, technological development, economic expansion, and individual initiative, will almost certainly continue during the foreseeable future.

In the last decade, however, we have begun to recognize that a number of problems are associated with the process and patterns of growth.

Policies are needed to deal with these problems and to insure that future growth is both orderly and balanced. As Ex-President Nixon said, "The growth which this Nation will inevitably experience in the coming decades will be healthy growth only if it is balanced growth—and this means growth which is distributed between both urban and rural areas." Orderly growth requires overcoming the problems associated with past growth and preventing their repetition in the future. This will necessitate action by all parts of our society—individuals and families, private enterprise, and government at the local, state, and Federal levels.

The Nation's total rural population—that is, the number of persons living in open country or in places with less than 2,500 inhabitants—has remained relatively constant over most of this century. Nevertheless, there have been changes in population composition for many small, nonmetropolitan towns and other rural areas.

Since the 1940's, farm population has declined so rapidly that it now constitutes less than one-fifth of total rural population. At the same time, the number of market and service centers needed by this shrinking segment of rural America has fallen, meaning that many small towns are no longer able to serve their original function.

While some growth in nonfarm employment did occur in nonmetropolitan areas during the decade of the 1960's, the increase was unevenly distributed. In fact, half of the Nation's counties did not experience any growth in nonfarm employment, due to such factors as their remoteness from large volume markets, lack of natural resources and skilled labor, inadequate public facilities, absence of recreational and cultural activities, the financial difficulties of local governments, and limited pools from which to draw effective leadership.

Where employment opportunities have failed consistently to match the number of jobseekers, many younger and better educated persons have sought jobs in larger towns and cities, leaving behind an older and less skilled population in the midst of deteriorating economies. Often, the result is a tax base inadequate to finance basic public services or to attract new job producing investment (which would augment the tax base).

Consequently, many indicators show nonmetropolitan areas lagging behind metropolitan areas in terms of economic and social conditions. For example, in 1970, 13.8 percent of nonmetropolitan families were below the official poverty level compared with 7.9 percent of metropolitan families; and the median income of families in nonmetropolitan areas was $2,000 less than that of families in metropolitan areas. The percentage of high school and college graduates in the rural population is smaller. Rural areas have fewer medical and dental personnel in proportion to their population. The incidence of substandard housing is about three times higher in nonmetropolitan areas (where three-fifths of the Nation's substandard housing units were located in 1970). And in many rural areas, vital public services and facilities—such as police and fire protection, a clean water supply, sewage disposal, air transportation facilities, and recreational and cultural opportunities—are unavailable, inadequate, or provided only at high cost.

1. The author lists all of the following as benefits of growth except
   I. The population has been relocated to where there are employment opportunities
   II. Economic expansion
   III. Decrease in rural population

   (A)   I only
   (B)   II only
   (C)   III only

   (D)   I and III only
   (E)   I, II, and III

2. In the passage the phrase "healthy growth" refers to

   (A) urban growth
   (B) rural growth
   (C) balanced urban and rural growth
   (D) planned urban growth
   (E) planned economic growth

3. It may be inferred from the passage that in order to achieve healthy growth

   (A) present methods of growth must continue
   (B) new methods of organizing growth must be devised
   (C) action will be required by some parts of our society
   (D) individuals and families must take action
   (E) the Federal government will have the chief responsibility for change

4. According to the passage, since the 1940's farm population has changed so rapidly that it now constitutes

   (A) less than 1/5 of the urban population
   (B) less than 1/5 of the suburban population
   (C) more than 3/5 of the rural population
   (D) less than 1/5 of the rural population
   (E) 1/5 of the population of the U.S.

5. It may be inferred from the passage that rural towns and cities are in economic trouble because

   (A) they lack skilled leadership
   (B) the number of nonfarm jobs in rural areas is not sufficient to give a sound economic base to the community
   (C) the farming jobs in rural areas do not produce enough income to give a sound economic base to the community
   (D) most major industries have their home offices on the East coast
   (E) many years of drought have hurt rural economies

6. According to the passage the main reason that many young and well-educated persons have sought jobs in large towns and cities is that

   (A) employment opportunities in rural areas have often failed to match the number of job seekers
   (B) the jobs in rural areas tend to be noncreative and mundane
   (C) recruiters from urban based companies go out of their way to hire rural applicants
   (D) rural areas do not need the skills which the well-educated offer
   (E) the anti-intellectual climate of rural areas tends to repel well-educated job applicants

Reading Passage II

The key to successful treatment of cancer is to diagnose it at a stage when the cancer can be removed entirely from the body. We have at our disposal two methods by which such removal can be accomplished—surgery and X ray. These are not alternative techniques for all forms of cancer. Some forms of cancer are "radio resistant," or not responsive to such doses of X rays as can be safely administered. Other forms are sensitive to X rays and are called "radio curable" or "radio sensitive."

Among the radio-resistant cancers, which must be treated by surgery, are the cancers of the gastrointestinal tract and the associated organs, including the stomach, small and large intestines, gall bladder, pancreas, and liver. Surgical resection is also the primary curative approach to brain tumors, cancers of the breast, kidney, testis and ovary, and bone and muscle.

Very radio sensitive cancers, such as those arising from the lymph nodes and blood-forming tissues, of which Hodgkin's disease and lymphosarcoma are examples, are usually best treated by X rays. For cancers of the mouth and the face, the uterine cervix and the urinary bladder, either surgery or X rays may be selected as the primary treatment.

There are, of course, many modifications of techniques used by surgeons and radiotherapists. The ideal management of most patients with cancer is by a smooth working team of a surgeon, radiotherapist, pathologist and internist, with frequent consultations among the specialists regarding treatment and progress. In medicine, responsibility for a patient is not safely divided among doctors, and at any given time the primary management of a patient must remain in the hands of one of the clinicians.

Inadequate surgery or radiotherapy, which in the initial course of treatment does not include the total extent of the cancer, is not only doomed to failure but may well spread cancer cells and speed up the fatal course of the patient. That is why even the ancients, whose experience with cancer was usually limited to cancer of the breast, followed the principle of Hippocrates, "primum non nocere," meaning, "first do not harm."

Surgical resections of internal cancers became possible following the discoveries of two great boons to mankind, anesthesia and asepsis, during the 19th century. The German surgeon, Theodor Billroth, remains a giant of the early era, especially for his operations on the stomach and intestines. During the 20th century, with further improvements of surgical techniques and the introduction of blood transfusions and antibiotics, all portions of the human body became surgically approachable. American surgeons played an important role in the developments with Harvey Cushing's operations on the brain, and Evarts Graham's surgical removal of the lung for cancer.

Increasingly extensive operations for cancer have been perfected, and cancers of the cervix, head, and neck that were previously considered beyond operation are now accepted for surgery. The use of heart-lung pumps, artificial kidneys, and the replacement of bones and blood vessels were forerunners of transplantation of whole organs and surgical miracles at the same time. Experiences with more conservative resections of cancers of the breast, thyroid, and other sites show that these more limited procedures also have a definite place in the treatment of cancer. The question is not whether radical or more limited surgery is superior, because both have their place. The question is what procedures are best under what circumstances and in what patients with what tumors.

7. According to the passage the phrase "radio resistant" means

   (A) X-ray treatment will have no effect on a particular cancer
   (B) a particular cancer is super-sensitive to X-ray treatment
   (C) a particular cancer is not responsive to doses of X rays that can safely be given to a patient
   (D) X-ray treatment will be unable to affect a particular cancer because of its location
   (E) a particular patient may react allergically to X rays

8. According to the passage one prime difference between cancers of the gastrointestinal tract and associated organs and cancers of the brain is

   (A) cancers of the gastrointestinal tract are radio resistant while cancers of the brain are primarily treated by surgery but do not have to be treated exclusively in this fashion
   (B) cancers of the gastrointestinal tract are radio resistant but cancers of the brain are always treated by X rays
   (C) cancers of the gastrointestinal tract are treated by surgery
   (D) cancers of the gastrointestinal tract are treated by either surgery or X rays while cancer of the brain is always treated by surgery
   (E) there is no real difference between cancer of the gastrointestinal tract and cancer of the brain

9. The passage states that "responsibility for a patient is not safely divided among doctors;" however, it suggests that the ideal management of most cancer patients is

   (A) by one trained specialist with a knowledge of the patient's history
   (B) by one doctor in charge of several nurses
   (C) by a team of surgeons, radiotherapists, pathologists, and internists, with consultation throughout the case
   (D) by the teamwork of a surgeon and the family physician
   (E) by the cooperative efforts of a surgeon, a radiotherapist, and the patient who has been trained in cancer detection

10. As used in the passage, the phrase "first do not harm" means

   (A) the physician should be careful not to spread the cancer by inadequate treatment
   (B) a trained hand is essential to skillful surgery
   (C) an antiseptic environment is necessary in order not to spread bacteria
   (D) a skillful surgical team is necessary so that mistakes are made nowhere along the line
   (E) a hospital must be adequately equipped in order to treat a particular cancer properly

11. The passage mentions all of the following men as contributors to the fight against cancer except

   I. Theodor Billroth
  II. Hans Mayor
 III. Luis Vanteur

(A) I only
(B) II only
(C) III only
(D) I and III only
(E) II and III only

12. The author's primary purpose in this passage is to

(A) prove that X-ray therapy is more effective than surgery
(B) prove that surgery is more effective than X-ray therapy
(C) compare the use of X-ray therapy with surgery
(D) prove that the only effective treatment of cancer is a combination of X-ray therapy and surgery
(E) give the history of cancer surgery

13. It can be inferred from the passage that use of heart-lung pumps and artificial kidneys

(A) will be greatly expanded in the future
(B) will be handed over to specialists
(C) will become more expensive
(D) will become more complicated
(E) will eventually be replaced by the transplantation of living organs

Reading Passage III

Human beings are born with a desire to communicate with other human beings. They do this in many ways. A smile communicates a friendly feeling; a clenched fist, anger; tears, sorrow. From the first days of life, babies express pain or hunger by cries and actions. Gradually they add expressions of pleasure and smiles when a familiar person comes near. They begin to reach out to be picked up.

Human beings also use words to communicate. Babies eventually learn the words of their parents. If the parents speak in English, the baby will learn to speak English. If the parents speak Spanish, their baby will speak Spanish. An American baby who is taken away from his own parents and brought up by a family who speaks Chinese, Urdu, Swahili, or any other language will learn the language of the people around him instead of English.

Whatever the language, once young children learn to use it, the doors to communication open wider. Children can then tell other people what they want, how they feel, and who they are. At the same time, they can understand the words of other people and absorb new knowledge.

Words are important tools of learning. Children can ask questions and understand the answers; they can tell about their discoveries and express their likes and dislikes. A knowledge of language helps a child to develop complex processes of thinking and to find solutions to problems.

Words also help children grow socially. A child who cannot use language to communicate with others remains locked away in his own little world. No one knows what he wants to do or what his particular needs are because he cannot express himself. As the children around him become more proficient at language, they talk together. Friendships grow. But the silent child without language is left out. The other children are likely to ignore him or even make fun of him. He falls farther and farther behind.

Learning to speak is an important step toward learning to read. Children who cannot speak their language have difficulties comprehending the written word. They are poor readers in school. As they advance to harder subjects, they must be able to read textbooks in history, geography, social studies, and science. Even math books are full of problems and explanations that must be read. Much of our education is based on language. The child who cannot use his language comfortably and freely is handicapped throughout his entire school life.

We must go back to the beginnings to see that young children have a solid base of language. In the relaxed and warm atmosphere of a loving home or good child care center, language can develop naturally. Every normal child has the ability to speak a language well. But each needs encouragement from the grownups around him. Each one must be allowed to speak and must know that someone is listening.

Man may be the only animal to use spoken or written words to communicate, but he is not the only animal that is able to communicate. Every dog lover knows that animals can reveal their feelings quite clearly. A dog wags its tail, and by this action it says, "I'm happy you're home again." It jumps up at the master's legs and begs, "Please pet me." Some dogs run to the kitchen every time the refrigerator door is opened and wait patiently for a snack. Dogs can express all these meanings without a word or even a bark.

Of course, dogs have lived with man for many, many years, so it may be natural that they have learned to communicate with their human masters. Do animals in nature communicate with one another as well? They certainly do. A starling will give out a danger cry to alert the entire flock when it sees a hawk or other enemy. On hearing the cry, the flock flies away.

Bees tell one another about the nectar they have found by doing a special dance. One movement says that the nectar is close by. A different movement says the nectar is far away and even informs the other bees how far away.[1]

Many animals communicate to attract a mate and ensure a new generation. Grasshoppers and crickets search for a mate by singing songs that only other grasshoppers and crickets can understand. Butterflies recognize members of the opposite sex by their colors and movements. Some fish develop bright colors in the mating season to attract a mate, but are dull and difficult to see at other times of the year to protect them from their enemies.

---

[1] *Signals in the Animal World,* Dietrich Brukhardt, Wolfgang Schleidt, Helmut Altner and collaborators, tr. Kenneth Morgan, McGraw Hill Book Co., New York, 1967.

14. It can be inferred that the author holds all of the following opinions except

   (A)   a child is influenced by many different factors
   (B)   a child will probably reflect the characteristics of the predominant influences in his life
   (C)   a child's language is acquired from the people around him
   (D)   language may be subject to a small number of innate influences
   (E)   language helps a child develop socially

15. According to the author language is useful for all of the following reasons except

   I.   Words are the tools of learning.
   II.   Words aid a child's social development.
   III.   Some languages make communication easier than other languages.
   IV.   Language gives a child a broader range of communication.
   V.   Once a child learns one language it is more difficult for him to learn a second language.

   (A)   I only   (D)   III and V only
   (B)   II only   (E)   II and V only
   (C)   III and IV only

16. The passage states that one of the dangers of a child not being able to use language is

   (A)   a child who cannot communicate may remain locked in his own world
   (B)   a child who cannot use language may have a stilted fantasy life
   (C)   the use of language is essential for developing mechanical skills
   (D)   words are the means of developing legal knowledge
   (E)   language helps to reduce a man's aggressive tendencies

17. It may be inferred from the passage that the basis of friendship is

   (A)   physical interaction between children
   (B)   nonverbal communication between children
   (C)   verbal communication between children
   (D)   a child's natural tendencies to form groups
   (E)   the human need for companionship

18. A child will be handicapped in which of the following school subjects if he cannot read?

   I.   History and Social Studies
   II.   Mathematics
   III.   Geography

   (A)   I only   (D)   I and III only
   (B)   II only   (E)   I, II, and III
   (C)   III only

19. The author implies that dogs may be able to communicate so easily with man because

(A) dogs are intelligent animals
(B) dogs have long lived in association with man
(C) dogs can be easily trained
(D) dogs can understand the language of men
(E) dogs learn in much the same way as parrots learn

Reading Passage IV

One of the little-known tribes of central Texas was the Tonkawa. Few objects made and used by the Tonkawa are preserved in museum collections, and no description of traditional Tonkawa culture, based upon a study of actual specimens, has appeared in literature. Nevertheless, a small but unique collection of Tonkawa materials has been a part of the ethnological collection of the Smithsonian Institution for a century. It is unique, not only because it is the earliest known Tonkawa collection, predating the extermination of the bison on the Southern Plains, but also because the time, place, and conditions under which the collection was made in the field are well documented. In order to place this collection in a meaningful cultural and chronological context, I have prefaced my description of the specimens with a brief historical sketch of the Tonkawa, with particular emphasis upon the year immediately preceding the acquisition of these materials by Dr. McElderry at Fort Griffin, Texas, in 1868.

Although the Tonkawa call themselves Titskan walitch, "the most human people," the tribal name is derived from the Waco name for these people, Tonkaweya, meaning "they all stay together." The Comanche and Kiowa, northwestern neighbors and longtime enemies of the Tonkawa, knew them by names which, in translation, meant "man-eating men" or "maneaters." The Tonkawan language apparently was affiliated with Karankawa, Comecrudo, and Cotoname through the common Coahuitecan stock, although too little is known of the languages of those extinct tribes to establish with certainty the closeness of their relationship to Tonkawan.

Available data on Tonkawa population, covering a period of nearly 200 years, indicate that the Tonkawa were not a large tribe. A Spanish estimate in 1778 gives 300 warriors. Sibley estimated the Tonkawa at but 200 men in 1805, and the tribal population continued to decline thereafter. Heavy war losses, epidemics, and loss of tribal identity through marriages outside the tribe were among the factors contributing to this decline. Of the sixty-two Tonkawa Indians on the tribal rolls in 1961, only three individuals were believed to be full-blooded Tonkawa.

If archaeological evidence of the Tonkawa exists, it may be represented in the Toyah Focus of the Central Texas aspect. Dr. Edward B. Jelks states that if the Toyah Focus material excavated at the Kyle Site, located on the Brazos River just above Whitney Dam in Hill County, Texas, can be related to an historic group, it is probably Tonkawa and/or Jumano. But he also believes that this focus may have come to an end in the late prehistoric period and another, yet undescribed, group may have taken its place. This later group, represented by triangular arrow points, Goliad Plain pottery, and other artifact styles, "may represent the archaeological remains of the historic and protohistoric Tonkawa ...," Radiocarbon dates from the Toyah Focus at the Kyle Site range from A.D. 1276 ± 130 years.

The historic record of the Tonkawa Indians begins with Francisco de Jesus Maria. In 1691 he included them with the Yojuane as enemies of the Hasinai. (Hodge, 1910, p.779). Earlier meetings between the Tonkawas and Europeans are questionable. Gabeza de Vaca may have encountered a Tonkawa subgroup in his flight through Texas in 1542, and Joutel of LaSalle's party reported hearing about a group called the Meghy, possibly the Mayeye, another subgroup, in 1687.

The first French encounter came in 1719, when Bernard de la Harpe, while carrying out orders to enter into trade with the Spanish and to explore western Louisiana, came into contact with the Taneaoye, the Tonkawa. M. Du Rivage, La Harpe's lieutenant, met these Indians, along with representatives of several other tribes seventy leagues up the Red River from Kadohadocho. Herbert E. Bolton, in his discussion of the Tonkawa in the *Handbook of the American Indians,* states that the Red River may have been a temporary location for the Tonkawa. During the early period of Spanish contact with the Tonkawan-speaking Mayeye, Yojuane, Ervipiane, and Tonkawa, these Indians were living a nomadic life along a broad belt from the San Antonia and Nacogdoches. They are reported being seen frequently along this road between 1727 and 1730, and from 1745 to 1762 three missions were established for the Tonkawas on the San Xavier River, San Gabriel River today.

20. In the first paragraph of this passage the mood the author attempts to create is one of

(A) suspicion
(B) suspense
(C) straightforward description
(D) hostility
(E) determination

21. It may be inferred from the passage that the names by which the Tonkawa Indians were known to other groups of people were dependent upon

(A) how the Tonkawa Indians viewed themselves
(B) how other people understood the Tonkawa language
(C) the pronunciation of Tonkawa speech by other people
(D) how other people viewed the Tonkawa Indians
(E) a misunderstanding involving several factors

22. It may be inferred from the passage that the Karankawa and Cotonane Indians lived

(A) in the same area as the Tonkawa Indians
(B) before the period covered in the passage
(C) at the same time as the Tonkawa Indians
(D) after the Tonkawa Indians
(E) with but were hostile to the Tonkawa Indians

23. It may be inferred that the reader should regard the Tonkawa Indians as a

    (A) popular Indian tribe
    (B) tribe which has traveled greatly
    (C) tribe famed for its heroism in war
    (D) tribe that is nearly extinct
    (E) tribe that is known for its ritualistic ceremonies

24. According to the passage the Toyah Focus of the Central Texas Aspect is

    (A) a school of archaeological thought
    (B) a place where archaeological evidence of the Tonkawa Indians exists
    (C) a place where archaeological evidence of the Tonkawa Indians may exist
    (D) world famous for the Kyle Site
    (E) a town located near the Kyle Site

25. According to the passage a characteristic that the Tonkawa had in common with the Yojuane was that they

    (A) both lived near the Brazos River
    (B) were both related by blood ties with the Ervipiane
    (C) were influenced by the French explorers
    (D) both were enemies of the Hasinai
    (E) both were first reported by Cabeza de Vaca

END OF TEST

Go on to do the following Test in this Examination, just as you would be expected to do on the actual exam. You will find correct answers for the entire Examination following the last question. Check your answers carefully after you have completed the whole Examination.

TEST II. PRINCIPLES AND CASES

TIME: 55 Minutes. 40 Questions.

Correct and explanatory answers are provided at the end of the exam. After you have completed the entire exam, read the explanations carefully. They'll reinforce your strengths and pinpoint your weaknesses so that you know just what to study to raise your score.

PART A. APPLYING SEVERAL PRINCIPLES TO A CASE

DIRECTIONS: Each law case described below is followed by several legal principles. These principles may be either real or imaginary, but for purposes of this test you are to assume them to be valid. Following each legal principle are four statements regarding the possible applicability of the principle to the law case. You are to select the one statement which most appropriately describes the applicability of the principle to the law case and blacken the space beneath the letter of the statement you select.

These questions do not presuppose any specific legal knowledge on your part; you are to arrive at your answers entirely by the ordinary processes of logical reasoning.

Case One

Doc Watson recently bought a hunting lodge and five hundred acres of property in Maine. Fred and Ned wrote Doc and asked if they could come and hunt on his property. Doc rented them both rooms for the following weekend. However, Ned began feeling a little ill so he asked Roger if he wanted to go in his place. Roger accepted. When Fred and Roger arrived in Maine, Doc allowed Fred to come onto his property but he refused to admit Roger.

Roger had bought a car from Doc and he decided to go onto the property to pick it up despite Doc's refusal to admit him with Fred. When Roger went onto Doc's land to get the car, Doc accused him of trespassing and turned his guard dog Fang loose. Fang took a large chunk out of Roger's leg.

While hunting, Fred proved himself to be a very poor shot. In the interest of safety, Doc told Fred that he would no longer be allowed to hunt on the property.

One night during this fateful weekend, while Doc was drinking socially with his friend, Sesame Carib, who owned the local health food store, Sesame asked if she could erect a billboard on Doc's property to advertise her store.

Doc gave her permission, and within a week she had the sign erected at great expense to herself. After seeing the sign, Doc decided that it was an eyesore and told Sesame to have it torn down.

Sesame refused to comply and Doc became infuriated. He told her that she was henceforth forbidden to use the old swimming hole on his property which the members of the community had used as far back as anyone could remember.

1. *Unless it has become irrevocable, a privilege is considered to be personal to the one to whom it is extended and it cannot be transferred without the permission of the grantor.*

   In a suit by Roger against Doc to recover his lost expenses because Doc would not allow him to stay in the hunting lodge, Roger will

   (A) win because Fred had transferred his right to stay in Doc's lodge to Roger
   (B) win because Doc's hunting lodge was semipublic property and it would be discrimination to deny anyone admission
   (C) lose because the privilege to stay in Doc's lodge had been extended to Fred, not Roger.
   (D) lose because Roger had never asked Doc for permission to stay in the hunting lodge

2. *A right to property brings with it the limited privilege to go onto the land of another to claim that property but such entry onto the other's land must be done peacefully by the one entering.*

   In a suit by Roger against Doc to recover for the injuries sustained from Fang, Roger will

   (A) win because he had been denied the right to stay in the lodge for the weekend
   (B) win because he was on Doc's property justifiably
   (C) lose because he did not enter Doc's property peacefully
   (D) lose because Doc had already denied him permission to come onto his property

3. *A privilege to use the land of another is revocable at any time by the owner of the land as long as the owner revokes such privilege reasonably.*

   In an action by Fred against Doc for damages due to Fred's loss of hunting rights, Fred will

   (A) win because Doc did take away his privilege reasonably
   (B) win because Doc's real motive in denying Fred the right to hunt was dislike of Roger
   (C) lose because Fred only had a right to hunt on a limited part of Doc's property
   (D) lose because Doc revoked Fred's privilege reasonably

4. *If a person with a privilege to perform some act on the property of another expends a substantial sum of money in the performance of that act, the property owner will not be allowed to revoke the privilege.*

If Sesame brings suit in order to be allowed to retain the billboard on Doc's land, Sesame will

(A) win because she spent a substantial sum to erect the sign
(B) win because it was irrelevant whether Doc thought the sign was an eyesore
(C) lose because Doc thought the sign was an eyesore
(D) lose because the sign discouraged tourists from staying at Doc's hunting lodge

5. *A privilege to use the land of another normally may be revoked at any time except if such privilege has been the right of an entire community for a substantial number of years.*

If Sesame brings suit against Doc to be allowed to use the old swimming hole, Sesame will

(A) win because Doc's refusal to let her use it was irrational
(B) win because the use of the community swimming hole had been a community right for a long period of time
(C) lose because Sesame was not a member of the community
(D) lose because Sesame had not brought the suit in the name of the community

Case Two

Brag Broker was preparing to give a cocktail party in his apartment. He told his ten-year-old son Eclipse to paste little plastic flowers onto a sliding glass door in the bedroom so that no one would walk into it. Eclipse went into the bedroom but instead of taking care of the door he began playing on the floor with his toy cars. Brag, while straightening a painting on the wall, noticed that the string on which it hung looked frail but he paid no attention to it.

That evening the party appeared to be going successfully. Luther Thario, enchanted with Cybil Sheep, lured her into the bedroom where he slipped on one of Eclipse's toy cars and broke his leg. Cybil became very upset and rushed for help. Not noticing the glass door, she smashed into it cutting her arms, face, and legs.

Doctor Dan Dashing heard screams from the bedroom and ran to help. He quickly set Luther's leg and then turned to Cybil. He warned Cybil that if he treated her now she might be scarred, but if she came to his office, he might be able to treat her cuts so that they would leave no scars. Cybil cried out, "I'm in pain, Doctor!" so Dan treated her immediately. Cybil's cuts eventually turned into scars.

Meanwhile, back in the living room, Mr. Stock, Broker's boss reached out to pet the family dog. Broker warned him that the dog had been known to bite, but Stock ignored the warning and the dog bit his hand. Archie Bald leaned back in his chair to light his pipe. A spark from the pipe touched the frail string supporting the painting above his head. The string broke and the painting fell, ruining Archie's recent nose job.

6. *A person will be liable on the basis of criminal negligence if he willfully and maliciously allows a known safety hazard to exist on his property.*

If Cybil Sheep brings suit against Brag Broker on the basis of criminal negligence, she will

(A) win because Brag should have inspected the glass door
(B) win because Brag should not have sent Eclipse to put the plastic flowers on the door
(C) lose because Brag did not purposefully fail to mark the glass door
(D) lose because Brag did everything that a reasonable man would have done

7. *A doctor will be guilty of malpractice if he knowingly treats a patient when he realizes that some future injury may result from his treatment.*

If Cybil Sheep brings suit against Doctor Dan Dashing for malpractice, Cybil will

(A) win because her injuries were only superficial
(B) win because Dan Dashing knew that there was a possibility of future injury
(C) lose because Dan warned her that there was a possibility of scars
(D) lose because Dan only treated Cybil at Cybil's insistence

8. *A person will be liable for any injury caused by an animal on his property unless the injured party is contributorily negligent.*

If Stock brings suit against Broker for the damages done by Broker's dog to his hand, Stock will

(A) win because a dangerous dog should not have been allowed at a social gathering
(B) win because strict liability attaches to the action of dangerous animals
(C) lose because Stock knew the dog had been known to bite but still he petted it
(D) lose because Stock treated the dog badly

9. *If a person induces another to come into a situation which he knows might cause such other person bodily harm, he will be liable for all damages suffered by such other person.*

If Cybil brings suit against Luther for the injuries that she suffered, Cybil will

(A) win because Luther induced her into the bedroom
(B) win because Luther should have known of the possible danger
(C) lose because Luther did not have ethical motives in inducing Cybil to the bedroom
(D) lose because Luther did not know of any possible danger

10. *If a person has reason to know of a possible hazard on his premises, he has a duty to warn any invitee of the possible hazard unless an invitee can be said to have knowingly assumed the risk.*

If Archie Bald brings suit against Broker for the damage done to his nose, Archie will

(A) win because Broker did not warn him of the frail string on the painting
(B) win because Broker should have fixed the painting before the party
(C) lose because Archie was contributorily negligent
(D) lose because Archie assumed the risk by sitting under the painting

Proceed directly to the next Part.

PART B. APPLYING ONE PRINCIPLE TO SEVERAL CASES

DIRECTIONS: Each principle of law given below is followed by several law cases: These principles may be either real or imaginary, but for purposes of this test you are to assume them to be valid. Following each law case are four statements regarding the possible applicability of the principle to the law case. You are to select the one statement which most appropriately describes the applicability of the principle to the law case decision. Blacken the space beneath the letter of the statement you select. These questions do not presuppose any specific legal knowledge on your part; you are to arrive at your answers entirely by the ordinary processes of logical reasoning.

Principle One

First-degree murder is any killing with malice aforethought which is willful, deliberate, and premeditated, or perpetrated by poisoning or lying in wait, torture or bombing, or committed in the perpetration or attempted perpetration of arson, rape, mayhem, burglary, or robbery.

Second-degree murder is any killing with malice aforethought other than first-degree murder.

Malice aforethought can be shown by any one of the following acts:
  1. Intent to kill.
  2. Intent to resist arrest.
  3. Intent to mislead others into any action in which there is grave danger of serious bodily harm.

11. Dr. Edward Eldum was the chief surgeon in a New Canaan Hospital. Mary Unfortunate was six months pregnant, but if she delivered her baby, possible grave damage could be done to her health. Dr. Eldum did not normally perform abortions, but since he knew Mary's family, he decided to treat Mary himself. During the operation such grave damage was done by Eldum's unpracticed hand that both Mary and the fetus died.

If Eldum is charged with first-degree murder, Eldum will

(A) win because none of his actions was done with malice aforethought
(B) win because his actions were not premeditated
(C) lose because his actions were so negligent as to be considered torture
(D) lose because his actions were willful and deliberate

12. Riley Fast was a drag racing enthusiast. Riley met Berny Rubber, whom he had never liked, in a bar one night and after five or six drinks together, Riley challenged Berny to a drag race. Both Riley and Berny stumbled to their cars and roared off in search of an empty road. While making a particularly sharp turn, Riley accidentally bumped the side of Berny's car which sent it into a tree, killing Berny.

If Riley is charged with first-degree murder, Riley will

(A) win because he held no ill will toward Berny
(B) win because his actions were not willful, deliberate, and premeditated
(C) lose because Riley had an ingrained dislike for Berny
(D) lose because Riley's actions were done with malice aforethought and were willful, deliberate, and premeditated

13. Mike Muscles was a labor organizer who had called his union out on strike. Scrooge Tightwad, the owner of the local wicket manufacturing plant, refused to bargain with either Mike or his men. In order to frighten Scrooge into bargaining, Mike put a small bomb in the plant, which was set to explode at an hour when no one would be present. However, Scrooge decided to make a nocturnal check of the plant and was killed when the bomb went off.

If Mike is charged with first-degree murder, Mike will

(A) win because he had no intention of injuring anyone
(B) win because his real intention was to promote bargaining between a union and management
(C) lose because Scrooge was killed by a bomb
(D) lose because Mike acted willfully and with malice aforethought

14. Lois Rent had been having an affair with Harry Handsome. Her husband Clark Rent found out about this situation and decided to avenge his honor. Clark searched for Harry with the intent to beat Handsome until he became a lot less attractive. Clark found Harry and delivered him a blow to the jaw which sent him reeling into a lamppost with such force that Harry's skull was fractured and he died.

If Clark is charged with second-degree murder, Clark will

(A) win because he did not have malice aforethought
(B) win because he had acted with sufficient provocation and in the heat of passion
(C) lose because his actions were willful, deliberate, and premeditated
(D) lose because his actions were done with malice aforethought

15. Officer Chekofsky spotted a mugging taking place on a street corner and he rushed to the aid of the victim. Slugger the mugger saw Chekofsky coming and tried to run away. Chekofsky overtook him, but

while he was trying to handcuff Slugger, Slugger hit Chekofsky with a brick and Chekofsky died. Slugger was later arrested when he tried to mug a plainclothes policeman who was formerly a professional boxer.

If Slugger is charged with second-degree murder, Slugger will

(A) win because he did not intend to kill Chekofsky
(B) win because he did not intend to mislead Chekofsky into a dangerous activity
(C) lose because Slugger acted with malice aforethought
(D) lose because Slugger's actions were willful, deliberate, and premeditated

Principle Two

A successful action on the basis of negligence requires that the plaintiff show that the defendant owed him a duty of due care.

Generally, everyone owes a duty to exercise due care so as not to subject others to unreasonable risks of harm.

This duty arises when the defendant is doing an act which he can reasonably foresee might cause injury to the person or property of another.

Due care is that degree of care which a reasonable man would exercise in a similar situation to all those to whom injury is foreseeable.

16. Anna Collector had just purchased an expensive vase which she left in Ned's garage. Ned was an amateur carpenter who used his garage as a workshop. He realized that the blade on his electric saw was a little loose but nevertheless continued to saw wood for a new cabinet. The blade on the saw broke, flew across the garage, and shattered the vase.

If Anna brings suit against Ned, Anna will

(A) win because Ned was strictly liable for Anna's vase
(B) win because Ned should have known that his saw could do damage to things present in the garage
(C) lose because Ned would be responsible for Anna's person not for her property
(D) lose because Ned did not think that his saw would do damage

17. Fred Front was walking along a seaside boardwalk in July, casually tossing stones into the water. He spied a milk crate at his feet and tossed it over the railing. Web Wark, who was swimming beneath the pier, was hit by the crate and badly injured.

If Web brings suit against Fred, Fred will

(A) win because he could not see Web beneath the boardwalk
(B) win because it is common practice for people to throw things into the ocean
(C) lose because he should have known that someone might be swimming beneath the boardwalk
(D) lose because he knew that someone might be swimming beneath the boardwalk

18. Benny Fender was driving recklessly in his new sportscar on a winding country road. Joseph and Mary were having a picnic in a grassy spot close to the road. As he approached the picnickers, Benny lost control of his car. Mary became so frightened that she ran for the protection of a nearby tree. Just at that moment, lightning struck the tree and burned Mary severely.

If Mary brings suit against Benny for her injuries, Mary will

(A) win because Benny's driving endangered her life
(B) win because Benny's driving caused her to run beneath the tree
(C) lose because it was the lightning that injured her
(D) lose because Benny could not reasonably foresee injury to Mary by lightning

19. Red Rails, a trackman for the New York City subway system, fell on the tracks while working one day. Mike Motors, the engineer of the D train, was unaware of the accident because the warning sign in the tunnel malfunctioned. Mike did not see Red and ran over him without realizing what he had done. The safety switch under the first car was tripped and the train stopped. However, Mike reversed the train and moved forward several times before looking under the train and seeing Red's mangled body.

If Red's estate brings suit against Mike for negligence, Mike will

(A) win because it was not his fault that the warning signal malfunctioned
(B) win because he did eventually check to see what was under the train
(C) lose because Mike should not have hit Red
(D) lose because Mike should have realized that a man might be trapped under the train

20. Doctor Proctor was a renowned general surgeon who, as chief surgeon, was in charge of the actions of his staff while he was operating on Cary Ill. Proctor allowed a young medical student named Hem Stitch to close the wound. Hem did an excellent job of suturing but he forgot to take out a sponge that he had left inside of Cary. Cary needed a second operation to remove the sponge.

If Cary brings suit against Proctor for negligence, Proctor will

(A) win because it was Hem Stitch who left the sponge inside of Cary
(B) win because Cary should have joined Hem Stitch in his action against Proctor
(C) lose because Proctor should have known that a medical student might make a mistake
(D) lose because Proctor should have known that Hem Stitch, who had been negligent in the past, might make a mistake

PART C. CHOOSING THE NARROWEST JUSTIFYING PRINCIPLE

DIRECTIONS: In this section you will be given several groups of imaginary law cases. Each question will present a set of facts and a fictitious court holding, which you are to presume to be valid. Following each case are four legal principles, lettered (A), (B), (C), and (D). You are to choose the narrowest (most precise) principle which explains the court decision given. However, this principle may not conflict with the holdings given in any of the preceding cases in the same group. The correct answer to the first case in any group will always be the most precise principle which correctly explains the legal decision made. From the second question until the end of each group, you are to select the narrowest principle which does not conflict with any of the previous holdings.

These questions do not presuppose any specific legal knowledge on your part. They are to be answered entirely by the ordinary processes of logical reasoning. Indicate your choice by blackening the appropriate space on the answer sheet.

Group One

21. Rizzo, the publisher of *Scandal Magazine,* was being harrassed by the local police. In order to get the police to stop, Rizzo decided to put pressure on Mayor Peoples, who was running for re-election. Rizzo said in his magazine that Peoples was a constant drug user. Nevertheless, Mayor Peoples won re-election. Peoples brought suit against Rizzo for defamation. *Held,* for Rizzo.

    The *narrowest principle* that reasonably explains this result is:

    (A) The matter published must be of the type which would tend to lower a person's reputation.

    (B) The matter published must be known to be untrue by the person who published it.

    (C) The matter published must in fact lower the reputation of the defamed person in the eyes of a third party.

    (D) The matter published must tend to subject the plaintiff "to hatred, contempt or ridicule."

22. XYZ Educational Service was a partnership which trained people to take the sanitation workers exam. Consumer caused an article to be circulated which said, "XYZ Stinks!" Owing to this article, XYZ lost so many customers that it was forced to go out of business. XYZ brought suit against Consumer for defamation. *Held,* for Consumer.

    The *narrowest principle* that reasonably explains this result and is *not inconsistent* with the ruling given in the preceding case is:

    (A) An unincorporated association may bring suit in its own name as a legal entity.

    (B) An unincorporated association does not have sufficient status as an entity to sue for defamation.

    (C)   An unincorporated association is afforded the same legal status as a corporation.

    (D)   A partnership does not have sufficient status as an entity to sue for defamation.

23. Crabby Appleseed, the recently deceased owner of Appleseed's Real Estate Company, had been involved in several questionable deals. Barker erected a sign in front of the Appleseed home which said, "Crabby Appleseed was rotten to the core!" His sign caused the Appleseed Estate to lose several buyers for certain orchard property. The Appleseed Estate brought suit against Barker for defamation. *Held,* for Barker.

The *narrowest principle* that reasonably explains this result and is *not inconsistent* with the rulings given in the preceding cases is:

    (A)   Any living person, corporation, partnership or other legally recognized entity may sue for defamation.

    (B)   No action for defamation will lie unless the person defamed is capable of bringing the action in his own name.

    (C)   No member of a group defamed may bring an action unless the person bringing the action has been personally ridiculed.

    (D)   In matters involving grazing land the estate of the deceased owner will be allowed to bring an action in the deceased's name.

24. Factor was the sole owner of Canit Construction Company, Incorporated. Amps wrote untruthfully in a trade publication called *Circuit,* that Factor used second-rate material when he did work for a customer. Factor's company lost several potential contracts because of this article. Factor brought suit and charged Amps with defamation. *Held,* for Factor.

The *narrowest principle* that reasonably explains this result and is *not inconsistent* with the rulings given in the preceding cases is:

    (A)   Any corporation may bring a suit on behalf of one of its owners.

    (B)   A person has been defamed when actual damage has been done to a business in which he has a monetary interest.

    (C)   A person has been defamed when damage has been done to a business of which he is sole owner.

    (D)   A person has been defamed when damage has been done to a corporation of which he is the sole owner.

25. Artemus wrote a fictional article in which the main character, John Sawmount, spent much of his time associating with criminals. Unbeknown to Artemus there was a real John Sawmount who lost a prestigious job as the head of a University because of Artemus's article. Sawmount brought an action for defamation against Artemus. *Held,* for Sawmount.

The *narrowest principle* that reasonably explains this result and is *not inconsistent* with the rulings given in the preceding cases is:

(A) When a person's name is published, that person may sustain an action for defamation, even though the author of the defamation did not know that such a person existed, if such person suffered injury.

(B) There is no defamation unless it was the author's intent to damage the person defamed.

(C) A publication may clearly be defamatory of somebody, and yet on its face make no reference to that person.

(D) The author of a defamatory article is strictly liable if he maligns the reputation of a public official.

Group Two

26. Plates is a counterfeiter. Throughout the month of July he has been passing fake twenty-dollar bills to the merchants of Metropolis. One day Officer Hawk spots Plates about to give a twenty-dollar bill to a store clerk. Hawk mistakenly assumes that the bill is a fake and arrests Plates for attempt. The state brought an action against Plates. *Held,* for Plates.

The *narrowest principle* that reasonably explains this result is:

(A) The "Overt Action" which constitutes a criminal attempt might of itself be entirely legal.

(B) In order to constitute attempt the act in question must be a crime if it were completed.

(C) For the crime of attempt the criminal action in question must be completed.

(D) For an officer of the law to make a valid arrest for attempt, he must have reason to believe that a crime is about to be committed.

27. Mogul was the owner of a large but unprofitable factory, which he decided would become a better financial investment if he could have it burned to the ground and then collect an insurance payment. Torch, a well-known arsonist, agreed to burn Mogul's factory for a specified amount of cash. While Torch was in a gas station filling a five-gallon can with gasoline, Officer Shea decided that a crime was afoot and arrested Torch for attempted arson. The state brought an action against Torch for attempt. *Held,* for Torch.

The *narrowest principle* that reasonably explains this result and is *not inconsistent* with the ruling given in the preceding case is:

(A) In order to constitute a criminal attempt an overt act made toward the completion of the crime must be committed.

(B) In order to constitute an attempt the intended crime must be violent in nature.

156 / *Law School Admission Test*

(C)   In order to be guilty of an attempt the accused must commit an unequivocal act which goes beyond a mere equivocal act which goes beyond mere preparation.

(D)   In order to be guilty of a criminal attempt the act in question must be a step in the course of the planned conduct.

28.   Vertigo had an intense fear of tall buildings. He decided that the only way to rid himself of his anxiety was to destroy all buildings above forty stories tall. Vertigo was arrested for the attempted destruction of the Pinnacle Building, an office tower one hundred and ten stories tall. When Vertigo was arrested, he was standing at the base of the building swinging a baseball bat against one wall. The state brought an action against Vertigo for attempt. *Held,* for Vertigo.

The *narrowest principle* that reasonably explains this result and is *not inconsistent* with the rulings given in the preceding cases is:

(A)   For an attempt to be punishable, the act committed by the accused must have an apparent chance of success.

(B)   For an attempt to be punishable, the act committed by the accused must have a malignant nature.

(C)   For an attempt to be punishable, the accused must be capable of injuring a human being.

(D)   For an attempt to be punishable, the accused must have committed an act which is outside the course of human events.

29.   Plugger had been denied a raise by his boss Flint. Plugger decided to get even with Flint, so he went to a pawnshop and bought a gun. The firing pin on the gun was bent and the gun would not fire. However, when Flint saw Plugger pointing the gun at him he became extremely frightened and suffered a mild heart attack. The state brought an action against Plugger for attempted murder. *Held,* for the state.

The *narrowest principle* that reasonably explains this result and is *not inconsistent* with the rulings given in the preceding cases is:

(A)   If the accused's act is obviously and apparently inadequate to accomplish the crime, there can be no attempt.

(B)   If the accused's act is apparently adequate to accomplish a crime, there is an attempt.

(C)   If the accused's act is apparently adequate to accomplish a crime, there is an attempt if the victim suffers an adverse physical effect.

(D)   If the accused's act is responsible for an ill effect in the intended victim of the crime, there is an attempt.

30. Archer was paid $10,000 to murder Casper's wife. Archer skillfully assembled a bomb and placed it in Casper's house. Casper's wife was the only one present in the house. However, due to a leaky water pipe the bomb did not go off. After this Archer's conscience bothered him so much that he returned Casper's money and renounced any malignant thought toward Casper's wife. The state brought an action against Archer for attempt. *Held,* for the state.

The *narrowest principle* that reasonably explains this result and is *not inconsistent* with the rulings given in the preceding cases is:

(A)   Attempt is the commission of an act that narrowly falls short of harming the life, health, or property of another.

(B)   Once an act that could reasonably have caused harm to another has been committed, an attempt is complete and cannot be renounced.

(C)   An actor in a crime may renounce an attempt by informing the intended victim of the plot.

(D)   Once an act that could reasonably have caused harm to another has been committed, an act is complete.

Proceed directly to the next Part.

PART D. CHOOSING THE MAJOR FACTOR (CASE)

DIRECTIONS: In this test you are given a set of facts followed by several questions relating to them. Each question presents a different legal principle to be applied to the set of facts. All principles given are to be assumed to be valid even though they may be either real or imaginary. You are to apply the principle to the given statement of facts and then pick the one of the four alternatives which is the MAJOR FACTOR in the legal decision. Blacken the space on the answer sheet corresponding to the alternative of your choice. These questions do not relate to one another. You are to answer each one solely on the basis of the material given for that specific question. Arrive at your answers by ordinary logical reasoning alone. Do not be influenced by any outside legal knowledge that you may possess.

Case One

Professor Fuddle, after leaving a party at the home of his sister, Anita Bald, realized that he had left his umbrella behind. When he returned to fetch the umbrella, he found the house deserted. Professor Fuddle opened the door with the passkey that he knew his sister always left under the welcome mat. He found his umbrella but he also decided to borrow his sister's china tea set at the same time. When a passing policeman, Ed Catchum, on night patrol, tried to stop Professor Fuddle, the professor fled in fear. Catchum soon overtook Fuddle and arrested him.

31. A suit brought against Fuddle by the state on a charge of burglary was held for Fuddle on the following principle:

    Burglary is the breaking and entering of the dwelling house of another, in the nighttime, with the intent to commit a felony therein.

    Which of the following choices was the major factor in the disposition of this case?

    (A) Fuddle was not successful in carrying away the china tea set.
    (B) Anita Bald was Fuddle's sister.
    (C) Fuddle's original intent was only to reclaim his umbrella.
    (D) Fuddle had a right to take the china tea set.

32. A suit brought against Fuddle by the state, on a charge of resisting arrest, was held for the state on the following principle:

    Anyone who resists the normal approach of a policeman in the pursuit of his duty may be guilty of resisting arrest, if he intentionally flees from the police officer.

    Which of the following choices was the major factor in the disposition of this case?

    (A) Fuddle resisted the normal approach of a police officer.
    (B) Fuddle ran away from Officer Catchum.

(C)   Officer Catchum provoked Fuddle to run away.
(D)   Fuddle intentionally ran away from Officer Catchum.

33.   A suit brought against Fuddle by the state on a charge of larceny was held for Fuddle on the following principle.

Larceny is the trespassory taking and carrying away of the personal property of another with the intent to deprive the owner permanently of his property.

Which of the following choices was the major factor in the disposition of this case?

(A)   Fuddle carried the china tea set away.
(B)   Fuddle only wanted to borrow the china tea set.
(C)   Fuddle did not intend to return the china tea set.
(D)   Fuddle claimed ownership of the china tea set.

Case Two

Christianson was the kindly owner of the Wanda Widget factory. His plant was not unionized but Christianson nevertheless paid his employees union scale wages and gave them a bonus turkey every Christmas. However, this year the turkey rancher experienced an outbreak of disease which killed most of his turkeys. Since Christianson could not give his employees the customary Christmas turkey, he gave each one a chicken instead.

One day Christianson saw Johnson trying to organize the factory employees into a union. Immediately, Christianson gave all the men in his plant an automatic raise in pay, and all talk of unionization ceased.

However, Christianson truly believed that Johnson's activities had been disloyal and therefore he had Johnson dismissed. Not wanting to be cruel to Johnson's family, Christianson gave Johnson a separation check for three months' wages.

34.   A suit for damages brought by the employees against Christianson is held for the employees on the following principle:

Employers and Union must bargain collectively on matters of wages, hours, and other condition of employment. Bonuses and other forms of supplemental compensation will be included in the term "wages."

Which of the following was the major factor in the disposition of this case?

(A)   Christianson gave the employees a chicken instead of a turkey.
(B)   Christianson gave the employees a chicken instead of something equal in value to a turkey.
(C)   Christianson gave the employees a chicken without entering into collective bargaining with the employees.
(D)   Christianson was not obligated to give the turkey. He gave it as a gift every year.

35. A suit charging Christianson with an unfair labor act, brought by the National Labor Relations Board (NLRB) is held for the NLRB on the following principle:

An employer may not engage in any extraordinary action which encourages or discourages membership in a labor union.

Which one of the following choices was the major factor in the disposition of this case?

(A) Christianson raised the employees' salaries as soon as he saw Johnson trying to organize them.
(B) Christianson had always paid union scale wages.
(C) Christianson gave out bonus turkeys whenever they were available.
(D) There was no good reason for Christianson raising his employees' salaries.

36. A suit brought by Johnson against Christianson for reinstatement was held for Johnson on the following principle:

An employer may not discriminate in the hiring or firing of an employee on the basis of the employee's union or lack of union activity.

Which one of the following choices was the major factor in the disposition of this case?

(A) Christianson sincerely felt that Johnson's activities were disloyal.
(B) Christianson gave Johnson three months' separation pay.
(C) Christianson dismissed Johnson for his union activity.
(D) There was no reason to dismiss Johnson because the sentiment in support of a union died away after Christianson gave the employees a raise.

Case Three

Killer and Lefty were motorcyclists, both of whom were reputed by their respective followings to be the fastest motorcycle drivers in town. They decided to resolve the issue by racing on an old country road. As they raced past Becky Thatcher, a 96-year-old lady driving a Volkswagen, Becky became frightened and drove off the road into a tree. Nathan Hale, who was hanging from one of the tree limbs, was knocked onto the ground and broke his leg. When Nathan screamed for help, Becky became so upset that she suffered a minor heart attack.

An ambulance was called to take both Becky and Nathan to the hospital. However, as the ambulance proceeded toward the hospital, Farmer Green's cow Bessie walked into the road, causing the ambulance to swerve and knock Lefty, who just happened to be passing at the time, off his motorcycle. Lefty was severely bruised in the fall.

37. A suit for damage brought by Becky against Killer for the full damages to her car is held for Becky on the following principle:

If two parties are liable for a plaintiff's injuries, the law does not attempt to make a distinction between them but regards them as jointly and severally liable for the plaintiff's entire recovery.

Which one of the following choices was the major factor in the disposition of this case?

(A) Becky did not sue Lefty at the same time she sued Killer.
(B) Becky, under the above principle, could sue either Killer or Lefty, or both.
(C) Becky was frightened by both Killer and Lefty.
(D) A feeble old lady like Becky really should not have been driving a car.

38. A suit for damages brought by Nathan Hale against Becky was held for Becky on the following principle:

In order to be liable for damages, a defendant's negligent conduct must be the reason the plaintiff sustained his injuries.

Which one of the following choices was the major factor in the disposition of this case?

(A) Nathan would have fallen out of the tree even if Becky's car had not hit it.
(B) Lefty and Killer were the reasons that Becky drove off the road.
(C) Nathan should not have been hanging from the tree limb.
(D) Becky at the age of 96 was normally a very good driver.

39. A suit for damages brought by Becky Thatcher against Nathan Hale was held for Nathan on the following principle:

A person will be liable for an injury to another if his willful or voluntary act intentionally or negligently caused the injury.

Which one of the following choices was the major factor in the disposition of this case?

(A) Nathan's screams caused Becky to have a heart attack.
(B) Becky would have had the heart attack even if Nathan had not screamed.
(C) Nathan's screams were involuntary.
(D) Nathan's screams would not have caused a heart attack in a healthy person.

40. A suit for damages brought by Lefty against Farmer Green was held for Lefty on the following principle:

The owner of an animal which is the direct or indirect cause of injury to a person is responsible for the injuries sustained by that person.

Which one of the following choices was the major factor in the disposition of this case?

(A) In fact, the ambulance knocked Lefty off his motorcycle.
(B) Lefty was the original cause of the resulting mayhem.
(C) The cow caused the ambulance to swerve.
(D) Lefty should not have been riding so close to the ambulance.

END OF TEST

TEST III. PRACTICAL JUDGMENT

TIME: 20 Minutes. 20 Questions.

DIRECTIONS: In this test you will be presented with a detailed case study of a practical business situation. Read the study carefully. Then answer the two sets of questions based upon the reading. In the Data Evaluation questions, you will be asked to classify certain facts on the basis of their importance to the case presented. In the Data Application questions you will be asked to make judgments based upon your comprehension of the information.

Correct and explanatory answers are provided at the end of the exam. After you have completed the entire exam, read the explanations carefully. They'll reinforce your strengths and pinpoint your weaknesses so that you know just what to study to raise your score.

Business Situation . Jervis Toy Company

In January, Mr. Horace Nelson, president of Jervis Toy Company, considered a proposal to change to level monthly production for the coming year. The company's production schedules had previously been highly seasonal, reflecting the seasonal pattern of sales. Mr. Nelson can appreciate the improvement in production efficiency that the proposal promises, but he is uncertain of its impact upon other phases of the business.

Jervis Toy Company is a manufacturer of plastic toys for children. These include tea sets, billiard sets, space helmets, earth satellites, guns, automobiles, trucks, and a wide variety of other items.

The manufacture of plastic toys is a highly competitive business with many producers, most of which are not strongly financed. Capital requirements are not large, and technology is relatively simple, so that a number of new firms enter the business each year. On the other hand, competition is severe with respect to both price and design, resulting in a relatively high failure rate. There is sometimes a significant, temporary advantage in designing a popular new toy of the "fad" type. Margins tend to be high on such an item, until competitors are able to offer a similar product. For example, the successful introduction by Jervis Toy Company of plastic toy billiard sets had contributed significantly to profits two years ago. Last year eleven competitors offered a similar item, and its wholesale price was nearly halved.

Jervis Toy Company was founded in 1946 by Mr. John Jervis upon his release from naval service. Prior to World War II, Mr. Jervis had been employed as production manager by a large manufacturer of plastic toys. With his savings and those of his former assistant, Mr. Horace Nelson, Mr. Jervis established Jervis Toy Company. Originally a partnership, the firm had been incorporated in 1947, with Mr. Jervis taking 75% of the capital stock and Mr. Nelson, 25%. The latter served as production manager, and Mr. Jervis, as president, assumed responsibility for overall direction of the company's affairs. Mr. Jervis' health broke down two years ago and he was forced to retire from active participation in the business. Mr. Nelson assumed the presidency at that time. The next year, he hired Mr. James Hardy, a recent graduate of a prominent Eastern technical institute, as production manager. Mr. Hardy had worked during vacations in the plastics plant of a large diversified chemical company, and thus had a basic familiarity with plastics production processes.

Jervis Toy Company has experienced relatively rapid growth since its founding and has enjoyed profitable operations each year since 1949. Sales for the past year were $840,000 and are projected at $1,000,000 for the current year. Net profits reached $127,000 last year and are estimated at $152,000 for this year, under seasonal production, after taxes of 50%. The cost of goods sold in the past has averaged 60% of sales and is expected to maintain approximately that proportion for the current year under seasonal production. In keeping with the company's experience, operating expenses are considered likely to be incurred evenly throughout each month of the current year under either seasonal or level production.

Expanding operations have resulted in a somewhat strained working capital position for Jervis Toy Company. The year end cash balance of $86,000 is regarded as the minimum necessary for the operation of the business. The company has occasionally borrowed from its bank of account, Hood Trust Company, on an unsecured line of credit. A loan of $40,000 is outstanding at the moment. Mr. Nelson has been assured that the bank would be willing to extend a credit line of up to $150,000 for the coming year, with the understanding that the loan will be completely repaid and "off the books" for at least a 30-day period during the year. Interest will be charged at a rate of 6%, and any advances in excess of $150,000 will be subject to further negotiations.

The company's sales are highly seasonal. Over 80% of annual dollar volume is usually sold during the period from August to November. Sales are made principally to variety store chains and toy brokers on net 30-day terms. Large variety store chains are becoming increasingly important customers of Jervis Toy Company, accounting for over 65% of sales for the past year.

The company's production processes are not complex. Plastic molding powder, the principal raw material, is processed by injection molding presses and formed into the shapes desired. The plastic shapes are next painted at "merry-go-round" painting machines. The final steps in the process are assembly of the toy sets and packaging in cardboard cartons or plastic bags. Typically, all runs begun are completed in the same day so that there is virtually no work in process at the end of the day. Purchases on net 30-day terms are made weekly in amounts necessary for estimated production in the forthcoming week. Total purchases for the current year are forecast at $300,000.

Jervis Toy Company's practice has been to produce in response to orders. This means production at a small fraction of capacity for about the first seven months of the year in order to take care of the restricted demand during this period. Only one of the five injection presses is customarily in use at one time during this period.

The first sizable orders for Christmas business are usually received from variety store chains early in August. For the next four months all equipment is utilized for 12 hours per day. The work force is greatly increased and also put on a 12-hour day. Last year overtime premiums for this period amounted to $53,000. Shipments are made whenever possible on the day an order is produced. Hence, production and sales amounts in each month tend to be equivalent. A small inventory of representative finished goods, averaging $32,000 last year, is maintained in a nearby public warehouse, owing to lack of space in the plant. Storage costs of $800 were incurred last year.

As in the past, *pro forma* balance sheets and income statements based upon an assumption of seasonal production have been prepared for the current year and presented to Mr. Nelson for his examination.

Since coming to work at Jervis Toy Company, Mr. Hardy has been impressed by the many problems arising from this method of scheduling production. Overtime premiums reduce profits. Seasonal expansion of the work force brings difficulties in recruitment and training. Machinery is largely unused during eight months of the year and subjected to heavy usage during the remaining four months. Accelerated production schedules during the peak season necessitate frequent setup changes on the presses and painting machines with some seemingly unavoidable confusion in scheduling runs. Relatively short runs and frequent setup changes cause inefficiencies in the manual assembly and packaging operations as workers encounter difficulties in relearning their operations.

For these reasons, Mr. Hardy is urging Mr. Nelson to adopt a policy of level monthly production for the coming year. He has pointed out that estimates of sales volume have usually proved to be reliable in the past. Purchase terms will not be affected by the rescheduling of purchases. The elimination of overtime wage premiums will result in substantial savings, estimated at $60,000 for the coming year. Moreover, Mr. Hardy firmly believes that significant additional direct labor savings, amounting to about $47,000, will result from orderly production. Mr. Nelson speculated upon the effect that level production might have upon the company's funds requirements for the year. He assumed that except for profits, tax payments, and fluctuations in the levels of inventories, accounts receivable, and accounts payable, fund inflows and outflows will be approximately in balance. To simplify the problem, Mr. Nelson decided to assume that gross margin percentages would not vary significantly by months under either method of production.

DATA EVALUATION

DIRECTIONS: Based on your analysis of the Situation, classify each of the following items in one of five categories. On your answer sheet blacken the space under:

(A) *if the item is a MAJOR OBJECTIVE in making the decision; that is, one of the outcomes or results sought by the decision-maker.*

(B) *if the item is a MAJOR FACTOR in arriving at the decision; that is, a consideration explicitly mentioned in the passage that is basic in determining the decision.*

(C) *if the item is a MINOR FACTOR in making the decision; that is, a secondary consideration that affects the criteria tangentially, relating to a Major Factor rather than to an Objective.*

(D) *if the item is a MAJOR ASSUMPTION made in deliberating; that is, a supposition or projection made by the decision-maker before weighing the variables.*

(E) *if the item is an UNIMPORTANT ISSUE in getting to the point; that is, a factor that is insignificant or not immediately relevant to the situation.*

1. The seasonal nature of the business

2. Competition within the industry

3. Technology within the industry

4. The illness of Mr. Jervis

5. Past growth of the Jervis Toy Company

6. Year end cash balance

7. The availability of an unsecured line of credit

8. When operating expenses are likely to be incurred

9. Projected sales for the current year

10. Nature of the company's traditional outlets

11. Reduction of overtime premium and heightened seasonal costs

12. The way in which the plastic molding powder was processed

13. End of the year storage costs

14. The continued stability of accounts receivable and accounts payable.

DATA APPLICATION

DIRECTIONS: Based on your understanding of the Business Situation, answer the following questions testing your comprehension of the information supplied in the passage. For each question, select the choice which best answers the question or completes the statement.

15. Which of the following are reasons why several new toy firms enter the business each year?

    I. Capital requirements can be met with considerable effort.
    II. Technology is relatively simple.
    III. The manufacture of plastic toys is a highly competitive business.

    (A) I only
    (B) II only
    (C) I and II only
    (D) II and III only
    (E) I, II, and III

16. Sometimes a significant temporary advantage can be derived from devising a toy of the fad type but the advantage will disappear quickly because

    (A) fads often end as quickly as they begin
    (B) competitors will quickly offer a similar product
    (C) new toy companies are always coming into existence
    (D) fad toys are easy to improve upon by competitors
    (E) plastic is very inexpensive and easy to work with

17. Mr. Nelson's initial reaction to the proposal for a level monthly production schedule was

    (A) skeptical
    (B) optimistic
    (C) open-minded
    (D) frivolous
    (E) perturbed

18. Mr. Hardy offered many reasons for adopting a level production schedule one of which was estimated production and labor savings in the current year of

    (A) $60,000
    (B) $53,000
    (C) $47,000
    (D) $107,000
    (E) $300,000

19. Among the changes effected by the Jervis Company in order to meet the Christmas demand are:

    (A) All equipment is utilized twelve hours per day; the work force is expanded, and all vacations are cancelled.
    (B) The work shifts are lengthened to twelve hours a day and all overtime pay is cancelled.

(C)   The work force is put on a twelve hour day and all equipment is utilized during this period.

(D)   Shipments are made more frequently during this period but often any particular customer would have to wait two to three weeks for his order.

(E)   The first sizable orders for the Christmas season are generally received during August.

20.   What aspect of Jervis Toy's past performance best supports Mr. Hardy's recommendation to adopt a level production schedule?

(A)   Estimates of sales volume have usually proven reliable in the past.

(B)   The company's purchase terms have remained the same for the last five years.

(C)   The Christmas season has not always been the boom time for the Jervis Toy Company.

(D)   Since its beginning, the Jervis Toy Company has been one of the leaders in the industry.

(E)   The company's purchase terms have been very random for the last five years.

END OF TEST

Go on to do the following Test in this Examination, just as you would be expected to do on the actual exam. You will find correct answers for the entire Examination following the last question. Check your answers carefully after you have completed the whole Examination.

TEST IV. DATA INTERPRETATION

TIME: 30 Minutes. 25 Questions.

DIRECTIONS: This test consists of data presented in graphic form followed by questions based on the information contained in the graph, chart or table shown. After studying the data given, choose the best answer for each question and blacken the corresponding space on the answer sheet. Answer each group of questions solely on the basis of the information given or implied in the data preceding it.

Questions 1 to 6

Cigarette Smokers: 1970

Sex and age	Population (mil.)	Percent distribution			
		Present smoker	Former smoker	Never smoked	Unknown
Male	62	43	26	31	.6
17–24 years	12	41	9	49	1.4
25–44 years	23	51	23	26	.5
45–64 years	20	45	32	23	.3
65 years and over	8	23	40	37	na
Female	71	31	11	57	.5
17–24 years	14	30	7	62	1.0
25–44 years	24	39	15	46	.4
45–64 years	22	33	12	55	.5
65 years and over	11	11	8	81	.5

na   Not available.

Source: U.S. National Center for Health Statistics.

1. In 1970, what percent of the United States population over the age of 17 smoked cigarettes?

   (A) 63%   (D) 31%
   (B) 71%   (E) 37%
   (C) 43%

2. How many women between 25 and 44 years of age had quit smoking in 1970?

   (A) 15 million   (D) 23 million
   (B) 24 million   (E) 5.3 million
   (C) 3.6 million

3. How many more women are there over the age of 65 than men in that age group who have never smoked?

   (A) 3 million   (D) 6 million
   (B) 4.4 million   (E) 2.6 million
   (C) 44 million

4. Assuming that the percent distribution of smokers with age is constant over time, how many men between the ages of 17 and 24 can be expected to start smoking within the next 8 years?

(A) 1.2 million   (D) 5.5 million
(B) 1.3 million   (E) 2.5 million
(C) 6.12 million

5. Which of the following can be inferred from the table?

I. Since a greater percentage of people over 65 have never smoked, nonsmokers generally live longer.
II. Since there are more women than men in the total adult population, despite the fact that there are more men than women in the youngest age group, women generally live longer than men.
III. Since the percentage of women who are former smokers declines with age, while the number of men who are former smokers increases with age, men who stop smoking generally live longer than women who stop smoking.

(A) I only   (D) I and III only
(B) II only   (E) none
(C) III only

6. The age group for which the number of men smokers most nearly equals the number of women smokers is

(A) 17-24 years
(B) 25-44 years
(C) 45-64 years
(D) over 65 years
(E) There is not enough information to determine the answer.

Questions 7 to 13

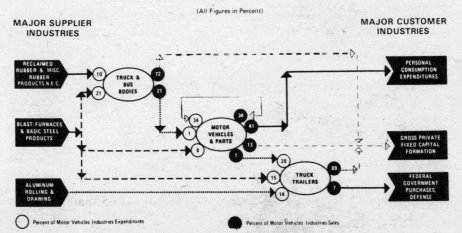

AUTOMOTIVE INDUSTRIES

(All Figures in Percent)

Truck and Bus Bodies --- 100% = $1.5 billion
Motor Vehicles & Parts - 100% = $40 billion
Truck Trailers --------- 100% = $2 billion

7. How much does the Defense Department spend on truck trailers annually?

(A) $890 million   (D) $105 million
(B) $70 million   (E) $2.8 billion
(C) $140 million

8. What is the total amount of purchases made by all three components of the automotive industry from the basic steel products industry?

(A) $3.2 billion   (D) $382 million
(B) $4.4 billion   (E) $3.82 billion
(C) $17.6 billion

9. What portion of the output of the motor vehicles & parts industry is sold to a producer in the automotive industry?

(A) 35%   (D) 21%
(B) 34%   (E) none of the above
(C) 1%

10. How many dollars of gross private fixed capital investment are spent on the automotive industry?

(A) $1.1 billion   (D) $13 billion
(B) $1.8 billion   (E) $8.1 billion
(C) $5.2 billion

11. How much rolled and drawn aluminum is purchased by the Defense Department indirectly through the truck trailer industry?

(A) $280 million   (D) $19 million
(B) $140 million   (E) $210 million
(C) $70 million

12. A 10% drop in personal consumption would probably reduce sales of motor vehicles and parts by

(A) $1.64 billion   (D) $4.1 billion
(B) $16.4 billion   (E) $410 million
(C) $164 million

13. An increase in the price of steel will probably have the greatest effect on the price of

(A) truck and bus bodies   (D) truck bodies
(B) motor vehicles   (E) motorcycles
(C) automotive parts

Questions 14 to 19

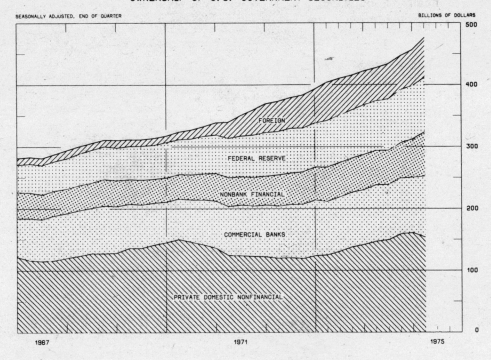

OWNERSHIP OF U.S. GOVERNMENT SECURITIES

14. From 1970 through 1972, which group increased the value of its holdings of U.S. Government securities the most?

    (A)   Private domestic nonfinancial institutions
    (B)   Commercial banks
    (C)   Nonbank financial institutions
    (D)   Federal Reserve System
    (E)   Foreigners

15. On March 31, 1975, what was the value of U.S. Government securities owned by commercial banks?

    (A) $250 billion   (D) $75 billion
    (B) $100 billion   (E) $50 billion
    (C) $150 billion

16. On December 31, 1969, what percent of outstanding U.S. Government securities was owned by nonbank financial institutions?

    (A) 20%   (B) 40%   (C) 12%   (D) 30%   (E) 18%

17. From January 1, 1967 through December 31, 1974, foreign holdings of U.S. Government securities increased by

    (A)   200%   (D)   70%
    (B)   400%   (E)   9%
    (C) $12.5 billion

18. From January 1, 1969 through December 31, 1972, what percent of the increase in outstanding U.S. Government securities was bought by the Federal Reserve System?

    (A) 16.1%   (B) 18.7%   (C) 22.5%   (D) 27.7%   (E) 50%

19. From January 1, 1967 through December 31, 1974, the share of U.S. Government securities owned by private domestic nonfinancial institutions

    (A) declined by 17.3%   (D) increased by 17.3%
    (B) declined by 7.4%   (E) increased by 25%
    (C) increased by 41.6%

Questions 20 to 25

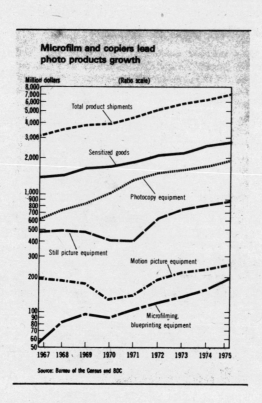

20. In 1975, photocopy equipment constituted what percent of the value of total product shipments?

    (A) 75%   (B) 51%   (C) 27%   (D) 20%   (E) 10%

21. The increase in value of still picture equipment shipments between 1967 and 1975 was how many times the increase in value of shipments of microfilming and blueprinting equipment?

    (A) 2   (B) 3   (C) 1/2   (D) 1/3   (E) 5

22. Shipments of which product group had a higher percentage change between 1967 and 1975 than the percentage change in total shipments in that period?

    (A) sensitized goods
    (B) photocopy equipment
    (C) still picture equipment
    (D) motion picture equipment
    (E) none of the above

23. The percentage change in shipments of microfilming and blueprinting equipment between 1967 and 1970 was what fraction of the percentage change in such shipments between 1970 and 1975?

    (A) 1/4   (B) 1/2   (C) 1/3   (D) 2/3   (E) 2/5

24. The increase in shipments of still picture equipment between 1967 and 1975 constituted what percent of the increase in total shipments in that period?

    (A) 11%   (B) 13%   (C) 17%   (D) 67%   (E) 75%

25. What was the value of photoproducts shipments in 1968?

    (A) $4,000
    (B) $4 million
    (C) $4 billion
    (D) $3 billion
    (E) $7.5 billion

END OF TEST

Go on to do the following Test in this Examination, just as you would be expected to do on the actual exam. You will find correct answers for the entire Examination following the last question. Check your answers carefully after you have completed the whole Examination.

174 / Law School Admission Test

TEST V. ERROR RECOGNITION

TIME: 20 Minutes. 35 Questions.

DIRECTIONS: *This is a test of your ability to recognize standard written English. Some of the sentences presented are acceptable as written English. Others contain errors of diction, verbosity or grammar. No one sentence contains more than one kind of error. Read each sentence carefully, then classify each according to the categories that follow. Mark your answer sheet:*

(A) *if the sentence contains an error in DICTION; that is, the use of a word which is incorrect because its meaning does not fit the sentence, or because it is not acceptable in standard written English.*

(B) *if the sentence is VERBOSE; that is, wordy or repetitious without justification by the need for emphasis.*

(C) *if the sentence contains FAULTY GRAMMAR; that is, errors in parallelism, number, case, tense, etc.*

(D) *if the sentence contains none of these errors.*

Correct and explanatory answers are provided at the end of the exam.

1. The purpose of this inquiry is to determine the true facts.

2. Holding one end of the rope in your right hand, two loops are made with the portion held in your left hand.

3. We must respect such a girl as her.

4. Morton's interest in philately is as keen and intense today as it was ten years ago.

5. I stopped overnight at a very expensive hotel.

6. Are you and your wife aware that John's wages is a dollar an hour?

7. He also said that he had often been a guest of John's.

8. Neither the elevator nor the escalator were in operation.

9. Polk governed with a single-minded energy, and it left him prematurely white-haired.

10. The Senator expressed the hope that his constituents agreed with and concurred in his views on inflation.

11. Although soft wheels cut quickly and are a joy to use in gemstone grinding, they are quite expensive.

12. I am glad you are done writing the article.

13. The State Department and the French Government have been leery of disengagement.

14. By hitting five home runs in one baseball game, Krandall established a new major-league record.

15. No house in America so compellingly evokes the manners, concerns and delights of a bygone age now past.

16. The Senator proposed diverting surplus waters of two northern California rivers hundreds of miles to the southward.

17. If a new war should come about in the Middle East, the Arab nations will surely unite together against Israel.

18. The killing occurred extremely sudden.

19. Your decision to buy a yacht is as impolitic as it is imprudent.

20. My father bought me a swell wristwatch for my birthday.

21. We both detest fascism, but I wonder if you hate it as much as me.

22. It is hoped that two-thirds of this cost will be borne by the Federal government.

23. Although Igor has been in this country for sixteen years, he clings to the customs of his native Transylvania, where he was born.

24. During the 1930s, there was a notable absence of intellectual activity on the part of the youth of Argentina.

25. The Senator, elated to learn that he had been reelected for another term, burst into tears of joy.

26. Several firms now manufacture machines designed to eliminate much of the tedious effort formerly necessary in the shaping and polishing of spheres.

27. Mr. Johnson was said to have falsely fabricated this case.

28. Smoke bellowed from the windows of the top floor of the four-story brick structure during the blaze.

29. Paul Cutler, who died last year, left a large estate of considerable size.

30. The report stressed the point that all three thousand members of the union had voted against the proposal.

31. Ohio as well as several other states, have a sales tax.

32. This was a windfall for the corporation and an unexpected acquisition.

33. It is obvious that you will derive no benefit or advantage from the research.

34. It are his parents that we admire.

35. Wrestlers must keep themselves in good shape.

END OF TEST

Go on to do the following Test in this Examination, just as you would be expected to do on the actual exam. You will find correct answers for the entire Examination following the last question. Check your answers carefully after you have completed the whole Examination.

TEST VI. SENTENCE CORRECTION

TIME: 20 Minutes . 25 Questions.

DIRECTIONS: Some part of each of the following sentences is un-derlined. After each sentence are five ways of stating the under-lined part. Choice A simply repeats the original sentence or phrase. If you think that the original sentence is more effective than any of the alternatives, pick Choice A. If you believe the underlined part is incorrect, select from the other choices (B, C, D, or E) the one you think is best and blacken the corresponding space on the answer sheet. In choosing the best alternative, consider grammar, sentence structure, punctuation and word usage. Do not choose an answer that changes the meaning of the original sentence.

Correct and explanatory answers are provided at the end of the exam. After you have completed the entire exam, read the explanations care-fully. They'll reinforce your strengths and pinpoint your weaknesses so that you know just what to study to raise your score.

1. There was such a crowd that he did not find his friends.

   (A) There was such a crowd that he did not find his friends.
   (B) The crowd was such that he did not find his friends.
   (C) There was such a crowd so that he did not find his friends.
   (D) There was such a crowd as to not find his friends.
   (E) Not finding his friends, there was such a crowd.

2. A child's foolish fears are on a plane with a savage.

   (A) A child's foolish fears are on a plane with a savage.
   (B) A child's foolish fears are on a plane with the fears of a savage.
   (C) A child's foolish fears and a savage's foolish fears are on a plane.
   (D) A child's fears, on a plane with a savage, are foolish.
   (E) A child's foolish fears are on a plane with a savage's.

3. A key note of sincerity runs through a well-built speech.

   (A) A key note of sincerity runs through a well-built speech.
   (B) A key-note of sincerity should be the mainspring of a well-built speech.
   (C) Sincerity should be the mainspring of a well-built speech.
   (D) Sincerity is the foundation of a well-built speech.
   (E) Sincerity is the key-note of a well-built speech.

4. Paul spoke to the stranger, and he was very surly.

    (A)   Paul spoke to the stranger, and he was very surly.
    (B)   He was speaking in a very surly manner, as Paul spoke to the stranger.
    (C)   Paul spoke to the stranger; he was very surly.
    (D)   The stranger and Paul spoke, and he was very surly.
    (E)   Paul spoke in a very surly manner to the stranger.

5. At first I believed that John was right, I came to realize, however, that he was wrong.

    (A)   I came to realize, however, that
    (B)   then coming to realize that
    (C)   finally I came to the realization that
    (D)   afterwards I came to realize that
    (E)   but I came to realize that

6. Mary has the sweetest voice I almost ever heard.

    (A)   Mary has the sweetest voice I almost ever heard.
    (B)   Mary almost has the sweetest voice I ever heard.
    (C)   Mary has almost the sweetest voice I ever heard.
    (D)   Mary has the sweetest voice I ever heard, almost.
    (E)   Mary has the sweetest voice I ever almost heard.

7. If I had of analyzed the situation more clearly I never would have come to that decision.

    (A)   If I had of analyzed the situation more clearly
    (B)   If I had analyzed the situation more clearly
    (C)   If I had've analyzed the situation more clearly
    (D)   If I analyzed the situation more clearly
    (E)   If I would have analyzed the situation more clearly

8. Like his Roman predecessor, his private life was profligate.

    (A)   Like his Roman predecessor, his private life was profligate.
    (B)   Like his Roman predecessor's life, his life was profligate.
    (C)   Like his Roman predecessor, he lead a profligate life.
    (D)   His life, like that of his Roman predecessor, was profligate.
    (E)   Like that of his Roman predecessor, he led a profligate life.

9. Both these authors have written short stories about his courtship.

    (A)   about his courtship.   (D)   about his courtships.
    (B)   about their courtship.   (E)   about they're courtship.
    (C)   about their courtships.

10. <u>You land at Bombay; many strange looking people are in the streets.</u>

   (A) You land at Bombay; many strange looking people are in the streets.
   (B) When you land at Bombay, you see many strange looking people in the streets.
   (C) You land at Bombay, you see many strange looking people in the streets.
   (D) When landing at Bombay, many strange-looking people are to be seen.
   (E) You land at Bombay, home of many strange-looking people.

11. <u>Men who cared only for their individual interests were now in a state of discouragement.</u>

   (A) Men who cared only for their individual interests were now in a state of discouragement.
   (B) Men who cared only for their individual interests were now in a discouraged state.
   (C) Men who cared only for their individual interests were now discouraged.
   (D) Selfish men were now discouraged.
   (E) Selfish men were now in a discouraged state.

12. <u>He gave a dime to the boy that brought him the newspaper that printed the news that the war was ended.</u>

   (A) He gave a dime to the boy that brought him the newspaper that printed the news that the war was ended.
   (B) He gave a dime to the boy bringing him the newspaper announcing that the war was ended.
   (C) He gave the boy a dime that brought him the newspaper with the news that the war was ended.
   (D) He gave the boy a dime for bringing him the newspaper with the news that the war was ended.
   (E) He gave the boy a dime for bringing him the newspaper that printed the news that the war was ended.

13. The size of the plantations <u>vary</u>.

   (A) vary. (D) varies.
   (B) tend to vary. (E) is a variant.
   (C) is a variable.

14. He called upon such soldiers <u>that</u> would volunteer for this service to step forward.

   (A) that (B) who (C) as (D) which (E) what

15. Like all pioneers, Stouker's work is neglected.

    (A)   Like all pioneers, Stouker's work is neglected.
    (B)   Like that of all pioneers, Stouker's work is neglected.
    (C)   Like all pioneer's work, Stouker's work is neglected.
    (D)   Like all pioneers' work, Stouker's work is neglected.
    (E)   Stouker's, like other pioneers', work is neglected.

16. At school he never understood his lessons and undoubtedly did not please his teachers.

    (A)   he never understood his lessons and undoubtedly did not please his teachers.
    (B)   he never caught on to his lessons and undoubtably did not make a hit with his teachers.
    (C)   he never caught on to his lessons and undoubtedly did not please his teachers.
    (D)   he never understood his lessons and undoubtably did not please his teachers.
    (E)   he never caught on to his lessons and undoubtably did not please his teachers.

17. When we had taken our seats, the play began.

    (A)   When we had taken our seats, the play began.
    (B)   Having taken our seats, the play began.
    (C)   Our seats having been taken by us, the play began.
    (D)   When our seats had been taken, the play began.
    (E)   Our seats taken, the play began.

18. No sooner had the class begun but John started talking to his friend.

    (A)   but John started talking
    (B)   when John started talking
    (C)   John started talking
    (D)   than John started talking
    (E)   and John started talking

19. What use of an education could a girl who married a pauper and afterward knew nothing but hard work, make?

    (A)   What use of an education could a girl who married a pauper and afterward knew nothing but hard work, make?
    (B)   What use could a girl make of an education who married a pauper and afterward knew nothing but hard work?
    (C)   What use could a girl who married a pauper and afterward knew nothing but hard work, make of an education?
    (D)   What use could a girl make of an education who married a pauper and afterward knew nothing but hard work?
    (E)   What use of an education could a girl make who married a pauper and afterward knew nothing but hard work?

20. Eating starchy food, working long <u>hours, and without recreation makes</u> any employee less efficient than he might otherwise be.

    (A) hours, and without recreation makes
    (B) hours, and without recreation make
    (C) hours, and to avoid recreation makes
    (D) hours, and avoiding recreation make
    (E) hours, and avoiding recreationg makes

21. The Mound Builders <u>fashioned not only elaborate ornaments but also made excellent pottery.</u>

    (A) fashioned not only elaborate ornaments but also made excellent pottery.
    (B) not only fashioned elaborate ornaments but also made excellent pottery.
    (C) not only fashioned elaborate ornaments but they also made excellent pottery.
    (D) not only fashioned elaborate ornaments but they made excellent pottery.
    (E) not only fashioned elaborate ornaments but also they made excellent pottery.

22. The giraffe is a tall animal with hoofs; <u>their necks are long and slender.</u>

    (A) their necks are long and slender.   (D) it's neck is long and slender.
    (B) his neck is long and slender.   (E) its neck is long and slender.
    (C) their neck is long and slender.

23. <u>One should do their best.</u>

    (A) One should do their best.   (D) One should do the best they can.
    (B) One should do the best one can do. (E) One should do what he can do best.
    (C) One should do his best.

24. <u>The total effect of all this discussion is to return back to our point of departure.</u>

    (A) The total effect of all this discussion is to return back to our point of departure.
    (B) The total effect of this discussion has been to return back to our point of departure.
    (C) The effect of this discussion has been to return back to our point of departure.
    (D) The effect of this discussion has been to return to our point of departure.
    (E) The effect of this discussion has been to return to our departure.

25. <u>He thinks hard, as his father did.</u>

    (A) He thinks hard, as his father did. (D) He thinks hardly, like his father did.
    (B) He thinks hardly, as his father did (E) He thinks as hard as his father did.
    (C) He thinks hard, like his father did.

TEST VII. LOGICAL REASONING

TIME: 25 Minutes. 20 Questions.

This is a test of your ability to evaluate the reasoning contained in a statement or reading passage. Each statement or passage is followed by one or more questions. Answer each question solely on the basis of information stated or implied in the reading. If more than one choice seems possible, then you must select the one answer that does not require making implausible or superfluous assumptions. Blacken the space on the answer sheet that corresponds to the letter of your choice.

Correct and explanatory answers are provided at the end of the exam.

1. The biographical novel is based on the conviction that the best of all plots lies in human character; and that human character is endlessly colorful and revealing. It starts with the assumption that those stories which have actually happened can be at least as interesting as those which have been imagined.

   The author would probably consider which of the following aspects of a biographical novel to be most deserving of critical attention?

   (A) Its fast moving plot.
   (B) Its historical accuracy.
   (C) Its lucid language.
   (D) Its philosophical implication.
   (E) Its character development.

Questions 2 and 3

Today's consumers are evidencing greater interest in beauty treatment products and rates are increasing faster for these products than for two other major categories of beauty goods: cosmetics and fragrances. An apparent cause of this phenomenon is the current emphasis on youth and the natural look, which requires the skin itself to be basically attractive and youthful in texture and appearance.

2. Of the following, what logical contradiction does the above paragraph suggest?

   (A) Cosmetics can create the same natural look as beauty treatment products so there is no reason for the cosmetic sales decline.
   (B) The youth market is expanding; nevertheless, it is the youths' parents who earn the money.
   (C) People are buying more manufactured products in order to achieve natural beauty.
   (D) If a fragrance represents a natural scent there is no reason for it to experience a sales decline.
   (E) Youthful skin normally has acne; therefore, why would anyone want youthful skin.

3. If everything in the above passage is true, then the beauty treatment products that have the highest sales rate should be

   (A) inexpensive and within the means of young buyers
   (B) products made from milk, eggs, vegetable juices, etc., and packaged in boxes with pictures of wildlife and/or fruits, flowers, and vegetables
   (C) easy to carry and convenient to apply
   (D) products which have been in the market a long time and have had a chance to be tested
   (E) products that anyone can buy out of their disposable personal income

4. Poe conceived of God as a poet. The universe therefore was an artistic creation, a poem composed of God.

   The reader may conclude Poe felt that man's proper response to God would be

   (A) logical   (D) aesthetic
   (B) mystical   (E) reproachful
   (C) submissive

5. One times one equals one, but a one which is also a third thing, which is fixed in the mind, in the looking of one working on the other Emotions can be like plot and underplot. If we put two emotions of the established sorts in association we get an artistic emotion differing from either but with attributes common to both.

   Which of the following best expresses the author's attitude toward the emotions?

   (A) The emotions are like other natural properties; mixing fire and water is very difficult.
   (B) The emotions are what make the actions of one man dramatic.
   (C) The emotions must be tamed like wild stallions bursting at their stalls.
   (D) The emotions are unusual because the whole is often greater than the sum of its parts.
   (E) The emotions must be kept separate from one another because to mix them is dangerous.

6. Do you think that farmers should plant more corn when we already have more than we can consume?

   In terms of its logical feature the question above most closely resembles which of the following?

   (A) Do you think that the president of a university should beg for money?
   (B) Should the churches be taxed for their excess wealth?

      (C)   Do you think that a fat man should go on a diet?

      (D)   Do evil men live longer than good men?

      (E)   Should the state control the economic production of a country?

7. Since I have seen only a few exceptional plays, all the plays I have not seen must be exceptional.

   Which of the following most closely parallels the kind of reasoning used in the sentence above?

   (A)   Since only a few of the scientists in this area are geniuses, there must be only a few geniuses among scientists.

   (B)   Since most of the trees in the forest are tall there must only be a few short trees.

   (C)   Since the standards to get into Harvard are so high there must be no one in Harvard.

   (D)   Since only few policemen can speak Spanish all firemen must speak Spanish.

   (E)   Since I have met only a handful of well-trained campanologists all the campanologists I have not met must be well trained.

8. Experience is not in the impressions we receive; it is in making sense. And poetry is the foremost sense shaper of experience. It renders actual ever new sectors of the apparently inexhaustible field of potential experience.

   In light of the above statement which of the following is probably true about the poet and the common man?

   (A)   The poet lives in the world of the unreal while the common man lives in the world of the real.

   (B)   For the poet that which is systematic in a system is merely the trivial aspect of true order.

   (C)   The poet is probably easier prey to doubt and uncertainty than people content to live within the sense made by others.

   (D)   The poet experiences greater rewards for his work than the common man receives for his ordinary work.

   (E)   The poet is better able to delve into the world of archetypes than the common man.

9. You see before you an American author, six feet tall, 195 pounds, grey at the temples, two weeks short of fifty-two years of age, obviously unaccustomed to public speaking, afflicted with an Eastern Pennsylvania twang, writer of several best-sellers, writer also of an equal number of non-sellers, occasionally banned in Detroit, Michigan, Akron, Ohio, and East Germany; and almost completely ill at ease on the platform.

   For those whose curiosity can be so easily satisfied I now suggest a quick and quiet departure, and I make that suggestion with no bitterness and without prejudice—and indeed with some envy.

Which of the following sentences would provide the most logical continuation of the above paragraph?

(A) After all there's a football game on one TV station tonight and the first showing of a star-studded movie on another channel.

(B) This is an informal talk but let's not get carried away with the spirit of informality.

(C) I now have given you a glimpse of the novelist at work, and, rather sneakily, I have eased myself into my topic for the evening which somewhat to the surprise of no one is: the Novel.

(D) The florid recital of categories which I have just offered may have had a certain air of making fanfare.

(E) A good deal of literature is always organ-grinding, and some of it can be very good, as it reminds us of or extends the sense of our common predicament.

10. Judging from the tenor of the following statements and the apparent authoritativeness of their sources which is the most reasonable and trustworthy?

(A) Army Sergeant: The men in my outfit are the best soldiers on this base.

(B) Doctor: Mrs. Jones, your baby is one of the brightest children I've ever seen.

(C) Night Watchman: I spotted a man trying to get out of the yard, by climbing a barbed wire fence, at about three o'clock in the morning.

(D) Car dealer: The new Sangusto V8 is probably the smoothest riding car on the road.

(E) Teacher: The school where I work is without question the finest in Reedville.

11. There is only one barber in this town and he shaves every man who does not shave himself. Who shaves the barber?

The apparent paradox above can be resolved if one realizes that:

(A) The barber may have a beard.
(B) The barber may go to a different town for a shave.
(C) The initial statement cannot be true.
(D) The barber may be a woman.
(E) The barber may also shave men who do shave themselves.

12. Judging from the tenor of the following statements and the apparent authoritativeness of their sources, which is most reasonable and trustworthy?

(A) Teachers' Union president: If our teachers are forced to give up their preparation periods, the education of our children will be irremediably damaged.

(B) Vascular Surgeon: I don't think that your phlebitis requires surgery; we should be able to control it with drugs.

   (C)   Auto Mechanic: We ought to socialize medicine. My doctor charged me $100 just to tell me I was healthy.

   (D)   Research Scientist: This new Federal Revenue Sharing is obviously unconstitutional.

   (E)   College Freshman: We students should have as much say in how this school is run as the faculty. After all, we're as intelligent as they are.

Questions 13 and 14

The main difference between the literature of the United Stated and that of the Soviet Union is that while one can speak of American short stories without mentioning President Carter, it is out of the question to appraise Russian fiction without referring to Premier Kosygin.

13. The most logical continuation of this paragraph is:

   (A)   However, any country would be proud to claim Tolstoy as a native son.

   (B)   Yet in the United States, one of our recent presidential candidates was a poet of no mean skill.

   (C)   Creative writing in the Soviet Union is a public function and as such is controlled by the Party and the Government.

   (D)   This is a result of the fact that our political system rewards the average man rather than the truly creative artist.

   (E)   This is another example of how our well-intentioned guarantee of freedom of the press has an unfortunate side-effect.

14. The author's position is *least* likely to be supported by reference to American

   (A)   lyric poetry   (D)   musical comedies
   (B)   political satire   (E)   best-selling novels
   (C)   folk songs

15. John: You have to have a high LSAT score to get into law school these days.

Bill: That's not so. My cousin got a 795 and was rejected by three Ivy League schools.

Bill's response shows that he has interpreted John's remark to mean:

   (A)   All law schools require high LSAT scores for admission.
   (B)   Some law schools require high LSAT scores for admission.
   (C)   A high LSAT score is one over 700.
   (D)   A high LSAT score is sufficient for admission into law school.
   (E)   Ivy League schools do not have the same admission requirements as other law schools.

16. Restlessness such as ours, success such as ours, do not make for beauty. Other things must come first: good cookery, cottages that are homes, not playthings; gardens, repose. These are first-rate things, and out of first rate stuff art is made. It is possible that machinery has finished us as far as this is concerned. Nobody stays at home any more; nobody makes anything beautiful any more.

The author's argument is predicated on the assumption that

    (A)   an artist must be a gourmet
    (B)   beauty depends on utility
    (C)   there are no successful artists any more
    (D)   the true artist can never know peace
    (E)   industrialization is inimical to excellence.

17. American labor ceased being a hotbed of social reform some time ago—back when the money started to get good. At its top rung, no hierarchy is more devoted to preserving the status quo in its own arrangements, and few are more conservative politically. There is no room there for a labor politician who doesn't know when to sell out his own membership in an effort to ingratiate himself with his adversaries, be they employers or politicians. They call such behavior "unstatesmanlike."

The author's method of argument in the passage is most similar to that used in which of the following passages?

    (A)   It's no surprise that the same doctors who were most set in their opposition to Medicare are the ones who are most in favor of national health insurance. The Hippocratic Oath is irrelevant when one's personal financial interests are involved.
    (B)   The President is just proposing a new tax cut because as a politician he's more interested in what the people want than in what his principles dictate.
    (C)   American automobile manufacturers only decided to make small cars when they could no longer con the American people into buying those gas-guzzling monsters.
    (D)   The development of the detente between the Communist and the Western nations is a necessary result of the related needs of the two groups. Even the strictest Marxist realizes that the proletariat must eat before it can dictate.
    (E)   Walter Reuther represented the inherent contradictions of the American labor movement. After his union split from the AFL-CIO because of his personal disagreements with the entrenched hierarchy, he was the lowest paid president of a major American labor union.

18. This is a piece of perverse and sickening adulation of trash, in which Smith says that Patterson is "a pop artist whose whole tendency is classical of the likes of Joyce, Eliot, Pound, and Pynchon." Of course, our jesuitical juggler hedges his bets: "Patterson's particular way of expressing nostalgia needs to be taken as seriously, as studiously as some of the other literary manifestations I've mentioned, though this does *not* mean that we need think of it as equivalently good or satisfying."

The flaw in the author's attack on Smith's position is:

(A) He does not offer an alternative point of view.
(B) He uses emotionally charged words rather than logic to discredit Smith.
(C) He attacks Smith's religion which is not relevant to the topic under debate.
(D) He points out Smith's uncertainty about his own views.
(E) He uses the names of famous writers rather than logic to buttress his own position.

19. The world's experience of professed seers has on the whole been very unfortunate. In the main they are a bad lot with a shady reputation. The odds are so heavily weighted against any particular prophet that apart from some method of testing, perhaps it is safer to stone them, in some merciful way.

The point the author is making in his rather light-hearted manner is:

(A) We should not try to prepare for the future for there is no way to tell what it will be.
(B) The prophet is without honor in his own country.
(C) The future will forever be unknowable and ineluctable.
(D) The risk of harm from mistaken prediction is greater than the chance of good from correct prediction.
(E) Prophecy is born of suffering.

20. Should the people who decide on our transportation priorities continue to ignore the fact that the last thing we want or need or will tolerate is more expressways?

The rhetorical technique most similar to the one used in the passage is the one used in which of the following examples?

(A) Should those who decide our environmental policy decide that the last thing we need is expensive pollution control equipment?
(B) Do those who decide on our war strategy believe that what we need most is a quick victory?
(C) Should those who direct our health care policies close their eyes to the fact that the last thing we need is more specialists?
(D) When will those who choose our foreign policy accept the fact that the last thing we will tolerate is more imperialistic adventurism?
(E) When will those who fix our military policy see that the infantryman is the backbone of our army?

END OF EXAMINATION

CORRECT ANSWERS FOR VERISIMILAR EXAMINATION II.

TEST I. READING COMPREHENSION

1.C	5.B	9.C	13.E	17.C	21.D	25.D
2.C	6.A	10.A	14.D	18.E	22.B	
3.B	7.C	11.E	15.D	19.B	23.D	
4.D	8.A	12.C	16.A	20.B	24.C	

TEST II. PRINCIPLES AND CASES

1.C	6.C	11.A	16.B	21.C	26.B	31.C	36.C
2.B	7.B	12.B	17.C	22.D	27.C	32.D	37.B
3.D	8.C	13.C	18.D	23.B	28.A	33.B	38.B
4.A	9.D	14.A	19.D	24.D	29.C	34.C	39.C
5.B	10.A	15.C	20.C	25.A	30.B	35.A	40.C

TEST III. PRACTICAL JUDGMENT

1.B	4.E	7.B	10.E	13.E	16.B	19.C
2.B	5.B	8.B	11.D	14.D	17.C	20.A
3.C	6.C	9.D	12.E	15.B	18.D	

TEST IV. DATA INTERPRETATION

1.E	5.E	9.A	13.A	17.B	21.B	25.C
2.C	6.D	10.E	14.E	18.D	22.B	
3.D	7.C	11.D	15.B	19.A	23.D	
4.A	8.E	12.A	16.C	20.C	24.A	

TEST V. ERROR RECOGNITION

1.B	6.C	11.D	16.B	21.C	26.D	31.C
2.C	7.D	12.A	17.B	22.D	27.B	32.B
3.C	8.C	13.A	18.C	23.B	28.A	33.B
4.B	9.D	14.B	19.B	24.D	29.B	34.C
5.A	10.B	15.B	20.A	25.B	30.B	35.A

TEST VI. SENTENCE CORRECTION

1.A	5.E	9.C	13.D	17.A	21.B	25.A
2.E	6.C	10.B	14.C	18.D	22.E	
3.D	7.B	11.D	15.B	19.E	23.C	
4.E	8.C	12.D	16.A	20.D	24.D	

TEST VII. LOGICAL REASONING

1.B	4.D	7.E	10.C	13.C	16.E	19.D
2.C	5.D	8.C	11.E	14.B	17.A	20.C
3.B	6.C	9.A	12.B	15.D	18.B	

EXPLANATORY ANSWERS FOR VERISIMILAR EXAMINATION II.

Here you have the heart of the Question and Answer Method. . .getting help when and where you need it. Where one of your Key Answers differs from ours you have a problem which can easily be remedied by reading the explanation. Then, if you have time, you might be able to pick up points on the exam by reading the other explanations, even where you wrote the Key Answers correctly. These explanations stress fundamental facts, ideas, and principles which just might pop up as questions on future exams.

TEST I. READING COMPREHENSION

1. **(C)** Alternatives I and II are mentioned as positive benefits in the first paragraph of the passage, while alternative III is merely stated without mentioning whether or not it has a good or bad effect. Going to where the jobs are is a good effect but the effect of leaving the rural environment may or may not be healthy as seen in paragraph 3.

2. **(C)** Paragraph 3 states that "healthy growth . . . means growth which is distributed between both urban and rural areas."

3. **(B)** Paragraph 3 implies that healthy growth, which is both orderly and balanced, is best achieved by overcoming the problems associated with past growth in order to prevent their repetition in the future.

4. **(D)** See paragraph 5: "farm population now constitutes less than one-fifth of total rural population."

5. **(B)** It is stated that half the nation's counties did not experience any growth in non-farm employment due to remoteness from large-volume markets, lack of resources, etc. Therefore, (B) would appear to be a logical inference. (C), while true, is not the primary cause of the economic trouble.

6. **(A)** See the first sentence in paragraph 7. It is not that the skills of the better educated are not needed (as in choice D), but rather that the economic situation makes it difficult to provide the jobs for these skilled people.

7. **(C)** Radio resistant cancers do not respond to safe doses of X rays. (A) is incorrect because the cancer might respond to an unsafe dose of X rays.

8. **(A)** Paragraph 2 states that cancers of the gastrointestinal tract *must* be treated by surgery while cancers of the brain are *primarily* treated by surgery, which does not rule out alternative methods of treatment.

9. **(C)** Paragraph 4 specifically states that the ideal management of cancer patients is "by a smooth working team of a surgeon, radiotherapist, pathologist and internist."

10. **(A)** Paragraph 5 deals with inadequate surgery and radiotherapy and states that used improperly these techniques may actually spread cancer. Therefore, it is essential that a physician anticipate and refrain from choosing those which might do more harm than good. (B), (C), (D), and (E) are part of and included in choice (A).

11. **(E)** Neither Major nor Vanteur are mentioned in the passage.

12. **(C)** X-ray therapy and surgery, alone or in combination, are the major weapons in the battle against cancer. Even though some history is dealt with, the comparative aspects of radiotherapy and surgery is the major theme.

13. **(E)** It is stated that, "The use of heart-lung pumps, artificial kidneys .... were forerunners of transplantations of whole organs." Taking this one step further, we might infer that living organ transplants would eventually replace the use of mechanical devices. There is no evidence in the passage that would refute this assumption.

14. **(D)** This topic is not discussed, and the author's stated views would lead us to believe that he might dispute the idea of innate knowledge.

15. **(D)** Alternative I is stated in paragraph 4. Alternative II is stated in paragraph 5. Alternative IV is stated in paragraph 3. Alternatives III and V are never dealt with in the passage.

16. **(A)** As stated in paragraph 5, "A child who cannot use language remains locked away in his own little world."

17. **(C)** Paragraph 5 states that "as the children around him become more proficient at language, they talk together. Friendships grow." Therefore, verbal communication may be assumed to be the basis of friendship. Choices (D) and (E) are both true to certain extents but neither topic is dealt with directly in the passage.

18. **(E)** Alternatives I and III are mentioned in the passage. Alternative II is never mentioned, however, it may be inferred from the comment about math books.

19. **(B)** As stated in Paragraph 9, "dogs have lived with man for many years, so it may be natural that they have learned to communicate with their human masters." (C) is true but is not the prime reason as stated in (B).

20. **(B)** The author tells us just enough about the Tonkawa Indians to make us want to know more. For example, he mentions that he wishes to date the artifacts' collection and then tells us how he is going to set the scene by relating part of the Tonkawan history.

21. **(D)** Paragraph 2 cites several examples of the names by which the Tonkawas were known. They called themselves "the most human people." Their enemies called them "man-eating men." Another group called them a name which meant "they all stay together." It is obvious that alternative (D) must be correct.

22. **(B)** Paragraph 2 states that the Tonkawan language is in the same family as that of the Karankawa and Cotoname and refers to these two tribes as extinct. Since we are given considerable information about the Tonkawa, we must assume that these extinct tribes lived in a period before white men could make good records of their culture.

23. **(D)** Paragraph 3 tells us that the Tonkawa were never a populous tribe and that due to war losses and the loss of tribal identity, the tribe had dwindled to only 3 full-blooded Tonkawans by 1961.

24. **(C)** The first sentence in paragraph 4 mentions the Toyah focus as the one place where archaeological evidence of the Tonkawa *may* exist.

25. **(D)** As stated in paragraph 5, Francisco de Jesus Maria recorded the Tonkawas and Yojuanes as enemies of the Hasinai. Although it is mentioned that the Tonkawa and Yojuane Indians shared a common language, there is no mention of blood ties between the tribes.

TEST II. PRINCIPLES AND CASES

1. **(C)** is correct because, according to the principle, a privilege cannot be transferred. (A) is incorrect because Doc had extended the invitation to Fred, not Roger. (B) is incorrect because the principle does not deal with semi-public property. (D) is incorrect because the principle deals with the transfer of privilege.

2. **(B)** is correct because the principle grants Roger the right to go onto Doc's land in order to claim his property. (A) is incorrect because the principle is based on the right to claim personal property. (C) is incorrect because it is contrary to the facts. Roger did enter the property peacefully. (D) is incorrect because the principle grants Roger the right to go onto Doc's land to claim his car.

3. **(D)** is correct because Fred had proved himself to be a poor shot and therefore it is reasonable that his hunting rights be revoked. (A) is incorrect because according to the principle Fred cannot win if Doc takes away his privilege reasonably. (B) is incorrect because the principle is not concerned with motives. (C) is incorrect because it does not comply with the facts; there was no mention of hunting within specified bounds.

4. **(A)** is correct because Sesame did spend a large sum of money to erect the sign on Doc's property. (B) and (C) are incorrect because what Doc thought of the sign is irrelevant. (D) is incorrect because the principle concerns the economic burden of a person other than the property owner.

5. **(B)** is correct because Sesame was a member of the community. (A) is incorrect because Doc's state of mind is irrelevant to the principle. (C) is incorrect because it is contrary to the facts. (D) is incorrect because the principle does not require Sesame to bring suit in the name of the community.

6. **(C)** is correct because Brag made some attempt at marking the door by asking Eclipse to do it. (A) is incorrect because the principle does not call for inspection. (B) is incorrect because the principle does not require Brag to mark the danger zone himself. (D) is incorrect because the principle concerns willful and malicious negligence without mention of what a reasonable man would do.

7. **(B)** is correct because the principle ony calls for knowledge of possible future harm. (A) is incorrect because the severity of the injury is not important to the principle. (C) is incorrect because warning the patient of future harm is irrelevant to the principle. (D) is incorrect because a request by the patient is irrelevant to the principle.

8. **(C)** is correct because Stock was contributorily negligent. (A) is incorrect because the principle does not call for absolute exclusion of all harmful animals. (B) is incorrect because it excludes the possibility of contributory negligence. (D) is incorrect because there is no evidence that Stock treated the dog badly.

9. **(D)** is correct because Luther had no reason to suspect danger. (A) is incorrect because the principle calls for knowledge of possible danger. (B) is incorrect because the principle calls for absolute knowledge. (C) is incorrect because Luther's motives are not important.

10. **(A)** is correct because Brag knew the string was hazardous and the principle does not make an exception for contributory negligence. (B) is incorrect because there is only an obligation to warn of and not necessarily to repair a hazardous condition. (C) is incorrect because contributory negligence is not important to this principle. (D) is incorrect because Archie did not know that the string was frail, and therefore, did not knowingly assume any risk.

11. **(A)** is correct because none of the requirements for malice aforethought is met. (B) is incorrect because he did intend to perform the abortion. (C) is incorrect because we have no knowledge of pain on Mary's part. (D) is incorrect because there was no malice aforethought.

12. **(B)** is correct because Riley had no intention of killing Berny. (A) is incorrect because it is stated that Riley did not like Berny, but ill will, or the lack of it, alone cannot convict a man of first-degree murder. (C) is incorrect because dislike does not necessarily imply intention to kill. (D) is incorrect because this is not true to the facts.

13. **(C)** is correct because death by bombing is enough for first-degree murder. (A) and (B) are incorrect because when a bomb is involved intention is not important. (D) is incorrect because other motives are irrelevant where a bombing is concerned.

14. **(A)** is correct because Clark did not have any of the three elements required for malice aforethought. (B) is incorrect because provocation and passion are not key points in second-degree murder. (C) is incorrect because willful, deliberate and premeditated actions alone do not constitute malice aforethought. (D) is incorrect because Clark's actions did not satisfy the requirements for malice aforethought.

15. **(C)** is correct since all that is necessary for second-degree murder is malice aforethought. (A) is incorrect because intention is not necessary if there is malice aforethought. (B) is incorrect because intention to resist arrest is sufficient to establish malice aforethought. Intention to mislead is irrelevant in this case. (D) is incorrect because these elements are not necessary for second-degree murder.

16. **(B)** is correct because under the principle a duty of due care was owed. (A) is incorrect because this principle mentions nothing about strict liability. (C) is incorrect because the principle calls for a duty of due care to the property of another. (D) is incorrect because Ned should have known of the possibility of damage.

17. **(C)** is correct because Fred owed a duty of due care. (A) is incorrect because it is reasonable to assume that someone might be swimming in July. (B) is incorrect because the principle requires the exercise of due care where the danger of injury exists. (D) is incorrect because Fred had no absolute knowledge of a swimmer.

18. **(D)** is correct because it takes into account the forseeability of the injury. (A) is incorrect because she was not harmed by the driving. (B) is incorrect because it was an outside force which injured her. (C) is incorrect because it is not how she was injured that is important, but rather Benny's responsibility for the injury.

19. **(D)** is correct because it takes into account Mike's duty after the train had come to a stop. (A) is incorrect because the case is concerned with the reversing and moving forward of the train after it was stopped by the safety switch. (B) is incorrect because he checked too late. (C) is incorrect because the original hitting of Red was unavoidable.

20. **(C)** is correct because a medical student should only work under the direct supervision of a chief surgeon. (A) is incorrect because it does not deal with Proctor's responsibility. (B) is incorrect because joinder of parties is not at issue here. (D) is incorrect because there is no indication that Hem Stitch had been negligent in the past.

21. **(C)** is correct because Mayor Peoples was obviously not hurt by the article. (A) is incorrect because the matter published was of the type which would tend to lower someone's reputation and therefore Rizzo would lose by the principle. (B) is incorrect because the facts do not reveal Rizzo's state of knowledge. (D) is incorrect even though it might give the proper result because the words "in fact" in (C) are narrower than the words "tend to" in (D).

22. **(D)** is correct because it narrowly excludes a partnership from bringing suit in a defamation action. (A) is incorrect because it only allows XYZ to bring suit; it does not determine the result. (B) is incorrect because it is not as precise as (D). An unincorporated association may include business entities other than partnerships. (C) is incorrect because like (A) it only deals with the ability to bring suit.

23. **(B)** is correct because it lets Barker win and takes into account that Crabby Appleseed is dead. (A) is incorrect because it concerns only the ability to bring suit, not the outcome. (C) is incorrect because it is far less precise than (B). (D) is incorrect because we are not dealing with grazing land.

24. **(D)** is correct because Factor was the sole owner of the corporation. (A) is incorrect because it is too broad and does not deal with the facts of the case. (B) and (C) are incorrect because they are not as precise as (D).

25. **(A)** is correct because it mentions that knowledge is not required for a defamation action to be brought and that real damage must be done. (B) is incorrect because Sawmount would lose by this principle. (C) is incorrect because reference was made to John Sawmount. (D) is incorrect because Sawmount was not a public official.

26. **(B)** is correct because according to the case Plates was spending a real twenty-dollar bill. (A) is incorrect because it would convict Plates for spending a genuine twenty-dollar bill. (C) is incorrect because there is no criminal action involved here. (D) is incorrect because there was reason for Hawk to believe a crime was in process and Plates would be held guilty.

27. **(C)** is correct because the filling of gasoline cans is not unequivocable. (A) is incorrect because an overt act was committed and this would convict Torch. (B) is incorrect because arson is a violent crime and this principle would convict Torch. (D) is incorrect because filling a gasoline can might be considered one of the steps in committing arson and Torch would be found guilty.

28. **(A)** is correct because it is impossible to knock down a skyscraper with a baseball bat, and this choice is consistent with the facts of the case. **(B)** is incorrect because there was malignity but nevertheless Vertigo won. **(C)** is incorrect because, while it is unlikely that Vertigo will injure anyone, it is possible that he could hit someone by accident. Thus, according to this principle Vertigo would lose. **(D)** is incorrect because according to this principle Vertigo will probably be found guilty.

29. **(C)** is correct because the gun looked real and Flint suffered a heart attack. **(A)** is incorrect because the gun looked real and its ineffectiveness was not apparent. **(B)** is incorrect because there is no apparent inadequacy and it conflicts with the ruling given in question 28. **(D)** is incorrect because it is not as precise as **(C)**.

30. **(B)** is correct because it holds Archer guilty and it takes into account the facts of the case. **(A)** is incorrect because it does not deal with the matter of apparent renunciation. **(C)** is incorrect because by this principle the state would lose. **(D)** is incorrect because it is not as precise as **(B)** and because it does not mention an attempt.

31. **(C)** is correct because the principle requires intent to burglarize upon entry. **(A)** is incorrect because apprehension of a felon does not mitigate the crime. **(B)** is incorrect because a filial relationship does not mitigate the crime. **(D)** is incorrect because we are given no evidence of the truth of this statement.

32. **(D)** is correct because it concerns the key matter of Fuddle's intent. **(A)** is incorrect because according to this law there must be an intentional flight to be guilty of this crime. **(B)** is incorrect since it does not say anything about Fuddle's intent. **(C)** is incorrect because Catchum was in the normal pursuit of his duty.

33. **(B)** is correct because Fuddle had no intention of permanently depriving the owner of her tea set. **(A)** is incorrect because it does not deal with intention. **(C)** is incorrect because Fuddle did intend to return the tea set. **(D)** is incorrect because it is contrary to the facts.

34. **(C)** is correct because the principle calls for collective bargaining when there is a change in a regularly given gift. **(A)** is incorrect because this might have been permissible with collective bargaining. **(B)** is incorrect because Christianson might have bargained over this point. **(D)** is incorrect because since the turkey was given with regularity, Christianson was obliged to give a turkey or something of equal value.

35. **(A)** is correct because immediately after the raising of their salaries the employees forgot all thoughts of unionization. **(B)** is incorrect because his present actions came suddenly and in response to union activity. **(C)** is incorrect because giving turkeys is not the act that we are

concerned with. The unfair practice is the sudden increase in pay to discourage unionization. (D) is incorrect because giving turkeys is not the major issue, although Christianson's reason was probably to discourage unionization.

36. **(C)** is correct since it deals with Christianson's attitude toward unionization. (A) is incorrect because we are not concerned with Christianson's feelings about Johnson but rather with his intentions concerning unionization. (B) is incorrect because the only adequate remedy under this principle would be reinstatement. (D) is incorrect because the only matter we are concerned with is Johnson's initial unionization activity.

37. **(B)** is correct because the principle regards each negligent party as totally responsible for his actions. (A) is incorrect because she did not have to sue Lefty. (C) is incorrect because Becky's injury and not Becky's fear is the key issue. (D) is incorrect because the principle makes no presumption about Becky's age.

38. **(B)** is correct because Killer and Lefty were the true causes of Nathan's injuries. (A) is incorrect because there is no evidence of this, and if it were true, Becky would not be the negligent party. (C) is incorrect because the principle does not concern itself with this factor. (D) is incorrect because it is irrelevant to the principle.

39. **(C)** is correct because Nathan was in agony. (A) is incorrect because Nathan did not scream intentionally. (B) is incorrect because we have no knowledge of this and the principle is concerned with Nathan's intention.

40. **(C)** is correct because the cow was the immediate cause of the accident. (A) is incorrect because the ambulance could not help but swerve. (B) is incorrect because we are concerned with immediate causation. (D) is incorrect because the principle does not deal with contributory negligence.

TEST III. PRACTICAL JUDGMENT

DATA EVALUATION

(A) means that the Conclusion is a Major Objective;
(B) means that the Conclusion is a Major Factor;
(C) means that the Conclusion is a Minor Factor;
(D) means that the Conclusion is a Major Assumption;
(E) means that the Conclusion is an Unimportant Issue.

1. **(B)** This would be a prime consideration in changing monthly production levels since the business is highly seasonal. Bulk sales come only during certain periods.

2. **(B)** Competition is intense within the industry so this will be an important element in making the decision.

3. **(C)** The technology in the industry is relatively simple so this will not be a major part of the decision.

4. **(E)** No problems were mentioned as a result of the transfer of leadership so this will not be an important consideration.

5. **(B)** The past growth of the company has been considerable and therefore this factor will be an important consideration in any decision to change traditional production schedules.

6. **(C)** There is a minimum, necessary year-end cash balance and this will be one of many factors considered in making any change.

7. **(B)** To meet the necessary excess cost contingencies these extra funds will be essential if the production schedules are changed.

8. **(B)** Because of the seasonal nature of the business, these are highly fluctuant, and it will be necessary to know that adequate funds are available.

9. **(D)** Mr. Hardy's whole scheme of level monthly production is based on the forecast that the cost of goods sold will average the same percentage of sales as in the past.

10. **(E)** The company is not considering any change in its traditional outlets and all trends, especially to variety chain stores, probably will not be affected by a change of production schedules.

11. **(D)** The new production schedule is expected to accomplish this.

12. **(E)** No change is planned for this production process.

13. **(E)** The end of the year storage costs are not large enough to be considered an important issue.

14. **(D)** This is an essential assumption because it is one of the cornerstones on which the plan for level monthly production is based.

DATA APPLICATION

15. **(B)** It is stated that many new firms enter the business each year because "capital requirements are not large and technology is relatively simple." While competition is heavy, this is not a reason for entering a business.

16. **(B)** Increased competition reduces profit margins as illustrated by Jervis' experience with toy billiard sets.

17. **(C)** Look at the last paragraph. Mr. Nelson listened to the idea and then began a process of taking the new alternatives into consideration in an open-minded fashion; however, to say that he was optimistic would be jumping to a conclusion.

18. **(D)** In the last paragraph Mr. Hardy estimates savings of $60,000 in wage premiums plus $47,000 in production costs.

19. **(C)** This is the only alternative which is fully supported by the reading. (See paragraph 9.) (A) is incorrect because the passage gives no information about vacations being cancelled.

20. **(A)** Since it is stated that estimates of sales volume have usually proved to be reliable in the past, it can be assumed that they will likewise be reliable in the future, and thus a good basis for determining a sound, level production schedule.

TEST IV. DATA INTERPRETATION

1. **(E)** Since 43% of the men over 17 and 31% of the women over 17 were smokers, the overall percentage must lie between these two limits; there is only one such choice—37%.

2. **(C)** The former smokers in this group are 15% of 24 million = 3.6 million women.

3. **(D)** There are 37% of 8 million = 2.96 million men; and 81% of 11 million = 8.91 million women over 65 who have never smoked. The difference is nearly 6 million.

4. **(A)** In 8 years, the twelve million men who were between 17 and 24 in 1970 will all have passed into the next higher age group. In this group, the percent who smoke is 51%, so of the 12 million new members, 6.12 million can be expected to be smokers. In the younger group, only 41% or 4.92 million were smokers. The increase is 1.2 million.

5. **(E)** (I) cannot be inferred from the chart because it is equally probable that there are more older non-smokers because there were fewer smokers when those who are now old were young. An example of the same logical error would be drawing the inference that having a native tongue other than English causes people to live longer, since a higher percentage of older Americans are not native English speakers. (II) is not a valid inference because there are not more men than women in the youngest age group. (III) cannot be inferred because it ignores the fact that more women than men never smoked.

200 / Law School Admission Test

6. **(D)** The number of smokers in each age group is:

	Men	Women
17-24	.41 × 12 = 4.92 M	.30 × 14 = 4.2 M
25-44	.51 × 23 = 11.7 M	.39 × 24 = 9.36 M
45-64	.45 × 20 = 9.0 M	.33 × 22 = 7.26 M
65 and over	.23 × 8 = 1.84 M	.11 × 11 = 1.21 M

Therefore, the smallest difference between men and women smokers occurs in the 65 and over age group.

7. **(C)** The Defense Department purchases 7% of the $2 billion output of the truck trailer industry, or $140 million.

8. **(E)** Truck and bus bodies industry spends 21% of $1.5 billion = $0.315 billion on steel. Motor vehicles and parts industry spends 8% of $40 billion = $3.2 billion. Truck trailers industry spends 15% of $2 billion = $0.3 billion. The total is $3.815 billion.

9. **(A)** 1% of the output is sold to the truck trailer industry and 34% of the output is sold to the motor vehicles and parts industry, for a total of 35%.

10. **(E)** Gross private fixed capital formation consumes 72% of the $1.5 billion output of truck and bus bodies, or $1.08 billion; 13% of the $40 billion output of motor vehicles and parts, or $5.2 billion; and 89% of the $2 billion output of truck trailers, or $1.78 billion. The total is $8.06 billion.

11. **(D)** The defense department spends $140 million on truck trailers annually (see question 7), of which 14% goes to purchase aluminum, for a total indirect purchase of $19.6 million.

12. **(A)** 41% of the $40 billion output of motor vehicles and parts goes to personal consumption (.41 × $40 billion = $16.4 billion). A 10% drop in personal consumption would reduce this amount by 10% or $1.64 billion.

13. **(A)** Truck and bus bodies are the industry group that is most dependent on steel, 21% of expenditures as compared to 8% of expenditures for motor vehicles and parts, and 15% of expenditures for truck trailers.

14. **(E)** Foreign holdings of U.S. Government securities went from about $10 to about $50 billion, a greater increase than any of the other groups.

15. **(B)** The width of the commercial bank segment of the graph at this date is the distance from $150 to $250 billion, or $100 billion.

16. **(C)** The holdings of nonbank financial institutions at this date were $40 billion which is 12% of the total of $320 billion.

17. **(B)** Foreign holdings of U.S. Government securities went from $10 billion to $50 billion, which is a 400% increase.

18. **(D)** During this period, the Federal Reserve Board increased its holdings from $60 to $80 billion while the total increase was about $70 billion. $\frac{20}{70} = 28\%$

19. **(A)** At the beginning of 1967 the share owned by private nonfinancial institutions was about $120 billion of a total of $280 billion or 42%. In 1974, the share was $160 billion out of a total of about $450 billion, or 35%. This is a decline of about 17% $\left(\frac{42-35}{42} = 17\%\right)$.

20. **(C)** Photocopy equipment was $2 billion, which is about 28% of total shipments of $7 billion.

21. **(B)** Shipments of still picture equipment grew by about $500 million, while microfilming equipment grew by about $150 million; so the ratio is 3:1.

22. **(B)** The simplest way to answer this question is to look for the line that has a steeper slope than the line for total shipments. This is a necessary consequence of the fact that this is a ratio scale where equal slopes mean equal percentage changes. By inspection, the correct answer is (B) photocopy equipment.

23. **(D)** The percentage change in the first period is $\frac{90-50}{50} = 80\%$. The percentage change in the second period is $\frac{200-90}{90} = 122\%$. The answer to the question is obtained by dividing the percentage change for the first period by the percentage change for the second period: $\frac{80}{122} = \frac{2}{3}$

24. **(A)** The increase in still picture equipment was $400 million and the total increase was about $3,600 million. $\frac{4}{36} = 11\%$.

25. **(C)** The answer to this question is available directly from the graph: $3.6 billion.

TEST V. ERROR RECOGNITION

(A) *means the sentence contains an error in DICTION;*
(B) *means the sentence is VERBOSE;*
(C) *means the sentence contains FAULTY GRAMMAR;*
(D) *means the sentence contains NO ERROR.*

1. **(B)** "—— to *determine the facts*." There are no such things as false facts.

2. **(C)** "Holding one end of the rope in your right hand, *you make* two loops with the portion held in your left hand." In the original sentence, which is incorrect, the participle *holding* modifies *loops,* which is nonsense; *loops* did not do the holding. A participle must attach itself immediately to the noun with which it has a logical association. In the corrected sentence, *holding* does attach itself immediately to *you,* the noun it logically modifies.

3. **(C)** "We must respect such a girl as *she*." There is ellipsis in this sentence. The full sentence is "We must respect such a girl as she *is*."

4. **(B)** "———is *as keen today* as it was———." *Keen* and *intense* are synonyms.

5. **(A)** "I *stayed* overnight———." *To stop* is used colloquially for *to stay.*

6. **(C)** "———John's wages *are* a dollar———." When the subject (*wages*) and complement (*a dollar*) differ in number, the verb must follow the number of the subject.

7. **(D)** No errors.

8. **(C)** "Neither the elevator nor the escalator *was* in operation." When the subjects of both *neither* and *nor* are singular, the verb must be singular as well.

9. **(D)** No errors.

10. **(B)** "———his constituents *agreed with his views*———." *Agreed with* and *concurred in* are synonyms.

11. **(D)** No errors.

12. **(A)** "I am glad you are *finished* writing the article." *Done* in the sense of *completed* or finished is colloquial.

13. **(A)** "———have been *wary* of disengagement." *Leery* is slang for *wary*.

14. **(B)** "———*a major-league record*." If Krandall established the record, it was *new*.

15. **(B)** "———of a *bygone age*." *A bygone age* is *an age now past*.

16. **(B)** "———hundreds of miles *southward*." The suffix *-ward* denotes "direction to" or "motion toward."

17. **(B)** "———will surely unite against Israel." *To unite* is *to act together*.

18. **(C)** "———extremely *suddenly*." What is needed to modify the verb *occurred* is an adverb. *Sudden,* an adjective, must therefore be changed to the adverb *suddenly*.

19. **(B)** "Your decision to buy a yacht *is imprudent*." *Imprudent* and *impolitic* are synonyms.

20. **(A)** "———*an excellent* wristwatch———." *Swell* is slang for *excellent*.

21. **(C)** "———as much as *I*." If you hate fascism *as much as me,* you hate it as much as you hate me. On the other hand, if you hate fascism *as much as I,* you hate it as much as I hate it. The latter meaning is implied in the sentence.

22. **(D)** No errors.

23. **(B)** "———of his *native Transylvania.*" *His native Transylvania* means *Transylvania, where he was born*.

24. **(D)** No errors.

25. **(B)** "———elated to learn that he *had been reelected, burst*———." *Reelected* means *elected for another term*.

26. **(D)** No errors.

27. **(B)** "———*to have fabricated* this case." *Fabricate* means invent or devise *falsely*.

28. **(A)** "Smoke *billowed*———." *To bellow* is to cry out loudly or to roar. *To billow* is to rise in a large, swelling mass.

29. **(B)** "———left *a large estate.*" *Large* and *of considerable size* mean approximately the same thing.

30. **(B)** "The report *stressed that*———." The expression *the point* can be omitted without changing the meaning of the sentence.

31. **(C)** "———*has* a sales tax." A singular subject followed by such an expression as *with, together with, as well as*, plus a noun, takes a singular verb.

32. **(B)** "This was a windfall for the corporation." A *windfall* is *an unexpected acquisition.*

33. **(B)** "———that you will derive no *benefit from*———." *Benefit* and *advantage* are synonyms.

34. **(C)** "It *is* his parents———." The subject of the sentence is *it*, not *parents*. The verb must agree with its subject in number and gender.

35. **(A)** "———in good *condition.*" *Shape* is used colloquially for *condition.*

TEST VI. SENTENCE CORRECTION

1. **(A)** is correct. Choice (B) changes the meaning of the original sentence. *Such* is completed by *that*, rather than *so that*, when a result clause follows; for this reason, (C) is incorrect. Choices (D) and (E) are meaningless.

2. **(E)** is correct. *A child's fears* are compared to a *savage's fears*, not to a savage. Therefore, Choices (A) and (D) are wrong. (B) and (C) are wordy. In Choice (E), *savage's* is elliptical, meaning *savage's fears.*

3. **(D)** is correct. Choices (A), (B), (C), and (E) call up conflicting mental images: *key-note* suggests music; *mainspring* suggests mechanics; *well-built* suggests carpentry. Choice (D) maintains one image.

4. **(E)** is correct. In Choices (A), (B), (C), and (D) *he* could refer to either *Paul* or *the stranger*.

5. **(E)** is correct. Choices (A), (B), (C), and (D) are run-on sentences.

6. **(C)** is correct. Choice (A) makes no sense. (B) suggests that Mary almost has a voice. (D) is awkward, and (E) gives the impression that I almost heard Mary's voice.

7. **(B)** is correct. The past contrary-to-fact conditional form is *had analyzed*. Only Choice (B) uses this verb form.

8. **(C)** is correct. Choice (A) compares two unlike things, *predecessor* and *life*. (B) unnecessarily repeats the word *life*. In Choice (D) there is an awkward separation between subject and verb. Choice (E) makes no sense.

9. **(C)** is correct. A pronoun (*their*) must agree in number with its antecedent (*both*). In (A) and (D), *his* does not agree in number with *both*. If the two authors have written about *their courtship* (B), they courted each other. *They're* (E) means they are.

10. **(B)** is correct. In Choice (A), there is an awkward change of subject. (C) is a run-on sentence. (D) implies that the strange looking people are the ones landing at Bombay. Choice (E) changes the meaning of the original sentence.

11. **(D)** is correct. Since *men who cared only for their individual interests* are *selfish men*, and since *in a discouraged state* means *discouraged*, the simplest way of expressing the thought is *selfish men were now discouraged*.

12. **(D)** is correct. Choice (A) is a confusing series of elements beginning with *that*. In (B) it is unclear whether the boy or the newspaper is announcing the war's end. Choice (C) suggests that the dime brought the newspaper and (E) is awkward.

13. **(D)** is correct. A verb (*varies*) agrees with its subject (*size*) despite intervening expressions (*of the plantations*). Choices (B), (C), and (E) change the meaning of the original sentence.

14. **(C)** is correct. *Such* is completed by *as* when a relative clause follows.

15. **(B)** is correct. Not *pioneers* but their *work* is neglected. Choice (A) implies the contrary. The work of pioneers is pioneers' work, so (C) is incorrect. (D) and (E) are awkward.

16. **(A)** is correct. *To catch on to* and *to make a hit with* are colloquial usages, and *undoubtably* is an illiterate expression.

17. **(A)** is correct. The participle *having* illogically modifies *the play* in (B). Choice (C) is awkard and in (D) and (E), we are unsure who has taken the seats.

18. **(D)** is correct. The expression is *no sooner . . . than*.

19. **(E)** is correct. In (A) and (C) the subject and verb are awkwardly separated. Choices (B) and (D) suggest that *education* married a pauper.

20. **(D)** is correct. Since the first two members (*eating* and *working*) of the compound subject are gerunds (*-ing* forms of verbs, used as nouns) the third member should also be a gerund (*avoiding*). Since a compound subject normally takes a plural verb, Choice (E) is incorrect.

206 / *Law School Admission Test*

21. **(B)** is correct. The construction *not only . . . but also* requires parallelism. In Choice (A) an adjective follows *not only,* but a verb follows *but also.* In (E), a verb follows *not only,* but a pronoun follows *not also.* The use of the word *they* in Choices (C) and (D) unbalances the sentence.

22. **(E)** is correct. An animal is referred to as *it,* unless it has been given a name; therefore, Choice (B) is incorrect. The pronoun *its* agrees with *giraffe;* Choices (A) and (C) incorrectly substitute *their* for *its. It's* in Choice (D) means *it is.*

23. **(C)** is correct. There is no reason for the change in number (*one, they*) in Choices (A) and (D). (B) is wordy and (E) changes the meaning of the original sentence.

24. **(D)** is correct. *Total effect, total effect of all this,* and to *return back* are redundant expressions. (A), (B), and (C) each contain at least one of these tautologies. In (E), *departure,* meaning the act of going away, is incorrectly substituted for *point of departure,* meaning starting point.

25. **(A)** is correct. Choices (C) and (D) use the preposition *like* instead of the conjunction *as.* One thinks *hard* not *hardly* as in (B) and (D). Choice (E) changes the meaning of the original sentence.

TEST VII. LOGICAL REASONING

1. **(B)** is correct because the passage is primarily concerned with how interesting historical truth can be. (A), (C), (D), and (E) are only characteristics which help to enliven historical truth.

2. **(C)** is correct because natural beauty implies nothing added to make the skin attractive, but people are buying more and more beauty treatment products just to achieve this effect. (A), (B), (D), and (E) are not logical contradictions to the paragraph.

3. **(B)** is correct because this type of product and packaging would highlight the trend toward the natural look. (A) and (E) are incorrect because the emphasis of the passage is not on price but on general appeal. (C) is irrelevant to the facts presented. (D) is incorrect because a new trend would indicate new products.

4. **(D)** is correct since the passage states that Poe "conceived of God as a poet." (A), (B), (C), and (E) deal with ideas not touched on in the passage.

5. **(D)** is correct because the implication is that when two emotions are joined they become something greater as stated in the first sentence: "One times one equals one, but a one which is also a third thing . . ." (A) is incorrect because no implication of difficulty is given. (B) is incorrect because while drama is an attribute of the emotions it may not be a necessary attribute. (C) is incorrect because violent emotions are not implied. (E) is incorrect because the reader may infer from the passage that the mixing of emotions is a good thing.

6. **(C)** is correct because it deals with the reduction of an excess as does the original question (an excess of corn and an excess of fat). (B) is incorrect even though it is very close to (C) merely because it does not deal with food or food products. (A), (D), and (E) are incorrect because they do not deal with the reduction of an abundance.

7. **(E)** is the best of all the alternatives because it uses the personal "I" as does the original dialogue, and it follows the same structure as the example. (A), (B), (C), and (D) are not as good because they do not follow the same pattern as the original passage.

8. **(C)** is correct because the passage states that the poet is the foremost "sense shaper of experience." That means the poet's experience changes more rapidly than that of other people, and therefore he should be easier prey to doubt and uncertainty because he is the one who must recognize a new reality. (A) is incorrect because the poet is always rendering new experience actual or real. (B) is incorrect because there is no evidence of this. (D) is incorrect because the passage does not mention reward. (E) is incorrect because archetypes are not mentioned in the passage.

9. **(A)** is correct because it offers a suggestion for what the listener can do should he choose to make the "quick and quiet departure" the speaker has just mentioned. (B), (C), (D), and (E) are all incorrect because they do not follow as logically from the last sentence of the passage given.

10. **(C)** is correct because the night watchman has a vested interest in reporting accurately the events that occur during his tour of duty. (B) is incorrect because a doctor would want to please a new mother regardless of the accuracy of his statement. (A) is incorrect because a sergeant's responsibility is to train his men well and to say that he did not have well-trained men would reflect on his own ability. (D) is incorrect because a car dealer will probably say good things about the car that he is trying to sell. (E) is incorrect because the teacher has a vested interest in praising her school.

11. **(E)** is correct because "every man who does not shave himself" does not mean "only men who do not shave themselves," so the barber may shave himself without contradicting the terms of the paradox. (A) and (D) contradict the statement that "*He* shaves *every* man who does not shave himself." (B) and (C) only avoid the paradox, not resolve it.

12. **(B)** is correct because a vascular surgeon has the knowledge to make the judgment contained in the statement and a surgeon does not stand to profit from advising against surgery. (A) is incorrect because the statement is self-serving even if the union president has the expertise to justify our respect for his opinion. (C) and (D) are incorrect because the speakers can be presumed to lack expert knowledge of the subject matter. (E) is incorrect because it is entirely self-serving.

13. **(C)** is correct because it explains the difference described in the passage. (A) is a non-sequitur. (B) misinterprets the reference to a lack of political content in American literature to mean a lack of literary content in American politics. (D) and (E) are value judgments which are not supported by the passage.

14. **(B)** is correct because it would be illogical for the author to illustrate the non-political character of American literature by reference to those works which use American politics as their central theme.

15. **(D)** is correct. Since Bill uses his cousin's rejection despite a high LSAT score to refute John's remark, he must think John has implied that a high score is all that is required. John has actually said a high score is *necessary* and no valid inference can be drawn about whether or not it is sufficient. (A) and (B) are incorrect because they are consistent with what John actually said and, therefore, do not explain Bill's remark. (C) and (E) deal with issues which are not raised by the dialogue.

16. **(E)** is correct because the author's conclusion follows from his premises only if the mechanization of modern society precludes "first-rate things." (A), (C), and (D) are incorrect because the passage discusses the social climate for appreciating beauty, not the characteristics of artists. (B) is incorrect because the passage describes the prerequisites for the creation of beauty, not a definition of it.

17. **(A)** is correct because it is the only alternative which accuses a class of people of placing their personal interests ahead of the interests of those whom they have a duty to serve. (B), (C), and (D) are incorrect because they all state that the subjects of the criticism are surrendering their self-interest to the needs of the majority. (E) does not focus on the divergence between personal advantage and the general welfare.

18. **(B)** is correct because the validity of Smith's position does not depend on the author's opinion of it but on its internal consistency or lack of it. (A) is incorrect because one need not offer an alternative point of view to demonstrate the mistakes in a theory. (C) is incorrect because the reference to Smith as a "jesuitical juggler" does not refer to Smith's religion but to his style of rhetoric. (D) is incorrect because this is not a flaw in the attack. (E) is incorrect because the author of the statement does not use the names of famous writers, Smith does.

19. **(D)** is correct because the author feels that it is *safer* to destroy prophets since we cannot test the accuracy of their predictions. Obviously, it is not safer for the prophets, but for society. (A) and (C) are incorrect because the selection deals with the relationship between those who claim to know the future and society, not the relationship between the future and society. (B) and (E) are incorrect because they ignore the effect of prophecy on society.

20. **(C)** is correct because it is the only one which, like the stem question, poses a question to which either an affirmative or a negative answer constitutes an admission of the truth of the questioner's actual point. (A) and (B) are incorrect because they can be answered without conceding the questioner's argument. (D) and (E) are incorrect because they can not be answered "Yes" or "No" and are merely rhetorical phrasings rather than logical traps.

Law School Admission Test

THIRD VERISIMILAR EXAM

This professionally-written Examination enables you to display and exercise the important test-taking abilities leading to high scores . . . judgment, coolness, and flexibility. The various Tests fairly represent the actual exam. They should help in jogging your memory for all kinds of useful and relevant information which might otherwise be lost to you in achieving the highest exam rating possible.

Time allowed for the entire Examination: 3½ Hours

In order to create the climate of the actual exam, that's exactly what you should allow yourself . . . no more, no less. Use a watch to keep a record of your time, since it might suit your convenience to try this practice exam in several short takes.

ANALYSIS AND TIMETABLE: VERISIMILAR EXAMINATION III.		
This table is both an analysis of the exam that follows and a priceless preview of the actual test. Look it over carefully and use it well.		
SUBJECT TESTED	*Time Allowed*	*Questions*
READING COMPREHENSION	30 minutes	25
PRINCIPLES AND CASES	55 minutes	40
PRACTICAL JUDGMENT	40 minutes	40
DATA INTERPRETATION	30 minutes	25
ERROR RECOGNITION	20 minutes	35
SENTENCE CORRECTION	20 minutes	25
QUANTITATIVE COMPARISON	15 minutes	25
TOTALS EXAM III	210 minutes	215

ANSWER SHEET FOR VERISIMILAR EXAMINATION III.

Consolidate your key answers here just as you would do on the actual exam. Using this type of Answer Sheet will provide valuable practice. Tear it out along the indicated lines and mark it up correctly. Use a No. 2 (medium) pencil. Make only ONE mark for each answer. Additional and stray marks may be counted as mistakes. In making corrections erase errors COMPLETELY. Make glossy black marks.

TEST I. READING COMPREHENSION

TEST II. PRINCIPLES AND CASES

TEST III. PRACTICAL JUDGMENT

TEST IV. DATA INTERPRETATION

TEST V. ERROR RECOGNITION

1 A B C D E	2 A B C D E	3 A B C D E	4 A B C D E	5 A B C D E	6 A B C D E	7 A B C D E	8 A B C D E
9 A B C D E	10 A B C D E	11 A B C D E	12 A B C D E	13 A B C D E	14 A B C D E	15 A B C D E	16 A B C D E
17 A B C D E	18 A B C D E	19 A B C D E	20 A B C D E	21 A B C D E	22 A B C D E	23 A B C D E	24 A B C D E
25 A B C D E	26 A B C D E	27 A B C D E	28 A B C D E	29 A B C D E	30 A B C D E	31 A B C D E	32 A B C D E
33 A B C D E	34 A B C D E	35 A B C D E	36 A B C D E	37 A B C D E	38 A B C D E	39 A B C D E	40 A B C D E

TEST VI. SENTENCE CORRECTION

1 A B C D E	2 A B C D E	3 A B C D E	4 A B C D E	5 A B C D E	6 A B C D E	7 A B C D E	8 A B C D E
9 A B C D E	10 A B C D E	11 A B C D E	12 A B C D E	13 A B C D E	14 A B C D E	15 A B C D E	16 A B C D E
17 A B C D E	18 A B C D E	19 A B C D E	20 A B C D E	21 A B C D E	22 A B C D E	23 A B C D E	24 A B C D E
25 A B C D E	26 A B C D E	27 A B C D E	28 A B C D E	29 A B C D E	30 A B C D E	31 A B C D E	32 A B C D E

TEST VII. QUANTITATIVE COMPARISON

1 A B C D E	2 A B C D E	3 A B C D E	4 A B C D E	5 A B C D E	6 A B C D E	7 A B C D E	8 A B C D E
9 A B C D E	10 A B C D E	11 A B C D E	12 A B C D E	13 A B C D E	14 A B C D E	15 A B C D E	16 A B C D E
17 A B C D E	18 A B C D E	19 A B C D E	20 A B C D E	21 A B C D E	22 A B C D E	23 A B C D E	24 A B C D E
25 A B C D E	26 A B C D E	27 A B C D E	28 A B C D E	29 A B C D E	30 A B C D E	31 A B C D E	32 A B C D E

TEST I. READING COMPREHENSION

TIME: 30 Minutes. 25 Questions.

DIRECTIONS: Below each of the following passages, you will find questions or incomplete statements about the passage. Each statement or question is followed by lettered words or expressions. Select the word or expression that most satisfactorily completes each statement or answers each question in accordance with the meaning of the passage. Write the letter of that word or expression on your answer paper.

Correct and explanatory answers are provided at the end of the exam.

Reading Passage I

One of the more important functions of the Foreign Service of the United States is the administration of our immigration laws. The responsibility for issuing visas to certain aliens was first placed by Congress on consular officers in the Act of July 5, 1884. In 1917, during the First World War, a general requirement that all aliens seeking to enter the United States obtain visas was instituted and has continued since that time under successive immigration laws. With certain exceptions, therefore, aliens desiring to come to the United States are required to obtain appropriate visas from U.S. consular officers stationed at 253 posts throughout the world.

Although consular officers are directly responsible under the law for the issuance or refusal of visas, the Department of State is responsible for the general administration of the immigration laws insofar as they concern the Department and the Foreign Service. In fulfilling this responsibility, the Visa Office of the Bureau of Security and Consular Affairs of the Department prepares regulations which are published in the Federal Register, instructs consular officers regarding interpretations of the laws, establishes standardized procedures, provides on-the-spot guidance through regional meetings and field trips, and furnishes advisory opinions concerning all phases of visa work. A review procedure is set in motion when a consulate requests the Department's advice on material points of law or when the department requests a report from a consular post with a view to determining whether the action taken or proposed in a specific case is reasonable and in accordance with the applicable provisions of the law. Although most visas are issued at overseas posts, certain categories of nonimmigrant visas may be issued or revalidated by the Accreditation and Issuance Branch of the Visa Office.

For many people in foreign lands, the call at the American consular office is the first actual contact with the United States. A courteous reception by an American official and his considerate attention to the application for a visa serve to create an atmosphere of good will and help to promote good relations with foreign countries.

S-3272

In recent years successive Presidents have stressed the importance of facilitating international travel. The procedures for the issuance of visas to persons wishing to visit the United States have been made as simple as possible. Every effort is made to expedite the necessary action, and, in many cases, the personal appearance of the applicant is not required. Before a visa is issued, an applicant's written application is reviewed or he is interviewed by a consular officer to determine his eligibility for a visa appropriate to the purpose of his journey to the United States. If necessary, documentary evidence is requested to establish that the applicant has a residence abroad to which he will return, that he does not come within any of the excludable classes, and that he has adequate financial resources for the proposed journey. To further facilitate the travel of nonimmigrants, the granting of a visitor visa of indefinite validity has been authorized for nationals of countries who on a reciprocal basis permit the waiver of visa fees and the issuance of visas valid for multiple entry within a period of 48 months. Such visas while still valid may be transferred from an expired passport to a new passport. If the visa is of a specific validity and is submitted to a consular office within a year of expiration, it may be revalidated under a procedure that does not require the personal appearance of the visa applicant. Necessary clearance checks are handled expeditiously.

Applicants who are entitled to one of the immigrant classifications and who are chargeable to an oversubscribed foreign state or category are registered on waiting lists in the order in which they have qualified, in order to establish a priority for consideration when visa numbers become available. Although nonpreference and Western Hemisphere applicants are accorded the date on which they have met the requirement of section 212 (a) (14), which is prerequisite to those classifications, by law the priority date for preference applicants is that on which the petition to establish a preference was filed with the Immigration and Naturalization Service.

Aliens who receive visas are subject to examination at the port of entry by inspectors of the Immigration and Naturalization Service and by medical officers of the U.S. Public Health Service to establish their eligibility for admission into the United States. The jurisdictions of the Foreign Service, the Immigration and Naturalization Service, and the Public Health Service do not overlap in most respects but close liaison is maintained to insure a uniform interpretation of the law and to coordinate practices. At a number of posts abroad officers of the U.S. Public Health Service are on duty to conduct the medical examinations. At other posts, the examinations are conducted by approved local physicians. Similarly, officers of the Immigration and Naturalization Service are stationed at a number of Foreign Service posts abroad, in order that they may take action more expeditiously in those matters which call for action by that service.

In preparation for their visa duties abroad, consular officers take a course in visa instruction at the Foreign Service Institute as a part of their Foreign Service training. A correspondence course in visa work is also available for officers and clerical personnel assigned to overseas posts.

1. It may be inferred that the author considers the visa functions of the Foreign Service

    (A) a nuisance both to the taxpayer and the government
    (B) a task of significant import
    (C) a function that could be better handled by a different department
    (D) a task incompetently handled by the State Department
    (E) a function that is better handled by our State Department than any other department of state in the world

2. According to the passage what exceptions exist to the visa requirements?

    (A) Consular officials are exempt.
    (B) Military personnel and consular officials are exempt.
    (C) Only consular officials of particular countries are exempt.
    (D) No exemptions are ever made without the approval of the President.
    (E) The passage does not make clear what exemptions exist to the visa requirements.

3. According to the passage who is directly responsible for the issuance or refusal of visas?

    (A) Department of State
    (B) Foreign Service
    (C) The Federal Register Bureau
    (D) Consular officers
    (E) Accreditation and Issuance Branch of the Visa office

4. It may be inferred from the passage that the Federal Register

    (A) is a device for recording visa problems
    (B) is a textbook for consular officials
    (C) is a reference source for many issues concerning visas
    (D) keeps the news concerning the Bureau of Consular Affairs current
    (E) is a very comprehensive reference source

5. It may be inferred from the passage that consular officials may act as emissaries to the people of other nations because

    (A) consular officials are in charge of propaganda in other countries
    (B) consular officials have often been known to aid democratic insurgents
    (C) the consular official in many cases makes the first contact with people of foreign lands
    (D) consular officials often offer political asylum to people who may be wanted by the authorities in their own land
    (E) consular officials attempt to maintain friendly relations with foreign governments

6. It may be inferred from the passage that the reason the procedure for obtaining travel visas has been made simple is to

(A) lighten the workload of the consular officials
(B) improve relations with foreign countries
(C) encourage the lagging steamship passenger business
(D) stem the flow of gold from the United States
(E) encourage travel from Latin America

7. According to the passage all the following steps may possibly be required in order to obtain a visa except

I. The applicant must submit to a medical examination by the embassy doctor.
II. The applicant may be interviewed by an embassy official.
III. Documentary evidence may be requested to prove that the applicant has a residence abroad.

(A) I only
(B) II only
(C) III only
(D) I and II only
(E) II and III only

Reading Passage II

In the winter of 1844 the citizens of Boston voluntarily cut a path through the ice of East Boston harbor to free the Cunard line's Britannia and allow her to sail to sea. While the people of Boston were so extravagantly demonstrating their high regard for the British steamship line, Congressmen in Washington were contemplating it with a growing concern. It was not that Cunard's performance had been unsatisfactory. It had, in fact, exceeded all expectations. Since 1840 its passage time between Liverpool and Boston, via Halifax, had averaged only fourteen days, and sailings were being maintained with great regularity. It was, rather, the success of the Cunard line that was forcing Congress to take a critical view of the whole situation involving postal communication with Europe.

The advent of the steam packet had blunted American prestige. For many years American sailing packets had dominated the "Atlantic shuttle." Although the sailing packets were still carrying the bulk of European emigrants and freight—including coal being shipped to America for use by the steam packets—most of the mail, cabin passengers, and fine freight were now carried by the British steamships. Their progress appeared inevitable, and the American flag would soon take second place on the "Atlantic Ferry." American pride, inflated by a surge of new nationalism, was piqued. But Congress was concerned with far more than piqued pride. The United States was becoming increasingly dependent upon the British for its postal communication with Europe. Additionally, the Cunard line was under contract to the British Admiralty, subsidized at 81,000 pounds sterling annually, to carry the mails, and each of its ships carried on board an off-duty officer of the British navy as an agent of the Admiralty. The close tie between the British Admiralty and the contract mail packets was noted by Congress.

During the 1840's there was a great expansion of American foreign trade. Total foreign trade averaged $197 million annually during the first five years of the decade and $259 million for the last five years. The second half of the decade was characterized by a general tendency toward freer trade. In 1846 Great Britain repealed its Corn Laws, and in the same year the United States reduced its tariff. Increased industrialization in Great Britain, coupled with the high prices for foodstuffs caused by crop failures, particularly in Ireland, were also important causes of the increased American foreign trade.

The representatives of American commercial interests, now prosperous, began to flex their political sinews. Interested as they were in the rapid transmission of business information, particularly in regard to prices, they were also concerned about the cost of disseminating such information. The postal reform achieved in Great Britain stimulated them to press for lower and more uniform rates of postage in the United States. As early as June 10, 1840, Daniel Webster introduced a resolution in the Senate calling for lower rates of postage and the use of postage stamps. A British General Post Office order of February, 1841 announced the inauguration of the Cunard packet service, with "the Postage remaining as at present, viz. an Uniform Charge of 1s. the Single Letter . . . ." A later General Post Office order of February, 1841 applied the one shilling packet rate to a letter whose weight did not exceed half an ounce, instead of a single letter consisting of one sheet of paper. Although this British packet rate represented a considerable reduction in postage in comparison with the rates of 1837, American postal rates remained high, and agitation for postal reform in the United States was beginning to attract the attention of the public.

Important as this reduction in postal rates was to American business, it was not the only savings made possible by the Cunarders. Their relatively rapid crossings, together with the regularity and certainty of their sailings, were obviating the necessity for sending many duplicate copies of the same letter by different ships in order to be certain that a copy would arrive as early as possible, or would arrive at all. This had resulted in a considerable saving in clerical cost as well as in postage.

There were, however, other aspects of the foreign mail service that inconvenienced and annoyed merchants. Since the Cunarders ran to Liverpool, letters addressed to other parts of Europe were forwarded from England, often with great difficulty. American businesses usually employed a British banking, merchandising, or brokerage firm to act as their agent for forwarding mail. Agents on the continent were also employed. The agents paid the necessary postage and attended to the expeditious routing of letters. The act of March 3, 1845 authorized the Postmaster General or the Secretary of

State to empower United States consuls to pay foreign postage and forward letters. Certain consuls were so empowered, but the consular service in general was not used for this purpose. The cost and cumbersomeness of forwarding mail through agents was an annoyance to American merchants who exerted political pressure upon Congress to eliminate the necessity for this procedure.

8. According to the passage Congressmen in Washington considered the Cunard line with growing concern because

   (A) it had failed repeatedly to live up to its claim to the public
   (B) the success of the Cunard Line forced Congress to take a critical look at postal connection with Europe
   (C) the loss of mail on steamships could reach crisis levels
   (D) the cost of intercontinental mail delivery could rise in the future
   (E) the United States might be faced with a shortage of fuel with which to supply its steamships

9. It may be inferred from the passage that the majority of American freight companies were affected in what way because of the success of the Cunard line?

   (A) A huge number of bankruptcies swept the industry.
   (B) American ships lost the majority of the freight business to English steamships.
   (C) American ships were no longer considered as safe as English ships.
   (D) American shipping lost some of its prestige, fine freight, and passenger business.
   (E) American shipping only barely managed to maintain the bulk of the intercontinental mail.

10. According to the passage what was the "Atlantic Ferry"?

   (A) An American clippership
   (B) A British steamship
   (C) The name for the passage between North America and Europe
   (D) The name that referred to the shipment of cargo between the continents
   (E) The name that referred to the shipment of passengers between the United States and England

11. It may be inferred that the main reason for the concern by Congress with the rise of the steamship was

   (A) the loss of American prestige
   (B) the threat that steamships would become effective warships
   (C) the great rapidity with which the British were building steamships
   (D) the United States' dependence on the British for postal communications
   (E) the close tie between the British admirals and the contract mail business

12. According to the passage all the following were important causes of increased American foreign trade in the 1840's except

  I. Great Britain exercised greater control and organization over the flow of grain.
 II. U.S. tariffs became less of a burden because of world-wide inflation.
III. Ireland became industrialized freeing it from its agrarian culture.

(A) I only
(B) II only
(C) I and III only

(D) II and III only
(E) I, II, and III

13. The author's primary purpose in the passage is to

(A) show the development of postal communication between the United States and Europe
(B) demonstrate the importance of steamshipping to commercial goods
(C) illustrate the industrial success of the Cunard Steamship Company
(D) illustrate the inefficiency with which the United States government reacts to crises
(E) give a brief history of the first half of the 19th century

Reading Passage III

In the brief history of this nation, we have always claimed that progress and the "good life" are connected with population growth. In fact, population growth has frequently been regarded as a measure of our progress. If that were ever the case, it is not now. There is hardly any social problem confronting this nation whose solution would be easier if our population were larger. Even now, the dreams of too many Americans are not being realized; others are being fulfilled at too high a cost. Accordingly, this Commission has concluded that our country can no longer afford the uncritical acceptance of the population growth ethic that "more is better." And beyond that, after two years of concentrated effort, we have concluded that no substantial benefits would result from continued growth of the nation's population.

The "population problem" is long run and requires long run responses. It is not a simple problem. It cannot be encompassed by the slogans of either of the prevalent extremes: the "more" or the "bigger the better" attitude on the one hand, or the emergency crisis response on the other. Neither extreme is accurate nor even helpful.

The "population problem" can be interpreted in many ways. It is the pressure of the populace reaching out to occupy open spaces and bringing with it a deterioration of the environment. It can be viewed as the effect on natural resources of increased numbers of people in search of a higher standard of living. It is the impact of population fluctuations in both growth and distribution upon the orderly provision of public services. It can be seen as the concentration of people in metropolitan areas and depopulation of rural America, with all that implies for the quality of life in both places. It is the instability over time of proportions of the young, the elderly, and the productive. For the family and the individual, it is the control over one's life with respect to the reproduction of new life—the formal and informal pronatalist pressures of an outmoded tradition, and the disadvantages of and to the children involved.

Unlike other great public issues in the United States, population lacks the dramatic event—the war, the riot, the calamity—that galvanizes attention and action. It is easily overlooked and neglected. Yet the number of children born now will seriously affect our lives in future decades. Population growth produces a powerful effect in a double sense: its fluctuations can be strong and difficult to change; and its consequences are important for the welfare of future generations.

There is scarcely a facet of American life that is not involved with the rise and fall of our birth and death rates: the economy, environment, education, health, family life and sexual practices, urban and rural life, governmental effectiveness and political freedoms, religious norms, and secular lifestyles. If this country is in a crisis of spirit—environmental deterioration, racial antagonisms, the plight of the cities, the international situation—then population is part of that crisis.

Although population change touches all of these areas of our national life and intensifies our problems, such problems will not be solved by demographic means alone. Population policy is no substitute for social, economic and environmental policy. Successfully addressing population requires that we also address our problems of poverty, of minority and sex discrimination, of careless exploitation of resources, of environmental deterioration, and of spreading suburbs, decaying cities, and wasted countrysides. By the same token, because population is so tightly interwoven with all of these concerns, whatever success we have in resolving these problems will contribute to easing the complex system of pressures that impel population growth.

Consideration of the population issue raises profound questions of what people want, what they need—indeed, what they are for. What does this nation stand for and where is it going? At some point in the future, the finite earth will not satisfactorily accommodate more human beings—nor will the United States. How is a judgment to be made about when that point is to be reached? Our answer is that now is the time to confront the question: "Why more people?" The answer must be given, we believe, in qualitative not quantitative terms.

The United States today is characterized by low population density, considerable open space, a declining birth rate, and movement out of the central cities, but that does not eliminate the concern about population. This country, or any country, always has a "population problem," in the sense of achieving a proper balance between size, growth, and distribution on the one hand, and, on the other, the quality of life to which every person in this country aspires.

Nor is this country alone, in the world, demographically or in any other way. Many other nations are beginning to recognize the importance of population questions. We need to act prudently, understanding that today's decisions on population have effects for generations ahead. Similarly, we need to act responsibly toward other people in the world: This country's needs and wants, given its wealth, may impinge upon the patrimony of other, less fortunate peoples in the decades ahead. The "population problem" of the developing countries may be more pressing at this time, as in the longer perspective, it is both proper and in our best interest to participate fully in the worldwide search for the good life, which must include the eventual stabilization of our numbers.

14. It may be inferred from the passage that the commission investigating population growth would be in favor of

   (A) increasing the food production of the U.S.
   (B) either leveling off or reducing the population of the U.S.
   (C) supporting the policy of many religious groups
   (D) increasing job opportunities in the U.S.
   (E) leaving it up to the individual to define her role as a person concerned with population growth

15. According to the passage what do the "bigger the better attitude" and the "emergency-crisis response" have in common?

   (A) They both have certain appealing aspects which must be investigated.
   (B) Each point of view takes in certain meaningful aspects of the overall problem.
   (C) Both points of view are too extreme to be useful.
   (D) The "emergency crisis response" has greater significance to our age than the "bigger the better" approach.
   (E) A little can be gained from each point of view but not much.

16. According to the author the problem of population can be interpreted in all of the following ways except:

   I. Its effect on natural resources.
   II. Its effect on the fluctuating amounts of oxygen in the atmosphere.
   III. Its effect on ocean life in coastal waters.

   (A) I only   (D) II and III only
   (B) II only   (E) I, II, and III
   (C) I and II only

17. According to the passage, the reason why population does not arouse much public interest is

   (A) it is not as pressing a problem as some other issues
   (B) the problem is downplayed by the news media

(C) the public has been overexposed to the problem

(D) it lacks the drama of a war or similar crisis

(E) there is very little that the public can do about the problem

18. It may be inferred from the passage that family life is affected by

(A) the urban environment

(B) the effect of mass communication

(C) the rise and fall of the population

(D) the density of the population

(E) the political struggles of ethnic urban groups

19. The author's main purpose in this article was

(A) to put the spotlight on the population problem

(B) to put the population problem in perspective with some of the other problems facing the country

(C) to strengthen the case for abortion

(D) to promote the effectiveness of planned parenthood groups

(E) to talk about the plight of the urban dweller

Reading Passage IV

Gertrude Stein is supposed to have explained to Hemingway that "remarks are not literature." Tonight I am offering some remarks, and I make no claim for them whatsoever. A writer's views on other writers may have a certain interest, but it should be clear that he reads what they write almost always with a special attitude. If he should be a novelist, his own books are also a comment on his contemporaries and reveal that he supports certain tendencies and rejects others. In his own books he upholds what he deems necessary, and usually by the method of omission he criticizes what he understands as the errors and excesses of others.

I intend tonight to examine the view taken by recent American novelists and short-story writers of the individual and his society, and I should like to begin by telling you the title of a new book by Wylie Sypher. It is *Loss of the Self in Modern Literature and Art*. It do not propose to discuss it; I simply want to cite the title of Mr. Sypher's book, for in itself it tells us much about the common acceptance of what the Spanish critic Ortega y Gasset described some years ago as "the dehumanization of the arts." One chapter of Mr. Sypher's book is devoted to the Beats, but, for the most part, he finds, as we might have expected, that the theme of the annihilation of Self, and the description of an "inauthentic" life which can never make sense, is predominantly European and particularly French. The names he most often mentions are those of Andre Gide, Sartre, Beckett, Sarraute, and Robbe-Grillet. These are writers whose novels and plays are derived from definite theories which make a historical reckoning of the human condition and are peculiarly responsive to new physical, psychological, and philosophical theories. American writers, when they are moved by a similar spirit to reject and despise the Self, are seldom encumbered by such intellectual baggage, and this fact pleases their European contemporaries, who find in them a natural, that is, a brutal or violent acceptance of the new universal truth by minds free from intellectual preconceptions. In the early twenties D. H. Lawrence was delighted to discover a blunt, primitive virtue in the first stories of Ernest Hemingway, and 20 years later Andre Gide praised Dashiell Hammett as a good barbarian.

European writers take strength from German phenomenology and from the conception of entropy in modern physics in order to attack a romantic idea of the Self, triumphant in the 19th century but intolerable in the 20th. The feeling against this idea is well nigh universal. The First World War with its millions of corpses gave an aspect of the horrible to romantic overvaluation of the Self. The leaders of the Russian Revolution were icy in their hatred of bourgeois individualism. In the Communist countries millions were sacrificed in the building of socialism, and almost certainly the Lenins and the Stalins, the leaders who made these decisions, serving the majority and the future, believed they were rejecting a soft, nerveless humanism which attempted in the face of natural and historical evidence to oppose progress. A second great assault on the separate Self sprang from Germany in 1939. Just what the reduction of millions of human beings into heaps of bone and mounds of rag and hair or clouds of smoke betokened, there is no one who can plainly tell us, but it is at least plain that something was being done to put in question the meaning of survival, the meaning of pity, the meaning of justice and of the importance of being oneself, the individual's consciousness of his own existence.

It would be odd, indeed, if historical events had made no impression on American writers, even if they are not on the whole given to taking the historical or theoretical view. They characteristically depend on their own observations and appear at times obstinately empirical. But the latest work of writers like James Jones, James Baldwin, Philip Roth, John O'Hara, J.F. Powers, Joseph Bennett, Wright Morris, and others show the individual under a great strain. Laboring to maintain himself, or perhaps an idea of himself (not always a clear idea), he feels the pressure of a vast public life, which may dwarf him as an individual while permitting him to be a giant in hatred or fantasy. In these circumstances he grieves, he complains, rages, or laughs. All the while he is aware of his lack of power, his inadequacy as a moralist, the nauseous pressure of the mass media and the weight of money and organization, of cold war and racial brutalities. Adapting Gresham's theorem to the literary situation one might say that public life drives private life into hiding. People begin to hoard their spiritual valuables. Public turbulence is largely coercive, not positive. It puts us into a passive position. There is not much we can do about the crises of international politics, the revolutions in Asia and Africa, the rise and transformation of masses. Technical and political decisions, invisible powers, secrets which can be shared only by a small elite, render the private will helpless and lead the individual into curious forms of behavior in the private sphere. Public life, vivid and formless turbulence, news, slogans, mysterious crises, and unreal configurations dissolve coherence in all but the most resistant minds, and even to such minds it is not always a confident certainty that resistance can ever have a positive outcome. To take narcotics has become in some circles a mark of rebellious independence, and to scorch one's personal earth is sometimes felt to be the only honorable course. Rebels have no bourgeois certainties to return to when rebellions are done. The fixed points seem to be disappearing. Even the self is losing its firm outline.

20. It may be inferred that the author regards novels as critical commentaries because

    (A)   many novels deal with matters of social import
    (B)   in a novel an author accepts certain literary tendencies and rejects others
    (C)   all novels deal with the society the writer lives in
    (D)   the excitement of a novel comes from the social issues with which it deals
    (E)   novels are born in the social conscience of an author

21. Ortega y Gasset most probably meant by the phrase "the dehumanization of the arts" that

    (A)   novels of his day dealt with cruel and immoral deeds
    (B)   the writers of his period dealt only with the nobility of the era
    (C)   no one appreciated the great art of his era
    (D)   writers often dealt with an inauthentic life which can never make sense in reality
    (E)   the writers of his period wrote only about themselves

22. According to Wylie Sypher what do Andre Gide and Sartre have in common with "The Beats"?

    (A)   A love of music.
    (B)   They often write about an unreal sort of life.
    (C)   A flowing and mellow style of writing.
    (D)   They nearly always write about the working classes of their societies.
    (E)   They have a common bond with the young revolutionaries of their societies.

23. According to the author how do American writers differ from European writers, particularly French writers?

    (A)   Americans have a blunt, primitive style close to the tradition of Hemingway.
    (B)   American writers do not have the same encumbrances of philosophical and psychological theories that Europeans have.

(C) European authors tend to stay close to the style of Sartre.

(D) French writers intentionally differ from their American counterparts.

(E) European authors have been afflicted by the struggles of the continent.

24. According to the passage all the following are true about American writers *except*:

   I. They are less encumbered by modern physical theories than European writers.
   II. They always avoid the tendency to reject the self.
   III. Some of the greatest American writers have had so called primitive virtues.

   (A) I only
   (B) II only
   (C) III only
   (D) I and II only
   (E) II and III only

25. The author implies that World War I and the Russian Revolution had what effect on twentieth-century European literature?

   (A) They gave it a tendency to seek individual virtue.
   (B) European literature became more escapist.
   (C) These events helped to destroy the romantic idea of the self.
   (D) These events started a trend of rugged individualism.
   (E) European literature became more self-reflective.

END OF TEST

Go on to do the following Test in this Examination, just as you would be expected to do on the actual exam. You will find correct answers for the entire Examination following the last question. Check your answers carefully after you have completed the whole Examination.

TEST II. PRINCIPLES AND CASES

TIME: 55 Minutes. 40 Questions.

These questions do not presuppose any specific legal knowledge on your part; you are to arrive at your answers entirely by the ordinary processes of logical reasoning.

PART A. APPLYING SEVERAL PRINCIPLES TO A CASE

DIRECTIONS: Each law case described below is followed by several legal principles. These principles may be either real or imaginary, but for purposes of this test you are to assume them to be valid. Following each legal principle are four statements regarding the possible applicability of the principle to the law case. You are to select the one statement which most appropriately describes the applicability of the principle to the law case and blacken the space beneath the letter of the statement you select.

Correct and explanatory answers are provided at the end of the exam.

Case One

Dashing Dan, a passenger, was running to catch a Long Island Railroad train which had just pulled out from the platform. Casey Jones, an employee of the railroad, saw Dashing Dan trying to catch up with the train. As Dan came close, Casey reached out to help Dan aboard, and, in the process, dislodged an innocent looking package from Dan's arms. The package contained fireworks which exploded so violently that the concussion loosened some scales many feet away at the other end of the platform.

Betty Bystander was staring at the beautiful cloud formation when she heard the violent explosion. The loosened scales fell upon her and broke her leg. The shock of the explosion so startled her that she acquired a nervous twitch which has lasted to this day. Dan suffered a few nicks and bruises.

1. *A duty of due care is owed only to those whom a reasonable man might foresee as being in the zone of danger created by his negligent action.*

   In an action by Betty against Casey to recover for her broken leg, Betty will

   (A) win because Casey was negligent in dislodging the package
   (B) win because scales can be expected to fall on bystanders
   (C) lose because Casey was not responsible for knocking the package from Dan's arms
   (D) lose because she was not in the foreseeable zone of danger

2. *Damages for emotional injury are not recoverable unless the emotional injury is accompanied by a physical manifestation.*

When Betty sues Casey for $5000 for emotional injuries, Betty will

(A) win because she was severely frightened by the explosion
(B) win because her emotional damage was accompanied by physical symptoms
(C) lose because she was not in the foreseeable zone of danger
(D) lose because a nervous twitch is not a physical response

3. *An employer is responsible for the results of the actions of his employees done while in the course of their employment.*

If Dan sues the Long Island Railroad (L.I.R.R.) for his injuries, Dan will

(A) win because the L.I.R.R. is responsible for the results of the actions of Casey Jones
(B) win because he was in the foreseeable zone of danger
(C) lose because he should have brought suit against Casey and not against the L.I.R.R.
(D) lose because he should not have been running to catch the train in the first place

4. *Reckless behavior on the part of the plaintiff is a defense against any action for damages brought against a defendant.*

When Dan sues Casey for his injuries, Dan will

(A) win because Casey was negligent in knocking the package from his arms
(B) win because running after a moving train is a reasonable action
(C) lose because he should not have been running after the moving train
(D) lose because it was not foreseeable that he would be injured

5. *A person is liable for damages done by any explosives in his possession if the damage is done directly by the blast of such explosives.*

If Betty sues Dan for damages resulting from her broken leg, Betty will

(A) win because the damage was done by explosives in Dan's possession
(B) win because Dan should have realized that he was being a menace both to himself and others
(C) lose because she was contributorily negligent in standing so close to the scales
(D) lose because she was not injured directly by the fireworks

Case Two

Buster Fender wanted to impress his girlfriend Billie Joy Ride with the speed of his car. However, as Buster and Billie were speeding down a lonely country road, a cow crossed the road, causing Buster to swerve into an apple tree. The apple tree fell and hit Iris Newton. Iris sustained internal injuries for which surgery was required.

Iris was rushed to General Hospital, a hospital which had been cited several times by the State Health Commissioner for lack of cleanliness. In the course of surgery on Iris, bacteria from the air entered the open wound and infected it, leading to her death.

Billie suffered a mild concussion and a broken arm, but she recovered from both injuries. Buster was merely emotionally shaken and vowed never to speed on country roads again.

6. *A person is responsible for any damages caused directly by his negligence or for any damages caused by a foreseeable indirect result of his negligence.*

   When the estate of Iris Newton brings an action for wrongful death damages against Buster, the estate will

   (A)   win because when a person is seriously injured complications resulting from surgery for such injuries are foreseeable
   (B)   win because Buster should not have been driving so fast
   (C)   lose because such complications resulting from the surgery were not foreseeable
   (D)   lose because Iris should not have been sitting under the apple tree

7. *A passenger in a motor vehicle may not recover for injuries suffered during the normal operation of such motor vehicles.*

   When Billie sues Buster for damages due to her injuries, Billie will

   (A)   win because she never told Buster to drive so fast
   (B)   win because Buster was not operating the car normally when Billie was injured
   (C)   lose because a passenger may not recover for injuries sustained during the normal operation of a motor vehicle
   (D)   lose because she was also at fault in allowing Buster to drive so fast

8. *Owners of livestock are responsible for damages directly caused by their livestock when such livestock enter upon public roads.*

   When Buster sues the owner of the cow for damages done to his car, Buster will

   (A)   win because the cow should not have been on the highway
   (B)   win because it was the cow which caused him to go off the road

    (C)   lose because the damage done to his car was not directly caused by the cow

    (D)   lose because in reality he was responsible for the damage done to his car since he was speeding

9. *If a hospital does not keep its facilities up to a normal standard of cleanliness, it will be held responsible for all injuries caused by infection, except where there is contributory negligence on the part of the patient.*

When the estate of Iris Newton sues General Hospital for damages on her wrongful death, the estate will

    (A)   win because the negligent surgery of the doctors allowed the bacteria to infect the wound

    (B)   win because the hospital facilities were not kept to a normal standard of cleanliness

    (C)   lose because Iris was negligent for sitting under the apple tree in the first place

    (D)   lose because the hospital was as clean as the staff could make it under present conditions

10. *Trespassers are liable for any damages to an owner's property unless the trespass is unavoidable or unintended.*

When the owner of the apple tree sues Buster for damages, the owner will

    (A)   win because Buster trespassed on his property

    (B)   win because the trespass onto his property was not unavoidable

    (C)   lose because Buster did not intend to enter his property

    (D)   lose because Buster could not have avoided going off the road and onto the owner's property

Proceed directly to the next Part.

PART B. APPLYING ONE PRINCIPLE TO SEVERAL CASES

DIRECTIONS: Each principle of law given below is followed by several law cases: These principles may be either real or imaginary, but for purposes of this test you are to assume them to be valid. Following each law case are four statements regarding the possible applicability of the principle to the law case. You are to select the one statement which most appropriately describes the applicability of the principle to the law case decision. Blacken the space beneath the letter of the statement you select. These questions do not presuppose any specific legal knowledge on your part; you are to arrive at your answers entirely by the ordinary processes of logical reasoning.

Principle One

A person is privileged to use deadly force—force which is likely to cause death or serious bodily harm—in self-defense if all of the following conditions are met:

I. *The actor reasonably believes that the other person is about to inflict an immediate harmful or offensive contact upon him.*

II. *The actor reasonably believes that such contact would cause the actor's death or serious bodily harm.*

III. *The actor retreats, if possible, before using deadly force.*

11. Peter was an avid gambler. However, he had recently gone through a long losing streak and he was heavily in debt to his bookie, Snapper. Snapper came to Peter's house waving a gun and saying, "I'm going to blow your head off, unless you pay me immediately." Peter became quite frightened, ran to the back of his house in order to get his hunting rifle and then went out on his front porch and shot Snapper fatally.

    In the action of the State against Peter, Peter will

    (A) win because all the elements required for the use of deadly force were present
    (B) win because he shot Snapper in self-defense
    (C) lose because he did not retreat before shooting Snapper
    (D) lose because he shot to kill Snapper and not merely to wound him

12. Morgan bought a cigarette lighter which looked just like a gun. When he went to work the next day he burst into Sampson's office and yelled, "Give me the money you owe me, Sampson, or I'll shoot!" Sampson first pulled a gun out of his desk drawer but then fled to the executive washroom. Morgan beat on the metal door of the washroom saying, "Come out! Come out!" Sampson threw the door open and fatally shot Morgan.

In the action of the State against Sampson, Sampson will

(A) win because he was in fear of immediate, serious bodily harm, and he retreated before he reacted

(B) win because he had no way of knowing that Morgan did not have a real gun

(C) lose because he could not have reasonably believed that he could have been shot by a cigarette lighter

(D) lose because while he was locked in the washroom he was not in present danger

13. Thompson, a judo expert, was walking through a bad neighborhood when he was attacked by a knife-wielding thug named Jones. Thompson at first tried to run away but he was quickly overtaken by Jones. However, when Jones lunged at Thompson with the knife, Thompson threw Jones into the street where he was hit by a gypsy cab and killed.

In the suit of the State against Thompson, Thompson will

(A) win because he did not use deadly force

(B) win because he complied with all the requirements for the use of deadly force

(C) lose because he did not warn his attacker that he was a judo expert

(D) lose because as a judo expert he was relatively certain that he could defend himself

14. Becky, a sixty-two-year-old lady, was just coming home from the super-market. She was unaware that she was being followed by Kane, a mugger. Kane followed Becky into her elevator. He demanded that Becky give him her money and said that he would not let her out of the elevator until she did. Becky became quite angry and slapped Kane's face, not realizing that Kane had a plate in his head. Kane died from the blow.

In the action of the State against Becky, Becky will

(A) win because she did not use deadly force

(B) win because she was in immediate fear of serious bodily harm

(C) lose because she did not retreat before she hit Kane

(D) lose because she was not in immediate fear of bodily harm

15. Racer was riding his ten-speed bike in Central Park. While he was struggling to get up a very steep hill, Lurky jumped in front of him and grabbed onto his bike. Racer succeeded in temporarily breaking away but Lurky caught Racer's bike again. Racer took a bicycle wrench from his pocket and hit Lurky, killing him. Racer rode off to get help.

In the action of the State against Racer, Racer will

(A) win because he tried to flee before he hit Lurky

(B) win because he complied with all the requirements for the use of deadly force

(C) lose because he was never in fear of serious bodily harm

(D) lose because he did not try hard enough to flee from Lurky

Principle Two

Robbery is the unlawful taking and carrying away of the personal property of another, from his person or in his presence, by violence or by putting him in fear, with the intent to deprive the owner permanently of his property.

The taking must always be accompanied by force or by threats and must always be from the person or in the presence of the owner.

16. Fingers is walking along the beach one day when he spots a transistor radio on Bather's blanket. Fingers picks up the radio and walks off, undetected by Bather who is one hundred yards away talking to the lifeguard. When Bather returns he notices his radio is missing from his blanket and spots it on Fingers' blanket. Bather calls a cop and has Fingers arrested.

    In the action of the State against Fingers for robbery, Fingers will

    (A) win because he did not use force or threats against Bather
    (B) win because he did not take the radio in Bather's presence
    (C) lose because he carried away the personal property of another
    (D) lose because he intended to permanently deprive Bather of his property

17. Oscar wanted a stereo for his party. He went to Gracy's apartment and asked to borrow her stereo. When Gracy refused, Oscar replied that he would hit her if she didn't give it to him. Gracy became frightened and let Oscar take the stereo. The next day Oscar returned the stereo to Gracy's apartment. Gracy later had Oscar arrested. He admitted to the police that he had taken Gracy's stereo by threatening her with bodily harm.

    In the action of the State against Oscar for robbery, Oscar will

    (A) win because Gracy did not try to restrain him physically
    (B) win because he did not intend to deprive Gracy of her property permanently
    (C) lose because all of the elements of the crime of robbery were present
    (D) lose because he took property in the presence of its owner

18. Snooker spent much of his time in Clipper's rigged gambling parlor. Snooker had been losing heavily for weeks and was upset about it, especially since his rent was due. He met Clipper in an alley and said, "Give me back my money, you cheat, or I'll hit you!" Clipper, in fear, gave Snooker the money and went to the police.

    In the action of the State against Snooker for robbery, Snooker will

    (A) win because it was his own money he took back
    (B) win because Clipper was engaged in illegal gambling

(C) lose because he intended to deprive Clipper permanently of his property

(D) lose because he used force in order to take the personal property of another

19. Weasel was a pickpocket who usually operated in Alexander's basement. While browsing amid the factory-second blue jeans, he bumped into Groovy and lifted the hand-made leather wallet from Groovy's back pocket. Groovy saw Weasel put the wallet into his pocket and he yelled for the guard. Weasel used force to overpower the guard but was soon captured by three brawny salesgirls.

In the action of the State against Weasel for robbery, Weasel will

(A) win because he did not carry the wallet away from the scene of the crime

(B) win because he did not use force or threats to take the wallet

(C) lose because he took the wallet while in the presence of the owner

(D) lose because he used force in his attempted escape

20. Punk met Wealthy on the street and said, "Give me your money or I'll kick you in the kneecap!" Wealthy, a former heavyweight wrestler, merely pushed Punk aside and walked on. Punk vowed to get even with Wealthy. He later broke into Wealthy's bedroom, while Wealthy was sleeping soundly, and took Wealthy's wallet from the night table. However, while he was crawling out of the window, Punk was caught by a neighbor.

In the action of the State against Punk for robbery, Punk will

(A) win because he did not take the wallet from the person of Wealthy

(B) win because Wealthy was not frightened by him

(C) lose because he had a specific intent to deprive Wealthy of his property

(D) lose because he took Wealthy's personal property

Proceed directly to the next Part.

PART C. CHOOSING THE NARROWEST JUSTIFYING PRINCIPLE

DIRECTIONS: In this section you will be given several groups of imaginary law cases. Each question will present a set of facts and a fictitious court holding, which you are to presume to be valid. Following each case are four legal principles, lettered (A), (B), (C), and (D). You are to choose the narrowest (most precise) principle which explains the court decision given. However, this principle may not conflict with the holdings given in any of the preceding cases in the same group. The correct answer to the first case in any group will always be the most precise principle which correctly explains the legal decision made. From the second question until the end of each group, you are to select the narrowest principle which does not conflict with any of the previous holdings.

These questions do not presuppose any specific legal knowledge on your part. They are to be answered entirely by the ordinary processes of logical reasoning. Indicate your choice by blackening the appropriate space on the answer sheet.

Group One

21. Arthur and Marty decide to rob a bank. They go to Marty's house and draw up a floor plan of the bank and a projected getaway route. Arthur, however, becomes nervous as the plotting goes on. He tries to convince Marty to give up the idea but Marty persuades him to go on. Unknown to Marty and Arthur, the house has been bugged, and both men are arrested and charged with conspiracy to rob a bank. At the trial, Arthur and Marty move that the charges be dropped. *Held*, for Arthur and Marty.

The *narrowest principle* which upholds this legal decision is:

(A) It is the unlawful combination or agreement that constitutes the crime of conspiracy.

(B) It is the unlawful combination or agreement to rob a financial institution that constitutes the crime of conspiracy.

(C) An overt act beyond the preparation stage must be made before any person or persons can be found guilty of a crime.

(D) An overt act must be made before any person or persons can be found guilty of conspiracy.

22. Reginald and Arturo are members of the international jet set. Reginald insults Arturo's girlfriend and Arturo slaps him in retaliation. They decide to settle the dispute with pistols. Arturo shoots Reginald in a fair fight in the wilds of Staten Island. In the action against Arturo for conspiring to commit a felony, Arturo's lawyer moves for dismissal. *Held*, for Arturo.

The *narrowest principle* that reasonably explains this result and is *not inconsistent* with the ruling given in the preceding case is:

(A) For those crimes in which agreement or concerted action by two persons is an essential element of the offense, it will take more than two persons to be guilty of conspiring to commit such an offense.

(B) A person will be guilty of conspiracy if any overt act is performed in furtherance of the conspiracy.

(C) For those crimes in which agreement or concerted action by two persons is an essential element of the offense, an overt act will be necessary for the completion of the crime.

(D) In those crimes in which agreement or concerted action by two persons is an essential element of the offense, it will take more than two persons to be guilty of conspiring to commit such an offense, except in crimes where firearms are involved.

23. Crafty is a lieutenant stationed at Fort Top Secret. Crafty conspires with Boris, a Soviet diplomat, to steal the plans for the new atomic-powered electric can opener. However, their conversation is overheard by Eves. Crafty and Boris are arrested and charged with conspiracy. Crafty's lawyer moves that the charges be dropped. *Held,* for Crafty.

The *narrowest principle* that reasonably explains this result and is *not inconsistent* with the rulings given in the preceding cases is:

(A) One person cannot be convicted of conspiring with another who is immune from prosecution, such as a diplomat.

(B) A person can be convicted of conspiracy when he conspires with another who is merely immune from prosecution, such as a diplomat.

(C) For those crimes in which agreement or concerted action by two persons is an essential element of the offense, an overt act will be necessary for the completion of the crime.

(D) Conspiring with an agent of a foreign nation is punishable absolutely.

24. Mack and Bruiser are friends. Mack is a likable person but a little retarded. Bruiser talks Mack into walking into a liquor store and stealing a case of Yago Sangria. However, when Mack comes out of the store in clear sight of a policeman, he hands the case of Sangria to Bruiser. When Bruiser is charged with conspiring with Mack to rob the liquor store, Bruiser's lawyer moves for dismissal of the charge. *Held,* for Bruiser.

The *narrowest principle* that reasonably explains this result and is *not inconsistent* with the rulings given in the preceding cases is:

(A) One person cannot be convicted of conspiring with another who lacks criminal capacity.

(B) A person can be convicted of conspiracy when he uses another person as an innocent instrumentality to commit acts planned by him.

(C)   One person cannot be convicted of conspiring with another who has any sort of mental deficiency or who lacks criminal capacity.

(D)   The crime of conspiracy is punishable when any sort of combination exists to rob or loot a retail merchant.

25.   Percy the Shoplifter was one of the most successful people in the business. He always worked alone. He got rid of his loot by putting it in an abandoned mailbox. George the Fence would pick up the loot from the mailbox, sell it, and put the money back into the box after making the appropriate deductions. Percy never met George. When Percy was finally arrested, his lawyer moved that the charge of conspiracy against him be dismissed. *Held,* Percy is convicted of conspiracy.

The *narrowest principle* that reasonably explains this result and is *not inconsistent* with the rulings given in the preceding cases is:

(A)   Conspiracy is the combination of two or more parties to commit a criminal act.

(B)   Conspiracy is the combination of two or more parties to commit a criminal act, but unless at least one party is aware of the other's identity, conspiracy has not been committed.

(C)   Conspiracy is the combination of two or more parties to commit a crime. The identity of all parties must be known to each of the conspirators, except in cases of petty theft and shoplifting where identities need not be known.

(D)   Conspiracy is the combination of two or more parties to commit a grossly immoral action. Gross immorality is to be defined by the court.

Group Two

26.   Harry bought a new car which was much admired by his friend Peter. Peter had just met Mary at the beach and he wanted to make a good impression with her on the first date, so he asked to borrow Harry's car. While Peter was driving to the Lonely Drive-In Theater with Mary, the steering mechanism went awry. The car went off the road and Peter was seriously injured. Peter sues the manufacturer of the car. *Held,* for Peter.

The *narrowest principle* which upholds this legal decision is:

(A)   If the average, reasonable man would have foreseen that a chattel would create a risk of harm to human life or limb, if not carefully made or supplied, then the manufacturer or supplier of such chattel is under a duty of due care in the manufacture or supply thereof, and this duty of care is owed to the owner.

(B)   The manufacturer of any product owes a duty of due care in manufacture to any foreseeable user of the product.

(C)   The manufacturer of any automobile product owes a duty of due care in manufacture to any foreseeable user of the product.

(D)   The manufacturer of any automobile product owes a duty of due care in manufacture to the owner of the product.

27. Speedy got a new motorcycle for his birthday and decided to go touring the countryside. Speedy was known to take unreasonable chances with his life and the lives of others. While speeding down a country road the drive chain, which had been negligently made, broke. The bike went off the road and hit Larry. Larry sued the manufacturer. *Held*, for Larry.

The *narrowest principle* that reasonably explains this result and is *not inconsistent* with the ruling given in the preceding case is:

(A) The manufacturer of any automotive product is liable to any foreseeable user of his product for damages due to its negligent manufacture.
(B) The manufacturer is liable to all foreseeable users of the product for damages due to its negligent manufacture.
(C) Operators of motor vehicles are personally liable for accidents in which their vehicles leave the public roadway.
(D) The manufacturer is liable not only to foreseeable users but to all persons foreseeably within the scope of use of a defective product.

28. Ronald was using his new electric rotary saw when a defective blade broke and flew through the new Tiffany vase which he was storing in his garage. Ronald's wife was quite upset and caused him to bring a suit against the manufacturer of the saw. *Held*, for Ronald.

The *narrowest principle* that reasonably explains this result and is *not inconsistent* with the rulings given in the preceding cases is:

(A) The manufacturer is liable not only to foreseeable users but to all persons foreseeably within the scope of use of a defective product.
(B) A manufacturer is liable for negligent design of his product including failure to test adequately or to install safety features.
(C) As long as a risk of harm to human life is foreseeable, the manufacturer will be liable for property damages even though no personal injury occurs.
(D) A manufacturer cannot be held liable for the negligent manufacture of a product which is only the cause of property damage.

29. Max Motors, a manufacturer, assembles its cars using parts manufactured by ABC Incorporated. A defective steering column manufactured by ABC was installed by Max Motors which was unaware of the defect. George, who bought the Max Motors car with the steering column defect, was nearly killed because of it. George sued Max Motors. *Held*, for George.

The *narrowest principle* that reasonably explains this result and is *not inconsistent* with the rulings given in the preceding cases is:

(A) The manufacturer is liable for personal injuries even though he has merely assembled components produced by others.

(B)   The manufacturer is liable for personal injuries even though he has merely assembled components produced by others, if a defective component causes the injury.

(C)   Negligence in the manufacture of any consumer product may make the manufacturer liable for any damages caused by the product.

(D)   Negligence in the manufacture of any automotive product may make the manufacturer liable for any damages caused by the product.

30.   Sam Dealer sold the car which was assembled by Max Motors with the defective ABC steering column. Sam's workmen always checked the cars he sold, but they did not find the defective steering column on the car sold to George. George brought a suit against Sam for selling him the defective car. *Held,* for Sam.

The *narrowest principle* that reasonably explains this result and is *not inconsistent* with the rulings given in the preceding cases is:

(A)   If a dealer fails to make a reasonable inspection of a product, he will be liable to the purchaser.

(B)   If a dealer inspects a car with reasonable care but does not discover a hidden defect, he will not be liable for the malfunction.

(C)   Manufacturers are absolutely liable for all defects whether caused during production, shipment, or sale of the product.

(D)   Car dealers are responsible for all defects in the cars they sell.

Proceed directly to the next Part.

PART D. CHOOSING THE MAJOR FACTOR (CASE)

DIRECTIONS: In this test you are given a set of facts followed by several questions relating to them. Each question presents a different legal principle to be applied to the set of facts. All principles given are to be assumed to be valid even though they may be either real or imaginary. You are to apply the principle to the given statement of facts and then pick the one of the four alternatives which is the MAJOR FACTOR in the legal decision. Blacken the space on the answer sheet corresponding to the alternative of your choice. These questions do not relate to one another. You are to answer each one solely on the basis of the material given for that specific question. Arrive at your answers by logical reasoning alone.

Case One

Green Monster Associates, Inc. manufactures power lawn mowers. Green Monster sells its lawn mowers for one hundred dollars per mower, and on that hundred dollars it makes ten dollars profit. Green Monster buys many of its parts from Rexite Casting Co. Green Monster has already geared the machinery in the factory to use a certain type of housing for the lawn mower and cannot change it this season. The president of Rexite realizes this and decides to raise the price for the housings ten dollars. However, there is a contract between Rexite and Green Monster to purchase the housings at the old price. In order to still make a profit, Green Monster raises its prices by ten dollars. This causes the profits from the sale of lawn mowers to go down by five thousand dollars for the year. Beyond this, Rexite induced six of Green Monster's best men to break their existing employment contracts and to go to work for Rexite. This action caused Green Monster's profit to go down by an additional two thousand dollars.

The housings on the lawn mowers are defective. Many people are injured when they accidentally fall on the lawn mowers, the housing breaks, and their hands are caught in the gears.

31. A contract action by Green Monster against Rexite concerning the mower housings is held for Green Monster on the following principle:

Damages are recoverable for breach of contract only if such breach causes one of the parties to the contract to be in a weakened financial position.

Which of the following was the major factor in the disposition of this case?

(A) Rexite raised the price of its mower housings by ten dollars.
(B) Rexite had a contract to sell Green Monster the housings at the old price.
(C) Green Monster lost five thousand dollars because it was forced to raise its prices.
(D) Green Monster was forced to raise its selling price to one hundred and ten dollars.

S-3272

32. A suit brought by one of the injured purchasers of a Green Monster mower against Green Monster is held for Green Monster on the following principle:

    A manufacturer is not liable for defects in a product if the defective parts were produced by a supplier under an invalid contract.

    Which of the following was the major factor in the disposition of this case?

    (A) Rexite was the one responsible for the defective part, not Green Monster.
    (B) Rexite did not have a valid contract with Green Monster at the time it produced the parts.
    (C) Rexite raised its prices on its parts because it knew it had Green Monster over a barrel.
    (D) Green Monster had a duty to inspect the parts it purchased from Rexite.

33. A suit brought by Green Monster against Rexite, for inducing Green Monster's employees to quit and join Rexite, is held for Green Monster on the following principle:

    One who induces an employee to break his contract of employment will be liable to the employer for damages only if such employee enters the employ of another.

    Which of the following was the major factor in the disposition of this case?

    (A) Green Monster lost two thousand dollars because of the loss of key employees.
    (B) The six employees went to work for Rexite.
    (C) The six employees were responsible for designing the defective mower housings.
    (D) The six employees went to work for another employer after leaving Green Monster.

34. A suit for damages brought by one of the purchasers of a Green Monster mower against Rexite is held for the purchaser on the following principle:

    A supplier or material manufacturer will be held responsible for damages caused by any defect in a safety device.

    Which of the following was the major factor in the disposition of this case?

    (A) The housing of a mower is designed to keep hands and appendages out of the moving parts of the machine.
    (B) Tough, durable plastic would have been the best material to use in the manufacture of the housing.
    (C) A valid contract did not exist between Rexite and Green Monster at the time of the manufacture of the housing.
    (D) A purchaser must bring a suit for damages against the manufacturer of a defective safety feature and not merely the person who assembles such feature.

35. A suit for damages for duress brought by Green Monster against Rexite is held for Green Monster on the following principle:

Damages are recoverable if one willfully and knowingly takes advantage of another's weakened bargaining position.

Which of the following was the major factor in the disposition of this case?

(A)　The president of Rexite knew that Green Monster needed his mower housings.

(B)　The president of Rexite knew that Green Monster needed his mower housings and that he could get at least ten dollars more for the housings.

(C)　Green Monster was responsible for putting itself into such a weak bargaining position.

(D)　Rexite deliberately broke a contract with Green Monster.

Case Two

Wendel the welder is working on a pier welding steel plates together. Sparks from the welding activity are falling into the water. The *Hapless,* an oil tanker, is tied up at an adjacent pier. Oil and sludge are falling into the water off the side of *Hapless.* Greasy McGuirk, the captain of the *Hapless,* notices the sludge falling into the water but says, "What the heck, it's only a harbor and there are a lot more where this one came from."

The men of *Hapless,* while cleaning the ship, throw their old rags, mops and undershirts into the water. Wendel notices the junk floating toward him and, fearing the possibility of fire, stops welding and goes to consult with his supervisor, Slide Rule, the chief construction engineer for the firm that owns the pier. Slide looks at the junk floating in the water and decides that the oil is of the heaviest and muckiest variety and therefore there is very little possibility that it will catch fire. He tells Wendel to continue welding. Wendel reluctantly resumes his work and the sparks created ignite the rags floating in the water. The rags act as a wick and ignite the oil. The pier and the *Hapless* are both badly damaged by the resulting fire. Greasy McGuirk is seriously burned and Wendel is slightly charred.

36. A suit for damages brought by the owner of the *Hapless* against Slide Rule is held for the owner of the *Hapless* on the following principle:

Damages are recoverable if the defendant is aware of some possible danger under his control that might lead to property damage.

Which of the following was the major factor in the disposition of this case?

(A)　The *Hapless* was the one responsible for the initial spillage of oil.

(B)　Slide Rule realized that there was some possibility of fire.

(C)　Wendel, the welder, continued to weld, even after seeing the muck floating in the water.

(D)　Greasy McGuirk knew that oil was spilling into the water.

37. A suit for damages brought by the owner of the pier against the owner of the *Hapless* is held for the owner of the *Hapless* on the following principle:

    The damage that occurs must be of the type that a reasonable person in the defendant's position would have foreseen and must result directly from the defendant's actions.

    Which of the following was the major factor in the disposition of this case?

    (A) It was foreseeable that the muck would do some damage to the pier.
    (B) It was foreseeable that the sparks from the welding might ignite the oily water.
    (C) The sparks from Wendel the welder's torch actually caused the fire.
    (D) The chief engineer realized that there was some possible danger from fire.

38. A suit for damages brought by Wendel against Greasy McGuirk is held for McGuirk on the following principle:

    Damages are recoverable if the defendant is responsible for the direct cause of the damage and the plaintiff is not responsible for any intervening action which causes the damage.

    Which of the following is the major factor in the disposition of this case?

    (A) Greasy McGuirk was directly responsible for the spillage of the oil into the water.
    (B) The sparks from Wendel's torch caused the fire.
    (C) The rags were thrown into the water by the crew of the *Hapless*.
    (D) Slide Rule told Wendel to continue welding.

39. A suit for damages brought by Greasy McGuirk against the owner of the pier is held for Greasy on the following principle:

    A party is liable for the damages caused by the actions of his agent, if at the time the party or the agent could foresee that his actions might cause damage of the type which, in fact, ensued.

    Which of the following was the major factor in the disposition of this case?

    (A) Wendel was the pier owner's agent.
    (B) Slide Rule was the agent of the owner of the pier and he knew that there was some chance of fire.
    (C) There was some danger of fire due to the fact that oil was floating in the water.
    (D) Slide Rule told Wendel, who was the pier owner's agent, that there was some danger of fire, and Wendel continued to weld.

40. A suit for damages brought by Wendel against Slide Rule is held for Wendel on the following principle:

If a person relies on the advice of another, who has the role of an expert concerning the matters upon which advice is asked, that person should reasonably be able to rely on the expert's advice, except in matters in which the advice is outside the expert's field of expertise.

Which of the following was the major factor in the disposition of this case?

(A) Slide Rule was an expert in matters of construction.
(B) Slide Rule was an expert in the matters of construction and Wendel relied on his advice.
(C) Slide Rule should have known, because he was an expert, that danger of fire was greater than he thought it was.
(D) Slide Rule should not have told Wendel to continue welding.

END OF TEST

Go on to do the following Test in this Examination, just as you would be expected to do on the actual exam. You will find correct answers for the entire Examination following the last question. Check your answers carefully after you have completed the whole Examination.

TEST III. PRACTICAL JUDGMENT

TIME: 40 Minutes. 40 Questions.

DIRECTIONS: In this test you will be presented with a detailed case study of a practical business situation. Read the study carefully. Then answer the two sets of questions based upon the reading. In the Data Evaluation questions, you will be asked to classify certain facts on the basis of their importance to the case presented. In the Data Application questions you will be asked to make judgments based upon your comprehension of the information.

Correct and explanatory answers are provided at the end of the exam.

Business Situation I. Weatherstrip, Inc.

Weatherstrip, Inc. manufactures aluminum molding for sale to makers of storm windows and screens. In early February, Mr. Martin Schultz, the president of the company, reviewed the past year's results and considered future growth prospects.

The company had operated at or near capacity for the first six months of the year and had been forced to turn away business because of inability to get sufficient raw material. Starting last July, the company had been put on an allocation basis by the government for its raw material supplies. It was permitted to procure only 75% of its aluminum consumption during the prior calendar year. Consequently, the company could have sold more than it was allowed to produce.

Mr. Schultz recognized that the aluminum quotas would be lifted at some time in the future; and, following a period of "catching up" on the shortages brought on by the quotas, he forecast that there would be intense competition within the industry on the basis of both price and service. He therefore concluded that the company would fare best in this period and in the future if it could cut costs and offer rapid delivery service even on orders which called for unusually shaped extrusions and special finishing. If Weatherstrip were to acquire an extrusion machine it could:

1. Reduce the cost of raw material.
2. Accomplish the same volume of business with a smaller inventory of standard shapes.
3. Make unusually shaped extrusions to fit customer specifications more quickly and at lower cost than he could under existing arrangements.
4. Manufacture extrusions for other machine shops not equipped to make dies or to extrude aluminum.

Upon investigation, Mr. Schultz learned that an extrusion machine would cost about $100,000 and delivery could not be expected before 18 months. He also learned, however, that the essential components (the press, the pump, the stretcher, the billet, the heating oven, and the die-heating oven) could be purchased from several different manufacturers for much less. Delivery of these components could be expected in about six months.

Mr. Schultz had viewed several extrusion installations and was confident that he could do the expensive and time-consuming engineering work of installing and hooking up the components, using his regular employees. He further believed that certain parts, such as a billet conveyor, could be made in his own machine shop. He estimated the total cost of components and parts both purchased and manufactured at $43,000 and the labor on the installation and assembly at $7,000. He did not calculate his own time in terms of dollars. Mr. Schultz expected cash outlays for the acquisition and installation of the extrusion machine would run as follows:

February	$ 1,000	May	14,000
March	5,000	June	3,000
April	22,000	July	3,000

Both Weatherstrip, Inc. and Mr. Schultz were short of available capital to finance the extrusion machine project. He ruled out an equity issue, since he believed that the machine would shortly pay for itself, and therefore concluded that a short term loan from the bank would be the most appropriate solution to the problem of financing the project.

Mr. Schultz' personal savings of $6,000 had not been sufficient to purchase the assets of the predecessor company upon discharge from military service many years before, so he had sold $16,000 worth of stock in Weatherstrip to family and friends in order to raise the additional funds needed. From time to time, Mr. Schultz had negotiated small, unsecured loans for working capital purposes with the Special Trust Company, where his company maintained an account. To finance the costs of moving and to provide more working capital for the larger volume of business in the new location, Mr. Schultz had arranged for an increase in the outstanding loan to $14,000. Later this loan was gradually increased to $34,000, the amount outstanding in February of the current year.

Mr. Schultz estimates that he can probably reduce his inventory from the $75,000 level at which it now stands to about $25,000 once the extrusion machine is in operation, for the inventory would then be made up primarily of billets of pure aluminum with a small amount of finished standard stock items. Although he anticipates that the machine could thus pay for itself once in operation, he recognizes that he will have to get interim financing to pay for the machine until inventory reduction is possible. Thus, Mr. Schultz went to the Special Trust Company and talked to Mr. Beam, who had arranged the outstanding loan, to explain his planned expansion of fixed assets and its anticipated savings in the costs of operation and investment of inventory.

Mr. Bean acknowledged the progress that Weatherstrip had made up to that time and stated that he was impressed with the advantages cited by Mr.

Schultz. However, he pointed out that Weatherstrip was already getting liberal treatment from the bank and cautioned against too rapid an expansion on borrowed funds. He commented that borrowing on a short term basis to finance a long term investment would drag the net working capital position of the company below $35,000, a reasonably safe level for Weatherstrip's current volume of business. Nevertheless, Mr. Beam stated that his mind was not closed on the matter. He asked Mr. Schultz to bring in the figures for the company's most recent quarter and also projections of his needs for the coming year.

DATA EVALUATION

DIRECTIONS: Based on your analysis of the Situation, classify each of the following items in one of five categories. On your answer sheet blacken the space under:
(A) if the item is a MAJOR OBJECTIVE in making the decision; that is, one of the outcomes or results sought by the decision-maker.
(B) if the item is a MAJOR FACTOR in arriving at the decision; that is, a consideration explicitly mentioned in the passage that is basic in determining the decision.
(C) if the item is a MINOR FACTOR in making the decision; that is, a secondary consideration that affects the criteria tangentially, relating to a Major Factor rather than to an Objective.
(D) if the item is a MAJOR ASSUMPTION made in deliberating; that is, a supposition or projection made by the decision-maker before weighing the variables.
(E) if the item is an UNIMPORTANT ISSUE in getting to the point; that is, a factor that is insignificant or not immediately relevant to the situation.

1. Financial position of Weatherstrip, Inc.

2. Education of Mr. Martin Schultz

3. Reducing the cost of manufacturing unusually shaped extrusions

4. Ability of the extrusion machine to quickly pay for itself

5. Lifting of aluminum quotas

6. Rapid delivery of low cost and unusually shaped extrusions

7. Availability of low cost components for an extrusion machine

8. Ability of Weatherstrip's employees to assemble and install the components of an extrusion machine

9. Existence of equity investors to provide capital for the purchase of the extrusion machine

10. Mr. Schultz' personal assets

11. Past loans from the Special Trust Company

12. Reduction of inventory

13. Weatherstrip's progress up to the present time

14. Special Trust Company's willingness to lend Weatherstrip an additional $50,000

DATA APPLICATION

DIRECTIONS: Based on your understanding of the Business Situation, answer the following questions testing your comprehension of the information supplied in the passage. For each question, select the choice which best answers the question or completes the statement.

15. It can be inferred that the difference between the cost of the components of an extrusion machine and the cost of a complete machine is primarily due to

   (A) the engineering required to install and assemble the separate components into a single machine
   (B) the labor required to install and assemble the separate components into a single machine
   (C) the labor and materials required to make the separate components
   (D) the profits of the component manufacturers
   (E) the shipping cost of the complete machine

16. Mr. Schultz predicted that areas of the greatest competition once the quotas were lifted would be in

   (A) rate of production   (D) delivery and installation
   (B) installation and maintenance (E) efficiency of the operating plant
   (C) price and service

17. All of the following are true concerning the purchase of an extrusion machine except

   I. The machine would cost $5,000.
   II. Delivery would take 18 months.
   III. The essential components had to be purchased from the same manufacturer as the extrusion machine.

   (A) I only   (D) I and III only
   (B) II only   (E) I, II and III
   (C) I and II only

18. Mr. Schultz was confident that he could purchase the components and do the work of installing and hooking up the components in his own shop, using his own employees at what estimated cost?

(A) $7,000   (D) $50,000
(B) $23,000   (E) $60,000
(C) $43,000

19. The initial capital used to purchase the assets of Weatherstrip's predecessor company, including Mr. Schultz' own money and that from outside investors amounted to what percentage of the money needed for the components and installation of the extrusion machine?

(A) 12%   (B) 32%   (C) 38%   (D) 44%   (E) 50%

20. Mr. Beam was impressed with the progress of Weatherstrip but he confessed certain reservations concerning additional loans, which dealt mainly with

(A) Weatherstrip's excess of surplus capital
(B) too rapid an expansion on borrowed funds
(C) the vagaries of the molded aluminum market
(D) the vagaries of the economy as a whole
(E) the expected recession

Business Situation II. Weyburn Wax Company

In early 1974 the treasurer and production manager of the Weyburn Wax Company were considering the advisability of changing the method of filling and capping cans of paste wax, one of the company's several products. The paste wax, a quality wax that could be used to polish many types of flooring material, was packaged in five standard sizes ranging from one-half to eight pounds.

Sales of the paste wax had been increasing over the past few years (see Exhibit 1) and amounted to $210,000 in 1973. The sales manager believed that sales would probably continue to increase in the future.

The mechanism currently used to fill the cans to the proper weight looks like a large cupcake baking tin. For each size can there is a trough with several standard-sized pockets in it. When wax is poured into the trough, these pockets fill up and the excess wax is allowed to drain off. There is a hole in the bottom of each pocket, which is plugged by a stopper when wax is being poured in. Since all the stoppers are ganged together, all the pockets can be emptied at one time, each into a can placed beneath it.

The system operates in the following manner. When one-pound cans are to be filled, a trough containing thirty-two pockets, each exactly large enough to hold one pound of wax, is put into a frame. Thirty-two cans are placed under the trough on a tray so that there is a can directly under each pocket. Wax is poured into the trough until all thirty-two pockets are filled and all the excess wax has drained off. The stoppers are then removed from the bottom of the pockets, and each can is filled with the wax from the pocket above it. The tray of filled cans is placed on a hand conveyor and travels a few feet into a storage area where the wax is allowed to harden. After the proper hardening time, the trays are conveyed to a capping machine where lids are pounded on.

Based on several years' experience, the company has found that three men, working in a group, perform the filling and capping operations most efficiently. The procedure is for these three men to alternate between the filling operation and the capping operation; that is, they work together filling and storing cans until enough cans of wax have hardened, and then they switch to the capping operation. Each of these three men receives $3.00 per hour. The company pays approximately 4% of the payroll for social security and unemployment compensation taxes.

With the company's current production and sale of paste wax amounting to 368,400 pounds in 1973, the filling and capping operation is not a full-time job for the three men. The men, in fact, are taken off other jobs or temporarily employed for a couple of days when the filling and capping operations are to be performed. Because of the seasonal nature of the business, the work force at the Weyburn Wax Company is very fluid; that is, persons are frequently employed or laid off, depending on the volume of work. Workers are paid only for the hours they work.

It is not the company's policy to manufacture an excessively large inventory of paste wax at any one time because the company does not wish to tie up a large amount of cash in inventory. The company has found, however, that it is most economical to produce at least enough wax in one production run to fill orders for a two- or three-week period because the workers involved take a few hours to reach an efficient work pace and because the company receives quantity discounts on larger orders of raw materials which are purchased only as required.

The following operating data was available for 1973 regarding the number of cans of wax produced and the cans filled per minute by the three men working together:

CAN SIZE	ANNUAL PRODUCTION OUTPUT (IN CANS) IN 1953	NO. OF MIN. SPENT BY 3 MEN FILLING CANS	CANS PER MIN.
½ lb.	3,900	280	14
1 lb.	176,400	12,600	14
2 lbs.	17,600	2,500	7
4 lbs.	35,200	8,800	4
8 lbs.	1,750	440	4
Total	234,850 cans	24,620 min.	9.54

The average number of all cans filled per minute by three men was 234,850 cans divided by 24,620 minutes = 9.54 cans per minute.

In 1973, the three men together capped an average of twenty cans per minute; cans could be capped at this rate regardless of their size.

As an alternative to replacing the present hand filling equipment, the production manager was considering the purchase of an automatic filling machine. The company could purchase this machine for about $5,300 delivered. This machine could be readily adjusted to fill any size can. It could fill 50 one-pound or half-pound cans per minute, and also could increase proportionately the production of other can sizes (*i.e.*, 50/14 of the current output per minute). This machine could not be used for any other product made by the company.

The automatic filling machine was expected to have a useful life of ten years. It was estimated that the maintenance cost on the machine for oil and adjustments would be $120 per year. Use of the machine would also add about $40 to the annual power bill of the plant. The present equipment had no scrap value, and one man would need eight hours to remove it and to prepare the area for the new machine. He would have to be paid $4 an hour. Since the new machine is a self-contained unit, the only other installation cost would be for electrical connections to be installed by an electrical contractor. This cost would amount to approximately $20.

The new machine would be operated by two skilled machine operators who would be transferred, as required, from other manufacturing departments. Such operators were currently being paid $4 per hour.

Under the proposed arrangement the capping operation would not be changed. Even though the number of cans filled per minute by the new machine would outstrip the number of cans capped per minute, the storage area was sufficient in size to store a large quantity of uncapped cans. It was the production manager's belief that if too large a bank of uncapped cans were built up, the filling operators could temporarily stop and go back to their other jobs while the men on the capping operation continued working. When the storage area was almost cleared of uncapped cans, the two filling machine operators could return and start filling additional cans until the storage area was again filled, or until the production run was completed.

One of the faults of the present system is the loss of wax because many cans are overfilled. Out of a batch of wax weighing 673 pounds in the first operation, about four pounds are lost due to overfilling. The automatic machine would practically eliminate this loss. The processing cost of paste wax up to the filling operation averaged $0.31 per pound in 1973; the average direct material cost per pound was $0.11; the average direct labor cost per pound was $0.04; and the indirect costs averaged $0.19 per pound variable costs and $0.09 per pound nonvariable costs.

Before presenting to the president of the company a proposal to authorize the purchase of one of the automatic machines, the production manager consulted with the company treasurer. The treasurer, after hearing how much the machines would cost, expressed concern as to whether the company could afford such a large cash outlay. The company was currently hard pressed for cash because of recent sizable capital expenditures. The treasurer stated that any further loans would be very difficult to obtain.

The treasurer also mentioned the fact that if the automatic machine were purchased, it would require much less than a month of one shift operation to fill all the cans of paste wax produced at the 1973 level of output. "As a result," the treasurer said, "we will have an idle machine on our hands for more than eleven months a year." Moreover, the treasurer thought capital expenditures should be deferred until the income tax situation was clarified. The company had paid income taxes at a 52 percent rate in 1973. In 1974 the rate was scheduled to drop to 47 percent; however, the treasurer believed that Congress would probably rescind this decrease. In 1975 and thereafter he thought the rate would probably go down somewhat.

EXHIBIT 1

Weyburn Wax Company

Paste Wax Sales

YEAR	PASTE WAX SALES
1967	$ 91,700
1968	89,500
1969	112,000
1970	129,000
1971	163,000
1972	197,000
1973	210,000

DATA EVALUATION

DIRECTIONS: Based on your analysis of the Situation, classify each of the following items in one of five categories. On your answer sheet blacken the space under:

(A) *if the item is a MAJOR OBJECTIVE in making the decision; that is, one of the outcomes or results sought by the decision-maker.*

(B) *if the item is a MAJOR FACTOR in arriving at the decision; that is, a consideration explicitly mentioned in the passage that is basic in determining the decision.*

(C) *if the item is a MINOR FACTOR in making the decision; that is, a secondary consideration that affects the criteria tangentially, relating to a Major Factor rather than to an Objective.*

(D) *if the item is a MAJOR ASSUMPTION made in deliberating; that is, a supposition or projection made by the decision-maker before weighing the variables.*

(E) *if the item is an UNIMPORTANT ISSUE in getting to the point; that is, a factor that is insignificant or not immediately relevant to the situation.*

21. Increase in future sales of paste wax

22. Difference between hourly wage rates paid hand filling machine operators and that paid automatic filling machine operators

23. Seasonal nature of Weyburn's business

24. Cost of a new machine

25. Reduction of labor costs for filling paste wax cans

26. Useful life of the new machinery

27. Imminent changes in the tax law

28. Cost of Weyburn's paste wax inventory

29. Elimination of waste in the filling operation

30. Cost of the capping operation

31. Weyburn's cash position

32. Utilization of the machine for filling cans of other Weyburn Wax Company products

33. Amount of storage space available for filled but uncapped cans

34. Difference between the number of workers required for the hand filling and machine filling operations

DATA APPLICATION

DIRECTIONS: Based on your understanding of the Business Situation, answer the following questions testing your comprehension of the information supplied in the passage. For each question, select the choice which best answers the question or completes the statement.

35. The Sales Manager's attitude towards the future rate of paste wax sales could be classified as

    (A) pessimistic   (D) concerned
    (B) anxious   (E) enthusiastic
    (C) optimistic

36. According to the information given about the company's manual filling and capping operation, the present work force consisted of

    (A) three part-time men   (D) five full-time men
    (B) one part-time and two full-time men   (E) four full-time men
    (C) five part-time men

37. It was not the company's policy to manufacture an excessively large inventory of paste wax at any one time, nevertheless it always kept at least a two to three week supply on hand. This policy was reasonable because

    (A) the company never knew when a large demand for its product might sweep the market
    (B) the workers always worked at an efficient pace
    (C) the warehouse facilities could easily store this much wax
    (D) the workers took a few hours to reach an efficient pace
    (E) the old machinery needed time to slow down before it could be stopped

38. Based on sales in 1973, the total labor cost of the automatic filling operation would have been approximately what percent of the labor cost for the manual operation?

    (A) 25%   (B) 28%   (C) 72%   (D) 89%   (E) 133%

39. In 1973, the cost of the wax wasted through overfilling was approximately

    (A) $3.00   (D) $3,000.00
    (B) $150.00   (E) There is not enough information available to
    (C) $1,500.00   determine the answer.

40. If the company had attempted to reduce costs in 1973 by using 2 pound cans for the wax then sold in 1 pound cans, then the labor costs for the filling operation would have decreased by about

    (A) 0%   (B) 15%   (C) 25%   (D) 50%   (E) 75%

TEST IV. DATA INTERPRETATION

TIME: 30 Minutes. 25 Questions.

DIRECTIONS: This test consists of data presented in graphic form followed by questions based on the information contained in the graph, chart or table shown. After studying the data given, choose the best answer for each question and blacken the corresponding space on the answer sheet. Answer each group of questions solely on the basis of the information given or implied in the data preceding it.

Questions 1 to 6

Women in the Labor Force

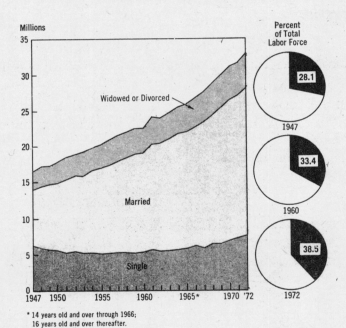

* 14 years old and over through 1966;
16 years old and over thereafter.

1. What was the size of the labor force in 1947?

   (A) 6.5 million
   (B) 28.1 million
   (C) 33.0 million
   (D) 58.7 million
   (E) It is impossible to tell from the information available.

2. Between 1947 and 1972, the number of married women in the labor force increased by

   (A) 10.4%   (B) 16.1%   (C) 74%   (D) 100%   (E) 152%

3. In 1972, the number of single women in the labor force was how many times the number of widowed or divorced women?

    (A)   1.5 times
    (B)   5 times
    (C)   0.2 times
    (D)   15 times
    (E)   0.7 times

4. Between 1947 and 1972, for every man added to the labor force, how many women entered?

    (A)   4
    (B)   1.7
    (C)   1.0
    (D)   0.5
    (E)   It is impossible to tell from the information available.

5. In 1960 the number of married women in the labor force was approximately

    (A)   33.4 million
    (B)   20 million
    (C)   15 million
    (D)   22.5 million
    (E)   3 million

6. In 1972, what percent of the labor force was composed of widows or divorcees?

    (A)   38.5%
    (B)   5.8%
    (C)   15.1%
    (D)   33%
    (E)   It is impossible to tell from the information available.

Questions 7 to 12

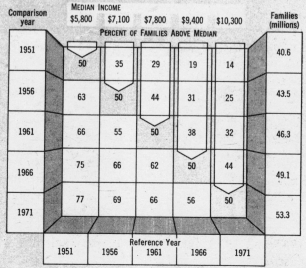

Trends in Median Family Income
(in 1971 Dollars)

Percent of families above median in comparison year related to percent above median in reference year.

Comparison year	$5,800	$7,100	$7,800	$9,400	$10,300	Families (millions)
1951	50	35	29	19	14	40.6
1956	63	50	44	31	25	43.5
1961	66	55	50	38	32	46.3
1966	75	66	62	50	44	49.1
1971	77	69	66	56	50	53.3

Reference Year: 1951, 1956, 1961, 1966, 1971

Source: U.S. Bureau of the Census

7. In 1971, how many families had incomes between $5,800 and $7,100?

   (A)   8 million
   (B)   53.3 million
   (C)   5.7 million
   (D)   4.3 million
   (E)   4.5 million

8. In 1971, how many more families had incomes over $7,800 than had incomes over $7,800 in 1961?

   (A)   10 million
   (B)   12 million
   (C)   16 million
   (D)   18 million
   (E)   It is impossible to tell from the information available.

9. As compared to 1956, the number of families who had an income in excess of the median income in 1961 was

   (A)   the same
   (B)   6% greater
   (C)   6.4% greater
   (D)   10% greater
   (E)   2.8 million greater

10. Between 1961 and 1966, total family income increased by

   (A) $1600
   (B) $2.8 million
   (C) $37.9 billion
   (D) $44.8 billion
   (E)   It is impossible to tell from the information available.

11. In what year did the fewest families have incomes below $5,800?

   (A) 1951   (B) 1956   (C) 1961   (D) 1966   (E) 1971

12. In what year did the largest number of families have incomes between $9,400 and $10,300?

   (A)   1956
   (B)   1961
   (C)   1966
   (D)   1971
   (E)   It is impossible to tell from the information available.

Questions 13 to 19

Sanitary paper products' market share rises
Shipments of converted products
Billions of dollars

13. From 1967 to 1974, the dollar value of shipments of coated and glazed paper

    (A) declined by 3%   (D) increased by 64%
    (B) declined by 10%   (E) It is impossible to determine the answer
    (C) increased by 48%   from the available information.

14. For how many categories was there no change in the share of total shipments?

    (A) 1   (B) 2   (C) 3   (D) 4   (E) 5

15. What portion of the overall increase in shipments was due to increased shipments of sanitary paper products?

    (A) 4%   (B) 29%   (C) 33%   (D) 39%   (E) 7.5%

16. What were the combined shipments of stationery products and envelopes in 1974?

    (A) $1.2 billion   (D) $740 million
    (B) $720 million   (E) none of the above
    (C) $464 million

17. For which product did the dollar value of shipments increase by the largest percentage?

(A) sanitary paper products
(B) coated and glazed paper
(C) pulp goods
(D) die cut paper and board
(E) stationery products

18. From 1967 to 1974 shipments of pulp goods

(A) remained constant
(B) increased by $200 million
(C) increased by $135 million
(D) increased by $87 million
(E) none of the above

19. For how many products did the dollar value of shipments decline?

(A) 0 (B) 1 (C) 2 (D) 3 (E) 4

Questions 20 to 25

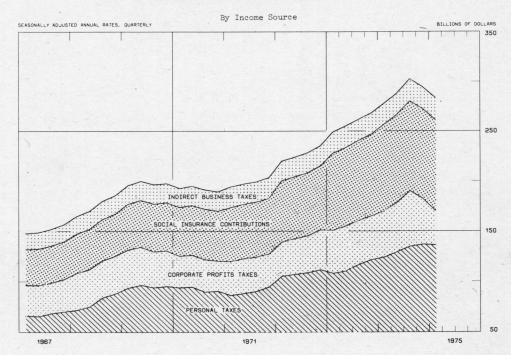

FEDERAL GOVERNMENT RECEIPTS

By Income Source

20. From 1967 through 1974, the source of Federal government income which grew by the largest percentage was

(A) indirect business taxes
(B) social insurance contributions
(C) corporate profits taxes
(D) personal taxes
(E) It is impossible to tell from the information given.

21. From 1967 through 1974, the income source whose percentage of total receipts declined the most was

    (A) indirect business taxes
    (B) social insurance contributions
    (C) corporate profits taxes
    (D) personal taxes
    (E) It is impossible to tell from the information available.

22. In the last quarter of 1972, the seasonally adjusted annual rate of corporate profits taxes collected was approximately

    (A) $150 billion
    (B) $100 billion
    (C) $75 billion
    (D) $50 billion
    (E) none of the above

23. In which year was the amount of social insurance contributions less than in the previous year

    (A) 1969
    (B) 1970
    (C) 1971
    (D) 1972
    (E) none of the above

24. From 1967 through 1974, total Federal government receipts increased by

    (A) 100%
    (B) 150%
    (C) 133%
    (D) $100 billion
    (E) $150 million

25. What percent of the growth in total Federal government receipts was due to the increase in indirect business taxes?

    (A) 0%   (B) 25%   (C) 50%   (D) 75%   (E) 100%

END OF TEST

Go on to do the following Test in this Examination, just as you would be expected to do on the actual exam. You will find correct answers for the entire Examination following the last question. Check your answers carefully after you have completed the whole Examination.

TEST V. ERROR RECOGNITION

TIME: 20 Minutes. 35 Questions.

DIRECTIONS: This is a test of your ability to recognize standard written English. Some of the sentences presented are acceptable as written English. Others contain errors of diction, verbosity or grammar. No one sentence contains more than one kind of error. Read each sentence carefully, then classify each according to the categories that follow. Mark your answer sheet:

(A) if the sentence contains an error in DICTION; that is, the use of a word which is incorrect because its meaning does not fit the sentence, or because it is not acceptable in standard written English.

(B) if the sentence is VERBOSE; that is, wordy or repetitious without justification by the need for emphasis.

(C) if the sentence contains FAULTY GRAMMAR; that is, errors in parallelism, number, case, tense, etc.

(D) if the sentence contains none of these errors.

Correct and explanatory answers are provided at the end of the exam.

1. The behavior of our company's representatives in foreign countries are being investigated.

2. John dived into the river and swam in the direction of the drowning woman.

3. Although Herbert is a talented fellow, he has few ambition, and I feel he will be a failure in life.

4. The ship's commander, along with most of the officers, was spending the evening ashore and thus was happily spared.

5. The article we wrote together was a joint effort.

6. During the 1880's, the American architect and furniture designer Henry Hobson Richardson designed numerous public buildings in the Boston area.

7. Six of our employees will be fired tomorrow.

8. The Green Bay Packers, as immured to the elements as Eskimos, easily defeated the New Yorkers.

9. That year, elm beetles ravished thousands of trees in New England.

10. His original views, which had never before been conceived, earned Mr. Jasper the praise of philosophers and psychologists.

11. It was noted that mathematics was one of the poorest taught subjects on the elementary and secondary levels of education.

12. The theories of the Greeks is my major interest.

13. Everybody must make up their mind to strive for success.

14. The cunning manager's craftiness was matched by that of his assistant.

15. Benjamin Franklin's practicable mind made him an ideal statesman.

16. Soon everyone knew that Walter had won his brother at ping-pong.

17. Everybody is to be admitted before eight o'clock.

18. There appear to be no variables relevant to the practice of informal education in England that are ignored in Professor Harde's description.

19. Until then, most American architecture, whether ecclesiastical or secular, had been mere stage carpentry.

20. Mr. Jones made the arrangements with Mr. Harris and myself.

21. By 1923 his creative abilities were widely recognized.

22. The Chinese diplomat charged the Americans with "unilateral action" flaunting the authority of the United Nations Command.

23. I did not invite Theodore to my party because I find him incredulously rude.

24. I have been told that there was a row last night at the *Jumping Horse Saloon.*

25. I have, at the end of the book, provided an appendix listing books and articles that go into greater detail than I have been able to here.

26. Mr. Watson, who is thirty years old, and his wife, who is twenty-eight, each is subject to sentences of five years in prison.

27. Most formidable was his posture, his voice, and his mustache.

28. I thought the tall girl was her.

29. The Sultan luxuriated opulently in a villa close to the capital.

30. Mr. Mantino explained to us some of the principals of the monetary system.

31. Deaf to the pleas of family and friends, he continued to abase and degrade himself.

32. None of these apples are ripe.

33. It is difficult for me to decide what to eat, for all the dishes served in this restaurant are unappetizing.

34. The chief lament of the average amateur photographer is his lack of spare time.

35. It is such advantages that we value.

END OF TEST

TEST VI. SENTENCE CORRECTION

TIME: 20 Minutes. 25 Questions.

DIRECTIONS: Some part of each of the following sentences is underlined. After each sentence are five ways of stating the underlined part. Choice A simply repeats the original sentence or phrase. If you think that the original sentence is more effective than any of the alternatives, pick Choice A. If you believe the underlined part is incorrect, select from the other choices (B, C, D, or E) the one you think is best and blacken the corresponding space on the answer sheet. In choosing the best alternative, consider grammar, sentence structure, punctuation and word usage. Do not choose an answer that changes the meaning of the original sentence.

Correct and explanatory answers are provided at the end of the exam. After you have completed the entire exam, read the explanations carefully. They'll reinforce your strengths and pinpoint your weaknesses so that you know just what to study to raise your score.

1. For the girls, a skirt or a dress <u>is usually required; for the boys, a white shirt and a tie are normally needed.</u>

   (A) is usually required; for the boys, a white shirt and a tie are normally needed.
   (B) are usually required; for the boys, a white shirt and a tie is normally needed.
   (C) are usually required; for the boys, a white shirt and a tie are normally needed.
   (D) is usually required; for the boys, a white shirt and a tie is normally needed.
   (E) being usually required, for the boys, a white shirt and tie is normally needed.

2. The heavy adobe soil is different <u>than</u> the sandy soil to which you are accustomed.

   (A) than
   (B) from
   (C) to
   (D) then
   (E) with

3. Habit grips a person <u>in much the same way as an octopus does.</u>

   (A) in much the same way as an octopus does.
   (B) like an octopus does.
   (C) like an octopus.
   (D) in much the same way as an octopus.
   (E) in an octopus-like fashion.

4. <u>Except for Eunice, we are all ready to start rehearsals.</u>

   (A) Except for Eunice, we are all ready to start rehearsals.
   (B) Except for Eunice, we are already to start rehearsals.
   (C) Accept for Eunice, we are all ready to start rehearsals.
   (D) Accept for Eunice, we are already to start rehearsals.
   (E) We are already, except for Eunice, to start rehearsals.

5. Not enough attention is devoted to oral English, <u>giving talks only three times a year.</u>

   (A) giving talks only three times a year.
   (B) as talks are given by the students only three times a year.
   (C) the students giving talks only three times a year.
   (D) for the students talk only three times a year.
   (E) talks being given by the students only three times a year.

6. Many observers believe that Senator Elanso <u>is not as good a politician like Senator Handake.</u>

   (A) is not as good a politician like
   (B) is not so good a politician as
   (C) is not so good a politician like
   (D) is not quite the politician as is
   (E) does not possess the qualities of a politician to the extent they are possessed by

7. <u>The money of a person who leaves no relatives and dies without having made a will, goes to the state.</u>

   (A) The money of a person who leaves no relatives and dies without having made a will, goes to the state.
   (B) A person who dies leaving no relatives, and without having made a will, finds that his money goes to the state.
   (C) The money of a person who dies without having made a will and who leaves no relatives, goes to the state.
   (D) If a person dies without having made a will and leaves no relatives, his money goes to the state.
   (E) The state gets a person's money that dies without having made a will and who leaves no relatives.

8. <u>Having rained heavily today, James found that the sewers were overflowing.</u>

   (A) Having rained heavily today, James found that the sewers were overflowing.
   (B) James found that the sewers were overflowing after having rained heavily today.
   (C) It rained heavily today; James found that the sewers were overflowing.
   (D) The sewers were overflowing, James found, after having rained heavily.
   (E) It having rained heavily today, James found that the sewers were overflowing.

9. <u>Driving south, in the final stretch, is Mount Bundler.</u>

   (A) Driving South, in the final stretch, is Mount Bundler.
   (B) Mount Bundler, driving South, is in the final stretch.
   (C) In the final stretch, driving South, is Mount Bundler.
   (D) Driving South, in the final stretch, you reach Mount Bundler.
   (E) Driving South, in the final stretch, Mount Bundler is reached.

10. <u>It is international in scope and informal in style.</u>

    (A) It is international in scope and informal in style.
    (B) It is international in style and informal in scope.
    (C) Its scope and style are international and informal.
    (D) It is international in scope and it is informal in style.
    (E) It is international in scope and its style is informal.

11. Place the seeds in water, and in a few days a <u>person will see that they have started to grow.</u>

    (A) a person will see that they have started to grow.
    (B) one will see that they have started to grow.
    (C) their growth will be obvious to the observer.
    (D) you will see that they have started to grow.
    (E) you will observe their having begun to grow.

12. <u>The enemy, while many in number, were absolutely annihilated by our troops.</u>

    (A) The enemy, while many in number, were absolutely annihilated by our troops.
    (B) The enemy, while numerous, were absolutely annihilated by our troops.
    (C) The enemy, while numerous, were annihilated by our troops.
    (D) The enemy, while many in number, were annihilated by our troops.
    (E) The enemy, while numerous, was annihilated by our troops.

13. For our picnic we had salad, potato chips, hamburgers, <u>also cold drinks.</u>

    (A)   also cold drinks.
    (B)   further, cold drinks.
    (C)   notwithstanding cold drinks.
    (D)   moreover, cold drinks.
    (E)   and cold drinks.

14. <u>A carhop is where somebody brings food from a restaurant to customers in their cars.</u>

    (A)   A carhop is where somebody brings food from a restaurant to customers in their cars.
    (B)   A carhop is when somebody brings food from a restaurant to customers in their cars.
    (C)   A carhop is somebody that brings food from a restaurant to customers in their cars.
    (D)   A carhop is a person, hired by a restaurant, bringing food to customers in their cars.
    (E)   A carhop is a bringer of food to customers in their cars.

15. Edward drives their car at sixty miles per hour, <u>whereas</u> his father drives it at about thirty miles per hour.

    (A)   whereas
    (B)   while
    (C)   on the other hand
    (D)   at the same time
    (E)   till

16. The little girl lacks <u>companions, especially children her own age.</u>

    (A)   companions, especially children her own age.
    (B)   companions, especially those of children her own age.
    (C)   children her own age.
    (D)   companionship, especially children her own age.
    (E)   companionship her own age.

17. <u>You are mad to throw away ten grand!</u>

    (A)   You are mad to throw away ten grand!
    (B)   You are nuts to throw away ten grand!
    (C)   You are nuts to throw away ten thousand dollars!
    (D)   You are mad to throw away ten thousand dollars!
    (E)   You are throwing away ten grand, you nut!

18. Having studied the problem, <u>it looked simple to Joseph.</u>

    (A)   it looked simple to Joseph.
    (B)   it posed no difficulties for Joseph.
    (C)   Joseph thought it was simple.
    (D)   Joseph found the problem simple.
    (E)   it seemed to Joseph that it was simple.

19. If I was the writer of that story, I am certain that I could have evolved a more logical conclusion.

    (A) If I was the writer of that story, I
    (B) If I could have been the writer of the story, I
    (C) If I would have been the writer of that story, I
    (D) If I had've been the writer of the story, I
    (E) If I had been the writer of the story, I

20. Mr. Collins said he was seriously considering to asking the Legislature to delay or abandon the inspection plan.

    (A) seriously considering to asking the Legislature to delay or abandon the inspection plan.
    (B) considering seriously asking the Legislature to delay the inspection plan or to abandon it.
    (C) seriously considering asking the Legislature to delay or abandon the inspection plan.
    (D) considering seriously asking the Legislature to delay or abandon the inspection plan.
    (E) seriously considering asking the Legislature to delay the inspection plan or to abandon it.

21. Francis asked for the privilege to get a driver's license.

    (A) the privilege to get a driver's license.
    (B) the privilege of a driver's license.
    (C) the privilege for to get a driver's license.
    (D) the privilege: a driver's license.
    (E) the privilege of getting a driver's license.

22. Among the questions that stumped aspirants was one asking him to identify grammatically correct sentences.

    (A) one asking him to identify grammatically correct sentences.
    (B) one asking them to identify grammatically correct sentences.
    (C) one asking to identify grammatically correct sentences.
    (D) one that asked to identify grammatically correct sentences.
    (E) one requiring to identify grammatically correct sentences.

23. His fellow playmates miss poor little Oscar now that he has ascended up to heaven.

    (A) His fellow playmates miss poor little Oscar now that he has ascended up to heaven.
    (B) His playmates miss poor little Oscar now that he has ascended to heaven.

(C)   His playmates miss poor little Oscar now that he has ascended up to heaven.

(D)   His fellow playmates miss poor little Oscar now that he has ascended to heaven.

(E)   Oscar has ascended up to heaven, being missed by his playmates.

24.   Freedom implies that <u>a man may conduct his affairs as he pleases so long as he does not injure anyone else.</u>

(A)   a man may conduct his affairs as he pleases so long as he does not injure anyone else.

(B)   a man may conduct his affairs as he pleases without injuring anyone else.

(C)   a man may conduct his affairs as he pleases so long as he did not injure anyone else.

(D)   a man may conduct his affairs as he pleases, lest he injure anyone else.

(E)   a man may conduct his affairs as he pleases so long as nobody is injured.

25.   <u>This is one of the largest, if not the largest, caves in the world.</u>

(A)   This is one of the largest, if not the largest, caves in the world.

(B)   This is one of the largest, if not the largest, cave in the world.

(C)   This is one of the largest caves in the world, if not the largest cave, in the world.

(D)   This is one of the largest caves in the world, if not the largest.

(E)   If not the largest, this is one of the largest caves in the world.

END OF TEST

Go on to do the following Test in this Examination, just as you would be expected to do on the actual exam. You will find correct answers for the entire Examination following the last question. Check your answers carefully after you have completed the whole Examination.

TEST VII. QUANTITATIVE COMPARISON

TIME: 15 Minutes. 25 Questions.

DIRECTIONS: For each of the following questions two quantities are given . . . one in Column A; and one in Column B. Compare the two quantities and mark your answer sheet with the correct, lettered conclusion. These are your options:

A: if the quantity in Column A is the greater;
B: if the quantity in Column B is the greater;
C: if the two quantities are equal;
D: if the relationship cannot be determined from the information given.

COMMON INFORMATION: In each question, information concerning one or both of the quantities to be compared is given in the Common Information column. A symbol that appears in any column represents the same thing in Column A as in Column B.

NUMBERS: All numbers used are real numbers.

FIGURES: Assume that the position of points, angles, regions, and so forth, are in the order shown.

Assume that the lines shown as straight are indeed straight. Figures are assumed to lie in a plane unless otherwise indicated.

Figures accompanying questions are intended to provide information you can use in answering the questions. However, unless a note states that a figure is drawn to scale, you should solve the problems by using your knowledge of mathematics, and NOT by estimating sizes by sight or by measurement.

Correct and explanatory answers are provided at the end of the exam. After you have completed the entire exam, read the explanations carefully. They'll reinforce your strengths and pinpoint your weaknesses so that you know just what to study to raise your score.

Common Information	*Column A.*	*Column B.*
1.	5^3	3^5
2.	$\sqrt{0.00025}$	$\dfrac{\sqrt{5}}{100}$
3.	$(1.2 \times 10^5)(1.3 \times 10^{-5})$	1.44

Common Information	Column A.	Column B.
4.	z	$\dfrac{y}{2}$
5. $\quad$ $3x + 2z = 4y$ $\quad\quad$ $x = y$	z	x
6.	z	3
7.	y	6
8.	$\dfrac{\dfrac{6}{0.2}}{5}$	$\dfrac{\dfrac{5}{0.2}}{6}$
9.	$\dfrac{\sqrt{1/5}}{\sqrt{2/7}}$	$\sqrt{.71}$
10.	$(7^6)^{1/3}$	50
11. $\quad$ $x^2 - 4x + 4 = y$	x	y
$\quad\quad\quad\quad y = 4$		
12.	x	0
13. $\quad$ $x > 1 \quad\quad y > 1$	$(\sqrt{x} - \sqrt{y})^2$	$x + y$
14.	$(\sqrt{x} + \sqrt{y})^2$	$4xy$
15.	y	x
16. $\quad$ $y = x^4$	$\dfrac{1}{y}$	$\dfrac{1}{x}$
17.	y^3	x^7
18.	$y^{1/4}$	x

	Common Information	Column A.	Column B.

19. $x = 5\sqrt{y^5}$ — $\dfrac{1}{x}$ — $\dfrac{1}{y-2}$

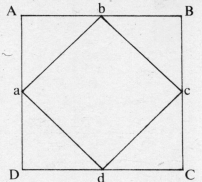

20. Distance $\overline{ab} + \overline{cd}$ — Distance $\overline{AC}$

21. Distance $\overline{AB}$ — $1.5 \times$ distance $\overline{ab}$

22. Area of square ABCD — $2 \times$ Area of square abcd

23. Perimeter of ABCD — $2 \times$ Perimeter of abcd

a,b,c, and d are the midpoints
of the sides of the square ABCD

---

24. $(1/2)^3$ — $(1/3)^2$

25. $\dfrac{(5/2)^7}{(2/3)^7}$ — 1

END OF EXAMINATION

Now that you have completed the last Test in this Examination, use your available time to make sure that you have written in your answers correctly on the Answer Sheet. Then, after your time is up, check your answers with the Correct Answers we have provided for you. Derive your scores for each Test Category and determine where you are weak so as to plan your study accordingly.

CORRECT ANSWERS FOR VERISIMILAR EXAMINATION III.

Now compare your answers with these Correct Key Answers. If your answers differ from these, go back and study the Practice Questions to see where and how you made your mistakes. In doing this, the following Explanatory Answers should prove helpful. They provide concise clarifications of the basic points behind the Key Answers. Even where your Key Answers are the same as ours, go over the explanations carefully because they may be quite useful in helping you pick up extra points on the exam.

TEST I. READING COMPREHENSION

1.B	5.C	9.D	13.A	17.D	21.D	25.C
2.E	6.B	10.C	14.B	18.C	22.B	
3.D	7.A	11.D	15.C	19.B	23.B	
4.C	8.B	12.E	16.D	20.B	24.B	

TEST II. PRINCIPLES AND CASES

1.D	6.A	11.C	16.B	21.C	26.C	31.C	36.B
2.B	7.B	12.D	17.B	22.A	27.D	32.B	37.B
3.A	8.C	13.B	18.A	23.C	28.C	33.D	38.B
4.C	9.B	14.A	19.B	24.C	29.B	34.A	39.B
5.D	10.D	15.C	20.B	25.C	30.B	35.B	40.B

TEST III. PRACTICAL JUDGMENT

1.B	6.A	11.C	16.C	21.D	26.D	31.B	36.A
2.E	7.C	12.A	17.D	22.C	27.C	32.E	37.D
3.A	8.C	13.E	18.D	23.E	28.E	33.E	38.A
4.D	9.E	14.B	19.D	24.B	29.A	34.C	39.C
5.D	10.C	15.A	20.B	25.A	30.E	35.C	40.A

TEST IV. DATA INTERPRETATION

1.D	5.C	9.C	13.C	17.E	21.A	25.A
2.E	6.B	10.E	14.B	18.D	22.D	
3.A	7.D	11.E	15.D	19.A	23.E	
4.B	8.B	12.D	16.A	20.B	24.A	

TEST V. ERROR RECOGNITION

1.C	6.D	11.C	16.C	21.D	26.C	31.A
2.D	7.A	12.C	17.D	22.A	27.C	32.D
3.A	8.A	13.C	18.D	23.A	28.C	33.D
4.D	9.A	14.B	19.D	24.A	29.B	34.D
5.B	10.B	15.A	20.C	25.B	30.A	35.D

TEST VI. SENTENCE CORRECTION

1.A	5.C	9.D	13.E	17.D	21.E	25.D
2.B	6.B	10.A	14.C	18.C	22.B	
3.A	7.D	11.D	15.A	19.E	23.B	
4.A	8.E	12.C	16.A	20.C	24.A	

TEST VII. QUANTITATIVE COMPARISONS

1.B	5.B	9.B	13.B	17.D	21.B	25.A
2.B	6.D	10.B	14.B	18.D	22.C	
3.A	7.D	11.D	15.D	19.D	23.B	
4.C	8.C	12.D	16.D	20.C	24.A	

EXPLANATORY ANSWERS FOR VERISIMILAR EXAMINATION III.

Here you have the heart of the Question and Answer Method...getting help when and where you need it. Where one of your Key Answers differs from ours you have a problem which can easily be remedied by reading the explanation. Then, if you have time, you might be able to pick up points on the exam by reading the other explanations, even where you wrote the Key Answers correctly. These explanations stress fundamental facts, ideas, and principles which just might pop up as questions on future exams.

TEST I. READING COMPREHENSION

1. **(B)** The first sentence states that "One of the more important functions of the Foreign Service of the United States is the administration of our immigration laws." A large part of the administration of immigration laws is the visa function; therefore, it must also be of significant import.

2. **(E)** Paragraph 1 mentions certain exceptions to the visa requirements, but never states what these exceptions are.

3. **(D)** The key word is *directly*. The first sentence of paragraph 2 states that "consular officers are directly responsible . . . for the issuance or refusal of visas . . ." (A), (B), (C), and (E) are all indirectly concerned with the issuance of visas.

4. **(C)** Paragraph 2 describes the Federal Register as a publication containing the regulations regarding the administration of immigration laws as prepared by the Visa Office of the Department of State. Therefore, to call the Federal Register a reference source is the best alternative. (A), (B), and (D) are probably at least partially correct, but not as precise as (C).

5. **(C)** In paragraph 3 it is stated that a call at the consular office is often the first contact with the United States, and the attitude of the consular officer contributes to the impression one forms of the U.S.

6. **(B)** Paragraph 3 deals with the consular officer's duty to "create an atmosphere of good will and help to promote good relations with foreign countries." The following paragraph discusses ways in which international travel has been facilitated. It is logical to assume that these measures, too, were adopted to promote good will.

7. **(A)** Alternative I is the only one not mentioned in the reading. Alternative II is referred to in paragraph 4 and alternative III in paragraph 6.

8. **(B)** The last sentence of the first paragraph states that the success of the Cunard Line forced Congress to take a critical look at the postal connection with Europe.

9. **(D)** The beginning of the second paragraph mentions that American prestige had been blunted by the advent of steam. Although American sailing packets still carried the bulk of freight, they were losing some of the prestige trade.

10. **(C)** The first half of the second paragraph justifies this conclusion. (D) and (E) are both correct as far as they go, but each takes in only part of what the "Atlantic Ferry" encompassed.

11. **(D)** It is stated in paragraph 2 that the prime reason for Congressional concern is the future dependence that the U.S. mail might have on British shipping and the close connection between British shipping and the British Admiralty. (A), (C), and (E) are all reasons for concern, but not the main reason.

12. **(E)** In paragraph 3 it is mentioned that in 1846 Britain repealed its Corn Laws which would have the effect of easing Britain's control over its flow of grain. Nothing is ever mentioned about Ireland becoming industrialized, but rather that Ireland suffered crop failures during this period. Paragraph 3 also mentions that the U.S. reduced its tariff but it does not mention that world inflation in any way affected the tariff. Therefore, none of the alternatives were mentioned as important causes of increased American foreign trade and the answer is (E).

13. **(A)** The entire passage deals with the effect of the steamship on postal communication with Europe. (B) and (C) are only small aspects touched upon by the passage. The focus of the passage is much too narrow to call it a brief history of the first half of the 19th century as in (E).

14. **(B)** The first paragraph states that "There is hardly any social problem confronting the nation whose solution would be easier if our population were larger." Therefore, it is safe to assume that the commission favors a leveling off or reduction in population. There is no support given in the passage for any other alternative.

15. **(C)** Paragraph 2 makes this explanation quite clear. Nothing definite is ever said about alternatives (A), (B), (D), or (E).

16. **(D)** Alternatives II and III might be true but they are never dealt with in the passage. Paragraph 3 states that the population problem can be interpreted in terms of its effect on natural resources.

17. **(D)** The first sentence in paragraph 4 states that population lacks the "dramatic event" of a war or riot that galvanizes attention. While it is implied that the population problem is not given the coverage it deserves (B), it is not stated that the problem is downplayed or suppressed.

18. **(C)** See paragraph 5, "There is scarcely a facet of American life that is not involved with the rise and fall of our birth and death rates . . ."

19. **(B)** When the author says in paragraph 4, "Unlike other great public issues . . . population lacks the dramatic event," he means to show the importance of population in comparison to those other issues of great concern.

20. **(B)** The first paragraph states that the novelist's books reveal "that he supports certain tendencies and rejects others." (A), (C), (D), and (E) are all possible facets of (B). A novel may deal with matters of social import or not. Society and social consciousness may influence the author, but it is his critical faculty which makes him choose one tendency or another.

21. **(D)** Paragraph 2 implies that Ortega y Gasset's phrase "dehumanization of the arts" means the same as "Loss of the Self in Modern Literature and Art" (the title of Sypher's book) which in turn results in "the description of an inauthentic life which can never make sense . . ."

22. **(B)** Paragraph 2 ties the Beats in with the theme of Mr. Sypher's book which is "annihilation of Self."

23. **(B)** According to the comparison made in paragraph 2, European writers are burdened by "intellectual preconceptions" (the historical reckoning of the human condition and new physical, psychological and philosophical theories). American writers "are seldom encumbered by such intellectual baggage." (A) and (C) are true but they both take in only part of the contrast which is made clear in (B). (E) is probably true but there is no supporting evidence provided it in the passage.

24. **(B)** In dealing with this type of question it is usually best to pick the answers which are wrong first. If you got question 23 correct, you know that I is true for American writers, and since paragraph 2 also states that an American writer possessed a "blunt, primitive virtue," III is also true. Therefore you can eliminate (A), (C), (D), and (E), so (B) must be correct.

25. **(C)** Paragraph 3 states that the First World War helped to destroy "the romantic overvaluation of the Self." This is juxtaposed with the Russian Revolution and the Communist rejection of "soft, nerveless humanism;" therefore, (C) is correct.

TEST II. PRINCIPLES AND CASES

1. **(D)** is correct because it is the only alternative that deals directly with the principle.

2. **(B)** is correct because Betty developed a physical response (*i.e.*, nervous twitch) to her emotional injury as required by the principle.

3. **(A)** is correct because the principle concerns the responsibility of an employer (L.I.R.R.) for his employee (Casey).

4. **(C)** is correct. A reasonable man would assume that it is a negligent action to run after a moving train.

5. **(D)** is correct because it was the scales which broke Betty's leg, not the fireworks.

6. **(A)** is correct because it is foreseeable that infection might set in an open wound after an injury. There is one continuous chain of causation.

7. **(B)** is correct because Buster was speeding and this is not reasonably understood as the normal operation of a motor vehicle.

8. **(C)** is correct because, while it is true that the cow caused Billie to swerve and go off the road, the damage to the car was not directly done by the cow.

9. **(B)** is correct because it is consistent with the facts and the principle. There is no evidence that Newton was contributorily negligent in any way.

10. **(D)** is correct because Buster had no intention of going onto private property. He was forced off the road.

11. **(C)** is correct because Peter was not retreating from Snapper. He was merely going to get his gun.

12. **(D)** is correct because the washroom door was made out of metal and Sampson was safe while he was locked behind it.

13. **(B)** is correct. Thompson had reason to believe that he was in danger (*i.e.*, Jones had a knife). It is reasonable to believe that a knife can cause serious bodily harm. Thompson did try to run away from Jones.

14. **(A)** is correct because it is not reasonable to interpret a slap in the face as a use of deadly force.

15. **(C)** is correct because at no time did Lurky threaten Racer with bodily harm. Lurky only grabbed onto Racer's bike.

16. **(B)** is correct because the key element in this case is that Fingers was one hundred yards away from Bather.

17. **(B)** is correct because Oscar only wanted the stereo for his party and the principle requires an intention to permanently deprive the victim of his property.

18. **(A)** is correct because we can be certain that Clipper was not in lawful possession of Snooker's money on the basis of the statement that Clipper's gambling parlor was rigged.

19. **(B)** is correct because the principle requires force or threats as an element of the crime and Weasel used neither in stealing Groovy's wallet.

20. **(B)** is correct because fear is a necessary element of the crime and Wealthy could not have been frightened since he was sleeping at the time of the robbery.

21. **(C)** is correct because it is the only alternative which recognizes the necessity of an act beyond the preparation stage. Therefore it is more precise (*i.e.*, narrow) than the other alternatives.

22. **(A)** is correct because it is the only principle which agrees with the holding.

23. **(C)** is correct because no overt act beyond conversation is committed by either Crafty or Boris.

24. **(C)** is correct because Mack was a little retarded and alternative (C) specifically uses the term mental deficiency.

25. **(C)** is correct because it deals specifically with shoplifting.

26. **(C)** is correct because it refers directly to the manufacturer of an automobile product rather than any product.

27. **(D)** is correct because it is the only principle which agrees with the holding by including not only users of the product but also persons within the foreseeable scope of the use of the product.

28. **(C)** is correct because there was a risk of harm to human life present and by dealing with this factor alternative (C) becomes the narrowest.

29. **(B)** is correct because even though Max Motors was not negligent in assembling its cars, the cars did have a defective component part made by another. Therefore by dealing with this factor, choice (B) is the most precise answer.

30. **(B)** is correct because Sam Dealer did make a reasonable inspection of the Max Motors car.

31. **(C)** is correct because the loss of $5000 is evidence of a weakened financial condition on the part of Green Monster.

32. **(B)** is correct because Rexite broke its contract with Green Monster by raising the price on its mower housings.

33. **(D)** is correct because going to work for another is the key element under the principle. It doesn't matter who they go to work for.

34. **(A)** is correct because it is the only alternative which directly states that a mower's housing is a safety device.

35. **(B)** is correct because it is the only alternative which takes into account the financial relationship between Rexite and Green Monster.

36. **(B)** is correct because Slide Rule thought that there was little possibility that the oil would catch fire. Therefore he must have realized that there was some possibility of fire no matter how small.

37. **(B)** is correct because it was fire which actually damaged the pier and the chance of fire was reasonably foreseeable.

38. **(B)** is correct because Wendel's own actions ultimately caused his injury. Therefore he cannot recover damages under this principle since he was the cause of his own injury.

39. **(B)** is correct because the agency relationship is the key element under this principle and it is true that Slide Rule was in the employ of the pier owner.

40. **(B)** is correct because it may be presumed that a construction engineer should know about both welding and combustibles.

TEST III. PRACTICAL JUDGMENT

DATA EVALUATION
(A) means that the Conclusion is a Major Objective;
(B) means that the Conclusion is a Major Factor;
(C) means that the Conclusion is a Minor Factor;
(D) means that the Conclusion is a Major Assumption;
(E) means that the Conclusion is an Unimportant Issue.

1. **(B)** This is a major factor since the company's lack of internal funds to purchase the extrusion machine forces Mr. Schultz to seek a bank loan and the bank's willingness to lend the money will depend greatly on Weatherstrip's financial position.

2. **(E)** Mr. Schultz' education has no bearing on the problem at hand which is whether or not to acquire an extrusion machine.

3. **(A)** This is one of the objectives mentioned at the beginning of the passage that Mr. Schultz hopes to achieve by acquiring an extrusion machine.

4. **(D)** This is a major assumption made by Mr. Schultz that makes a bank loan a feasible way of financing the acquisition of the machine.

280 / Law School Admission Test

5. (**D**) This is another major assumption made by Mr. Schultz since if the quotas are not removed, he will have no need for an extrusion machine.

6. (**A**) This is one of the major objectives that Mr. Schultz wants to accomplish by acquiring an extrusion machine.

7. (**C**) This factor is one of several minor factors which will determine how much capital is actually needed and, indirectly whether or not Weatherstrip can acquire the equipment and achieve its objectives.

8. (**C**) This, as in question 7, will help to determine the amount of capital needed.

9. (**E**) This is an unimportant factor since Mr. Schultz decided to exclude an equity issue in the belief that the machine would very shortly pay for itself.

10. (**C**) This is a minor factor, since Mr. Schultz' lack of capital forces him to seek outside financing.

11. (**C**) This is a minor factor because the past loans are one of several considerations that will influence the Special Trust Company in deciding whether or not to lend Weatherstrip the money for the extrusion machine.

12. (**A**) This is another of the goals that Mr. Schultz thinks the extrusion machine will help him achieve.

13. (**E**) This is unimportant because both Mr. Schultz and Mr. Beam are concerned primarily with the future. Since the decision to acquire an extrusion machine is based on assumptions that the business environment is going to change, past history is not a reliable guide to future results.

14. (**B**) This is a major factor because if the bank refuses to make the loan, Weatherstrip will be unable to acquire an extrusion machine, regardless of the advantages.

DATA APPLICATION

15. (**A**) Mr. Schultz estimated that the cost of the separate components plus the labor to assemble and install them would be $50,000, while the cost of a complete machine would be $100,000. The lower figure does not include the cost of the engineering work to be done by Mr. Schultz himself. He did not calculate a dollar value for this work but if he were to buy the machine from an outside source, he would have to pay for it. Therefore, that cost must be the reason for the $50,000 difference in prices.

16. (**C**) Once the quotas were lifted, Mr. Schultz forecast "that there would be intense competition within the industry on the basis of both price and service."

17. (**D**) The machine would cost between $50,000 and $100,000. Some components could be purchased from other manufacturers and some could be made in Weatherstrip's machine shop. There was no mention of delivery time.

18. (**D**) Mr. Schultz estimated the cost of both purchased and manufactured components to be $43,000 and the cost of labor for installation and assembly to be $7,000, for a total of $50,000.

19. (**D**) The components and installation of the machine amounted to $50,000. The capital required to purchase the predecessor company was $6,000 + $16,000 = $22,000. $22,000 is 44% of $50,000.

20. (**B**) Mr. Beam "cautioned against too rapid an expansion on borrowed funds."

DATA EVALUATION
(A) means that the Conclusion is a Major Objective;
(B) means that the Conclusion is a Major Factor;
(C) means that the Conclusion is a Minor Factor;
(D) means that the Conclusion is a Major Assumption;
(E) means that the Conclusion is an Unimportant Issue.

21. (**D**) A major assumption made by the sales manager, since an increase in sales will increase the savings to be realized by buying an automatic filling machine.

22. (**C**) This is a minor factor which reduces the savings with an automatic operation slightly because only two men are required at the higher wage rate, instead of three at the lower rate.

23. (**E**) The seasonal nature of the business has no effect on the savings to be achieved with the automatic filling machine.

24. (**B**) This is a major factor because the company will have to weigh the reduction of manufacturing costs against the cost of the new machine.

25. (**A**) This is one of the results that the production manager hopes to achieve by buying a new machine.

26. (**D**) This is a major assumption made by the production manager in order to compare the annual costs of an automatic filling system with those of the manual operation.

27. **(C)** This is a minor factor that the treasurer feels is a reason for postponing capital investments.

28. **(E)** The cost of the inventory is unimportant since it will be the same regardless of whether or not Weyburn buys the machine.

29. **(A)** This is one of the goals that the production manager expects to achieve by buying an automatic filling machine.

30. **(E)** Since the capping operation will be the same under both the automatic and the manual filling operations, its cost has no bearing on whether or not to buy a new machine.

31. **(B)** The company's cash shortage is a major factor in the decision of whether or not to make the $5,300 outlay for the new machine.

32. **(E)** Even though the treasurer comments that the machine will only be used for a month a year, this is unimportant because the ultimate decision will be made by weighing the cost of the machine against the savings to be realized.

33. **(E)** This is unimportant because if an excess of uncapped cans accumulated, the filling operation could be interrupted until the cans had been capped.

34. **(C)** This is a minor factor which increases the savings with an automatic operation only slightly because the two men required are paid more per hour than the three men they would be replacing.

DATA APPLICATION

35. **(C)** The second paragraph indicates that the sales manager was optimistic, but to call him enthusiastic is taking too strong a position.

36. **(A)** As stated in the 6th paragraph, "the filling and capping operation was not a full time job for the three men."

37. **(D)** This is one of the two reasons given for the inventory in paragraph 7. The second reason dealing with quantity discounts is not mentioned as one of the choices.

38. **(A)** Since the automatic filling machine can fill 50/14 as many cans per minute as the manual system, it will take only 14/50 as many man-hours to fill the cans. In addition, since the automatic system is operated by 2 men at $4.00 each per hour instead of 3 men at $3.00 per hour, the cost per man-hour of the new system is $8.00/$9.00 = 8/9 of the hourly cost of the old system. Hence, the labor cost of the new system is $8/9 \times 14/50 = 56/225 = 24.9\%$.

39. **(C)** Four pounds of wax are lost for each 673-pound batch, which is slightly less than 2/3 of 1%. ($4/673 < 4/600 = 4/6 \times 1/100 = 2/3$ of 1%)

    Total production in 1973 was 368,400 pounds, so about 2/3 of 1% of $368,400 = 2,456$ pounds were wasted.

Each pound costs $0.74	
Processing	$0.31
Direct material	.11
Direct labor	.04
Variable cost	.19
Nonvariable cost	.09
TOTAL	$0.74

    Thus, the cost of overfilling is 2,456 pounds at $0.74 each, or roughly $3/4 \times 2,456 = \$1,842$. **(C)** is the closest choice.

40. **(A)** The chart in the passage shows that 1-pound cans were filled at the rate of 14 per minute and 2-pound cans were filled at the rate of 7 per minute. 28 pounds could be canned per minute under either plan, so there would be no labor savings.

TEST IV. DATA INTERPRETATION

1. **(D)** In 1947 there were approximately 16 million women in the labor force and they constituted 28.1% of the total.
   .281 × Total Labor Force = 16 million
   Total Labor Force = 58.7 million

2. **(E)** In 1947 there were 8 million married women in the labor force. In 1972 there were 20 million.
   The percentage increase is $\dfrac{20 \text{ million} - 8 \text{ million}}{8 \text{ million}} = 150\%$

3. **(A)** $\dfrac{7.5 \text{ million single women}}{5 \text{ million widowed or divorced women}} = 1.5$.

4. **(B)** In 1972 the 33 million women were 38.5% of the labor force, therefore, as in question 1,
   Total Labor Force $= \dfrac{33 \text{ million}}{.385} = 85.7$ million
   From question 1 the 1947 Labor Force was 58.7 million. The increase in the Labor Force was
   85.7 million − 58.7 million = 27 million.
   The number of women in the Labor Force increased by 17 million (from 16 million to 33 million). Therefore the number of additional men must have been
   27 million − 17 million = 10 million
   $\dfrac{17 \text{ million women}}{10 \text{ million men}} = 1.7$ women per man

5. **(C)** The answer to this question can be read directly from the graph. It is the width of the central shaded region at 1960. The region extends from 5 million to 19 million for a width of 14 million or, approximately 15 million.

6. **(B)** In 1972 $\frac{5\text{ million}}{33\text{ million}}$ working women were widowed or divorced. Since women as a class were 38.5% of the Labor Force, widowed and divorced women were $\frac{5}{33} \times 38.5\% = 5.8\%$.

7. **(D)** In 1971, 77% of 53.3 million had incomes over $5,800; 69% had incomes over $7,100; therefore 8% of 53.3 million or 4.3 million families had incomes between $5,800 and $7,100.

8. **(B)** In 1971, 66% of 53.3 million or 35.2 million families had incomes over $7,800. In 1961, 50% of 46.3 million or 23.2 million families had incomes over $7,800. Hence, $35.2 - 23.2 = 12$ million more families who had incomes over $7,800 in 1971 than in 1961.

9. **(C)** By definition of the median, in 1956, 50% of 43.5 million families had incomes over the median. Thus:
$$\frac{50\%\text{ of }46.3\text{ million} - 50\%\text{ of }43.5\text{ million}}{50\%\text{ of }43.5\text{ million}} = \frac{23.15 - 21.75}{21.75} = \frac{1.4}{21.75}$$
Estimating this result shows that
$$\frac{1.3}{21.75} = 6\% < \frac{1.4}{21.75} < \frac{1.4}{21} = 0.67$$

10. **(E)** Total family income cannot be computed from the chart because that would require knowing the actual income of each family.

11. **(E)** In 1971, 23% of 53.3 million = 12.259 million families had incomes below $5,800. The only year that might have fewer families with incomes below $5,800 is 1966, so checking that years gives:
    25% of 49.1 million = 12.275 million.
Therefore, 1971 is the year with the fewest families with incomes below $5,800.

12. **(D)** Since in each year, 6% of the families had incomes between $9,400 and $10,300, the year with the greatest total number of families, 1971, must also have the greatest number in that income range.

13. **(C)** In 1967, coated and glazed paper shipments were 30% of $4.5 billion = $1.35 billion.

   In 1974, shipments were:
   27% of $7.4 billion = $1.998 billion.
   the percentage increase is
   $$\frac{1.998 - 1.35}{1.35} = \frac{.648}{1.35}$$
   Estimating the answer:
   $$\frac{.648}{.135} < \frac{.675}{1.35} = 50\%$$
   so the correct choice is (C), a 48% increase.

14. **(B)** Pulp goods were 3% of total shipments in 1967 and in 1974. "Other" was 10% of total shipments in 1967 and in 1974.

15. **(D)** The overall increase in shipments was $7.4 billion − $4.5 billion = $2.9 billion. The increase in shipments of sanitary paper products was $1.1 billion:
   33% of $7.4 billion = $2.4 billion
   29% of $4.5 billion = $1.3 billion
   $2.4 billion − $1.3 billion = $1.1 billion
   $$\frac{\$1.1 \text{ billion}}{\$2.9 \text{ billion}} = 39\%$$

16. **(A)** Stationery products were 7% and envelopes were 9% of total shipments, so combined they were 16% of $7.4 billion = $1.2 billion.

17. **(E)** The shortcut to doing this problem without checking each of the choices is to realize that the right answer must be a category whose percentage of total shipments increased, so you only have to check sanitary paper products and stationery products.
   sanitary paper products:
   Percentage Increase: $$\frac{33\% \text{ of } \$7.4 \text{ billion} - 29\% \text{ of } \$4.5 \text{ billion}}{29\% \text{ of } \$4.5 \text{ billion}}$$
   $$= \frac{\$2.442 \text{ billion} - \$1.305 \text{ billion}}{\$1.305 \text{ billion}} = \frac{\$1.137 \text{ billion}}{\$1.3 \text{ billion}} = 87.5\%$$
   stationery products:
   Percentage Increase: $$\frac{7\% \text{ of } \$7.4 \text{ billion} - 6\% \text{ of } \$4.5 \text{ billion}}{6\% \text{ of } \$4.5 \text{ billion}}$$
   $$= \frac{\$.518 \text{ billion} - \$.27 \text{ billion}}{\$.27 \text{ billion}} = \frac{\$.248 \text{ billion}}{\$.27 \text{ billion}} = 91.9\%$$

18. **(D)** Shipments of pulp goods were 3% of total shipments in both 1967 and 1974, so the change was:
   3% of $7.4 billion − 3% of $4.5 billion = 3% of ($7.4 − $4.5) billion
   = 3% of $2.9 billion = $.087 billion = $87 million.

19. **(A)** It is only necessary to check the category whose percentage of total shipments declined the most: coated and glazed paper.

    1967 Shipments: 30% of $4.5 billion = $1.35 billion

    1974 Shipments: 27% of $7.4 billion = $1.998 billion

Since shipments in this category did not decline, none of the others could have.

20. **(B)** Social insurance contributions went from about $40 billion (the width of that region in 1967, from $95 billion to $135 billion) to about $90 billion in 1974 (the distance from $170 billion to $260 billion) for a 125% increase $\left[\dfrac{90-40}{40} \times 100\right]$. The only sector that may be close is personal taxes, (from $70 billion to $135 billion) which was less than a 100% increase.

21. **(A)** In both 1967 and 1974, receipts from indirect business taxes were about $15 billion. Since there was virtually no change in this amount while total receipts went from $150 billion to almost twice that ($290 billion), the percentage of total receipts was nearly halved.

    $$\frac{15}{290} = 5.3\%, \quad \frac{15}{150} = 10\%$$

22. **(D)** The key to this question is recognizing that this is a cumulative line graph, so that the amount of receipts for corporate profits taxes is the distance between the top boundary of the region labeled personal taxes and the bottom boundary of the region labeled social insurance contributions. In the last quarter of 1972, the top of the corporate profits taxes region is $200 billion and the bottom is higher than $150 billion, so the closest answer is (D) $50 billion.

23. **(E)** This question is answered by observing that the region for social insurance contributions gets continuously wider from left to right, so that it is the one which never decreases.

24. **(A)** In 1967, total receipts were almost exactly $150 billion. In 1974, they were about $290 billion, for an increase of almost 100%.

    $$\frac{\$290 \text{ billion} - \$150 \text{ billion}}{\$150 \text{ billion}} = \frac{14}{15} = 93\,1/3\%$$

25. **(A)** Since indirect business taxes did not increase, no part of the increase in total receipts could have been due to the increase in indirect business taxes.

TEST V. ERROR RECOGNITION

(A) means the sentence contains an error in DICTION;
(B) means the sentence is VERBOSE;
(C) means the sentence contains FAULTY GRAMMAR;
(D) means the sentence contains NO ERROR.

1. **(C)** "———*is* being investigated." The verb always agrees with its subject (*behavior*) in person and number, whether or not there is a phrase or clause between the subject and the verb.

2. **(D)** No errors.

3. **(A)** "———he has *little* ambition———" *Few* answers the question "How many?" (He has *few* friends.) *Little* answers the question "How much?" (He has *little* ambition.)

4. **(D)** No errors.

5. **(B)** "The article was a joint effort." An article *written together* with someone is *a joint effort*.

6. **(D)** No errors.

7. **(A)** "———will be *dismissed* tomorrow." *Fired* is colloquial for *dismissed*.

8. **(A)** "———as *inured* to the elements as Eskimos———" *To immure* is to wall in or imprison. *To inure* is to accustom or habituate.

9. **(A)** "———*ravaged* thousands of trees———" *To ravish* is to seize and carry away forcibly, or to rape. *To ravage* is to destroy violently, to devastate.

10. **(B)** "His original views earned———." *Original* means *never before conceived*.

11. **(C)** "———one of the *most poorly* taught subjects———" What is needed to modify *taught*, a past participle used as an adjective, is an adverb. *Poorest* is an adjective.

12. **(C)** "———*are* my major interest." A verb agrees with its subject (*theories*), not with a subjective complement (*my major interest*).

13. **(C)** "Everybody must make *his* mind———" The indefinite pronoun *everybody* takes a singular verb. (Everybody was there.) Therefore, pronouns referring to *everybody* take the singular form. By convention, such pronouns are masculine.

14. (**B**) "The *manager's craftiness———*" *Cunning* and *crafty* are synonyms.

15. (**A**) "Benjamin Franklin's *practical* mind———" *Practicable* means feasible. *Practical* means dealing sensibly with everyday activities.

16. (**C**) "———had *beaten* his brother at ping-pong." One *wins* a game, but *beats* an opponent at the game.

17. (**D**) No errors.

18. (**D**) No errors.

19. (**D**) No errors.

20. (**C**) "———with Mr. Harris and *me*." Since *me* is the object of the preposition with, it has an object form (*me*).

21. (**D**) No errors.

22. (**A**) "———*flouting* the authority———" *To flaunt* is to wave or make a boastful display. *To flout* is to treat (someone or something) with contempt.

23. (**A**) "———*incredibly* rude." *Incredulous* means unbelieving, skeptical. *Incredible* means unbelievable.

24. (**A**) "———that there was a *brawl*———" *Row* is colloquial for *brawl*.

25. (**B**) "I have provided an appendix———" The appendix always appears at the *end* of a book.

26. (**C**) "———each *are* subject to———" When the word *each* is an adjective in apposition with a plural subject (Mr. Watson and his wife), the verb is plural. But when *each* is the subject of a sentence, it takes a singular verb. (*Each* of the defendants is subject to a sentence of five years in jail.)

27. (**C**) "Most formidable *were* his posture, his voice, and his mustache." A verb agrees with its subject (*posture, voice,* and *mustache*) even when the subject follows the verb.

28. (**C**) "I thought the tall girl was *she*." A personal pronoun functioning as a subjective complement is always of the same case as the substantive to which it refers. In this sentence, the personal pronoun *she* refers to the substantive *the tall girl,* which is in the nominative case. Therefore, *she* (nominative case) and not *her* (objective case) is correct.

29. **(B)** "The sultan luxuriated in a villa———" *To luxuriate* means to live in great luxury, and *opulence* is luxury.

30. **(A)** "———some of the *principles* of the monetary system." *Principal* means a chief or head. *Principle* means a fundamental truth.

31. **(A)** "———to degrade himself." *Abase* can be eliminated, since it is a synonym of *degrade*.

32. **(D)** No errors.

33. **(D)** No errors.

34. **(D)** No errors.

35. **(D)** No errors.

TEST VI. SENTENCE CORRECTION

1. **(A)** is correct. For singular subjects joined by *or*, a singular verb is usually required; for singular subjects joined by *and*, a plural verb is normally needed.

2. **(B)** is correct. One thing is different *from* another.

3. **(A)** is correct. (C) and (D) suggest that habit grips an octopus. (B) uses the preposition *like* for the conjunction *as*. (E) is awkward.

4. **(A)** is correct. *Except* is a preposition meaning with exclusion of; *accept* is a verb meaning receive with a consenting mind. *Already* means by this time or beforehand; *all ready* means everyone is ready or wholly ready. All choices except (A) make errors in the use of the above expressions; in addition, choice (E) is awkwardly structured.

5. **(C)** is correct. It is not made clear in choice (A) that the *students* give the talks. (B) and (E) are awkward. (D) changes the meaning of the original sentence.

6. **(B)** is correct. The expression is *not so . . . . as*. (A) and (C) incorrectly use *like* for *as*. (D) should read *is not quite the politician that Senator Handake is*. (E) is wordy.

7. **(D)** is correct. In choices (A) and (C), the subject and verb are awkwardly separated. (B) implies that a dead person can *find* something. (E) is awkward and suggests that *money* dies.

8. **(E)** is correct. (A) and (D) suggest that James, or the sewer, did the raining. (B) is meaningless. (C) does not indicate the causal relationship between the rainfall and the overflowing of the sewers.

9. **(D)** is correct. A participle (*driving*) must attach itself immediately to the noun with which it has a logical association (*you*). In (A), (B), (C), and (E) the participle is not so attached making it appear that *Mount Bundler* is driving.

10. **(A)** is correct. (B) changes the meaning of the original sentence. In (C) it is not made clear that *international* refers to *scope*, and *informal* to *style*. (D) is wordy and (E) lacks parallel construction.

11. **(D)** is correct. There is an unnecessary change of person in (A) and (B), and an awkward change of subject in (C). Choice (E) is clumsy.

12. **(C)** is correct. *Many in number* and *absolutely annihilated* are redundant expressions. (A), (B), and (D) each contain at least one of these tautologies. (E) neglects the rule that a collective noun, such as *enemy*, takes a plural verb if it is used to designate the members of a group taken separately.

13. **(E)** is correct. *Also, further, notwithstanding*, and *moreover* are conjunctive adverbs; their only use as conjunctions is between independent clauses. *And*, a simple coordinating conjunction, is appropriate in this sentence.

14. **(C)** is correct. A subordinate clause (other than a noun clause) cannot be used as a predicate noun; therefore, (A) and (B) are wrong. (D) is awkward and (E) does not specify that a carhop is a human being.

15. **(A)** is correct. Choices (C), (D), and (E) are run-on sentences. (B) and (D) suggest an impossible situation.

16. **(A)** is correct. The girl lacks companionship, not children; therefore, (C) and (D) are wrong. (D) should read *especially that of children her own age*. (B) and (E) make no sense.

17. **(D)** is correct. *Ten grand, nut*, and *nuts* are slang expressions.

18. **(C)** is correct. *Having studied the problem* logically modifies *Joseph*. It would seem otherwise in (A), (B), and (E). (D) is repetitious.

19. **(E)** is correct. A past contrary-to-fact condition sequence of tenses requires the past perfect form (*had been*) in the *if* clause. Only (E) uses this form.

20. **(C)** is correct. The *to* in choice (A) is incorrect. (B) and (D) are incorrect because of the misplacement of *seriously*. (E) is wordy.

21. **(E)** is correct. One asks for the privilege *of* doing, getting, having something. (D) contains a sentence fragment.

22. **(B)** is correct. Many aspirants were asked the questions. (A) suggests that only one person was questioned. (C), (D), and (E) do not indicate who was *asked* or *required* to answer questions.

23. **(B)** is correct. *Fellow playmates* and *ascended up* are redundant expressions. Choices (A), (C), (D), and (E) each contain at least one of these tautologies.

24. **(A)** is correct. (B) and (E) change the meaning of the original sentence. (C) contains a confusing shift in tense, and (D) makes no sense.

25. **(D)** The word *cave(s)* is given too much work in Choices (A), (B), and (E). One form of the word cannot express two separate thoughts (one of the largest *caves* in the world; the largest *cave* in the world). (C) is wordy.

TEST VII. QUANTITATIVE COMPARISONS

1. **(B)** $125 < 243$

2. **(B)** $\sqrt{0.00025} = \dfrac{\sqrt{2.5}}{100} < \dfrac{\sqrt{5}}{100}$

3. **(A)** $1.56 > 1.44$

4. **(C)** Since $x = y$, $2z = y$, $z = y/2$

5. **(B)** See 4.

6. **(D)** Since there are two variables and only one equation it is impossible to calculate a numerical result.

7. **(D)** See 6.

8. **(C)** $150 = 150$

9. **(B)** $\dfrac{\sqrt{1/5}}{\sqrt{2/7}} = \sqrt{\dfrac{1/5}{2/7}} = \sqrt{1/5 \times 7/2} = \sqrt{7/10} < \sqrt{.71}$

10. **(B)** $49 < 50$

11. **(D)** The two solutions to this equation are $x = 4$ and $x = 0$. Therefore the comparison cannot be determined.

12. **(D)** See 11.

13. **(B)** $(\sqrt{x} - \sqrt{y})^2 = x + y - 2\sqrt{xy} < x + y$

14. **(B)** $x + y < 2xy$, for $x > 1$, $y > 1$. $2\sqrt{xy} < 2xy$, for $x > 1$, $y > 1$.
Therefore $(\sqrt{x} + \sqrt{y})^2 = x + y + 2\sqrt{xy} < 4xy$.

15. **(D)** If $0 < x < 1$, then $x > x^4 = y$, if not, then $x \leq y$.

16. **(D)** See 15.

17. **(D)** See 15. $y^3 = x^{12}$, but if $0 < x < 1$, $x^7 > x^{12}$, if not, $x \leq x^{12}$

18. **(D)** If $x < 0$, then $y^{1/4} = (x^4)^{1/4} = -x > x$
If $x \geq 0$, then $y^{1/4} = x$

19. **(D)** If $y > 2$, then $1/x < 1/(y-2)$, *e.g.*, $1/3 < 1/(3-2)$
If $y = 1$, then $1/x = 1 > 1/(1-2) = -1$

20. **(C)** $\overline{ab} = \overline{cd} = 1/2\,\overline{BD}$.

21. **(B)** $\overline{AB} = \overline{ac} = \overline{ab} \times \sqrt{2} = 1.4 \times \overline{ab} < 1.5 \times \overline{ab}$

22. **(C)** Area of $\square$ ABCD $= (\overline{AB})^2 = (\overline{ab})^2 \times (\sqrt{2})^2$
$= 2 \times (ab)^2 = 2 \times$ area of $\square$ abcd.

23. **(B)** Perimeter of $\square$ ABCD $= 4 \times (\overline{AB}) =$
$4 \times (ab) \times \sqrt{2} = \sqrt{2} \times$ perimeter of $\square$ abcd

24. **(A)** $1/8 > 1/9$

25. **(A)** $(15/4)^7 > 1$

SCORE YOURSELF

Compare your answers to the Correct Key Answers at the end of the Examination. To determine your score, count the number of correct answers in each test. Then count the number of incorrect answers. Subtract ¼ of the number of incorrect answers from the number of correct answers. Plot the resulting figure on the graph below by blackening the bar under each test to the point of your score. Plan your study to strengthen the weaknesses indicated on your scoring graph.

EXAM III	Very Poor	Poor	Average	Good	Excellent
READING COMPREHENSION 25 Questions	1-4	5-10	11-17	18-22	23-25
PRINCIPLES AND CASES 40 Questions	1-7	8-17	18-28	29-35	36-40
PRACTICAL JUDGMENT 40 Questions	1-7	8-17	18-28	29-35	36-40
DATA INTERPRETATION 25 Questions	1-4	5-10	11-17	18-22	23-25
ERROR RECOGNITION 35 Questions	1-6	7-15	16-25	26-31	32-35
SENTENCE CORRECTION 25 Questions	1-4	5-10	11-17	18-22	23-25
QUANTITATIVE COMPARISON 25 Questions	1-4	5-10	11-17	18-22	23-25

EXAM IV	Very Poor	Poor	Average	Good	Excellent
LOGICAL REASONING 15 Questions	1-2	3-6	7-10	11-13	14-15
PRINCIPLES AND CASES 40 Questions	1-7	8-17	18-28	29-35	36-40
PRACTICAL JUDGMENT 40 Questions	1-7	8-17	18-28	29-35	36-40
DATA INTERPRETATION 25 Questions	1-4	5-10	11-17	18-22	23-25
ERROR RECOGNITION 35 Questions	1-6	7-15	16-25	26-31	32-35
SENTENCE CORRECTION 25 Questions	1-4	5-10	11-17	18-22	23-25
QUANTITATIVE COMPARISON 25 Questions	1-4	5-10	11-17	18-22	23-25

Law School Admission Test

FOURTH VERISIMILAR EXAM

In this comprehensive examination we have sought to predict the content of your test, and to provide you with the kind of practice you really require. It has approximately the same number of questions as the official test. The topics tested, the form of the questions, the level of difficulty, and the number of questions for each topic . . . all are quite similar to the official test. In every respect it simulates the actual conditions you will encounter. Test yourself to get an overview, to review your strengths and weaknesses, and to put yourself in the right frame of mind for scoring high.

Allow about 3½ hours for this Examination.

That's approximately how much time you'll have on the actual exam. Keep a record of your time, especially if you want to break up this practice into several convenient sessions. Then you'll be able to simulate actual exam conditions.

ANALYSIS AND TIMETABLE: VERISIMILAR EXAMINATION IV.		
This table is both an analysis of the exam that follows and a priceless preview of the actual test. Look it over carefully and use it well.		
SUBJECT TESTED	*Time Allowed*	*Questions*
LOGICAL REASONING	20 minutes	15
PRINCIPLES AND CASES	55 minutes	40
PRACTICAL JUDGMENT	40 minutes	40
DATA INTERPRETATION	30 minutes	25
ERROR RECOGNITION	20 minutes	35
SENTENCE CORRECTION	20 minutes	25
QUANTITATIVE COMPARISON	15 minutes	25
TOTALS EXAM IV	200 minutes	205

ANSWER SHEET FOR VERISIMILAR EXAMINATION IV.

Consolidate your key answers here just as you would do on the actual exam. Using this type of Answer Sheet will provide valuable practice. Tear it out along the indicated lines and mark it up correctly. Use a No. 2 (medium) pencil. Make only ONE mark for each answer. Additional and stray marks may be counted as mistakes. In making corrections erase errors COMPLETELY. Make glossy black marks.

TEST I. LOGICAL REASONING

1 A B C D E	2 A B C D E	3 A B C D E	4 A B C D E	5 A B C D E	6 A B C D E	7 A B C D E	8 A B C D E
9 A B C D E	10 A B C D E	11 A B C D E	12 A B C D E	13 A B C D E	14 A B C D E	15 A B C D E	16 A B C D E

TEST II. PRINCIPLES AND CASES

1 A B C D E	2 A B C D E	3 A B C D E	4 A B C D E	5 A B C D E	6 A B C D E	7 A B C D E	8 A B C D E
9 A B C D E	10 A B C D E	11 A B C D E	12 A B C D E	13 A B C D E	14 A B C D E	15 A B C D E	16 A B C D E
17 A B C D E	18 A B C D E	19 A B C D E	20 A B C D E	21 A B C D E	22 A B C D E	23 A B C D E	24 A B C D E
25 A B C D E	26 A B C D E	27 A B C D E	28 A B C D E	29 A B C D E	30 A B C D E	31 A B C D E	32 A B C D E
33 A B C D E	34 A B C D E	35 A B C D E	36 A B C D E	37 A B C D E	38 A B C D E	39 A B C D E	40 A B C D E

TEST III. PRACTICAL JUDGMENT

1 A B C D E	2 A B C D E	3 A B C D E	4 A B C D E	5 A B C D E	6 A B C D E	7 A B C D E	8 A B C D E
9 A B C D E	10 A B C D E	11 A B C D E	12 A B C D E	13 A B C D E	14 A B C D E	15 A B C D E	16 A B C D E
17 A B C D E	18 A B C D E	19 A B C D E	20 A B C D E	21 A B C D E	22 A B C D E	23 A B C D E	24 A B C D E
25 A B C D E	26 A B C D E	27 A B C D E	28 A B C D E	29 A B C D E	30 A B C D E	31 A B C D E	32 A B C D E
33 A B C D E	34 A B C D E	35 A B C D E	36 A B C D E	37 A B C D E	38 A B C D E	39 A B C D E	40 A B C D E

TEST IV. DATA INTERPRETATION

1 A B C D E	2 A B C D E	3 A B C D E	4 A B C D E	5 A B C D E	6 A B C D E	7 A B C D E	8 A B C D E
9 A B C D E	10 A B C D E	11 A B C D E	12 A B C D E	13 A B C D E	14 A B C D E	15 A B C D E	16 A B C D E
17 A B C D E	18 A B C D E	19 A B C D E	20 A B C D E	21 A B C D E	22 A B C D E	23 A B C D E	24 A B C D E
25 A B C D E	26 A B C D E	27 A B C D E	28 A B C D E	29 A B C D E	30 A B C D E	31 A B C D E	32 A B C D E

TEST V. ERROR RECOGNITION

This is an answer grid with columns labeled A B C D E for questions 1–40, arranged in rows of 8 (1–8, 9–16, 17–24, 25–32, 33–40).

TEST VI. SENTENCE CORRECTION

This is an answer grid with columns labeled A B C D E for questions 1–32, arranged in rows of 8 (1–8, 9–16, 17–24, 25–32).

TEST VII. QUANTITATIVE COMPARISON

This is an answer grid with columns labeled A B C D E for questions 1–32, arranged in rows of 8 (1–8, 9–16, 17–24, 25–32).

TEST I. LOGICAL REASONING

TIME: 20 Minutes. 15 Questions.

This is a test of your ability to evaluate the reasoning contained in a statement or reading passage. Each statement or passage is followed by one or more questions. Answer each question solely on the basis of information stated or implied in the reading. If more than one choice seems possible, then you must select the one answer that does not require making implausible or superfluous assumptions. Blacken the space on the answer sheet that corresponds to the letter of your choice.

Correct and explanatory answers are provided at the end of the exam. After you have completed the entire exam, read the explanations carefully. They'll reinforce your strengths and pinpoint your weaknesses so that you know just what to study to raise your score.

1. The test of obscenity is this: whether the tendency of the matter charged as obscenity is to deprave and corrupt those whose minds are open to such immoral influences, and into whose hands a publication of this sort may fall.

   A critic of the above test would consider which of the following a major flaw?

   (A) The test does not take into account that adolescents are more easily influenced than adults.
   (B) The test does not take into account the ultimate harm that obscene matter may cause.
   (C) The test might be applied without regard to the social purpose or value of the work in question.
   (D) The test does not take into account the way in which the publication may filter through society.
   (E) The test does not take into account that there will always be a certain number of depraved people in society.

2. Furthermore, if you become an accomplished manager the Department will have more need for you than it did for you as a substantive operator. Most of you bright people can analyze situations and report them faithfully. Most of you can write well. Seldom is the seventh floor misled by the cables and reports we receive. But we have a critical shortage of talented managers. Probably we always will have.

Which of the following is the main underlying presumption of the above memo?

(A) In order to be a good manager you must be able to communicate well.
(B) The Department has been reluctant to hire people with a strong leadership drive.
(C) The training programs in the Department for management personnel are inefficient.
(D) Managerial ability is a rare, natural talent.
(E) With the proper training most bright people can become good managers.

3. As diplomat; as scholar; as man of letters; as seeker of historical truth and political understanding; as teacher in the seminar and in the world; as a friend and human being—in all these aspects of his life, and in their unique union, he has been extraordinary and plenipotentiary.

The above farewell address was probably given to which of the following persons?

(A) A retiring clergyman from his role as teacher in a seminary
(B) A diplomat from his role as an ambassador
(C) A college president from his role as educator and fund raiser
(D) A respected member of a fraternal order from his role as society leader
(E) The father of a large family from his role as head of the PTA

4. The idea was to discourage tax competition among local governments over new industry, help jurisdictions incapable of helping themselves, and preserve the environment from over-industrialization at the same time.

The plan being described most likely called for

(A) increased laissez-faire capitalism
(B) revenue sharing among municipalities
(C) social support of health care programs
(D) an even disbursement of tax revenues among state governments
(E) a comprehensive program for institutions of higher learning

5. One of the basic themes underlying our analyses and policy recommendations is the substitution of quality for quantity; that is, we should concern ouselves with improving the quality of life for all Americans, rather than merely adding more Americans.

Which of the following sentences would provide the most logical continuation of this paragraph?

(A) And unfortunately, for many of our citizens that quality of life is still defined only as enough food, clothing and shelter.

(B)   Many other nations are beginning to recognize the importance of population questions.

(C)   Consideration of the population issue raises profound questions of what the people want, what they need and, indeed, what they are for.

(D)   "Why more people?" The answer must be given, we believe, in qualitative and not quantitative terms.

(E)   It is far easier to achieve agreement on abstract values than on their meaning or on the strategy to achieve them.

Questions 6 and 7

Shakespeare did not have to know the philosophical and scientific theorizing of his time to reflect the passionate individualism of the Renaissance. Dante, of course, was immensely learned in the theory of the universe of his age. The knowledge of his time was of a kind which interpreted the whole of existence within the unity of a single view of life. Knowledge and imagination were then one and the same. It is possible, of course, that the present revolution in science might arrive at the point where analytic and statistical inquiry broke down, and the behavior of infinitesimally small impulses, particles of energy, appeared entirely accidental, and their interpretation was inevitably subjective to the scientists.

6.   It may be inferred from the passage that the author feels that modern writers will probably follow the attitude of

(A)   Dante and combine scientific knowledge with the poetic conception of good and evil

(B)   Shakespeare and reflect on the values of their world as seen through the power of the imagination

(C)   Dante because in today's world knowledge and imagination have become fixed

(D)   both Shakespeare and Dante

(E)   the reactionary belief in materialistic determinism

7.   In the last sentence the author makes a prediction for the future. If that prediction were to come true the probable outcome would be that

(A)   the poetic imagination would separate from scientific research and technology

(B)   there would be a return to the Renaissance tradition as represented by Shakespeare

(C)   the poetic imagination would link up with the scientific and perhaps return to a culture based on a unity of logic and imagination

(D)   scientific logic would replace the poetic imagination as the theme in all art

(E)   authors would become more polarized in their thought than they are today

8. This response, or lack of response, basically avoids the issue or yields grudgingly in a kind of tokenism. It is not working very well, and if I am right that the youth revolt of today is something much more than the normal rebelliousness of the young then it will not work at all in the long run. We will constantly find ourselves peaked toward the brink of backlash.

The response (in line 1) that the author is most likely so frightened of is probably

(A) reactionary backlash   (D) apathy
(B) acceptance of radical ideas   (E) urban violence
(C) sympathy

9. Let the historic novelist create all the fictitious characters he cares to create. Fictitious scenes, fictitious utterances . . . let him erect and polish and garb the illusion that is in him . . . so long as he stays within the limits of his own creation. But let him not select the fact from where it lies, a dusty sapphire in the jewel box of time, and take it out and recut it, and reset it, and declare that he has an emerald.

The author would probably consider which of the following aspects of the historical novel to be the most important task of its author?

(A) To set a beautiful scene
(B) To investigate the philosophy of the period
(C) To be historically accurate
(D) To have a lucid style
(E) To keep the plot moving quickly

10. If you believe that man has free will then why does he so enjoy following orders?

In terms of its logical features the question above most closely resembles which of the following?

(A) Do you believe that evil men have evil purposes?
(B) Why does the end justify the means?
(C) If the computer cannot make a mistake why do you check it so frequently?
(D) Why do you believe the order is the keystone of efficiency?
(E) How can you believe that you are absolutely right?

11. How can God be all-good and all-powerful if He lets there be evil in the world?

In terms of the logical feature, the question above most closely resembles which of the following?

(A) How can the mayor be so concerned and so burdened by the problems of the city if he has time to play golf?
(B) How can the computer be completely efficient and absolutely accurate if it can't send me a proper monthly statement?

(C) How can one man be infallible and so precise at the same time?

(D) How can it be possible that you've travelled this route so often and now we're lost?

(E) How can I have flunked that test when I felt so good about it when I left the exam?

12. Italian society is difficult to write about because it does not lend itself to novel form. It is not a spiritually unified whole, whose various strata are in active relation one with the other through the common denominator of a language.

Which of the following opinions is the author least likely to hold about Italian society?

(A) It is politically stable because its members share common drives and desires.

(B) The Italian language promotes unity.

(C) Many different forces and groups make up Italian society.

(D) Italian art is among the most esteemed.

(E) Italian society though not unified now is thrust toward unification.

13. Transitions are skipped, and one has the impression that the writer wants to help the essential, and doesn't care to describe photographically the pimple of each one of his characters; nor does he want to necessarily tell of the gardener who wanted the tree of which the wood has been used to manufacture the door that his hero is about to open.

It may be inferred that the writer who is being discussed takes which of the following views towards literature?

(A) The minute details of an individual character are the most essential for character development.

(B) A work of literature must flow evenly from one scene to another.

(C) One moment is more valuable than one hour.

(D) An overview of life, emotions and events is aesthetically preferable to a meticulously realistic portrait of the human experience.

(E) A point of sensation is the ultimate experience.

14. The world of Newtonian science subtracts the qualities that are personal and immediate from human relationships. Instead of innocent contact with good, or guilt-ridden but still personal contact with evil, there is the screen between man and man of depersonalized values of power and materialism. The forces of nature are today screened from us as much by the inner processes of abstract thinking as by the outward appearances of industrial civilization.

A necessary premise of the author's argument is that

(A) power and materialism are evil

(B) abstract thought and direct experience are mutually exclusive

    (C)   industrialization cannot be described as good or evil

    (D)   men should not try to understand the processes of nature

    (E)   abstract thought is fundamental to modern civilization

15.   War in the twentieth century is only partially one of the ideologies and national interests. For those under the bombs, it is most immediately an epic struggle of the human spirit against a barbarous and unfeeling technology.

The author's position would be considerably weakened if it were pointed out that

    (A)   the American Revolution was won by an inferior number of ill-equipped American irregulars fighting a larger number of better trained, better equipped British and Hessian professionals

    (B)   over half of the United States' defense expenditures are for servicemen's pay

    (C)   the British response to German bombing of London in World War II was the bombing of Berlin

    (D)   the Israelis have won four wars against better equipped armies five times as large as theirs

    (E)   at the beginning of World War II, the German blitzkrieg required only a month to conquer Poland despite the courage of the Polish army

END OF TEST

Go on to do the following Test in this Examination, just as you would be expected to do on the actual exam. You will find correct answers for the entire Examination following the last question. Check your answers carefully after you have completed the whole Examination.

TEST II. PRINCIPLES AND CASES

TIME: 55 Minutes. 40 Questions.

Correct and explanatory answers are provided at the end of the exam. After you have completed the entire exam, read the explanations carefully. They'll reinforce your strengths and pinpoint your weaknesses so that you know just what to study to raise your score.

PART A. APPLYING SEVERAL PRINCIPLES TO A CASE

DIRECTIONS: Each law case described below is followed by several legal principles. These principles may be either real or imaginary, but for purposes of this test you are to assume them to be valid. Following each legal principle are four statements regarding the possible applicability of the principle to the law case. You are to select the one statement which most appropriately describes the applicability of the principle to the law case and blacken the space beneath the letter of the statement you select.
These questions do not presuppose any specific legal knowledge on your part; you are to arrive at your answers entirely by the ordinary processes of logical reasoning.

Case One

Wrongway Willie, Bumbling Bob, and Inept Ike decided to rob the payroll messenger for United Lathing Company. Willie and Bob purchased guns and the three of them set out in Ike's car along with Hapless Harry to find the messenger and rob him. After they had driven around upper Manhattan for several hours looking for the messenger, Harry got out of the car and went into a bar to relieve himself. Since there was no parking near the bar, the other three drove off. When Harry found he had been left behind, he took a cab home and spent the rest of the day watching television.

After they left Harry, the other three went to several sites where United Lathing Company was doing construction. They failed to find the messenger but they did attract the attention of two members of New York's finest. After the three prospective robbers went to two more sites, the police arrested them and warned them of their rights to remain silent and their right to counsel.

Bob told the police about the plan to rob the messenger and that it was all Harry's idea. Bob pleaded guilty to illegal possession of a firearm. Harry, Willie and Ike were tried for possession of firearms, attempted robbery, and conspiracy to commit robbery.

1. *The crime of attempt consists of an intent to do an act which is a crime and an act in furtherance of that intent which goes beyond mere preparation.*

    When Willie and Ike are tried for attempted robbery, the results will be:

    (A) They are both innocent because they could not find the messenger.
    (B) Willie is guilty because buying a gun is in furtherance of the intent to rob, but Ike is innocent because driving a car is not a criminal act.
    (C) Willie is guilty because buying a gun is more than mere preparation and Ike is guilty because driving the car is in furtherance of a criminal intent.
    (D) Willie is innocent because he was not driving the car.

2. *The crime of possession of an unregistered firearm is defined as being willingly in possession of a firearm which the possessor knows or should know to be unregistered.*

    At his trial for unlawful possession of firearms, Ike will be found

    (A) innocent because he was only driving the car
    (B) innocent because he did not buy the guns
    (C) guilty because his participation in a criminal activity implies that he knows the guns were unregistered
    (D) guilty because a driver is in possession of everything in his car

3. *The crime of conspiracy is the express or implied agreement of two or more persons to accomplish an unlawful purpose.*

    In Harry's trial for conspiracy to commit robbery, Harry will be

    (A) innocent because he was not in the car when the others were arrested
    (B) innocent because he did not buy a gun
    (C) guilty because the robbery was his idea
    (D) guilty because he went with the others to find the messenger

4. *At trial, statements of conspirators are admissible in evidence against each other only if there is some extrinsic evidence of the existence of the conspiracy.*

    Bob's testimony about Harry is

    (A) admissible because it is true
    (B) admissible because the presence of Bob, Willie, and Ike in the same car is evidence that they were members of a conspiracy
    (C) inadmissible because Harry was not in the car when the arrests were made
    (D) inadmissible because Bob is a convicted felon

5. *Withdrawal by a conspirator is a defense to the charge of conspiracy if there is a clear demonstration of the intent to withdraw given to all the other conspirators.*

   When Harry is tried for conspiracy to commit robbery, he will be

   (A) innocent because he went home
   (B) innocent because the others left him behind
   (C) guilty because he did not speak to the others after he went home
   (D) guilty because he never intended to withdraw

Case Two

St. Peter High is a Catholic boys' high school. The appropriate officials of St. Peter made an agreement with the local school board to have the students of St. Peter use the high school science rooms. The agreement provided that St. Peter pay for all materials used by its students in the lab, that St. Peter provide its own teachers and that St. Peter pay a set sum for the necessary cleaning and maintenance of the facility.

St. Peter students receive books on loan from the public school for all non-religious courses including the science courses. The local school district reimburses St. Peter for the costs of transportation of students to school under the same circumstances as public school children are given transportation—*i.e.,* certain distance from school attended, etc. Finally, school lunch programs are provided at St. Peter by local authorities under the same conditions as exist for such programs in public schools.

(A) P, a taxpayer in the affected public school district, sues in the state court to enjoin the enforcement of the agreement concerning the science room.

(B) F, the father of a Catholic girl who lives across the street from St. Peter but has to walk several blocks to Our Lady of Virgins, the Catholic girls' high school, sues St. Peter in Federal court to require it to admit his daughter. The daughter qualifies as to religion and all scholastic requirements.

6. *In order to have the right to sue to enjoin a state action, the person suing must show that he is directly injured by the action in question.*

   In the law suit by P, P will

   (A) win because his taxes are used to pay for the high school science facilities
   (B) win because of the freedom of religion
   (C) lose because the agreement does not cost the local school board anything
   (D) lose because the St. Peter students are already receiving state funds

7. *Publicly financed institutions may not exclude any citizen on the basis of race, religion, sex, or ethnic background.*

In the suit by F, F will

(A) win because discrimination by St. Peter's on the basis of sex is illegal
(B) win because his daughter is being denied the equal benefit of the state support of St. Peter's High
(C) lose because St. Peter's is not a public high school
(D) lose because his daughter is still a minor and not a citizen

8. *No state may deny to any citizen the equal protection of its laws.*

In the suit by F, F will

(A) win because discrimination on the basis of sex is illegal
(B) win because his daughter is being denied the equal benefit of the state support of St. Peter's High
(C) lose because St. Peter's is not a public school
(D) lose because his daughter is still a minor and not a citizen

9. *No one may assert the rights of another as the grounds for a lawsuit.*

In F's lawsuit, St. Peter's moves to dismiss on the basis of the principle above. F will

(A) win because he has the right to choose his daughter's school
(B) win because F's daughter has the right to go to the school of her choice
(C) lose because his daughter has no right to go to an all male school
(D) lose because the government has the right to decide how to spend its money

10. *Federal courts may not adjudicate any dispute between a taxpayer and a municipality except for actions where a violation of the Constitution is alleged.*

In P's lawsuit, the school board moves to dismiss. P will

(A) win because separation of Church and State is a Constitutional right
(B) win because Federal law is not applicable to the situation
(C) lose because the school board represents the municipality
(D) lose because he does not allege a violation of the Constitution

Proceed directly to the next Part.

PART B. APPLYING ONE PRINCIPLE TO SEVERAL CASES

DIRECTIONS: Each principle of law given below is followed by several law cases: These principles may be either real or imaginary, but for purposes of this test you are to assume them to be valid. Following each law case are four statements regarding the possible applicability of the principle to the law case. You are to select the one statement which most appropriately describes the applicability of the principle to the law case decision. Blacken the space beneath the letter of the statement you select. These questions do not presuppose any specific legal knowledge on your part; you are to arrive at your answers entirely by the ordinary processes of logical reasoning.

Principle One

Where an agreement has been reduced to a writing which the parties intend to be final, evidence of earlier oral or written expressions is not admissible to vary the terms of the writing. However, such extrinsic evidence is admissible to show forgery, fraud, or mistake and to explain or to interpret terms of the writing. Furthermore, extrinsic evidence is also admissible to show the existence of terms which are not inconsistent with the express or implied terms of the written agreement and which the parties would not ordinarily have included in the same agreement.

11. Dudly Dowery wishes to sell a piece of property to the Widow O'Reilly. There is an ugly icehouse on an adjacent piece of property and Dowery says that he will have it removed. Ms. O'Reilly buys the property and accepts the deed. Dowery does nothing with the icehouse. No mention of the icehouse is made in the deed or in the written contract of sale.

    In a suit for damages by Ms. O'Reilly against Dowery, evidence about the discussion of the icehouse is

    (A) admissible because it shows a mistake as to the terms of the deed
    (B) admissible because it explains the terms of the deed
    (C) inadmissible because it adds new terms to the written agreements
    (D) inadmissible because it shows fraud

12. Zell was a commission salesman for Seating Company; however to conceal the fact that his income depended on making sales the parties executed a written contract providing for a fixed monthly salary.

    When Zell sues for the commissions due him under the oral agreement, evidence about the oral agreement is

    (A) admissible because it shows the written agreement was a fraud
    (B) admissible because it explains what the parties meant by a fixed monthly salary

(C)   inadmissible because it is inconsistent with the written agreement
(D)   inadmissible because the parties would ordinarily have included those terms in the written agreement

13.   Jones contracts to sell the City Center Office Building which he owns to Smith. He tells Smith that the profits on the building are $10,000 a year. The contract contains no mention of profits, but does contain a clause stating that the parties intend the agreement to be final. After the contract is signed and Smith has paid his deposit, he finds that the building is actually unoccupied and that it loses money. In a suit by Smith for a refund of his deposit, evidence about Jones' statement is

(A)   admissible because it shows fraud
(B)   admissible because the contract would not ordinarily have included a mention of the profits
(C)   inadmissible because it varies the terms of the agreement
(D)   inadmissible because it neither shows forgery nor explains any term of the contract

14.   In June of 1974, Hayden agreed to repair Stone's roof. The written contract specified the materials, the price, and that the work was to be completed in a reasonable time. Stone paid in advance and, three months later, when the work still had not been done, Stone sued to get his money back. At the trial, Hayden attempts to introduce evidence to the effect that there was an oral agreement that the work was to be done by Christmas.

This evidence is

(A)   admissible because it explains what Hayden and Stone meant by a reasonable time
(B)   admissible because it is consistent with the express terms of the contract
(C)   inadmissible because it varies the terms of the written agreement
(D)   inadmissible because it does not prove forgery, fraud, or mistake

15.   Deadbeat hires Redbrick to plaster his house. A written agreement is signed which specifies the materials, the price and the date of completion. After the job is done, Deadbeat decides he wants a stucco finish and Redbrick agrees orally to refinish the walls for an additional $1,000. When Deadbeat refuses to pay the extra $1,000, Redbrick sues him.

Evidence about the oral agreement is

(A)   admissible because the oral agreement was made subsequent to the written agreement
(B)   admissible because "stucco finish" explains the terms of the written agreement
(C)   inadmissible because it varies the terms of the written agreement
(D)   inadmissible because it should have been included in the written agreement

Principle Two

The owner of a piece of real estate is liable to trespassers (those who enter the property without express or implied permission) only for injuries caused by hidden artificial conditions which are likely to cause death or serious bodily harm. The owner is liable to licensees (those with express or implied permission to enter the property for their own purposes) for injuries caused by any unusually dangerous condition or activity on the property which the owner knows about and fails to warn the licensee about. The owner is liable to invitees (those who enter the property at the request of the owner and for his benefit) for injuries caused by any condition or activity on the property.

16. Thom was hiking in upstate New York. He got lost, so in order to find his way home, he walked along the Pein Central railroad tracks. Unfortunately, he was struck by a freight train and seriously injured.

    When Thom sues to collect for his injuries, the railroad is found

    (A) liable because a freight train is an artificial condition which is likely to cause serious bodily harm
    (B) liable because it failed to warn Thom about the danger
    (C) not liable because Thom was contributorily negligent
    (D) not liable because Thom was trespassing

17. Letch's Fun City Adult Book Shop has a sign over the door which says, "Browsers Welcome." Heff, a farmer from the Midwest, goes in to look around. Because he is absorbed in the various Danish periodicals, he does not notice the stairs leading down to the Bargain Basement or the "Watch Your Step" sign over them. Heff falls down the stairs and breaks his leg.

    When Heff sues Letch, Letch is found

    (A) liable because stairs are a dangerous artificial condition
    (B) liable because Letch knew that a customer could fall down the stairs
    (C) not liable because there was a warning sign over the stairs
    (D) not liable because Heff was merely browsing, not buying

18. It is the middle of a blizzard, but Dr. Goodheart goes on a house call to the house of Hy Kondry. On his way up the walk, he slips on a patch of ice and fractures his coccyx.

    When Dr. Goodheart sues Kondry, Kondry is found

    (A) liable because Goodheart came at Kondry's request
    (B) liable because icy sidewalks are unusually dangerous
    (C) not liable because icy sidewalks in a blizzard are not an artificial condition
    (D) not liable because a well is natural on farmland

19. John Barleycorn was taking his usual short cut across Farmer Brown's North Forty on his way home from the local pub one night. Farmer Brown had started digging a well the day before and Barleycorn fell into the unfenced hole and suffered multiple injuries.

When Barleycorn sued Brown, Brown was found

(A) liable because Barleycorn had implied permission to walk across Brown's land
(B) liable because an unfenced hole is a dangerous hidden artificial condition at night
(C) not liable because Barleycorn was trespassing
(D) not liable because a well is natural on farmland

20. As a favor, Mary Sitwell is babysitting for the Joneses. After the children are in bed, she turns on the Jones' new television set. Unknown to the Joneses, there was a fault in the wiring. The set short circuits and Mary is badly burned.

When Mary sues the Joneses, the Joneses are found

(A) liable because they received a benefit from Mary's presence
(B) liable because they did not warn Mary about the television set
(C) not liable because they had no way of knowing that the television set was defective
(D) not liable because television sets are usually not dangerous

Proceed directly to the next Part.

PART C. CHOOSING THE NARROWEST JUSTIFYING PRINCIPLE

DIRECTIONS: In this section you will be given several groups of imaginary law cases. Each question will present a set of facts and a fictitious court holding, which you are to presume to be valid. Following each case are four legal principles, lettered (A), (B), (C), and (D). You are to choose the narrowest (most precise) principle which explains the court decision given. However, this principle may not conflict with the holdings given in any of the preceding cases in the same group. The correct answer to the first case in any group will always be the most precise principle which correctly explains the legal decision made. From the second question until the end of each group, you are to select the narrowest principle which does not conflict with any of the previous holdings.

These questions do not presuppose any specific legal knowledge on your part. They are to be answered entirely by the ordinary processes of logical reasoning. Indicate your choice by blackening the appropriate space on the answer sheet.

Group One

21. Wheeler, a New Yorker, was the president and chief stockholder of Wedonics Corporation. When he unexpectedly found himself short of funds, he sold some of his stock to Shyster, a Philadelphia lawyer. In order to convince Shyster to buy the stock, Wheeler falsified the corporation's financial records. Upon discovering the swindle, Shyster brought suit against Wheeler in federal court, claiming fraud under New York law and violations of the Federal Securities Law. Wheeler moved to dismiss for lack of jurisdiction. *Held* for Shyster.

    The *narrowest principle* which justifies this legal decision is:

    (A) Federal courts must hear any case which arises between citizens of different states.
    (B) Federal courts must hear any case which can only be decided by the application of both state and federal law to the same set of facts.
    (C) Federal courts must hear any case between citizens of different states if the litigation involves a question of federal law.
    (D) Federal courts must hear any case brought before them unless there is a compelling reason to decline jurisdiction in the interests of justice.

22. Granola, a young California entrepreneur, decided that the most direct way to acquire wealth beyond the dreams of avarice was to franchise a chain of Natural Fast Food stores. Granola sold the franchise for downtown Burbank to his neighbor, Dimwit. In the course of the negotiations, Granola misrepresented nearly every relevant fact, from the average number of customers per day to the cost of wheat germ. When

the Burbank store ultimately failed, Dimwit sued Granola in federal court claiming fraud under California law. Granola moves to dismiss for lack of jurisdiction. *Held,* for Granola.

The *narrowest principle* which justifies this legal decision and is *not inconsistent* with the ruling given in the previous case is:

(A)   Federal courts may not adjudicate any case concerning the sale of an interest in a business if the case involves a question of state law.

(B)   Federal courts may hear cases between citizens of the same state only if the plaintiff is asserting rights created by a federal law.

(C)   Federal courts may hear a case between citizens of the same state if the case must be decided by the application of both federal and state law to the same set of facts.

(D)   Federal courts must hear any case involving a commercial transaction which affects interstate commerce.

23.   Mammoth Motors, a Michigan car maker, uses its greater economic power to prevent Midget Cars, another Michigan automobile manufacturer, from selling vans and campers to Number 2 Car Rental Company. Midget, although weak in marketing and manufacturing, has a strong legal department, so it sues Mammoth in federal court claiming unfair competition under Michigan law and violations of the Federal Antitrust Law. Mammoth moves to dismiss for lack of jurisdiction. *Held,* for Midget.

The *narrowest principle* which reasonably explains this legal decision and is *not inconsistent* with the rulings given in the preceding cases is:

(A)   Federal courts must hear any case involving a commercial transaction which affects interstate commerce.

(B)   Federal courts may hear any case between citizens of the same state which arises under a state law regulating commerce.

(C)   Federal courts may hear cases which can only be decided by the application of both state and federal law to the same set of facts only if both parties are citizens of the same state.

(D)   Federal courts may hear a case between citizens of the same state only if the case involves a question of federal law.

24.   Codger, an elderly New Jersey resident, decided to retire to a more healthful climate. Dealer, an Arizona realtor, convinced Codger to buy ten allegedly wooded acres which included 200 yards of private beach on scenic Lake Mudhole. When Codger went to inspect his retirement estate, he discovered that Lake Mudhole had been desert since the age of the dinosaurs and that the nearest tree was over 20 miles away. Codger sues Dealer in federal court claiming fraud under Arizona law. Dealer moves to dismiss for lack of jurisdiction. *Held,* for Codger.

The *narrowest principle* which justifies this legal decision and is *not inconsistent* with the rulings given in the preceding cases is:

(A)   Federal courts may hear cases which do not involve a federal law only if the parties are citizens of different states.

(B) Federal courts may hear cases which do not involve a question of state law only if the parties are citizens of different states.

(C) Federal courts may hear a case between citizens of different states only if no question of federal law need be resolved to decide the case.

(D) Federal courts must hear any action brought by a citizen of one state against a citizen of another state.

25. Tony Deadbeat, a Texas businessman, is suffering an acute cash shortage. Since he has exhausted his local credit, he negotiates a loan at the usurious rate of 20% per week from Ponte O'Flesh, a Chicago financier. When Tony's financial position improves, he hires a Chicago lawyer and sues Ponte in Illinois' state court, claiming violations of the federal and Illinois usury laws. Ponte moves to transfer the case to Federal court. *Held,* for Tony.

The *narrowest principle* which justifies this legal decision and is *not inconsistent* with the rulings given in the preceding cases is:

(A) Federal courts may not decide any case which is originally brought in the state court of the state in which the defendant resides.

(B) Federal courts must refuse to hear a case between citizens of different states if the case cannot be decided without reference to state law.

(C) State courts may hear cases between citizens of different states if the case involves a question of state law.

(D) The plaintiff has the option of bringing his action in state or federal court.

Group Two

26. Gizmo is a widget distributor who has more widgets than he can sell. Waldo orders 1,000 widgets at $2.00 each. At that price, Gizmo will make a profit of $0.25 on each widget. Waldo suffers business reverses and decides that he cannot use that many widgets, so he cancels the order. The next day, Max, one of Gizmo's regular customers buys 2,000 widgets at $2.00 each. Gizmo sues Waldo for the $250 profit he would have made if Waldo had not cancelled his order. *Held,* for Gizmo.

The *narrowest principle* which explains this legal decision is:

(A) When the buyer breaches a contract for the sale of goods, the measure of damages is the loss suffered by the seller.

(B) In an action for breach of a sales contract, the measure of damages is the difference between the contract price and the resale price.

(C) When the buyer breaches a contract for the sale of goods, the measure of damages is the seller's expected profit on the transaction.

(D) In an action for breach of a sales contract, the nonbreaching party is entitled to damages sufficient to put him in as good a position as he would have been in if there had been no breach.

314 / *Law School Admission Test*

27. Grower contracts to sell his entire crop of oranges to Bryant for $15,000, a price which will give Grower a profit of $3,000. Bryant's squeezing machinery breaks down so she is unable to use the oranges and refuses to accept delivery. Grower resells the oranges to Linus for $15,000 and sues Bryant for the $3,000 profit he would have made. *Held*, for Bryant.

The *narrowest principle* which explains this legal decision and is *not inconsistent* with the ruling given in the preceding case is:

(A) A seller may not recover damages if, after the buyer breaches, he resells the goods for the contract price.

(B) When the buyer breaches a contract to buy a seller's entire output, then the measure of damages is limited to the difference between the contract price and the resale price.

(C) In an action for breach of a sales contract, the nonbreaching party is entitled to damages sufficient to put him in as good a position as he would have been in if there had been no breach.

(D) When the buyer breaches a sales contract, the measure of damages is the seller's out-of-pocket loss.

28. In August, Kane contracts to sell Baker his entire sugar harvest, 10 tons, for $10,000 to be delivered in November. However, in October, the price of sugar doubles and Kane sells the sugar to Fanny for $20,000. When he fails to deliver the sugar in November, Baker is forced to buy 10 tons on the open market for $22,000. Baker sues Kane for $12,000. *Held*, for Baker.

The *narrowest principle* which explains this legal decision and is *not inconsistent* with the rulings given in the previous cases is:

(A) The measure of damages for breach of a contract for the sale of a seller's entire output is the difference between the contract price and the resale price.

(B) When the seller breaches a contract for the sale of goods, the buyer is entitled to recover any profits which the seller makes as a result of the breach.

(C) In an action for breach of a sales contract, the nonbreaching party is entitled to damages sufficient to put him in as good a position as he would have been in if there had been no breach.

(D) When the selling party to a sales contract fails to make delivery when due, the buyer may recover damages.

29. In January, Tex contracts to sell Kurt's Slaughterhouse 200 head of cattle for delivery on or before June 30, at a price of $10,000. When the shipment doesn't arrive, Kurt buys 200 head of cattle on the open market for $10,000. When the cattle do arrive on July 3, Kurt refuses delivery and Tex resells the cattle for $10,000. Tex sues Kurt for $3,000, the profit he would have made if Kurt had bought the cattle. *Held*, for Kurt.

The *narrowest principle* which explains this legal decision and is *not inconsistent* with the rulings given in the previous cases is:

(A) A seller's damages under a sales contract are limited to his out-of-pocket loss.

(B) Breach by the seller is an absolute defense to the buyer's liability under a sales contract.

(C) The measure of the seller's damages for breach of a sales contract is the difference between the contract price and the price paid by the buyer.

(D) The seller's right to recover from the buyer is contingent upon the seller's timely performance of all his obligations under the contract.

30. In February, Farmer contracts to sell Broker 10,000 bushels of wheat at $2.00 per bushel to be delivered on or before May 1. When the shipment arrives on April 15, Broker discovers that there are only 9,500 bushels. Since the price of wheat has fallen, Broker refuses to accept delivery despite Farmer's offer to prorate the price or to send an additional 500 bushels before May 1. Farmer is forced to resell the wheat for $1.25 per bushel. Farmer sues Broker for the difference of $0.75 a bushel for 9,500 bushels. *Held,* for Farmer.

The *narrowest principle* which explains this legal decision and is *not inconsistent* with the rulings given in the previous cases is:

(A) If a buyer refuses to permit the seller to cure a minor breach of a sales contract, the seller may recover the damages to which he would have been entitled upon the breach by the buyer.

(B) A seller may recover damages for the buyer's breach of a sales contract only if the seller has performed all his obligations under the contracts.

(C) A buyer may only recover damages for breach of a sales contract if the seller is unable to cure the breach within a reasonable time.

(D) Breach by the seller is not a defense to the buyer's liability under a sales contract.

Proceed directly to the next Part.

PART D. CHOOSING THE MAJOR FACTOR (CASE)

DIRECTIONS: In this test you are given a set of facts followed by several questions relating to them. Each question presents a different legal principle to be applied to the set of facts. All principles given are to be assumed to be valid even though they may be either real or imaginary. You are to apply the principle to the given statement of facts and then pick the one of the four alternatives which is the MAJOR FACTOR in the legal decision. Blacken the space on the answer sheet corresponding to the alternative of your choice. These questions do not relate to one another. You are to answer each one solely on the basis of the material given for that specific question. Arrive at your answers by ordinary logical reasoning alone. Do not be influenced by any outside legal knowledge that you may possess.

Case One

The Jones family was once held captive in its home by three escaped convicts for 72 hours. Ultimately, the convicts were recaptured and the Joneses were released unharmed. Although the convicts had treated them courteously, the Joneses were so upset by the experience that shortly thereafter they sold their home and moved to another state. Three years later, Big Budget Films made a movie based loosely on these events, which depicted the convicts as vicious animals who savagely mistreated the family. *Scandal Rag Magazine* reviewed the movie and ran a picture section showing the cast performing scenes from the movie in the original Jones house. The review also included pictures of the Jones family and gave a brief description of the events on which the movie was based. Mr. Jones finds out about the article and sues *Scandal Rag* for damages for invasion of privacy.

31. A suit for damages brought by Jones against *Scandal Rag* is held for Jones on the following principle:

    Any business which uses the picture of a person for purposes of trade without the consent of such person is liable to that person for any damages suffered by him.

    Which of the following was the major factor in the disposition of this case?

    (A) Jones did not give his permission for *Scandal Rag* to use his picture in the magazine.
    (B) *Scandal Rag* invaded Jones' privacy by publishing the article.
    (C) *Scandal Rag* used pictures of actors portraying Jones without Jones' permission.
    (D) *Scandal Rag* used pictures of Jones' house without his permission.

32. A suit for damages brought by Jones against *Scandal Rag* is held for *Scandal Rag* on the following principle:

    A periodical which publishes a report of a news event is liable to the actors in that event only if it willfully or maliciously misrepresents the facts of that event.

    Which of the following was the major factor in the disposition of this case?

    (A) *Scandal Rag* gave an accurate review of the movie.
    (B) *Scandal Rag* did not intend that its readers think that the movie was literally true.
    (C) The only erroneous statements made were about the convicts, not about the Joneses.
    (D) Big Budget Films was responsible for the misrepresentations.

33. A suit for damages brought by Jones against *Scandal Rag* is held for *Scandal Rag* on the following principle:

    A person who was newsworthy can recover damages for defamation only by showing injury to his reputation arising out of false or misleading statements published by the defendant about the events which made him newsworthy.

    Which of the following was the major factor in the disposition of this case?

    (A) Three years after he was held hostage, Jones was no longer newsworthy.
    (B) Jones sued for the misrepresentations made about him by *Scandal Rag*.
    (C) Jones' only injury was to his peace of mind.
    (D) *Scandal Rag* was factually reporting about a movie.

34. A suit for damages by Jones against *Scandal Rag* is held for *Scandal Rag* on the following principle:

    In a suit for damages for unintentional injuries, the plaintiff must show that he suffered an economic loss.

    Which of the following was the major factor in the disposition of this case?

    (A) *Scandal Rag* did not intend to harm Jones.
    (B) *Scandal Rag* was reasonably careful in reporting the story of the Jones' ordeal.
    (C) Jones' business interests were hurt by the story and movie.
    (D) The only injury that Jones suffered was psychological.

35. A suit for damages brought by Jones against *Scandal Rag* is held for Jones on the following principle:

A periodical other than a newspaper or news magazine is unconditionally liable only for any misinformation it publishes about a non-newsworthy individual.

Which of the following was the major factor in the disposition of this case?

(A) Jones was no longer newsworthy three years after he was held hostage.
(B) The inaccuracies in the article were the result of *Scandal Rag*'s negligence.
(C) A movie review is not a news item.
(D) *Scandal Rag* is not a newspaper.

Case Two

Al Mundane is a specialist in cleaning and restoring paintings. J.P. Gotya has a collection of paintings he wants cleaned. They agree on a price of $24,000. Al offers his standard contract to J.P. to sign, but J.P. declines and says he will send Al one of his own standard contracts.

Two days later, Al receives J.P.'s signed contract and mails J.P. a letter accepting the terms. The next week Al realizes he cannot afford to charge only $24,000. Meanwhile, the letter of acceptance has been lost in the mail. Al calls J.P. to see if the letter has been received. When he finds out that it has been lost, he breathes a sigh of relief and tells J.P. that he will have to raise the price to $25,000. J.P. agrees and Al sends him a letter confirming the new price and agreeing to all the other terms in J.P.'s standard contract.

After the letter arrives, but before the paintings are delivered to Al, J.P. cancels the contract, but offers to pay the difference between the $24,000 he originally offered and Al's expenses on the job. Al sues for the profit he would have made on the later agreement: $25,000 less expenses.

36. A suit for damages brought by Al against J.P. is held for J.P. on the following principle:

In order to be enforced, a contract involving a payment of at least $1,000 must be embodied in a writing signed by the party against whom enforcement is demanded and specifying the sum of money due.

Which of the following was the major factor in the disposition of this case?

(A) J.P.'s signed contract set a price of $24,000.
(B) Al signed the second letter he sent J.P. confirming J.P.'s agreement to a price of $25,000.
(C) J.P. did not reply to Al's second letter in writing.
(D) Al's first letter set the terms of the contract.

37. A suit for damages brought by Al against J.P is held for Al on the following principle:

    If the parties intend for a contract to be in writing, then a contract is formed only when the offeror receives written acceptance.

    Which of the following was the major factor in the disposition of this case?

    (A) J.P.'s oral offer was accepted by Al's second letter.
    (B) The signed contract which J.P. sent Al was a written acceptance of Al's offer to do the job for $24,000.
    (C) J.P. cancelled the contract after he received Al's letter.
    (D) J.P. was not responsible for Al's first letter being lost in the mail.

38. A suit for damages brought by Al against J.P. is held for J.P. on the following principle:

    When a contract is concluded by mail, the contract becomes binding at the instant the acceptance is mailed.

    Which of the following was the major factor of the disposition of this case?

    (A) Al's right to damages was fixed when J.P. mailed his form contract.
    (B) The contract became binding when Al mailed his second acceptance.
    (C) A contract was created when Al mailed his first letter even though J.P. never received it.
    (D) Al's second letter was a unilateral change of contract.

39. A suit for damages brought by Al against J.P. is held for J.P. on the following principle:

    A change in the terms of a contract is not binding unless both parties receive some benefit from the change.

    Which of the following was the major factor in the disposition of this case?

    (A) No contract was formed until J.P. received Al's second letter.
    (B) The essential terms of the agreement were settled before J.P. sent Al the form contract.
    (C) J.P. received no greater services for $25,000 than for $24,000.
    (D) Al never accepted J.P.'s offer to do the job for $24,000.

40. A suit for damages brought by Al against J.P. is held for Al on the following principle:

Even though a contract is in writing, it can be amended orally if both of the parties agree.

Which of the following was the major factor in the disposition of this case?

(A) The contract was formed when the parties agreed orally on a price of $24,000.
(B) Al and J.P. intended that the contract be in writing.
(C) No contract was formed until J.P. had received Al's second letter.
(D) The final contract was the one formed over the telephone when J.P. agreed to Al's price increase.

END OF TEST

Go on to do the following Test in this Examination, just as you would be expected to do on the actual exam. You will find correct answers for the entire Examination following the last question. Check your answers carefully after you have completed the whole Examination.

TEST III. PRACTICAL JUDGMENT

TIME: 40 Minutes. 40 Questions.

DIRECTIONS: In this test you will be presented with a detailed case study of a practical business situation. Read the study carefully. Then answer the two sets of questions based upon the reading. In the Data Evaluation questions, you will be asked to classify certain facts on the basis of their importance to the case presented. In the Data Application questions you will be asked to make judgments based upon your comprehension of the information.

Correct and explanatory answers are provided at the end of the exam. After you have completed the entire exam, read the explanations carefully. They'll reinforce your strengths and pinpoint your weaknesses so that you know just what to study to raise your score.

Business Situation I. Conover Coupling Company

The Conover Coupling Company specializes in the manufacture of pipe couplings for use in industrial and residential construction. The company is a subsidiary of Houston Housing Supply, Inc., manufacturer of a large line of construction supplies including sewer and house connection pipes which employ Conover Couplings.

In the Conover Coupling plant, 3-inch to 8-inch diameter sewer and housing connection couplings are machined on two converted metal lathes. These lathes were purchased in used condition six years ago. Larger sewer couplings, of 10-inch to 16-inch diameters, are machined on a small boring mill which is fully depreciated. All three pieces of equipment (the two converted lathes and the boring mill) are badly worn, and considerable difficulty has been encountered recently in machining couplings to meet production specifications. In the opinion of the industrial engineering supervisor, it is necessary either to overhaul or to replace the machines. All three machines are considered to have zero salvage value.

One possibility is to replace the present lathes and boring mill with two new 3-inch to 16-inch diameter automatic lathes. The estimated cost of these lathes is $25,000 each; this figure includes a 10% allowance to cover installation and delivery costs. The engineering supervisor estimates that the new machines would have a physical life of 12 years each and that they would have 25% greater productivity than the old machines (*i.e.*, that they would permit a 25% increase in physical output with the same number of hours of labor). The engineer also believes that their installation in place of the old machines would free approximately 300 square feet of floor space. Rent, heat, light, and other overhead costs allocated on a space basis are charged at an annual rate of $2 per square foot.

S-3272

322 / *Law School Admission Test*

An overhaul of the old lathes, on the other hand, would involve the installation of new bedways, headstocks, carriages, and tool feeds—at an estimated cost of $7,700 in direct labor and parts for each lathe. Repairs needed to put the boring mill in satisfactory condition were estimated to cost an additional $1,100 in direct labor and parts. The engineering supervisor thought that these repairs would prolong the life of the lathes and boring mill approximately 12 years.

Direct labor costs with the present lathes and boring mill have been approximately $24,000 per year, but with the two new lathes it was estimated that these costs will be cut to about $18,000 per year (by eliminating the "graveyard" shift) for the same volume of production. "Normal" maintenance costs for the present two lathes together are approximately $1,700 higher than estimated maintenance costs for the two new lathes. The engineering supervisor believes that "normal" maintenance costs will remain roughly unchanged if the present lathes are repaired; an additional $500 per year maintenance outlay will be necessary, however, to reduce the rejection rate on both of the repaired lathes to that of the new lathes. Current maintenance for the boring mill is $700 annually.

In thinking about the alternatives, the supervisor considered a third possibility—the purchase of one new lathe to take the place of one old lathe. Shipping requirements for couplings are currently being met by operating the lathes and the boring mill six days a week, three eight-hour shifts per day. The same shipping requirements could be met by operating the new and old lathes and the boring mill on the average of two and one-half shifts per day; in other words, the "graveyard" shift would be eliminated on alternate nights. In the event of an increase in production requirements, additional part-time labor would be available to operate the machines on overtime.

With only one new lathe, breakdowns of a week or less would delay shipments, but breakdowns of a longer duration would undoubtedly result in increased handling charges and machining costs. The engineering supervisor estimates that it will cost $1,400 per annum to overcome this risk by maintaining the old discarded lathe as standby equipment. He thinks the lathe could serve this standby purpose without overhaul.

Looking ahead, company officials are confident that sales will equal, if not exceed, their current volume for the next seven years. Sufficient funds are available and will be allotted for repairs of new equipment when plans are approved by the treasurer of Houston Supply, Inc., the parent company.

DATA EVALUATION

DIRECTIONS: Based on your analysis of the Situation, classify each of the following items in one of five categories. On your answer sheet blacken the space under:

(A) if the item is a MAJOR OBJECTIVE in making the decision; that is, one of the outcomes or results sought by the decision-maker.

(B) if the item is a MAJOR FACTOR in arriving at the decision; that is, a consideration explicitly mentioned in the passage that is basic in determining the decision.

(C) if the item is a MINOR FACTOR in making the decision; that is, a secondary consideration that affects the criteria tangentially, relating to a Major Factor rather than to an Objective.

(D) if the item is a MAJOR ASSUMPTION made in deliberating; that is, a supposition or projection made by the decision-maker before weighing the variables.

(E) if the item is an UNIMPORTANT ISSUE in getting to the point; that is, a factor that is insignificant or not immediately relevant to the situation.

1. Salvage value of old lathes

2. Difference between maintenance costs for old and new lathes

3. Physical life of new lathes

4. Purchase price of new lathes

5. Lower rejection rate for machined couplings

6. Overhaul costs for old equipment

7. Difference between space requirements for old and new lathes

8. Productivity of new lathes

9. Labor supply for the "graveyard" shift

10. Demand for 16-inch couplings

11. Fluctuations in production requirements

12. Installation costs for new lathes

13. Meeting production specifications

14. Difference between labor costs with old and new lathes

DATA APPLICATION

DIRECTIONS: Based on your understanding of the Business Situation, answer the following questions testing your comprehension of the information supplied in the passage. For each question, select the choice which best answers the question or completes the statement.

15. The major advantage of acquiring new lathes instead of overhauling the old ones is

   (A) savings of space
   (B) lower initial cost
   (C) lower labor costs
   (D) lower maintenance costs
   (E) greater useful life

16. Which of the following is (are) NOT mentioned as a possible result of a breakdown if only one new lathe is purchased?

   I.   Delayed shipments
   II. Elimination of the "graveyard" shift
   III. Increased handling charges
   IV. Increased maintenance costs
   V.   Increased machining costs

   (A) II and IV only
   (B) I, III and V only
   (C) I, II, III and V only
   (D) I and V only
   (E) II, IV and V only

17. If Conover Coupling Co. buys two new lathes instead of overhauling its old ones, then it should realize annual savings of approximately

   (A) $2,200 (B) $6,000 (C) $9,000 (D) $18,000 (E) $32,000

18. An increase in the hourly wage rate paid lathe operators would most likely have the same effect on the engineering supervisor's decision as

   (A) a price increase for the new lathes
   (B) a decline in the demand for couplings
   (C) a lower price for the overhauling of the old lathes
   (D) a price decrease for the new lathes
   (E) the introduction of new materials that could be machined to greater tolerances on the old lathes

19. Overhaul of the old lathes requires replacement of all of the following EXCEPT

   (A) head stocks
   (B) boring mills
   (C) carriages
   (D) bedways
   (E) tool feeds

20. It can be inferred that which of the following would NOT be considered an overhead cost?

   (A) Rent
   (B) Cost of janitorial services
   (C) Real estate taxes on the plant
   (D) Fire insurance premiums for insurance on the plant
   (E) Fringe benefits paid to lathe operators

Business Situation II. Anscott Corporation

In October, Mr. L. Paul Manley, controller of Anscott Corporation, was trying to decide whether his company should lease its new data processing equipment from the manufacturer or from a third-party lessor. The decision concerning the type of equipment to acquire had been made in June, and during the intervening months the company had been preparing to convert its punched-card system to a combination card-and-magnetic-tape system involving an electronic computer. At the time that the equipment decisions were made, Anscott had deferred a final decision as to whether the equipment would be leased from the manufacturer or acquired in some other manner. This is the decision that now faces Mr. Manley.

Anscott's operations are sufficiently diversified and decentralized that management has not found it necessary to be an innovator in the use of electronic computers for data processing. The company has used XYZ punched-card equipment for many years and has watched the development of computers carefully. A year ago an intensive study of the potential benefits of electronic equipment was undertaken under Mr. Manley's direction. As a result of this study, Mr. Manley recommended that the company modernize its data processing operations by acquiring a medium-sized computer system, the XYZ 2001. This recommendation was justified by an analysis which indicated that annual costs with the new equipment (primarily costs for equipment rental and clerical personnel) would be approximately the same as the costs with existing equipment, so that the additional benefits of faster processing time and greater machine capacity would be obtained for practically no additional cost. After Mr. Manley's recommendation was approved, he began taking the necessary steps to convert to the new system. A new air-conditioning system and extensive modification and rewiring of the existing facilities were required. In addition, Mr. Manley established a programming group within his department to be responsible for the operation of the new equipment. Mr. Manley estimated that the total costs of installation and initial programming for the new system would require an expenditure of approximately $100,000 before the equipment was delivered.

In his initial analysis of computer systems, Mr. Manley had assumed that Anscott would lease any new equipment from XYZ in the same manner that it had leased its punched-card equipment in the past. The standard XYZ lease contract provides an initial lease period of one year, after which time the lease is automatically renewed. After the first year the contract can be cancelled at will by the lessee upon giving 90 days' notice of intention to cancel. Under the lease, XYZ also assumes all responsibility for maintenance of the equipment, and for paying the costs of insurance and property taxes.

In June, Mr. Manley received a letter from Bankers Leasing Corporation which made him wonder if he should consider another method of acquisition. The letter, reproduced in Exhibit 1, implied that it would be much cheaper to lease from Bankers than from XYZ, and Mr. Manley decided to investigate the possibility.

In response to Mr. Manley's letter of inquiry, Mr. Alvin Zises, president of Bankers Leasing Corporation, requested that Mr. Manley provide the following additional information:

1. A list of the equipment to be acquired indicating both the purchase price and the annual rental charged by XYZ.

2. The annual cost of the maintenance contract for each item of equipment which XYZ offered to purchasers of the equipment, and

3. Mr. Manley's estimate of the "economic life" of the equipment.

Mr. Manley had no trouble obtaining the first two pieces of information from the XYZ representative. He had somewhat more trouble, however, estimating the utilization period. The entire system that he planned for Anscott would be a collection of several items of equipment, some of it new (such as the computer), some of it which the company had been leasing for only a few months, and some of it (primarily key punch equipment) which the company had been leasing from XYZ for several years. Mr. Manley summarized Anscott's equipment requirements into categories by age, and sent a copy of that schedule to Mr. Zises.

In his covering letter, Mr. Manley said that it was his best guess that XYZ equipment would have an average life of about nine years. Therefore, he stated, the new equipment ought to last for nine years from the date of installation, the one-year-old equipment ought to be good for eight years, and the older equipment might have an average remaining life of about four years. In part, Mr. Manley based his nine year estimate on the fact that the XYZ trade-in schedule for used equipment (the amount which XYZ indicated it would allow the owner of used equipment against the purchase price of new equipment) showed that the equipment would have no value after seven years. Based on his own experience, Mr. Manley thought seven years might be too conservative because the property would have some resale value at the end of seven years, and that a nine-year life was more realistic. The trade-in schedule is shown below:

XYZ TRADE-IN SCHEDULE

AGE OF EQUIPMENT (IN MONTHS)	TRADE-IN VALUES AS PERCENT OF ORIGINAL COST
12	60%
24	48
36	36
48	24
60	15
72	7 1/2
84	1 1/2
Over 84	0

A couple of weeks after sending off the data, Mr. Manley received a letter from Bankers Leasing Corporation forwarding the schedule reproduced in Exhibit 2. In his letter, Mr. Zises made the following points:

1. Great savings would accrue to Anscott if it leased from Bankers. Assuming that all of the equipment was leased for nine years, and taking advantage of the favorable renewal options, total savings would amount to nearly half a million dollars. Even if the equipment were only leased for four, eight, or nine years, according to age, the savings would amount to over $333,000.

2. Because of Anscott's excellent credit standing, Bankers could offer a lease under which the interest cost was only 6-1/4% per year. While this rate was substantially higher than the 4-1/2% prime rate at the time, Mr. Zises pointed out that compensating balances raised the effective rate, that the money was being provided over a long term, and that Anscott would probably have to pay at least 5% for a loan of similar duration. In addition, by leasing, Anscott avoided all the extra "hidden costs" of debt such as legal fees, investment banker's fees, and the like.

3. The leasing proposal offered two tax advantages: (1) In effect, Anscott would be amortizing the cost of the equipment over its economic life, and this amortization would be tax deductible. Thus, for the new equipment, Anscott would amortize the full cost over nine years which would be more advantageous than depreciation under which Anscott would probably have to use a ten-year life and provide a 10% scrap value. (2) The monthly lease payments were composed of level amortization of the cost of the equipment plus interest of 6-1/4% of the unamortized balance. This meant that lease payments in the early years were higher than the payments in the later years, thus providing larger tax deductions in the early years than would be possible if a "level payment" lease were used. The monthly payments would be due at the beginning of each month.

4. The renewal provisions of the lease were quite favorable to Anscott. After the initial, noncancellable term, Anscott could continue to lease the equipment for an annual cost of one-half of 1 percent of the cost of the equipment, payable at the rate of one-twenty-fourth of 1 percent per month.

5. The lease contract would provide desirable flexibility for Anscott by permitting the lessee to dispose of any piece of equipment at any time by requesting Bankers to sell the equipment. In such an event, Anscott would be responsible for making sure that Bankers recovered the unamortized cost of the equipment, but if any excess over the unamortized cost were realized, Bankers would refund the excess to Anscott as an "adjustment of rent."

6. Anscott would receive the full benefit of any residual value of the equipment after the initial term of the lease. Any proceeds from the disposal of the equipment after it was fully amortized would be paid to Anscott as an "adjustment of rent."

Mr. Zises stated that the terms of this offer were firm, but were subject to adjustment in the event that the purchase price of the equipment were to change before execution of the agreement, in which event the terms of the lease would be adjusted pro rata. He also pointed out that the lease would be a "net lease," under which Anscott would be responsible for the payment of property taxes and insurance.

In examining the proposal from Bankers Leasing Corporation Mr. Manley could think of only three adjustments that needed to be made to the cost comparison. The cost of property taxes and insurance on the equipment, while minor, would probably amount to about 3% of the unamortized cost of the equipment. The maintenance costs included in the comparison were only the cost of the XYZ service contract, and Mr. Manley knew that, in addition, the owner of a piece of equipment might have to bear the cost of certain replacement parts which would be replaced free if the equipment were leased from XYZ. Finally, the cost comparison had ignored the federal excise tax on the equipment. This tax amounted to 10% of the purchase price of the equipment, or 10% of each year's lease payment when the equipment was leased from the manufacturer. The tax applied only to machines and not to "systems" which meant that all of the equipment with model numbers in the 2000 series would not be subject to the tax.

Mr. Manley knew that all of these minor considerations would have little impact on the calculations shown in Exhibit 2, and he was favorably impressed by the potential savings offered by the leasing company. Considering the heavy initial costs of installing the new system, Mr. Manley thought it was quite likely that Anscott would continue to use the equipment for many years, and he wondered if it would be wise for the company to pay a heavy "insurance premium" to XYZ in order to protect itself against obsolescence of the equipment.

EXHIBIT 1

LETTER FROM BANKERS LEASING CORPORATION

Dear Mr. Manley:

The rental charge set by most computer manufacturers must cover the following costs:

1.   Amortization of the cost of the equipment over as short a period as possible for quick recovery of the cost by the manufacturer. This period may be as short as 50 months for equipment with a possible life of eight to ten years.

2.   A reserve or "insurance premium" for obsolescence. In the ordinary rental program offered by some manufacturers, the reserve for obsolescence is sometimes sufficiently high to more than doubly recover any

possible obsolescence charges. As prudent businessmen, some manufacturers strive to achieve a "loss ratio" on obsolescence of less than 50% of the reserve.

3. A reserve for physical maintenance and service.

4. A cost-of-capital charge, which, depending upon the manufacturer, may run from over 15% to over 30% per annum (pretax) to enable the manufacturer's shareholders to receive an acceptable return on their investment in ownership of the equipment.

5. After fully recovering the cost of the asset the manufacturer usually may continue the rent at or near the same level.

6. Additional rents are charged for extra-shift operations.

In the leasing program which we offer to lessees of excellent credit, rent has the following components:

1. A lower monthly amortization charge because the asset is amortized over a period which closely corresponds to the economic life. For purposes of computing rent the amortization period may be eight or even ten years.

2. After full amortization, the monthly rent drops to an insignificant amount.

3. A cost-of-capital which is based not on the manufacturer's pretax equity requirements but on the excellent credit of your company. The cost-of-capital component compares not unfavorably with your total cost of debt financing.

EXHIBIT 2

YEAR	1	2	3	4	5
BANKERS LEASING					
9-YEAR RENT........	$49,782.08	$47,753.62	$45,725.16	$43,696.68	$41,668.20
8-YEAR RENT.......	7,629.59	7,305.51	6,981.42	6,657.31	6,333.23
4-YEAR RENT.......	3,248.84	3,082.58	2,916.33	2,749.74	53.20
MAINTENANCE.....	11,099.00	11,099.00	11,099.00	12,576.00	12,576.00
TOTAL	$71,759.51	$69,240.71	$66,721.91	$65,679.73	$60,630.63
XYZ	101,499.00	101,499.00	101,499.00	101,499.00	101,499.00
NET SAVINGS	$29,739.49	$32,258.29	$34,777.09	$35,819.27	$40,868.37

DATA EVALUATION

DIRECTIONS: *Based on your analysis of the Situation, classify each of the following items in one of five categories. On your answer sheet blacken the space under:*

(A) *if the item is a MAJOR OBJECTIVE in making the decision; that is, one of the outcomes or results sought by the decision-maker.*

(B) *if the item is a MAJOR FACTOR in arriving at the decision; that is, a consideration explicitly mentioned in the passage that is basic in determining the decision.*

(C) *if the item is a MINOR FACTOR in making the decision; that is, a secondary consideration that affects the criteria tangentially, relating to a Major Factor rather than to an Objective.*

(D) *if the item is a MAJOR ASSUMPTION made in deliberating; that is, a supposition or projection made by the decision-maker before weighing the variables.*

(E) *if the item is an UNIMPORTANT ISSUE in getting to the point; that is, a factor that is insignificant or not immediately relevant to the situation.*

21. Useful life of the equipment

22. Cost of initial programming

23. Noncancellable terms of the respective leases

24. Cost of replacement parts

25. Cost of installation

26. Rate of technological innovation in the computer industry

27. Modernization of Anscott's data processing system

28. Monthly rental amounts under the respective leases

29. Insurance premiums on the equipment

30. Maximum value for money spent

31. The prime interest rate

32. Risk of obsolescence of the new system

33. Cost of a maintenance contract

34. Wages paid to clerical personnel

DATA APPLICATION

DIRECTIONS: Based on your understanding of the Business Situation, answer the following questions testing your comprehension of the information supplied in the passage. For each question, select the choice which best answers the question or completes the statement.

35. An XYZ sales representative who calls on Mr. Manley would be most likely to offer which of the following rebuttals to Mr. Zises' letter?

    (A) Bankers Leasing is unable to provide the same high quality maintenance services as XYZ.
    (B) XYZ deserves a higher "cost-of-capital" charge because it took the risk of developing the equipment.
    (C) The amount of rent for extra shift operation is very low.
    (D) Since the rate of technological innovation in the computer industry is so rapid, the vast majority of computer users "trade up" to newer systems within four years, even though their equipment may still be operational for another four or five years.
    (E) The maintenance and service reserve built into the XYZ rental charge is no greater than the cost of a service contract which Mr. Manley expects to purchase anyway.

36. Mr. Zises used all of the following "hidden costs" to support his position that the 6-1/4% interest component in the Bankers Lease was not unreasonable despite the fact that the prime rate was only 4-1/2%, EXCEPT

    (A) legal fees
    (B) amortization of the cost of the equipment
    (C) compensating balances
    (D) premium interest paid for long term loans
    (E) investment bankers' fees

37. Which of the following is (are) given as reasons for Mr. Manley's decision to acquire an XYZ 2001:

    I. Equipment rental costs and clerical salaries with the 2001 would be no greater than those costs with the current equipment.
    II. Faster processing time with the 2001.
    III. The 2001 system is exempt from the excise tax.
    IV. Generous trade-in allowances for used equipment.

    (A) I only
    (B) III only
    (C) I and II only
    (D) III and IV only
    (E) I, II, and IV only

38. If Anscott Corp. leases through Bankers Leasing instead of directly from XYZ, how long will it be before the savings are greater than the costs of installation and initial programming?

    (A) 1 year 8 months
    (B) 2 years 2 months
    (C) 2 years 6 months
    (D) 2 years 11 months
    (E) 3 years 2 months

39. In addition to the rental, all of the following are differences between the XYZ lease and the Bankers lease EXCEPT

    (A) responsibility for the payment of excise taxes
    (B) responsibility for payment of property taxes
    (C) responsibility for insurance
    (D) responsibility for maintenance
    (E) cancellation clause

40. Mr. Manley would be most likely to decide against leasing through Bankers if he learned that

    (A) XYZ was offering a maintenance contract to purchasers (as opposed to direct lessees) which included replacement parts as needed at no extra charge
    (B) the excise tax on the equipment was being eliminated
    (C) actual resale prices for used XYZ equipment were much lower than the trade-in allowance offered by XYZ
    (D) XYZ was going to reduce the purchase price of its 2001 system
    (E) the equipment would be exempt from property taxes

END OF TEST

Go on to do the following Test in this Examination, just as you would be expected to do on the actual exam. You will find correct answers for the entire Examination following the last question. Check your answers carefully after you have completed the whole Examination.

TEST IV. DATA INTERPRETATION

TIME: 30 Minutes. 25 Questions.

DIRECTIONS: This test consists of data presented in graphic form followed by questions based on the information contained in the graph, chart or table shown. After studying the data given, choose the best answer for each question and blacken the corresponding space on the answer sheet. Answer each group of questions solely on the basis of the information given or implied in the data preceding it.

Correct and explanatory answers are provided at the end of the exam. After you have completed the entire exam, read the explanations carefully. They'll reinforce your strengths and pinpoint your weaknesses so that you know just what to study to raise your score.

Questions 1 to 6

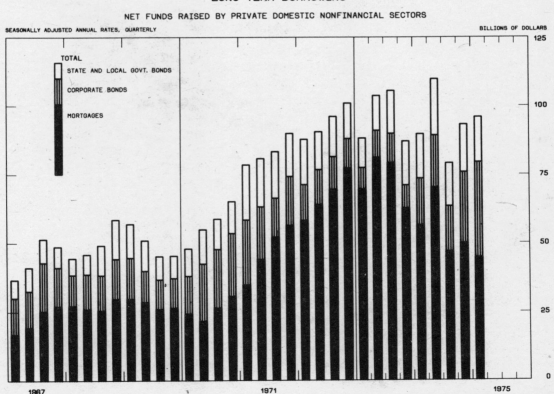

LONG-TERM BORROWING

NET FUNDS RAISED BY PRIVATE DOMESTIC NONFINANCIAL SECTORS

1. During the quarter that shows the greatest amount of any borrowing what percentage was raised through corporate bonds?

   (A) 18%
   (B) 28%
   (C) 50%

   (D) 57%
   (E) 70%

2. The value of state and local government bonds sold during the first quarter of 1968 was what percent of the amount sold during the peak quarter for sales of state and local government bonds?

   (A) 20%
   (B) 30%
   (C) 40%

   (D) 50%
   (E) 67%

3. From the second quarter of 1970 through the second quarter of 1973, the amount of funds raised through mortgages

   (A) increased 367%
   (B) more than quadrupled
   (C) doubled
   (D) was greater each quarter than in the previous quarters
   (E) increased 263%

4. In which year did mortgages account for less than half the total amount of funds raised?

   (A) 1967
   (B) 1969
   (C) 1971

   (D) 1973
   (E) in no year

5. By how much did the amount of money raised through mortgages decline between the third quarter of 1973 and the third quarter of 1974?

   (A) $4 billion
   (B) $8 billion
   (C) $20 billion
   (D) $35 billion
   (E) $52 billion

6. The longest period of uninterrupted quarter to quarter increases in total amount of funds raised was

   (A) 6 consecutive quarters
   (B) 9 consecutive months
   (C) 9 consecutive quarters
   (D) 10 consecutive quarters
   (E) 3 years

Questions 7 to 12

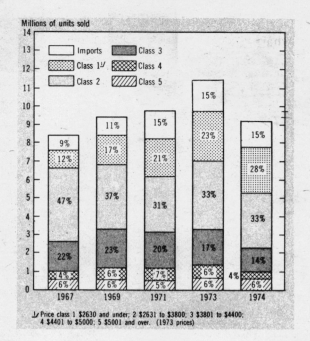

Consumers buying smaller cars

Source: Automotive News and BDC

Millions of units sold

Legend:
- Imports
- Class 1 ¹⁄
- Class 2
- Class 3
- Class 4
- Class 5

¹⁄ Price class 1 $2630 and under; 2 $2631 to $3800; 3 $3801 to $4400; 4 $4401 to $5000; 5 $5001 and over. (1973 prices)

7. For which class did unit sales decline the least between 1973 and 1974?

   (A) Imports   (B) Class 1   (C) Class 2   (D) Class 4   (E) Class 5

8. How many fewer Class 2 cars were sold in 1974 than in 1973?

   (A) 2.3 million   (D) 700,000
   (B) 1.8 million   (E) None, the same number were sold in each year.
   (C) 1 million

9. Between 1967 and 1973, the number of imported cars sold in the United States

   (A) increased by 6%   (D) remained approximately constant
   (B) increased by 67%   (E) It's impossible to tell from information
   (C) increased by 125%   available.

10. In 1973, what was the minimum dollar value of sales of Class 5 cars?

    (A) $3.4 billion   (D) $345 million
    (B) $690,000   (E) It is impossible to tell from the information
    (C) $3.4 million   given.

11. Between 1969 and 1971, which class had the largest percentage increase in unit sales?

    (A) Imports   (B) Class 1   (C) Class 3   (D) Class 4   (E) Class 5

12. What was the maximum total dollar volume of sales of imported cars in 1967?

    (A) $2.6 billion   (D) $1.5 billion
    (B) $1.9 billion   (E) It is impossible to tell from the information
    (C) $3.2 billion   available.

Questions 13 to 18

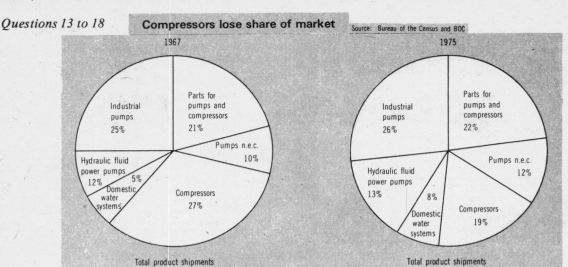

Compressors lose share of market Source: Bureau of the Census and BDC

1967 — Total product shipments $1.9 billion

Industrial pumps 25%
Parts for pumps and compressors 21%
Pumps n.e.c. 10%
Hydraulic fluid power pumps 12%
Domestic water systems 5%
Compressors 27%

1975 — Total product shipments $3.1 billion

Industrial pumps 26%
Parts for pumps and compressors 22%
Pumps n.e.c. 12%
Hydraulic fluid power pumps 13%
Domestic water systems 8%
Compressors 19%

13. How much did the dollar value of shipments of parts increase between 1967 and 1975?

(A) $1.2 billion (B) $120 million (C) $283 million (D) 1% (E) 4.7%

14. Between 1967 and 1975 the dollar value of compressor shipments

(A) declined by 8%   (D) increased by 15%
(B) declined by 30%   (E) increased by 63%
(C) remained nearly constant

15. The value of shipments of which product group increased by the largest percentage between 1967 and 1975?

(A) parts   (D) pumps n.e.c.
(B) hydraulic fluid power pumps   (E) domestic water systems
(C) industrial pumps

16. In 1975, shipments of industrial pumps were

(A) $806 million   (D) 1% greater than they were in 1967
(B) $475 million   (E) none of the above
(C) $12 million

17. The difference in the value of shipments between the two smallest categories of products in 1967 was

(A) $124 million   (D) $76 million
(B) $38 million   (E) $93 million
(C) $95 million

18. The dollar volume of shipments of hydraulic fluid power pumps in 1967 and 1975 combined was

(A) $775 million   (D) $619 million
(B) $631 million   (E) $403 million
(C) $1.25 billion

Questions 19 to 25

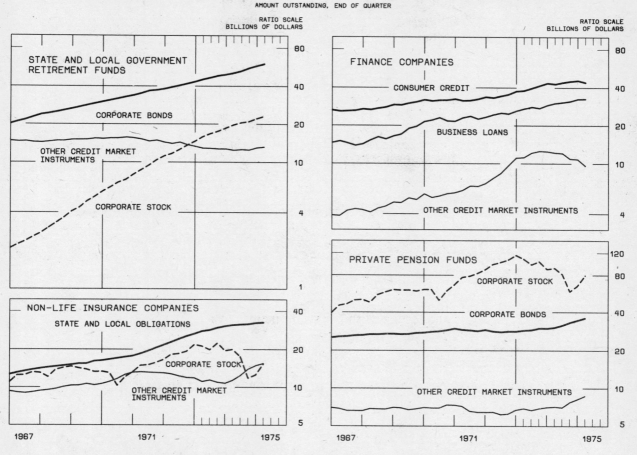

PRINCIPAL EARNING ASSETS OF SELECTED NONBANK FINANCIAL INSTITUTIONS

AMOUNT OUTSTANDING, END OF QUARTER

19. In the third quarter of 1974, state and local government retirement funds holdings of corporate stock were approximately what percent of their holdings of corporate bonds?

(A) 20%   (B) 33%   (C) 50%   (D) 75%   (E) 100%

20. In the first quarter of 1967, state and local government retirement funds owned corporate bonds whose total value was approximately how many times that of the corporate stock they owned?

(A) 4   (B) 34   (C) 8   (D) 20
(E)   It is impossible to tell from the information available.

21. From the end of 1972 until the end of 1974, the value of private pension funds holdings of corporate stocks

(A)   decreased by 25%   (D)   remained approximately constant
(B)   decreased by 35%   (E)   increased
(C)   decreased by 50%

22. At the beginning of 1970, the total value of credit market instruments held by non-bank financial institutions was approximately

   (A) $25 million
   (B) $39 million
   (C) $17 billion
   (D) $25 billion
   (E) $39 billion

23. From the beginning of 1967 through the end of 1974, the asset that grew by the largest percentages was

   (A) finance company holdings of credit market instruments
   (B) private pension fund holdings of corporate stock
   (C) non-life insurance company holdings of corporate stock
   (D) state and local government retirement fund holdings of corporate stocks
   (E) non-life insurance companies holdings of state and local obligations

24. The group of institutions with the highest amount of total assets at the end of 1974 was

   (A) state and local government retirement funds
   (B) non-life insurance companies
   (C) finance companies
   (D) private pension funds
   (E) It is impossible to tell from the information available.

25. Which of the following can one infer from the graph shown about the period from January 1, 1973 through December 31, 1974?

   I. Private pension funds sold more corporate stocks than they bought.

   II. Non-life insurance companies sold more corporate stock than they bought.

   III. Stock prices generally increased.

   (A) None
   (B) I and II only
   (C) III only
   (D) II and III only
   (E) I, II and III only

END OF TEST

Go on to do the following Test in this Examination, just as you would be expected to do on the actual exam. You will find correct answers for the entire Examination following the last question. Check your answers carefully after you have completed the whole Examination.

TEST V. ERROR RECOGNITION

TIME: 20 Minutes. 35 Questions.

DIRECTIONS: This is a test of your ability to recognize standard written English. Some of the sentences presented are acceptable as written English. Others contain errors of diction, verbosity or grammar. No one sentence contains more than one kind of error. Read each sentence carefully, then classify each according to the categories that follow. Mark your answer sheet:

(A) if the sentence contains an error in DICTION; that is, the use of a word which is incorrect because its meaning does not fit the sentence, or because it is not acceptable in standard written English.

(B) if the sentence is VERBOSE; that is, wordy or repetitious without justification by the need for emphasis.

(C) if the sentence contains FAULTY GRAMMAR; that is, errors in parallelism, number, case, tense, etc.

(D) if the sentence contains none of these errors.

Correct and explanatory answers are provided at the end of the exam. After you have completed the entire exam, read the explanations carefully. They'll reinforce your strengths and pinpoint your weaknesses so that you know just what to study to raise your score.

1. A number of steps should be taken in preparing to work on soft ground.

2. Single folks will certainly like Mr. Martin's new establishment.

3. I wish to buy a country home, irregardless of the cost.

4. The tanker was expected to skirt around submerged obstacles.

5. In Puritan New England, fiction was banned as evil and wicked until the end of the eighteenth century.

6. No question of there being any need for assistance has yet arisen.

7. Joseph and Mary is brother and sister.

8. This is a present from John and I.

9. The amount of money lost in the nursing home fraud is huge and massive.

10. Nobody was there outside of me and three of my friends.

11. When I learned that Henry had been lying to me, I became plenty angry.

12. A man who laughs at the right time will make friends.

13. Last Sunday I was so tired that I laid in bed the whole day.

14. The idea that London failed to produce art as vital as that of Paris during this period, because its society was less colorful and permissive, is somewhat undermined by Everett's exceedingly lively memoirs.

15. With a little advance planning, you can simplify your culinary chores for Easter.

16. If you use a power tool to cut the plates, it is obvious that you should be very careful of your fingers.

17. The new restaurant that has just opened serves French, Italian, and Thai cuisine at moderate prices.

18. Mr. Jones said it would be presumptive of him to suggest that his employer pay for the meal.

19. Although small in size, the *Beattlebottom* had a distinguished war record.

20. Such cases are rare, occurring infrequently.

21. In this area it is often exceedingly cold and frigid; for this reason there is little tourism here.

22. Every man, woman, and child are to be included.

23. Notify whomever is available.

24. Whom is the author of *Moby Dick*?

25. Did you loose a pearl necklace yesterday in this classroom?

26. In the era of the Great Rebellion, strange events were then reported at Baskerville Hall.

27. Many a town and village is rejoicing tonight.

28. It took me a long time to realize that William and me are incompatible.

29. Shortly after midnight Saturday the crowd had grown to several thousand.

30. Somehow, apparently, Mr. Smith's assistants got ahold of about a thousand copies of Mr. Jones' book.

31. Between 1890 and 1908, all but two of the Western territories became states, the number of stars on the American flag increasing from forty-three to forty-six.

32. Washington's confidence in closer Japanese-American relations was based on more than hopeful optimism.

33. We expected the path to be straight, but it was torturous instead.

34. The President addressed some forty-odd reporters at the press conference.

35. The Senator is certainly not adverse to reading about himself.

END OF TEST

TEST VI. SENTENCE CORRECTION

TIME: 20 Minutes. 25 Questions.

DIRECTIONS: Some part of each of the following sentences is underlined. After each sentence are five ways of stating the underlined part. Choice A simply repeats the original sentence or phrase. If you think that the original sentence is more effective than any of the alternatives, pick Choice A. If you believe the underlined part is incorrect, select from the other choices (B, C, D, or E) the one you think is best and blacken the corresponding space on the answer sheet. In choosing the best alternative, consider grammar, sentence structure, punctuation and word usage. Do not choose an answer that changes the meaning of the original sentence.

Correct and explanatory answers are provided at the end of the exam. After you have completed the entire exam, read the explanations carefully. They'll reinforce your strengths and pinpoint your weaknesses so that you know just what to study to raise your score.

1. The class studies many types of poetry, <u>such as</u> the ballad, the epic, and the lyric.

   (A) such as
   (B) as
   (C) such like
   (D) to include
   (E) which of

2. No one went except <u>father and me.</u>

   (A) father and me.
   (B) father and I.
   (C) father and myself.
   (D) father along with me.
   (E) I and father.

3. <u>On account of the winters are long and cold, nothing can live without shelter.</u>

   (A) On account of the winters are long and cold, nothing can live without shelter.
   (B) Because the winters are long and cold, nothing can live without shelter.
   (C) Nothing, the winter being long and cold, can live without shelter.
   (D) Without shelter nothing can live, the winters being long and cold.
   (E) The winters, long and cold, nothing can live without shelter.

4. <u>In the year of 1791 our house looked no different than the way it looks</u> <u>today</u>.

   (A)   In the year of 1791 our house looked no different than the way it looks today.

   (B)   In the year 1791 our house looked no different than the way it looks today.

   (C)   In the year of 1791 our house looked no different from the way it looks today.

   (D)   In the year 1791 our house was no different from today's.

   (E)   In the year 1791 our house looked no different from the way it looks today.

5. The lecture was concluded by <u>reciting a passage from Byron</u>.

   (A)   reciting a passage from Byron.

   (B)   the recision of a passage from Byron.

   (C)   a passage of Byron's being recited.

   (D)   a passage from Byron.

   (E)   the recitation of a passage from Byron.

6. When learning how to ride a bicycle, <u>practice is needed</u>.

   (A)   practice is needed.

   (B)   one thing you need is practice.

   (C)   you need practice.

   (D)   one thing you need will be practice.

   (E)   practice is to be done.

7. Even the men in the class had to admit that <u>both from the viewpoint of</u> <u>economics and history</u>, restrictions are disappearing.

   (A)   both from the viewpoint of economics and history,

   (B)   both from the viewpoints of economics and from that of history,

   (C)   both from the viewpoint of economics and from that of history,

   (D)   from the viewpoint both of economics and history,

   (E)   from the viewpoint of both economics and history,

8. Each of the <u>rocks which form the solid crust of our planet are</u> more than a billion years old.

   (A)   rocks which form the solid crust of our planet are

   (B)   rocks, which form the solid crust of our planet, are

   (C)   rocks which form the solid crust of our plant, is

   (D)   rocks which form the solid crust of our planet is

   (E)   rocks which form the solid crust of our planet have existed

9. Give everyone the credit <u>for having the courage of their convictions.</u>

    (A)   for having the courage of their convictions.
    (B)   for having the courage of their own convictions.
    (C)   for having courage.
    (D)   for having the courage of his convictions.
    (E)   because they have the courage of their convictions.

10. <u>Are you more interested in Dickens' life rather than in his art?</u>

    (A)   Are you more interested in Dickens' life rather than in his art?
    (B)   Are you more interested in Dicken's life or in his art?
    (C)   Are you interested in Dicken's life rather than in his art?
    (D)   Are you interested in Dickens' life rather than in his art?
    (E)   Are you interested in art or in the life of Dickens?

11. He picked up his report card, and was <u>unexpectedly surprised</u> to see that he had received excellent grades.

    (A)   He picked up his report card, and was unexpectedly surprised
    (B)   He picked his report card, and was unexpectedly surprised
    (C)   He picked his report card and was surprised
    (D)   He picked up his report card, and unexpectedly
    (E)   He picked up his report card, and was surprised

12. <u>It was an agreement to which all of them were parties to it.</u>

    (A)   It was an agreement to which all of them were parties to it.
    (B)   It was an agreement to which all of them were parties to.
    (C)   It was an agreement which all of them were parties to it.
    (D)   It was an agreement, all of them being parties to it.
    (E)   It was an agreement to which all of them were parties.

13. This is the man <u>of whom</u> I was telling you about.

    (A)   of whom
    (B)   of who
    (C)   as
    (D)   that
    (E)   what

14. I met the woman <u>who's dog this is.</u>

    (A)   who's dog this is.
    (B)   who'se dog this is.
    (C)   whose dog this is.
    (D)   of whom this is the dog.
    (E)   and this is her dog.

15. Their chief opponent was Carmins, <u>a shrewd politician, but who is now less popular than he was.</u>

    (A)   a shrewd politician, but who is now less popular than he was.
    (B)   a shrewd, but less popular politician.
    (C)   a shrewd politician and less popular than he was.
    (D)   a shrewd politician, who is now less popular than he was.
    (E)   a shrewd politician, yet one who is now less popular than he was.

16. <u>Dorothy was so enamored of William that she would not comply to</u> her father's wish that she stay away from the lad.

    (A)   Dorothy was so enamored of William that she would not comply to
    (B)   Dorothy was so enamored of William that she would not comply with
    (C)   Dorothy was so enamored with William that she would not comply with
    (D)   Dorothy was so enamored with William that she would not comply to
    (E)   Dorothy, enamored with William, would not comply to

17. <u>To learn tennis, a good teacher should help you.</u>

    (A)   To learn tennis, a good teacher should help you.
    (B)   When learning tennis, a good teacher should help you.
    (C)   To receive instruction in tennis, a good teacher should help you.
    (D)   To learn tennis, you should have the help of a good teacher.
    (E)   When learning tennis, it is always advisable to enlist the aid of a good teacher.

18. <u>A beautiful green vine of some kind; growing up the west side of the house it was.</u>

    (A)   A beautiful green vine of some kind; growing up the west side of the house it was.
    (B)   Growing up the west side of the house, it was a beautiful green vine of some kind.
    (C)   Growing up the west side of the house, a beautiful green vine of some kind.
    (D)   A beautiful green vine of some kind it was growing up the west side of the house.
    (E)   A beautiful green vine of some kind was growing up the west side of the house.

19. Although Griboyedov wrote great and original plays, <u>neither he nor Gogol used his talents to create</u> a school of Russian drama.

    (A)   neither he nor Gogol used his talents to create
    (B)   neither he nor Gogol used their talents to create
    (C)   neither he or Gogol used their talents to create
    (D)   neither he nor Gogol used his talents creatively for
    (E)   neither he nor Gogol used their talents in order to create

20. Parents are the ones <u>whom we believe ought to insist upon their childrens'</u> obeying orders.

    (A) whom we believe ought to insist upon their childrens'
    (B) whom we believe ought to insist upon their children's
    (C) who we believe ought to insist upon their childrens'
    (D) who we believe ought to insist upon their children
    (E) who we believe ought to insist upon their children's

21. Margaret had two desires, of which the first <u>was money; in the second place, she wanted fame.</u>

    (A) was money; in the second place, she wanted fame.
    (B) was for money; the second for fame.
    (C) was money, the second for fame.
    (D) place was money, the second place fame.
    (E) was for money and the second for fame.

22. <u>In later years he was pursued by remorse.</u>

    (A) In later years he was pursued by remorse.
    (B) In later years, he was pursued by remorse for something he had done that he was ashamed of.
    (C) In later years, he was pursued by remorse for something he had done of which he was ashamed.
    (D) Afterward in later years, he was pursued by remorse.
    (E) Afterward in later years, he was pursued by remorse for something he had done of which he was ashamed.

23. Our orchard will bear no oranges, <u>on account of</u> the frost.

    (A) on account of
    (B) due to
    (C) caused by

    (D) because of the effect of
    (E) because of the affect of

24. It is necessary that the stock <u>is to be</u> sold.

    (A) is to be
    (B) will be
    (C) be

    (D) shall be
    (E) would be

25. I do not know <u>as</u> I understand you.

    (A) as
    (B) that
    (C) as though

    (D) as whether
    (E) as if

END OF TEST

TEST VII. QUANTITATIVE COMPARISON

TIME: 15 Minutes. 25 Questions.

DIRECTIONS: For each of the following questions two quantities are given . . . one in Column A; and one in Column B. Compare the two quantities and mark your answer sheet with the correct, lettered conclusion. These are your options:

A: if the quantity in Column A is the greater;
B: if the quantity in Column B is the greater;
C: if the two quantities are equal;
D: if the relationship cannot be determined from the information given.

COMMON INFORMATION: In each question, information concerning one or both of the quantities to be compared is given in the Common Information column. A symbol that appears in any column represents the same thing in Column A as in Column B.

NUMBERS: All numbers used are real numbers.

FIGURES: Assume that the position of points, angles, regions, and so forth, are in the order shown.

> *Assume that the lines shown as straight are indeed straight. Figures are assumed to lie in a plane unless otherwise indicated.*

Figures accompanying questions are intended to provide information you can use in answering the questions. However, unless a note states that a figure is drawn to scale, you should solve the problems by using your knowledge of mathematics, and NOT by estimating sizes by sight or by measurement.

Correct and explanatory answers are provided at the end of the exam. After you have completed the entire exam, read the explanations carefully. They'll reinforce your strengths and pinpoint your weaknesses so that you know just what to study to raise your score.

Common Information	Column A.	Column B.
1.	x	y
2. $7x - 3y = 0$ $\quad x > 0$	$\sqrt{\dfrac{1}{x}}$	$\sqrt{\dfrac{1}{y}}$
3. $\quad y > 0$	x^2	y^3
4.	$\dfrac{x^2}{y^2}$	$1/5$

Common Information	Column A.	Column B.
5.	$6 \times 10^{-6} + 5 \times 10^{-4}$	50×10^{-5}
6.	$\dfrac{5 + 10^{-3}}{5 + 10^{-6}}$	1.01
7.	$\dfrac{52}{.01}$	$.52$
8.	$\dfrac{.01}{52}$	2×10^{-4}
9.	$\dfrac{1}{7/4}$	$\dfrac{1}{7 \times 4}$
10.	$x^2 + 4x + 4 = y \qquad y = 0$	$x + 2$	$y + 1$

	Common Information	Column A.	Column B.
11.	Consider tossing two dice, each six sided (6 dots, 1 to 6).	2 (2 dots)	12 (2 sixes)
12.	Assess probability of throwing the following.	7	11

	Common Information	Column A.	Column B.
13.		Arc $\overset{\frown}{CBA}$ − Arc $\overset{\frown}{CD}$	Arc $\overset{\frown}{AD}$
14.		length $\overline{AC}$	length $\overline{AD}$
15.		length of Arc $\overset{\frown}{CD}$	length $\overline{CE}$
16.		length $\overline{OF}$	1/2 length $\overline{CE}$
17.	BC is parallel to AD < CAD = 30°	measure of angle OAF	Arc $\overset{\frown}{AB}$

Common Information	Column A.	Column B.
18.	x	z
19. $3x + 2z = 4y$ $y = 2$	x	y
20.	z	$8 - \dfrac{3x}{2}$
21.	$10^3 - 10^2$	10
22.	60 percent of 30	30 percent of 60
23.	$\sqrt{14.5762}$	3.5
24.	$(\sqrt{3})^3$	$(3\sqrt{8})^2$
25.	$\dfrac{\sqrt[5]{33}}{2}$	1

END OF EXAMINATION

Now that you have completed the last Test in this Examination, use your available time to make sure that you have written in your answers correctly on the Answer Sheet. Then, after your time is up, check your answers with the Correct Answers we have provided for you. Derive your scores for each Test Category and determine where you are weak so as to plan your study accordingly.

CORRECT ANSWERS FOR VERISIMILAR EXAMINATION IV.

TEST I. LOGICAL REASONING

1.C	3.B	5.A	7.C	9.C	11.B	13.D	15.C
2.D	4.B	6.B	8.D	10.C	12.A	14.B	

TEST II. PRINCIPLES AND CASES

1.C	6.C	11.C	16.D	21.C	26.C	31.A	36.A
2.B	7.A	12.C	17.D	22.B	27.B	32.B	37.A
3.D	8.B	13.A	18.A	23.D	28.C	33.C	38.C
4.B	9.A	14.A	19.B	24.A	29.D	34.D	39.B
5.C	10.B	15.A	20.A	25.A	30.A	35.A	40.D

TEST III. PRACTICAL JUDGMENT

1.E	6.B	11.E	16.A	21.D	26.D	31.E	36.B
2.C	7.C	12.C	17.C	22.E	27.A	32.B	37.C
3.D	8.D	13.A	18.D	23.B	28.B	33.C	38.E
4.B	9.E	14.B	19.B	24.C	29.C	34.E	39.A
5.A	10.E	15.C	20.E	25.E	30.A	35.D	40.C

TEST IV. DATA INTERPRETATION

1.A	5.D	9.C	13.C	17.C	21.C	25.A
2.B	6.C	10.A	14.D	18.B	22.E	
3.E	7.B	11.A	15.E	19.B	23.D	
4.A	8.D	12.E	16.A	20.C	24.E	

TEST V. ERROR RECOGNITION

1.D	6.D	11.A	16.D	21.B	26.B	31.D
2.A	7.C	12.D	17.B	22.C	27.D	32.B
3.A	8.C	13.C	18.A	23.C	28.C	33.A
4.B	9.B	14.D	19.B	24.C	29.D	34.B
5.B	10.A	15.B	20.B	25.A	30.A	35.A

TEST VI. SENTENCE CORRECTION

1.A	5.E	9.D	13.D	17.D	21.E	25.B
2.A	6.C	10.D	14.C	18.E	22.A	
3.B	7.E	11.E	15.D	19.A	23.A	
4.E	8.D	12.E	16.B	20.E	24.C	

TEST VII. QUANTITATIVE COMPARISONS

1.B	5.A	9.A	13.C	17.B	21.A	25.A
2.A	6.B	10.B	14.A	18.D	22.C	
3.D	7.A	11.C	15.B	19.D	23.B	
4.B	8.B	12.A	16.B	20.A	24.A	

EXPLANATORY ANSWERS FOR VERISIMILAR EXAMINATION IV.

Here you have the heart of the Question and Answer Method. . .getting help when and where you need it. Where one of your Key Answers differs from ours you have a problem which can easily be remedied by reading the explanation. Then, if you have time, you might be able to pick up points on the exam by reading the other explanations, even where you wrote the Key Answers correctly. These explanations stress fundamental facts, ideas, and principles which just might pop up as questions on future exams.

1. **(C)** is correct because any intrinsic value that any particular work might have is never mentioned. (A) is incorrect because "those whose minds are open to such immoral influences," may be considered to imply teenagers. (B), (D), and (E) would not be considered flaws by a critic of this test of obscenity.

2. **(D)** is correct because the memo implies that although there are many bright substantive operatives, there is a shortage of talented managers. It does not criticize the management training program in any way, and therefore, the only reasonable alternative offered is that managerial ability is rare.

3. **(B)** is correct because the title diplomat is mentioned in the first line of the passage and even though the rest of the characteristics stated do not necessarily have to relate to a diplomat, the last word, said in summary, ties the passage together and this is a word often applied to a diplomat.

4. **(B)** is correct since the purpose of the plan was to discourage tax competition among local governments. Revenue sharing would seem to be a reasonable way to accomplish this. (A) would only increase competition among local governments. (C) is incorrect because health care is never mentioned. (D) and (E) are wrong because the passage deals only with local government.

5. **(A)** is correct because of the repetition of the phrase "that quality of life" which appeared in the last half of the passage. (B) changes the emphasis entirely. (C) and (D) are too different in tone and substance from the passage given. (E) may seem a possible choice, but (A) follows more easily.

6. **(B)** is correct because Shakespeare was involved with individualism and it is implied by the second half of the passage that today objective science and subjective individualism are dealt with separately. This modern view was not held by Dante. He had a single holistic view of life.

7. **(C)** is correct because the possible future is described in terms similar to those used to describe Dante's unified view of the universe. At present the scientific mind and the imaginative mind are polarized. In the future it is suggested that this polarization might break down. (A), (B), and (E) all represent the polarized view of the world. (D) is incorrect because the future does not hold replacement of poetic imagination, but a joining of poetic imagination with scientific thought.

8. **(D)** is correct because the first line mentions "This response or lack of response." Apathy is a lack of response. The passage deals with the dangers of avoiding a major issue and therefore apathy is the only reasonable alternative.

9. **(C)** is correct because when the author warns about the recutting and resetting of valuable stones, he is implying that historical facts should be presented accurately—ungarnished and unchanged. This is the major theme of the passage.

10. **(C)** is correct because it is the only alternative which offers a theory and then states its obvious contradiction as the original dialogue does.

11. **(B)** is correct because it states an absolute and then its contradiction (*i.e.,* "completely efficient . . . absolutely accurate"). (A) is incorrect because phrases like "so concerned" and "so burdened" are not absolutes. (C) is incorrect because of its lack of irony. (D) and (E) do not deal with absolutes and so cannot be correct.

12. **(A)** is correct since it specifically contradicts the second sentence. (B) and (E) are predictions about the future which can be neither rebutted nor supported by the passage. (C) is a restatement of the second sentence and (D) is irrelevant.

13. **(D)** is correct because it explains the writer's lack of attention to detail. (A) and (B) are specifically contradicted by the passage. (C) and (E) indicate an interest in minuntiae that the passage says the author does not demonstrate.

14. **(B)** is correct because only if abstract thinking precludes direct experience can it screen us from the forces of nature. The author may very well agree with the statements in choices (A) and (D), but they are conclusions derived from his argument rather than assumptions on which it is based. Choice (C) is irrelevant to the arguments. Choice (E) is incorrect because the argument deals with the conflict between modern life and direct experience. Abstract thinking need not be fundamental to but merely co-existent with modern civilization.

15. **(C)** is correct because it refutes the description of war being between technology and the human spirit by giving an example of war between technology and technology. (A) is incorrect because it does not deal with war in the twentieth century. (B) is irrelevant. Choices (D) and (E) support the author's statement.

TEST II. PRINCIPLES AND CASES

1. **(C)** is correct. Willie and Ike are both guilty because they had the intent and each committed the required act in furtherance of that intent as stated in the principle. (A) and (B) are wrong because the principle does not require a criminal act. (D) is irrelevant.

2. **(B)** is correct. Since Ike did not buy the guns, there is no way to infer that he should have known they were unregistered. (A) is wrong because it does not deal with the issue of knowledge. (C) ignores the fact that it is possible to obtain a gun legally even if it is to be used for an illegal purpose. (D) is not supported by the principle.

3. **(D)** is correct. Joining the robbery attempt excursion implied that Harry had agreed to commit a crime. (A) and (B) are wrong because the principle requires agreement, not any particular act. (C) is wrong because the fact that Bob said the robbery was Harry's idea does not mean that it actually was.

4. **(B)** is correct. The principle does not require that there be evidence that each co-conspirator is a member of the conspiracy, but only evidence that a conspiracy exists. Three people in the same car may not be proof positive but it is evidence. (A) is wrong because the principle does not deal with the truth of the statement, but with corroborating evidence. (C) is wrong because the principle only requires evidence of the conspiracy, not proof of its membership. (D) is irrelevant.

5. **(C)** is correct. Since Harry did not speak to the others, he could not have demonstrated his intent to withdraw, so he does not have a defense. (A) and (B) are wrong because they do not answer the question of whether Harry clearly demonstrated his intent to withdraw. (D) is wrong because it cannot be proved by the facts in the case.

6. **(C)** is correct. Since the agreement costs the local school board nothing, it cannot directly injure P. (A) is wrong because it does not show how P is directly injured. (B) and (D) are wrong because they do not deal with the principle.

7. **(A)** is correct. The principle states that institutions which receive public money may not discriminate on the basis of sex. St. Peter is such an institution, so (A) is the correct answer. (C) is wrong because the principle says "public-financed" not "public." (B) and (D) are irrelevant to the principle.

8. **(B)** is correct because that is the only choice which deals with the principle.

9. (**A**) is correct. The principle requires that F assert his own rights in order to win. (A) is the only choice that expresses the right that F is asserting. (B) is wrong because it is F's right, not his daughter's, that the principle requires. (C) and (D) do not state whether F is asserting his own rights or those of another.

10. (**B**) is correct because P is bringing his lawsuit in state court and the principle only applies to Federal courts. The other choices are wrong because they are based on the inapplicable principle.

11. (**C**) is correct because if the oral agreement about the icehouse was fundamental to Ms. O'Reilly's decision to purchase the property, then it would ordinarily have been included in one of the documents. Since it was not included, the principle requires that evidence about it be excluded. (A) is incorrect because there was no mistake. (B) is incorrect because there are no terms which could be explained by reference to the icehouse. (D) is incorrect because if there were fraud then the evidence would be admissible.

12. (**C**) is correct because a commission arrangement is clearly inconsistent with a fixed salary. (A) is incorrect because mere concealment is not a fraud unless someone is injured by it. (B) is contrary to common sense. (D) is incorrect because the exception for omitted terms is available only if those terms are not inconsistent with the written agreement.

13. (**A**) is correct because Jones defrauded Smith by misrepresenting essential facts about the building and the principle provides an exception for evidence which shows fraud. Choices (B), (C), and (D) are incorrect because they are superceded by the exception for fraud.

14. (**A**) is correct because there is an exception for evidence which interprets the terms of a writing. (B) is incorrect because the exception for consistent agreements is conditioned on the fact that they would not ordinarily have been included in the written agreement and since the written contract mentions time, it ordinarily would have specified an exact time limit. (C) is incorrect because the oral agreement does not actually vary the terms of the written agreement. (D) is not germane to the facts of the case.

15. (**A**) is correct because the principle only applies to oral agreements made prior to the written agreement.

16. (**D**) is correct because Thom did not have permission to walk along the tracks, so the railroad is only liable for hidden dangers. (A) is incorrect because trains on train tracks are not a hidden condition. (B) is incorrect because the railroad is under no duty to warn trespassers. (C) is incorrect because the principle does not mention the behavior of the injured party as an excuse for liability.

17. **(D)** is correct because the basic issue is whether Heff was a licensee or an invitee. If Heff were an invitee, then the warning sign would not shield Letch from liability. Since Letch received no benefit from Heff's visit, Heff was only a licensee and Letch's duty was limited to posting a sign. (A) and (B) are incorrect because they do not resolve the licensee/invitee question. (C) is incorrect because it is superceded by (D).

18. **(A)** is correct because the principle makes the owner of land absolutely liable to those who come at his request. (B), (C), and (D) are incorrect because they don't touch on Goodheart's status as an invitee.

19. **(B)** is correct because a landowner is liable even to trespassers for injuries suffered as a result of hidden artificial conditions. Therefore, there is no need to decide whether Barleycorn was a licensee or not. (A) and (C) are incorrect because they are superseded by choice (B). (D) is incorrect because the test is the artificiality of the dangerous condition, not its naturalness.

20. **(A)** is correct because the principle states that landowners are liable to invitees for *any* condition on the property. No exception is made for conditions which are unknown to the owner. (B), (C), and (D) are incorrect because the only question is whether or not Mary is an invitee. (A) answers that question affirmatively, so it preempts the other choices.

21. **(C)** is the narrowest principle because it is the only one which depends both on the residences of the parties and on the law to be applied. (A) and (B) are incorrect because each only mentions one of these two elements. (D) is incorrect because it does not set forth a meaningful standard.

22. **(B)** is correct because it is the only alternative which is consistent with question 21 while explaining the result. (A) is inconsistent with the previous question. (C) does not explain why the federal court may not decide the case set forth in the question. (D) discusses issues which are not relevant to this case.

23. **(D)** is correct because it distinguishes this case from the previous one. (A) is too broad, (B) contradicts the case in question 22, and (D) contradicts the case in question 21.

24. **(A)** is correct because it is narrower than (D). Alternative (B) does not explain the result and (C) is inconsistent with the ruling given in question 21.

25. **(A)** is correct because it is the only choice which distinguishes this case from the others. (B) and (C) are logically equivalent to each other and both are inconsistent with the preceding cases. (D) does not explain why the defendant cannot have the case transferred.

26. **(C)** is correct because it is the only choice which specifically alludes to the measure of damages used in the case. (A) and (D) are incorrect because they are broader than (C). (B) is incorrect because it does not explain the result.

27. **(B)** is correct because it is the only choice which deals specifically with "entire output" contracts. (A) conflicts with the previous case. Choices (C) and (D) are broader than (B).

28. **(C)** is correct because it is the only choice which explains the measure of damages used in this case. (A) and (B) are incorrect because they set damages on the basis of the seller's profits, not on the buyer's loss. (D) is too broad.

29. **(D)** is correct because it refers specifically to Tex's failure to deliver the cattle by the June 30 deadline. (A) and (C) are inconsistent with the case in question 21. (B) is broader than choice (D).

30. **(A)** is correct because it distinguishes this case from the prior one. (B) and (C) do not explain the result. (D) conflicts with the previous case.

31. **(A)** is correct because the principle states that liability is created by the non-consensual use of an individual's picture. (B) is incorrect because it only restates the conclusion implied by Jones' winning the lawsuit. (C) and (D) are incorrect because the principle requires the use of a *person's* picture.

32. **(B)** is correct because the fact that *Scandal Rag* was not liable implies that it made no willful or malicious misrepresentations. (A) is incorrect because the principle deals with the news event, not subsequent events. (C) is incorrect because the principle speaks of misrepresentations about the event and relief is not limited to the actors about whom misrepresentations are made. (D) is incorrect because the principle applies to periodicals, not to movies.

33. **(C)** is correct because the principle makes damage to the plaintiff's reputation a necessary condition for the defendant's liability and this choice indicates that the condition was not met. (A) is wrong because the temporary nature of Jones' newsworthiness is not a necessary element of the principle. (B) does not explain why *Scandal Rag* escaped liability. (D) does not deal with the issue of the statements made about Jones.

34. **(D)** is correct because the principle requires economic loss as a condition for a finding of liability and the lack of economic loss explains why *Scandal Rag* was not liable. (A) and (B) are incorrect because the questions of *Scandal Rag*'s intent and care do not resolve the issue of liability. (C) is incorrect because it would lead to liability for *Scandal Rag*.

35. **(A)** is correct because the principle requires that the subject about whom the misinformation is published be non-newsworthy. (B) is incorrect because the degree of care exercised by the periodical is irrelevant under the condition of absolute liability. (C) is incorrect because the principle deals with the nature of the periodical not with the nature of the article. (D) does not exclude the possibility that *Scandal Rag* may be a news magazine.

36. **(A)** is correct because the principle demands a signed writing stating the amount to be paid and J.P.'s form contract is the only writing which meets this requirement. (B) and (C) are incorrect because the writing must be signed by the party to be charged. (D) is incorrect because it is superseded by (A).

37. **(A)** is correct because only this decision as to which was the offer and which the acceptance leads to liability for J.P. (B) would lead to J.P.'s escape from liability. (C) does not answer the basic question of "Which contract?" (D) is not relevant.

38. **(C)** is correct because the principle makes the moment of mailing the reference point for determining the rights of the parties. (A) is incorrect because it is the mailing of the acceptance that the principle requires, not the mailing of an offer. (B) would lead to liability for J.P. (D) does not reach the critical issue of when the contract was formed.

39. **(B)** is correct because it is the only alternative which justifies J.P.'s avoidance of liability. (A) and (D) imply that the contract formed was for $25,000 so there would have been no modification to permit J.P. to invoke the principle. (C) does not resolve the issue of whether or not there was a change in the terms of a contract.

40. **(D)** is correct because it is the only alternative that relies on the principle to create liability for J.P. (A) and (B) do not justify the holding. (C) does not relate to the principle's reference to an oral modification.

TEST III. PRACTICAL JUDGMENT

DATA EVALUATION

(A) means that the Conclusion is a Major Objective;
(B) means that the Conclusion is a Major Factor;
(C) means that the Conclusion is a Minor Factor;
(D) means that the Conclusion is a Major Assumption;
(E) means that the Conclusion is an Unimportant Issue.

1. **(E)** The zero salvage value of the old lathes has no bearing on the decision of whether to rebuild or replace them.

358 / *Law School Admission Test*

2. **(C)** This minor factor is one of several ways that Conover will save money if they decide to replace rather than rebuild the lathes.

3. **(D)** The estimated 12 year useful life of the new equipment is a major assumption that the engineering supervisor must make in order to compare the total savings achieved by purchasing new lathes to the added expense involved.

4. **(B)** The purchase price is a major factor that the supervisor weighs against the anticipated savings.

5. **(A)** One objective of replacing or rebuilding the lathes is to lower the rejection rate for couplings.

6. **(B)** The overhaul costs are a major factor that the supervisor considers in comparing the cost of rebuilding the old equipment to the cost of replacing it.

7. **(C)** This is a minor factor that adds $600 to the savings expected from replacing rather than rebuilding the equipment.

8. **(D)** This is a major assumption made by the supervisor since he projects that replacing the old equipment will result in substantially reduced labor costs.

9. **(E)** This is unimportant because there is a sufficient labor supply and the supervisor is not concerned about a possible shortage.

10. **(E)** No mention is made about the demand for 16-inch couplings in particular or about any effect that it might have on the decision.

11. **(E)** Although the possibility of an increase in production requirements is mentioned, any of the alternatives is capable of meeting it, so it will not influence the decision made by the engineering supervisor.

12. **(C)** The cost of installation is a minor factor which increases the cost of replacing the equipment by about 10% and, hence, slightly reduces the desirability of that alternative.

13. **(A)** The difficulty in meeting production specifications is one of the problems that the supervisor intends to solve by replacing or rebuilding the old lathes.

14. **(B)** The lower labor costs associated with the new lathes are a major factor which makes replacement a reasonable alternative to overhaul despite the substantially greater initial cost.

DATA APPLICATION

15. **(C)** The $6,000 in annual labor costs that would be saved if Conover buys new lathes far outweighs any of the other advantages. Choice (A) amounts to $600, and choice (D) only totals $2,200. (B) and (E) are contradicted by the passage.

16. **(A)** The next to last paragraph mentions items I, III, and V. Item II is one of the benefits of buying new lathes, not one of the hazards of failing to do so. Item IV is not mentioned in the passage. Therefore, the answer is (A).

17. **(C)** Expected savings are:

Labor	$6,000
"Normal" maintenance	1,700
Additional maintenance	500
Boring mill maintenance	700
TOTAL	$8,900

18. **(D)** An increase in the hourly wage rate paid lathe operators will increase the dollar value of the 25% reduction in man-hours per unit of production made possible by the new lathes, hence it will make buying new lathes more attractive than overhauling the old ones. (D) is the only one of the choices that makes the new lathes more desirable.

19. **(B)** A boring mill is a separate piece of equipment, not a part of a lathe. All of the others are listed in the passage.

20. **(E)** Fringe benefits paid hourly employees will vary with the level of production. All of the other choices describe costs that are independent of production just as are rent, heat and light which are mentioned in the passage as examples of overhead costs.

DATA EVALUATION

(A) means that the Conclusion is a Major Objective;
(B) means that the Conclusion is a Major Factor;
(C) means that the Conclusion is a Minor Factor;
(D) means that the Conclusion is a Major Assumption;
(E) means that the Conclusion is an Unimportant Issue.

21. **(D)** This is a major assumption made by Mr. Manley since the rent charged by Bankers Leasing depends on the term of the lease and the term of the lease is based on Mr. Manley's projections of "economic life" of the equipment.

22. **(E)** This is an unimportant issue because regardless of which lease plan is chosen, the equipment and the initial cost of programming it will be the same.

23. **(B)** This is a major factor which, in conjunction with the rental charges, determines the differences between the two leasing plans. Since the non-cancellable term of the Bankers' lease is long as compared to the one year term of the XYZ lease, the rent charged by Bankers is lower because it includes less of an "insurance premium" for obsolescence.

24. **(C)** This is a minor factor that Mr. Manley must add to the rent charged by Bankers Leasing to equate it to the rent charged by XYZ.

25. **(E)** This is unimportant because, as in question 21, the cost of installation is unrelated to the choice of lessors.

26. **(D)** This is a major assumption which Mr. Manley must make in order to decide whether a long lease at a lower rent is more economical than a short lease at a higher rent.

27. **(A)** This is the objective that Anscott intends to achieve by acquiring the XYZ 2001.

28. **(B)** This is a major factor which, as in question 23, Mr. Manley must balance against the risk of obsolescence when he makes his decision.

29. **(C)** This minor factor must be added to the rent charged by Bankers in order to equate it to the rent charged by XYZ.

30. **(A)** This is a goal which every business person hopes to accomplish whenever he or she spends money.

31. **(E)** Despite the reference to it in Mr. Zises' letter, the prime rate is used only as a standard of comparison which is not relevant to Mr. Manley's decision. Anscott is not borrowing money at the prime rate. In making his decision, Mr. Manley will compare the rents under the respective leases to each other, not to a theoretical bank loan.

32. **(B)** This is the major factor that Mr. Manley must weigh against the difference in rents to decide which lease is more attractive.

33. **(C)** This minor factor, like those in questions 24 and 29, must be added to the rent charged by Bankers to make a valid comparison of the two leases.

34. **(E)** The cost of clerical personnel will be unaffected by the lease chosen, so it is unimportant.

DATA APPLICATION

35. **(D)** The basic question before Mr. Manley is whether or not the higher rent that XYZ charges is justified by the fact that XYZ will assume the risk that Anscott will want to change equipment in less than 9 years. The XYZ representative can be expected to emphasize this risk to make the rent differential seem reasonable. (A) and (E) are irrelevant because the comparison assumes that XYZ will provide maintenance in either case and the cost of that maintenance has been included. (B) is wrong because Mr. Manley is not likely to be motivated to reward XYZ at Anscott's expense. (C) avoids the main issue.

36. **(B)** Amortization is the rental component which is added to the interest component, not part of it.

37. **(C).** I and II are mentioned in the second paragraph. III and IV are mentioned as cost factors, not in connection with the basic decision to acquire the 2001 system.

38. **(E)** The cost of installation and initial programming are estimated to be $100,000. From Exhibit 2, we can see that the savings over the first three years total under $97,000, so the answer must be over three years. (E) is the only choice in that category.

39. **(A)** The only information in the passage about excise taxes is the basis on which they are computed and the exemption for "systems." Nothing is said about who is responsible for paying them.

40. **(C)** Mr. Manley bases his estimate of useful life on the XYZ trade-in schedule. If he were to find that the trade-in allowances were more than the actual resale value, then he would realize that he was overestimating the useful life. Since the low rent charged by Bankers is based on a long term lease, a shorter term would result in a higher rent and make the Bankers' lease relatively less attractive. (A), (D), and (E) would all have the effect of lowering the cost to Anscott of leasing from Bankers. (B) is irrelevant.

TEST IV. DATA INTERPRETATION

1. **(A)** The quarter with the greatest amount of borrowing ($110 billion) was the second quarter of 1974. In that quarter, approximately $20 billion was raised by corporate bonds, so the percentage is:
$$\frac{\$20 \text{ billion}}{\$110 \text{ billion}} = 18\%$$

2. **(B)** In the first quarter of 1968, approximately $6 billion was raised through the sale of state and local government bonds. In the peak quarter (either first quarter of 1971 or first quarter of 1974) $20 billion worth were sold. The percentage is:

$$\frac{\$6 \text{ billion}}{\$20 \text{ billion}} = 30\%$$

3. **(E)** Choice (D) can be eliminated because less money was raised through mortgages in the first quarter of 1973 than in the last quarter of 1972, so you only need compare the second quarter of 1970 (about $22 billion) with the second quarter of 1973 (about $80 billion). 80 is less than 4 times 22, and more than 2 times 22; so (B) and (C) can be eliminated. The percentage increase is:

$$\frac{\$80 \text{ billion} - \$22 \text{ billion}}{\$22 \text{ billion}} \times 100 = 263\%$$

4. **(A)** In 1967, about $86 billion was raised through mortages ($16 + 19 + 25 + 26 billion) out of a total of $175 billion ($35 + 39 + 52 + 49 billion), which is less than half.

5. **(D)** $80 billion was raised through mortgages in the third quarter of 1973 and $45 billion was raised in the third quarter of 1974, so the decline was:

$$\$80 - \$45 \text{ billion} = \$35 \text{ billion}.$$

6. **(C)** The longest period of uninterrupted quarter to quarter increases was from the third quarter of 1969 through the fourth quarter of 1971, for a total of *nine* quarters of increase. (Note: you can't count the first one because it did not show an increase over the prior quarter.)

7. **(B)** The class which had the smallest decline in unit sales must be that class which increased its percentage of total sales—Class 1.

8. **(D)** In 1973 the number of Class 2 cars sold was 33% of 11.4 million units or 3.8 million cars. In 1974 there were 33% of 9.3 million or 3.1 million Class 2 cars sold, for a decrease of about 700,000 cars.

9. **(C)** In 1967, 9% of 8.4 million = .76 million Imports sold. In 1973, 15% of 11.4 million = 1.71 million Imports sold. The percentage increase was:

$$\frac{1.71 \text{ million} - .76 \text{ million}}{.76 \text{ million}} \times 100 = 125\%$$

10. **(A)** In 1973, 6% of 11.4 million = 680,000 Class 5 cars sold. Since Class 5 cars cost at least $5,001 each, the minimum dollar value of these cars was:

$$\$5,001 \times 680,000 = \$3.4 \text{ billion}.$$

11. **(A)** It is only necessary to compare the two classes whose percentage of total sales increased the most: Imports and Class 1 cars.

        Imports:
           1971   15% of 9.8 million units = 1.47 million
           1969   11% of 9.4 million units = 1.034 million

$$\text{Percent increase: } \frac{1.47 \text{ million} - 1.034 \text{ million}}{1.034 \text{ million}} \times 100 = 42\%.$$

        Class 1:
           1971   21% of 9.8 million units = 2.058 million
           1969   17% of 9.4 million units = 1.6 million

$$\text{Percent increase: } \frac{2.06 \text{ million} - 1.6 \text{ million}}{1.6 \text{ million}} \times 100 = 28.75\%.$$

Hence, the Class with the largest percentage increase in number of units sold is Imports.

12. **(E)** The price range for imported cars is not given, so it is impossible to tell if the 700,000 imports were $3,000 Volkswagens or $30,000 Rolls Royces.

13. **(C)** In 1975, parts shipments were 22% of $3.1 billion = $682 million. In 1967, they were 21% of $1.9 billion = $399 million, so the increase was $682 − 399 million = $283 million.

14. **(D)** Compressor shipments went from 27% of $1.9 billion = $513 million to 19% of $3.1 billion = $589 million. The percentage increase is:

$$\frac{\$589 \text{ million} - \$513 \text{ million}}{\$513 \text{ million}} \times 100 = 14.8\%$$

15. **(E)** Compare the two groups with the largest increase in percent of the market: domestic water systems and pumps n.e.c.

        Domestic water systems:
           1975:   8% of $3.1 billion = $248 million
           1967:   5% of $1.9 billion = $95 million

$$\text{Percent increase: } \frac{\$248 \text{ million} - \$95 \text{ million}}{\$95 \text{ million}} \times 100 = 161\%.$$

        Pumps n.e.c.
           1975:   12% of $3.1 billion = $371 million
           1967:   10% of $1.9 billion = $190 million

$$\text{Percent increase: } \frac{\$372 \text{ million} - \$190 \text{ million}}{\$190 \text{ million}} \times 100 = 95.7\%.$$

Thus, shipments of domestic water systems increased by the largest percentage.

16. **(A)** In 1975, shipments of industrial pumps were:
26% of $3.1 billion = $806 million

17. **(C)** The two smallest categories in 1967 were domestic water systems and pumps n.e.c. The difference was:
10% of $1.9 billion − 5% of $1.9 billion =
(10% − 5%) of $1.9 billion = 5% of $1.9 billion
= $95 million.

18. **(B)** In 1967 hydraulic fluid power pumps shipments were 12% of $1.9 billion; in 1976 they were 13% of $3.1 billion. The sum is:
(.12 × $1.9 billion) + (.13 × $3.1 billion), but
consider: .13 × $3.1 billion = (.12 × $3.1 billion)
+ (.01 × $3.1 billion) so the sum can be written:
(.12 × $1.9 billion) + (.12 × $3.1 billion) +
(.01) × $3.1 billion = (.12 × $5 billion) +
(.01 × $3.1 billion) = $631 million.

19. **(B)** In the third quarter of 1974, state and local government retirement funds holdings of corporate stock were $20 billion and their holdings of corporate bonds were about $60 billion, so the percentage is:
$$\frac{\$20 \text{ billion}}{\$60 \text{ billion}} = 33\%$$

20. **(C)** In the first quarter of 1967, corporate bonds owned by state and local government retirement funds totalled $20 billion and corporate stock owned by them totalled $2.5 billion, so $20 billion = 8 × $2.5 billion.

21. **(C)** At the end of 1972, private pension funds owned stock valued at $120 billion. By the end of 1974, the value of their stock holdings had dropped to $60 billion, so the percentage decrease was:
$$\frac{\$120 \text{ billion} - \$60 \text{ billion}}{\$120 \text{ billion}} \times 100 = 50\%$$

22. **(E)** To answer this question you must add up the value of the credit market instruments held by each of the four types of institutions at the beginning of 1970.

State and Local Government Retirement Funds	$16 billion
Non-Life Insurance Companies	11 billion
Finance Companies	5 billion
Private Pension Funds	7 billion
TOTAL	$39 billion

23. **(D)** Since all of these graphs are on ratio scales, the size of the percentage change can be measured by the steepness of the line which joins the value at the beginning of 1967 with the value at the end of 1974. By inspection, it is obvious that the steepest line is the one for state and local government retirement fund holdings of corporate stocks.

24. **(E)** Since the graphs only measure *earning* assets, nothing can be inferred about *total* assets, which may include differing amounts of *non*-earning assets.

25. **(A)** Although the value of non-life insurance companies' holdings of stock and the value of the holdings of private pension funds both declined in the two year period 1973-1974, the decline could have resulted either from a general decline in stock market prices or from an excess of sales over purchases. There is no way to tell from the information available which cause or combination of causes was responsible.

TEST V. ERROR RECOGNITION

(A) means the sentence contains an error in DICTION;
(B) means the sentence is VERBOSE;
(C) means the sentence contains FAULTY GRAMMAR;
(D) means the sentence contains NO ERROR.

1. **(D)** No errors.

2. **(A)** "Single *people* will———" *Folks* is colloquial for *people*.

3. **(A)** "———regardless of the cost." *Irregardless* is an illiterate expression meaning *regardless*.

4. **(B)** "———to skirt submerged obstacles." *To skirt* means to pass *around* (something).

5. **(B)** "———banned as evil until———" *Evil* and *wicked* are synonyms.

6. **(D)** No errors.

7. **(C)** "Joseph and Mary *are* brother and sister." Singular nouns joined by *and* usually take a plural verb.

8. **(C)** "This is a present from John and *me*." The case of a pronoun (me) compounded with a substantive (John) is the same as that of the substantive. In this sentence, the substantive, John, being the object of the preposition *from,* is in the objective case. Therefore, the pronoun must also be in the objective case.

9. **(B)** "———is huge." *Huge* and *massive* are synonyms.

10. **(A)** "Nobody was there *except* me————" *Outside of* used for *except* is a colloquial expression.

11. **(A)** "————I became *quite* angry." *Plenty*, as used in the sentence, is a colloquial expression meaning *quite*.

12. **(D)** No errors.

13. **(C)** "————I *lay* in bed————" I *lay* in bed, but I *laid* the book on the table.

14. **(D)** No errors.

15. **(B)** "With a little planning————" *Planning* is the laying out of a future course; *advance* is therefore superfluous.

16. **(D)** No errors.

17. **(B)** "The new restaurant serves————" If the restaurant is *new*, it has obviously just opened.

18. **(A)** "————it would be *presumptuous* of him————" *Presumptive* means giving reasonable ground for belief. *Presumptuous* means bold or forward.

19. **(B)** "Although small, the *Brattlebottom*————" *Small* means limited in *size*.

20. **(B)** "Such cases are rare." *Rare* means *occurring infrequently*.

21. **(B)** "————it is often exceedingly cold; for this reason————" *Frigid* means *exceedingly cold*.

22. **(C)** "Every man, woman, and child *is* to be included." When singular subjects joined by *and* are introduced by *every, each, no, such a, many a*, the verb is singular.

23. **(C)** "Notify *whoever* is available." The case of a relative pronoun (who, which, that, etc.) is determined by its use in its own clause. In this sentence, the compound relative pronoun *whoever* is the subject of *is*. Since the subject is always in the nominative case, the correct form is *whoever*, which is nominative, not *whomever*, which is objective.

24. **(C)** "*Who* is the author————" The interrogative pronoun *who* has the form *whom* in the object position (To *whom* are you talking?) and *who* in the subject position (*Who* is the author of *Moby Dick*?).

25. **(A)** "Did you *lose* a pearl necklace————" *To loose* is to free. To *lose* is to become unable to find, to mislay.

26. (**B**) "In the era of the Great Rebellion, strange events were reported———" Since the expression "in the era of the Great Rebellion" has already indicated the period during which the strange events took place, there is no need for the word *then*.

27. (**D**) No errors.

28. (**C**) "———William and *I* are incompatible." Since *I* is part of the subject of the clause *William and I are incompatible,* it has a nominative form (I)—not an object form (me).

29. (**D**) No errors.

30. (**A**) "———Mr. Smith's assistants *obtained* about a thousand———" *Get ahold of* is dialectical for *obtain*.

31. (**D**) No errors.

32. (**B**) "———more than optimism." *Optimism* is the tendency to take the most *hopeful* view of matters.

33. (**A**) "———but it was tortuous instead." *Torturous* means causing extreme pain. *Tortuous* means full of twists, turns and curves.

34. (**B**) "———some forty reporters———" *Some forty reporters* and *forty-odd reporters* mean the same thing.

35. (**A**) "———certainly not *averse* to reading about himself." *Adverse* means opposed, antagonistic, hostile. *Averse* means disinclined, reluctant, loath.

TEST VI. SENTENCE CORRECTION

1. (**A**) is correct. *Such as,* not any of the other expressions, introduces an appositive.

2. (**A**) is correct. As part of the object of the preposition *except, me* (objective case) is correct.

3. (**B**) is correct. *On account of* is illiterate for *because,* so (A) is wrong. (C) and (D) are awkward, and (E) is a run-on sentence.

4. (**E**) is correct. (A), (B), and (C) violate the idioms *in the year* (*1791*) and *different from.* (D) is awkward.

5. (**E**) is correct. A gerund (reciting) should not refer to a noun (the speaker) unless the noun is named in the sentence; thus (A) is wrong. *Recision,* which means the act of cutting off or pruning, is used incorrectly in (B). (D) is wrong because the speaker, not the *passage,* concluded the lecture and (C) is awkward.

6. **(C)** is correct. In (A), (B), (D), and (E), either *practice* or *thing* seems to be doing the learning.

7. **(E)** is correct. The expression *both . . . and* requires parallel construction. Choices (A), (B), (C), and (D) lack such construction. (C) is also wordy.

8. **(D)** is correct. The sentence concerns not *rocks,* but *rocks which form the solid crust of our planet.* A phrase or clause needed to distinguish a substantive from all other members of its class is never set off with commas, therefore (B) and (C) are wrong. *Each* takes a singular verb; (A), (B), and (E) incorrectly use plural verbs. (E) also requires the deletion of *old* from the original sentence.

9. **(D)** is correct. The masculine personal pronoun *he* (*him, his*) is used to refer to the indefinite pronoun *everyone.* (A), (B), and (E) use *they, them, their.* (C) changes the meaning of the original sentence.

10. **(D)** is correct. (A) lacks parallel construction. (B) and (C) misuse the possessive which should be *Dickens'.* (E) changes the meaning of the original sentence.

11. **(E)** is correct. *Unexpectedly surprised,* a redundant expression, occurs in (A) and (B). One *picks up,* rather than *picks* a report card; therefore, (B) and (C) are wrong. (D) makes no sense.

12. **(E)** is correct. (A), (B), and (C) all violate the rules of grammar by repeating expressions needlessly or by inserting unnecessary words (to it, to, it). (D) is unclear.

13. **(D)** is correct. The relative pronoun *that* is used to introduce adjectival clauses (*that I was telling you about*).

14. **(C)** is correct. *Who's* as in (A) means *who is. Who'se* as in (B) is a misspelling of whose. (D) is awkward and (E) is unclear.

15. **(D)** is correct. (A), (C), and (E) needlessly introduce *but, and,* and *yet* between clauses. (B) changes the meaning of the original sentence.

16. **(B)** is correct. The idioms are *enamored of* and *comply with.*

17. **(D)** is correct. In (A), (B), and (C) it is not clear who is to learn—you or the teacher. (E) is unnecessarily wordy.

18. **(E)** is correct. (A) and (C) are sentence fragments, (B) is meaningless, and there is no reason for the insertion of *it* into Choice (D).

19. **(A)** is correct. A possessive adjective (his, theirs) following a *neither . . . . nor* construction takes the number of the *nor* subject noun; (B), (C), and (E) violate this rule. (D) changes the meaning of the original sentence.

20. **(E)** is correct. The relative pronoun *who* functions as the subject of the subordinate clause; thus it takes the nominative form *who,* not the objective form *whom.* (A) and (B) use *whom.* A noun preceding a gerund (an *-ing* form of a verb, used as a noun) takes the possessive case; therefore, (D) is wrong. The possessive of *children* is *children's;* for this reason (A) and (C) are incorrect.

21. **(E)** is correct. This sentence calls for parallel structure, which is lacking in (A) and (C). In (B), a semicolon is used in place of a comma, resulting in a sentence fragment. (D) makes no sense.

22. **(A)** is correct. *In later years* is *afterward;* if he was *ashamed of something he had done* he felt *remorse.* (B), (C), (D), and (E) contain these redundancies.

23. **(A)** is correct. *Due to* and *caused by* are adjectival constructions. They can modify a noun but not a whole clause, as they are made to do in (B) and (C). Choice (D) is redundant and (E) is meaningless. An *effect* is a result or consequence. An *affect* is a feeling or disposition.

24. **(C)** is correct. To express necessity, the subjunctive form of the verb is ordinarily used in the subordinate clause. *Be* is the appropriate subjunctive form.

25. **(B)** is correct. *That* and *whether* introduce noun clauses, such as *that I understand you.* Therefore, none of the other choices is correct.

TEST VII. QUANTITATIVE COMPARISONS

1. **(B)** $x = 3/7y, y > x.$

2. **(A)** Since $y > x, 1/y < 1/x, \sqrt{1/y} < \sqrt{1/x}.$

3. **(D)** $x^2 = \frac{9}{49} y^2.$ If $y < \frac{9}{49},$ then $x^2 > y^3,$ otherwise $x^2 \leq y^3.$

4. **(B)** $\frac{x^2}{y^2} = \frac{9}{49} < \frac{1}{5}$

5. **(A)** $6 \times 10^{-6} + 5 \times 10^{-4} > 5 \times 10^{-4}.$

6. **(B)** $\frac{5 + 10^{-3}}{5 + 10^{-6}} \cong 1 < 1.01.$

7. **(A)** $5200 > 0.52$.

8. **(B)** $\dfrac{.02}{104} < \dfrac{.02}{100}$

9. **(A)** $\dfrac{4}{7} > \dfrac{1}{28}$

10. **(B)** $x+2 = 0 < 1$.

11. **(C)** $\dfrac{1}{36} = \dfrac{1}{36}$

12. **(A)** $1/6 > 1/18$.

13. **(C)** $\overline{AC}$ is a diameter, so $\overset{\frown}{CBA} = 180° = \overset{\frown}{CDA}$.

14. **(A)** The diameter of a circle is the longest chord.

15. **(B)** $CD = \dfrac{\pi}{6}(\overline{AC}) = \dfrac{\pi}{6} \cdot \dfrac{\sqrt{3}}{2} \ (\overline{AE})$

    $\overline{CE} = 1/2 \ (\overline{AE})$

    $1/2 > \dfrac{\pi}{6} \dfrac{\sqrt{3}}{2}$.

16. **(B)** $\overline{OF} = 1/4 \ (\overline{AC}),\ \overline{CE} = \dfrac{\sqrt{3}}{3}(\overline{AC}),\ 1/4 < \dfrac{\sqrt{3}}{6}$.

17. **(B)** Since $\overline{BC}$ is parallel to $\overline{AD}$,
    $< CAD = < ACB = 1/2 \overset{\frown}{AB}$.

18. **(D)** There are two unknowns in one equation so it is impossible to solve for numerical values.

19. **(D)** See 18.

20. **(A)** $3x + 2z = 8,\ 2z = 8 - 3x,\ z = 4 - 3/2x$.

21. **(A)** $1000 - 100 = 900 > 10$.

22. **(C)** $18 = 18$.

23. **(B)** $(3.5)^2 = 12.25 < 14.5762$.

24. **(A)** $(\sqrt{3})^3 = 3\sqrt{3} > 4 = (\sqrt[3]{8})^2$.

25. **(A)** $\sqrt[5]{33} > 2$, since $2^5 = 32$.

Law School Admission Test

FIFTH VERISIMILAR EXAM

Based on all the information available before going to press we have constructed this examination to give you a comprehensive and authoritative view of what's in store for you. To avoid any misunderstanding, we must emphasize that this test has never been given before. We devised it specially to provide a final opportunity of employing all you've learned in a situation that closely simulates the real thing.

Time allowed for the entire Examination: 3½ Hours

In order to create the climate of the actual exam, that's exactly what you should allow yourself . . . no more, no less. Use a watch to keep a record of your time, since it might suit your convenience to try this practice exam in several short takes.

ANALYSIS AND TIMETABLE: VERISIMILAR EXAMINATION V.		
This table is both an analysis of the exam that follows and a priceless preview of the actual test. Look it over carefully and use it well.		
SUBJECT TESTED	*Time Allowed*	*Questions*
LOGICAL REASONING	15 minutes	10
PRINCIPLES AND CASES	55 minutes	40
PRACTICAL JUDGMENT	20 minutes	20
QUANTITATIVE COMPARISON	15 minutes	25
ERROR RECOGNITION	20 minutes	35
SENTENCE CORRECTION	20 minutes	25
VALIDITY OF CONCLUSION	30 minutes	50
PRACTICAL JUDGMENT	20 minutes	25
TOTALS EXAM V	195 minutes	230

SCORE YOURSELF

Compare your answers to the Correct Key Answers at the end of the Examination. To determine your score, count the number of correct answers in each test. Then count the number of incorrect answers. Subtract ¼ of the number of incorrect answers from the number of correct answers. Plot the resulting figure on the graph below by blackening the bar under each test to the point of your score. Plan your study to strengthen the weaknesses indicated on your scoring graph.

EXAM V	Very Poor	Poor	Average	Good	Excellent
LOGICAL REASONING 10 Questions	1-2	3-4	5-7	8-9	10
PRINCIPLES AND CASES 40 Questions	1-7	8-17	18-28	29-35	36-40
PRACTICAL JUDGMENT 45 Questions	1-7	8-19	20-32	33-40	41-45
QUANTITATIVE COMPARISON 25 Questions	1-4	5-10	11-17	18-22	23-25
ERROR RECOGNITION 35 Questions	1-6	7-15	16-25	26-31	32-35
SENTENCE CORRECTION 25 Questions	1-4	5-10	11-17	18-22	23-25
VALIDITY of CONCLUSION 50 Questions	1-8	9-20	21-35	36-44	45-50

ANSWER SHEET FOR VERISIMILAR EXAMINATION V.

Consolidate your key answers here just as you would do on the actual exam. Using this type of Answer Sheet will provide valuable practice. Tear it out along the indicated lines and mark it up correctly. Use a No. 2 (medium) pencil. Make only ONE mark for each answer. Additional and stray marks may be counted as mistakes. In making corrections erase errors COMPLETELY. Make glossy black marks.

TEST I. LOGICAL REASONING

TEST II. PRINCIPLES AND CASES

TEST III. PRACTICAL JUDGMENT

TEST IV. QUANTITATIVE COMPARISON

TEST V. ERROR RECOGNITION

373

TEST VI. SENTENCE CORRECTION

TEST VII. VALIDITY OF CONCLUSION

TEST VIII. PRACTICAL JUDGMENT

TEST I. LOGICAL REASONING

TIME: 15 Minutes. 10 Questions.

This is a test of your ability to evaluate the reasoning contained in a statement or reading passage. Each statement or passage is followed by one or more questions. Answer each question solely on the basis of information stated or implied in the reading. If more than one choice seems possible, then you must select the one answer that does not require making implausible or superfluous assumptions. Blacken the space on the answer sheet that corresponds to the letter of your choice.

Correct and explanatory answers are provided at the end of the exam.

1. We believe that the U.S. can successfully compete and win in this contest but we shall have to operate, in this field, more efficiently than we have been doing. We submit that to say long term commitment of foreign aid funds is incompatible with democratic controls is really to say that democracy cannot adjust its procedures to plain facts and plain needs.

    The "contest" referred to in the above passage is, most likely, in which of the following?

    (A)   The nuclear arms race
    (B)   The control of shipping lanes
    (C)   The advantageous use of foreign aid funds by democratic nations as opposed to authoritarian ones
    (D)   Field operation for tactical armed forces in the European theatre
    (E)   Agricultural development of underdeveloped countries

2. John: "I love Italian spaghetti."
    Mary: "That's too bad because we're having domestic spaghetti for dinner."

    Mary has interpreted John's remark to mean that

    (A)   John only likes spaghetti made in Italy   (D)   John is Italian
    (B)   John only likes spaghetti eaten by Italians (E)   John likes domestic spaghetti
    (C)   John only likes Italian food

3. I was in Iran 3 years ago and a year and a half ago I raised the question about money coming in here. It was creating real estate speculation and all sorts of fantastic industrial schemes. They want to build a big steel mill that the country cannot afford.

Concerning the above mentioned steel mill, it appears that

(A)   there may be a great need for it in the immediate future
(B)   it is not as important as a new hydroelectric plant
(C)   Iran, for the present, will probably be better off without it
(D)   it is already an accomplished fact and there is no use crying over spilt milk
(E)   three years ago the new steel mill had not been thought of yet

4.   A man who can read and write can be a better crook than a man who can't read and write. It is the literary people who have bled the country of Nepal.

It may most safely be inferred that the author of the above statement would be most in favor of

(A)   expanded agricultural programs for Nepal
(B)   a cutback in U.S. foreign aid to education
(C)   a monetary view of suecess
(D)   an all out effort to destroy institutions of higher education
(E)   giving technical assistance to foreign countries

5.   Based upon the speaker and what is being said, which of the following is the most believable statement?

(A)   Scientist: Lake Geneva is the most attractive resort in Europe.
(B)   Cab Driver: The gas shortage is due to a conspiracy among the oil companies.
(C)   Surgeon: My hospital gives the finest quality of health care.
(D)   Electrician: An overloaded circuit can cause the wires to burn up.
(E)   Indian Chief: The white men have pillaged our land unjustly.

6.   There are some who say that the missionary spirit of American democracy has lost its drive. We are often regarded abroad as a powerful, wealthy nation, concerned with others only when it serves our needs.

The author of the above passage would be most in favor of

(A)   more economically cooperative programs between the U.S. and other nations
(B)   rugged individualism on the part of all nations
(C)   suffrage for the common man
(D)   the right of all nations to contract for their own safety
(E)   more altruistic programs such as the Peace Corps

7.   Ten competitors in interstate commerce, controlling sixty per cent of the entire film business, have agreed to restrict their liberty of action by refusing to contract for display of pictures except upon a standard form which provides for compulsory joint action by them in respect of dealings with one who fails to observe such a contract with any distributor, all with the manifest purpose of coercing the Exhibitor and limiting freedom of trade.

Most simply stated the above passage says:

(A) Ten film distributors have agreed to take joint action against any exhibitor who violates their joint contract

(B) Ten film exhibitors have agreed to take joint action against any distributor who violates their joint contract

(C) The film distributors' employees union has agreed to take joint action

(D) The film exhibitors' employees union has agreed to take joint action with regard to distributors

(E) The film distributors have decided to flagrantly break the anti-trust laws

8. John: "Crab fishing is a wet and cold sport."
Mary: "Oh, it's too bad that we won't be near the sea on our vacation."

Mary has interpreted John's remark to mean that

(A) John doesn't like crab fishing
(B) John doesn't like wet and cold sports
(C) John only likes dry sports
(D) John never goes fishing
(E) John likes crab fishing

9. Where malaria, intestinal parasites, and trachoma are endemic you will not find stability and ordered solution of national problems.

The author of the above passage would most likely agree with which of the following statements?

(A) Sickness is due to a poor natural climate.
(B) Sick people invariably mean sick societies.
(C) Our laboratories must find new drugs with which to combat disease.
(D) There are no known cures for malaria.
(E) Progress must be based upon swords being beaten into plowshares.

10. His answer was that the plan was unlawful, even if the parties did not have the power to fix prices, provided that they intended to do so; and it was to drive home this point that he contrasted the case then before the court with monopoly, where power was a necessary element.

The man referred to in the passage above seems to feel that which of the following should be unlawful activity?

(A) Price fixing in fact
(B) The power to monopolize
(C) The intention to fix prices among different parties
(D) Predatory pricing structures
(E) The formation of trade associations

END OF TEST

TEST II. PRINCIPLES AND CASES

TIME: 55 Minutes. 40 Questions.

Correct and explanatory answers are provided at the end of the exam. After you have completed the entire exam, read the explanations carefully. They'll reinforce your strengths and pinpoint your weaknesses so that you know just what to study to raise your score.

PART A. APPLYING SEVERAL PRINCIPLES TO A CASE

DIRECTIONS: Each law case described below is followed by several legal principles. These principles may be either real or imaginary, but for purposes of this test you are to assume them to be valid. Following each legal principle are four statements regarding the possible applicability of the principle to the law case. You are to select the one statement which most appropriately describes the applicability of the principle to the law case and blacken the space beneath the letter of the statement you select.

These questions do not presuppose any specific legal knowledge on your part; you are to arrive at your answers entirely by the ordinary processes of logical reasoning.

Case One

Johnson suffered every time he ate, so he went to his doctor, Dr. Galen, a general practitioner, for treatment. When medication failed to relieve the symptoms, Dr. Galen diagnosed the problem as gall stones and advised Johnson to have his gall bladder removed. She had Johnson admitted to General Hospital, one of several hospitals where she had operating privileges. When Dr. Galen operated, she found the gall stones, as she expected. Since Johnson was already under the anesthetic and the incision had already been made, the doctor removed his appendix, a standard procedure whenever a patient undergoes abdominal surgery.

When Johnson awakened from the anesthetic, he complained of pain in his left shoulder. The resident on duty had never heard of that kind of pain following a gall bladder operation, so he examined Johnson and discovered that his collarbone was broken. It had not been broken before the operation. This additional injury caused Johnson to remain in the hospital for an extra week.

Johnson was understandably upset and became even more upset when he received Dr. Galen's bill. The bill included a charge of $500 for an appendectomy in addition to the $1,000 fee for the gall bladder removal. To add insult to injury, Johnson's insurance company informed him that the Limitation-of-Benefits clause (part of the fine print in his standard form policy which he had never read) limited its obligation to the usual cost of the single most expensive surgical procedure performed while the patient was anesthetized; therefore, it refused to pay for the appendectomy. The insurance company did send Johnson a check for $1,100, the standard fee for a gall bladder removal. Johnson was astonished, since the agent who had sold him the policy never mentioned any Limitation-of-Benefits clause.

1. *If a person suffers an injury for which there is no possible cause other than the defendant's lack of care, then in order to recover damages, that person need not prove that the defendant was in fact responsible for the injury, but he must prove that no other person could have been responsible.*

   When Johnson sues Dr. Galen for his broken collarbone, Johnson will

   (A) win, because only malpractice can cause a patient to suffer a broken collarbone during a gall bladder removal
   (B) win, because it was Dr. Galen's responsibility to see that no harm befell her patient
   (C) lose, because the fracture did not necessarily occur while Dr. Galen was operating
   (D) lose, because his collarbone was broken accidentally

2. *A hospital will only be held liable for those injuries to patients which are caused by the extreme carelessness of its full-time employees.*

   When Johnson sues General Hospital for the pain, suffering, and lost income which resulted from his broken collarbone, General Hospital will

   (A) win, because the fracture was caused by ordinary, not extreme, carelessness
   (B) win, because Dr. Galen could have performed the operation in another hospital
   (C) lose, because broken bones following surgery can only result from someone's gross disregard for ordinary standards of care
   (D) lose, because staff physicians at a hospital are the agents of the hospital

3. *A contract may be implied by the parties' customary manner of doing business with each other or by the common practices of the trade or business in which they are engaged.*

   When Dr. Galen sues Johnson for the $500 for the appendectomy, Dr. Galen will

   (A) win, because doctors generally perform appendectomies during abdominal operations
   (B) win, because as a physician she was under an implied obligation to do whatever she felt was necessary to preserve her patient's health

(C)   lose, because she never informed Johnson that she would remove his appendix

(D)   lose, because the insurance company, not Johnson, had the obligation to pay for any necessary surgery

4.   *If the two parties to a contract are of substantially unequal bargaining power and if the stronger party imposes terms on the weaker party which work to his unexpected detriment, then a court will reform the contract by eliminating the unjust terms.*

Assuming that Johnson pays Dr. Galen for the appendectomy, then when Johnson sues the insurance company to recover his $500, the insurance company will

(A)   win, because Johnson should have read the policy

(B)   win, because it was only required to pay for the gall bladder removal

(C)   lose, because Johnson could have gone to another insurance company for a policy without a Limitation-of-Benefits clause

(D)   lose, because Johnson had no opportunity to negotiate for a policy without a Limitation-of-Benefits clause

5.   *If one of the parties to a contract breaches an express or implied condition of the contract, then the other party has the option of refusing to perform his obligations under the contract or of performing and then suing the breaching party for damages.*

When Dr. Galen sues Johnson for refusing to pay her bill, Johnson will

(A)   win, because it is an implicit condition of a contract for medical services that the patient's health will be no worse after the services are performed than it was before

(B)   win, because he never specifically agreed to Dr. Galen's fee

(C)   lose, because his broken collarbone was the result of an accident

(D)   lose, because he must pay before he can sue for damages

6.   *The standards of care, skill, and competence required of a professional engaged in the practice of his profession are not as high as the highest level of care, skill and competence attained by any member of the profession, but are only as high as the average level attained by those members of the profession who have a similar degree of education and experience.*

When Johnson sues Dr. Galen for medical malpractice because his collarbone was broken, Dr. Galen will

(A)   win, because as a general practitioner, she will not be held to the level of competence of a specialist in abdominal surgery

(B)   win, because even the best doctor sometimes makes a mistake

(C)   lose, because as a general practitioner she was not competent to perform surgery

(D)   lose, because only an extraordinary degree of carelessness could cause an unconscious patient to break his collarbone

7. *If a contract for the sale of goods or services does not specify the price to be paid, then the contract will be understood to require that the price be the ordinary and reasonable price for similar goods and services.*

When Dr. Galen sues Johnson for the $1000 for removing his gall bladder, she will

(A) win, because Johnson did not pay her bill
(B) win, because the amount allowed by an insurance company is a reasonable fee
(C) lose, because Johnson never had an opportunity to negotiate the fee
(D) lose, because it is neither ordinary nor reasonable for an anesthetized patient to suffer a broken collarbone

8. *A person shall be liable for battery if he intentionally touches another in a manner which is neither typical of ordinary social contact between strangers nor consented to by the individual touched.*

When Johnson sues Dr. Galen for battery for removing his appendix, Johnson will

(A) win, because he did not authorize an appendectomy
(B) win, because broken bones do not result from ordinary social contact
(C) lose, because he consented to Dr. Galen's performing surgery on him
(D) lose, because a surgeon ordinarily performs an appendectomy during any abdominal surgery

Case Two

Puma was an independent oil driller who purchased some pipe from Briar for $10,000. He paid $1,000 down and agreed to pay the balance of $9,000 in 30 monthly installments of $300 each. Briar and Puma orally agreed that Briar would retain title to the pipe until the full purchase price had been paid, but that Puma could use it in his operations in the interim. Puma then purchased a drilling rig and some drill bits from Boring Drill Company (BDC) for $20,000. Puma signed the Boring Drill Company's standard time purchase contract. The contract called for a $2,000 down payment and 36 monthly installments of $500. In the event of a default in any one of the monthly payments Boring Drill Company had the right to repossess and sell the rig, the bits, and any other drilling equipment in Puma's possession. When Puma asked if this included the pipe to which Briar retained title, BDC's salesman replied that it was just a formality to protect Boring Drill Company and would not be enforceable until Puma had completely paid for the pipe. Puma signed the contract and Boring Drill Company delivered the drilling rig and bits. Six months later, Puma was unable to make his monthly payments on either the rig or the pipe.

Boring Drill Company sends two of its repossession specialists—Max, an ex-heavyweight boxer and Grunt, a former defensive center for the Green Bay Packers—out to Puma's drilling site. When they arrive at the site, they are unable to find Puma so they dismantle the rig and load it and the pipe into their truck. When they review their checklist they discover that they do not have the bits, so they go to the construction shack nearby which they find to be securely locked.

As they are standing there puzzling over their next move, Puma returns, followed by Briar who has come to get his money or his pipe. Max explains why he and Grunt are there and politely asks Puma for the key to the shed. Puma refuses and orders them to leave. Max shrugs his shoulders, breaks down the door to the shed, takes only the drill bits, and starts back to the truck. Briar then notices his pipe in the Boring Drill Company truck and demands that it be unloaded. Incensed at the prospect of losing both his pipe and his money, Briar tackles Max from behind and breaks his leg. Grunt rushes to the rescue and manages to subdue Briar. Grunt and Max leave, taking the rig, the bits, and the pipe with them.

9. *Although a time purchase contract may lawfully grant the seller the right to repossess the goods sold without a requirement of any judicial process, this self-help must be accomplished without any breach of the peace. If a breach of the peace occurs, the seller loses his right of repossession, he must return the goods, and his remedies are limited to money damages.*

   In a suit brought by Puma against Boring Drill Company for the return of the rig, bits, and pipe, Boring Drill Company will

   (A) win, because it was not responsible for Briar's attack on Max
   (B) win, because Puma did not have any money with which to pay damages
   (C) lose, because breaking into the shed was a breach of the peace
   (D) lose, because it failed to give Puma a reasonable opportunity to pay his debt before it repossessed the drilling equipment

10. *If a seller transfers the possession of property to a buyer but retains the title in himself, then in order to make this claim to the property superior to the claims of third parties, the reservation of title must be in a writing signed by the buyer, and the seller must make a reasonable effort to insure that third parties are alerted to the existence of his prior claim.*

   In a suit brought by Briar against Boring Drill Company for the return of his pipe, Briar will

   (A) win, because Puma told the salesman that Briar had title to the pipe
   (B) win, because the salesman impliedly agreed not to seize the pipe until Puma had completely paid for it
   (C) lose, because he committed a breach of the peace by attacking Max
   (D) lose, because Puma never signed a contract with Briar

11. *An individual has the right to use force which, in the light of all the circumstances, is reasonably necessary to recover, to protect, or to prevent the taking of property which he reasonably believes to be his; however, if he is in error either as to his ownership of the property or as to the permissible degree of force, then he is liable to one whom he injures for any damages suffered.*

In a suit brought by Max against Briar for damages due to his broken leg, Max will

(A) win, because Briar had no reason to believe that the pipe in the truck belonged to him

(B) win, because Briar need not have resorted to force to protect his right to the pipe

(C) lose, because it was reasonable for Briar to believe that pipe which was being transported away from a site where he was the sole supplier belonged to him

(D) lose, because more force may reasonably be used against a trained professional than would be reasonable if used against an untrained individual

12. *If one gives value in exchange for rights to property, in good faith and without knowledge of conflicting claims to that property, then, even if the seller had no right to sell the property and even if there is a third party with a prior claim to the property, the buyer acquires good title to the property and is not liable to any prior owner either for the property or for its value.*

In a suit brought by Briar against Boring Drill Company for the return of the pipe, Briar will

(A) win, because Boring's salesman knew of the existence of the prior oral agreements concerning the pipe

(B) win, because Boring Drill Company was acting in bad faith by using a form contract that gave it rights to repossess property supplied by another vendor

(C) lose, because Boring Drill Company gave value by extending credit to Puma against the collateral he offered

(D) lose, because he only has the right to collect an unpaid debt, not the right to take the pipe

13. *If a contract calls for future payments of more than $1,000, then the contract may be enforced only if there is a written memorandum of its terms signed by the party against whom enforcement is sought, unless one party has performed substantially all of his obligations under the agreement before he seeks to enforce it.*

In a suit brought by Briar against Puma for the balance due him of $7,200, Briar will

(A) win, because Puma acknowledged the existence of the contract to an independent third party

(B) win, because Puma had received virtually all that he had bargained for when Briar let him take possession of the pipe

(C) lose, because the total amount due is more than $1,000

(D) lose, because Puma never signed a contract with Briar

14. *If someone intentionally exercises dominion and control over the property of another in a manner which invades the other's ownership rights, then the wrongdoer must pay the owner an amount equal to the fair market value of the property.*

In a suit brought by Briar against Max and Grunt for the full fair market value of the pipe, Briar will

(A) lose, because Puma had already paid him a substantial part of the pipe's value

(B) lose, because Max and Grunt were not aware of Briar's interest in the pipe

(C) win, because Max and Grunt did not surrender the pipe to him when he demanded it

(D) win, because he retained title until he had received payment in full

PART B. APPLYING ONE PRINCIPLE TO SEVERAL CASES

DIRECTIONS: Each principle of law given below is followed by several law cases: These principles may be either real or imaginary, but for purposes of this test you are to assume them to be valid. Following each law case are four statements regarding the possible applicability of the principle to the law case. You are to select the one statement which most appropriately describes the applicability of the principle to the law case decision. Blacken the space beneath the letter of the statement you select. These questions do not presuppose any specific legal knowledge on your part; you are to arrive at your answers entirely by the ordinary processes of logical reasoning.

A principal is responsible for the authorized acts of his agent. The agent's authority may be either actual or apparent. Actual authority arises out of an express or implied agreement between the principal and the agent which empowers the agent to perform certain acts on behalf of the principal. The agent has the actual authority to do those acts which are expressly defined in the agency agreement and, also, to do those acts which, in view of the totality of circumstances surrounding the agency relationship, one may reasonably infer are helpful or necessary to him in the execution of his express functions. Apparent authority exists when, in the absence of actual authority, the principal, through his acts or omissions, has permitted innocent third parties to reasonably believe that the agent possesses authority which he in fact does not.

An agent is not liable to his principal or to third parties for acts which are within the scope of his actual authority. Both agent and principal are liable to third parties for acts for which the agent has apparent authority. In addition, an agent is liable to his principal for any loss the latter may suffer from an act by the agent outside the scope of his actual authority. Finally, the agent is under a duty to his principal to exercise the same degree of care and skill when acting on his principal's behalf as he would if he were acting on his own behalf.

15. Smith, a full-time agent for the Sleep Easy Life Insurance Company, sold Jones a $25,000 policy which contained a standard provision for triple indemnity in the event of Jones' death while a fare-paying passenger in a public conveyance. Smith's contract with the company specifies that he has no authority to bind the company for any risk in excess of $50,000 without prior approval by the vice president in charge of sales. Smith gives Jones a receipt for the first premium, tells him that his coverage is in force, and submits the policy for approval. Before the approval is received, Jones is killed in an airplane crash.

    In a suit by Jones' beneficiary against the insurance company for the $75,000 death benefit, the beneficiary will

    (A) win, because Sleep Easy is responsible for the actions of its agents
    (B) win, because it was reasonable for Jones to believe that Smith was permitted to sell standard form policies
    (C) lose, because the vice president never approved the contract
    (D) lose, because Smith did not announce the limits of his actual authority

16. Ankloff is a teller trainee at Fat City Bank. When Woodhen comes in to make his monthly car payment, he tells Ankloff that he has been laid off and is short of money. Ankloff, a sympathetic person, tells him to skip that month's payment and to make it up once he has a new job. Woodhen gratefully accepts Ankloff's offer. The bank repossesses Woodhen's car.

    In the suit between the bank and Woodhen for the car, Woodhen pleads his agreement with Ankloff as a defense. The bank will

    (A) lose, because a teller's authority to refuse payments is implied by his authority to accept them
    (B) lose, because Woodhen believed that Ankloff was authorized to renegotiate loans
    (C) win, because it was not reasonable for Woodhen to believe that Ankloff could waive a payment
    (D) win, because Ankloff had the implied authority to permit Woodhen to defer payment

17. Andrew is a stockbroker. His client, Mogul, has given him the power to make trades of up to $1,000 without Mogul's specific approval. Andrew gets a tip on Techno-Glamour, Inc. and buys 100 shares at $10 a share for Mogul's account. He also buys 200 shares for himself. Unfortunately, in his haste to make a killing, Andrew neglected to read the negative report on Techno-Glamour that had been circulated among the brokers in his office. Techno-Glamour drops from $10 to $2 a share.

If Mogul sues Andrew for his losses, Mogul will

(A) win, because Andrew should have asked Mogul before he bought the stock
(B) win, because Andrew should have read the report on Techno-Glamour
(C) lose, because Andrew was authorized to make such purchases
(D) lose, because Andrew bought Techno-Glamour stock for himself

18. Douglas is a real estate broker whom Owens hires to sell his house. Brown buys the house, but when he is about to move in he discovers that the house is structurally unsound because of an infestation of termites.

If Brown sues Douglas, Brown will

(A) win, because Douglas had a duty to make sure the house was inhabitable
(B) win, because it was reasonable for Brown to believe that the house would be termite-free
(C) lose, because Owens hired Douglas to sell the house
(D) lose, because Douglas did not know about the termites

19. Adams was the purchasing agent for XYZ Corp. After 40 years of faithful service, he retired and was succeeded by Jones. Jones wrote to all of XYZ's suppliers to inform them of the change in personnel. Adams felt he was entitled to more than a gold watch, so he booked an around-the-world trip on Twilight Airways and wrote a letter on XYZ stationery requesting that the trip be billed to the corporation. He signed his own name to the letter and typed "Purchasing Agent" under the signature. Neither XYZ nor Adams had had any prior dealings with Twilight Airways. When the bill for the trip arrives, XYZ refuses to pay.

If Twilight sues XYZ, XYZ will

(A) win, because XYZ cannot be held liable for fraud committed by its employees
(B) win, because XYZ had not used Twilight for travel in the past
(C) lose, because Jones should have notified Twilight of Adams' retirement
(D) lose, because purchasing agents normally have the authority to purchase services

20. Mike was maintenance supervisor for Fleet Trucking. He customarily contracted with outside shops for engine or body repairs that could not be done in the Fleet garage. Fleet refuses to pay for a paint job done by Sam's Garage because Mike had not received written approval from the treasurer before he ordered the paint job. Although this was the first time Sam had done any work for Fleet, the company had never before objected to paying for work ordered by Mike without the treasurer's consent.

If Sam sues Mike, Mike will

   (A) win, because his authority to make such contracts is implied by Fleet's practice of paying the bills
   (B) win, because it was reasonable for Sam to believe that Mike had the authority to order such work
   (C) lose, because he had never been expressly given the authority to make such contracts
   (D) lose, because he did not have the apparent authority to order the work done by Sam

21. Jerry is a salesman for Tricky Dick's Used Car Emporium. Only Roy, the manager, has the authority to offer credit or to approve applications for credit. One day when Roy was out to lunch, Thomas came in to buy a car. When he asked about financing, Jerry explained the various plans which were available and had Thomas fill out a credit application. Jerry initialed the application and forwarded it to the credit department. The loan was granted. Six months later Thomas finds he cannot keep up the payments.

If Tricky Dick sues Thomas, Thomas will

   (A) win, because Jerry did not have the authority to offer credit to Thomas
   (B) win, because Jerry had a duty to make sure that Thomas was not assuming too great a payment burden
   (C) lose, because Jerry was Tricky Dick's agent, not Thomas'
   (D) lose, because Jerry had apparent authority to offer financing

Principle Two

Hearsay evidence is testimony or written evidence, presented in court, of a statement made out of court, which is offered as proof of the truth of the matter asserted in the out-of-court statement.

Hearsay evidence is inadmissible except in four cases:

1. If the out-of-court statement contains information which the speaker knew, when he made the statement, was likely to be detrimental to his interests.

2. If the out-of-court statement was made as an immediate spontaneous reaction to an emotionally disturbing event.

3. If the person making the statement was about to die, was aware of the fact that he or she was about to die, and did, in fact, die.

4. If the written evidence being offered is the official record of the verdict in a judicial proceeding.

22. Harris was struck and seriously injured by a car in a hit and run accident. A week later, when he regained consciousness in the hospital, an officer questioned him about the accident. Harris described the car and gave the first four digits of the license plate number. The next day, while undergoing surgery, Harris died. However, acting on Harris' information, the police arrested Olfield and charged him with vehicular homicide.

    At Olfield's trial, the police officer's testimony about Harris' description is

    (A) admissible, because it was a spontaneous reaction to the accident
    (B) admissible, because Harris died the next day
    (C) inadmissible, because a police investigation is not a judicial proceeding
    (D) inadmissible, because it is offered to prove that Olfield's car hit Harris

23. Mr. and Mrs. Blackburn were driving home from a party when their car went out of control. Mrs. Blackburn was killed instantly. Mr. Blackburn was seriously injured. As he was being lifted into the ambulance, he saw his wife's body and cried out, "Oh my God, I've killed her." He dies before the ambulance reaches the hospital. Since the Blackburns had no children and neither of them had written a will, it is necessary to determine which of them died first to decide whose relatives will inherit the estate. At the probate proceedings, Mr. Blackburn's exclamation is offered as evidence that he was still alive when the ambulance arrived.

    The ambulance attendant's testimony about Mr. Blackburn's statement is

    (A) admissible, because it was spontaneous
    (B) admissible, because it was not offered as proof that Mr. Blackburn was at fault
    (C) inadmissible, because Mr. Blackburn was not aware that he was dying
    (D) inadmissible, because Mr. Blackburn did not know for sure that his wife was dead

24. Big Louie is a bookie. During an investigation, an undercover agent observed Smith hand Big Louie a twenty-dollar bill and say "Snookers, to win, in the eighth."

    At Big Louie's trial for bookmaking, the agent's testimony about this conversation is

(A) admissible, because it is not hearsay
(B) admissible, because it was against Smith's interest when he made it
(C) inadmissible, because it does not fall into one of the four exceptions
(D) inadmissible, because Smith did not intend for it to be repeated

25. John Tippler has one drink too many at a New Year's Eve party. On his way home, Tippler collided with Bob's parked car. After he staggers out to survey the damage, Tippler is arrested and charged with drunk driving. He contests the charge, but is convicted and fined $100. Bob then sues John for the damage to his car.

Bob seeks to introduce the guilty verdict as proof of John's inebriation. It is

(A) admissible, because it is not offered as proof of John's drunk driving but as proof of his drunkenness
(B) admissible, because judicial records are an exception to the general hearsay exclusion
(C) inadmissible, because the constitution prohibits double jeopardy
(D) inadmissible, because it is hearsay

26. Caples bought a life insurance policy on her life for $50,000 and on the application she designated her husband, Quincy, as the beneficiary. When she died five years later, her mother contested the payment of the policy proceeds to Quincy.

The application is introduced in evidence to prove that Quincy was the named beneficiary. This evidence is

(A) admissible, because Caples was about to die
(B) admissible, because the naming of Quincy in the application was the act that made him the beneficiary and was not merely proof of the fact
(C) inadmissible, because the application was an out-of-court statement
(D) inadmissible, because the application was a written record of an out-of-court statement

27. Bazely was a bookkeeper for the Alpha Corp. Unfortunately, he is a compulsive gambler and a heavy loser, so he embezzled $15,000 from the company to pay a loan shark. One bright spring day he narrowly escapes being hit by a bus. In gratitude for what seemed to be divine intervention, he decides to change his ways. His first act is to confess his crime to his boss, Ebenezer, the treasurer of Alpha Corp. Although Ebenezer is sympathetic, he recognizes his first loyalty is to the com-

pany. He advises Bazely to retain a lawyer and then reports him to the district attorney.

At Bazely's trial for embezzlement, Ebenezer's testimony about Bazely's confession is

(A) inadmissible, because it is hearsay
(B) inadmissible, because Bazely was not represented by counsel when he confessed
(C) admissible, because it was a spontaneous reaction to his near fatal accident
(D) admissible, because confessing was likely to lead to criminal prosecution

28. The police arrested Tony to question him about a series of liquor store robberies. After six hours of interrogation, Tony broke down and started to talk. "I didn't do nothing. It was all Joe's idea." Tony gasped between sobs. "I didn't even go into the store. I didn't carry a gun. I just hung around outside while Joe went in and did his thing."

At Tony's trial for being an accessory to robbery, the policeman's testimony about Tony's statement is

(A) admissible, because Tony admitted his involvement in a crime
(B) admissible, because it is not hearsay
(C) inadmissible, because Tony intended to convince the police of his innocence
(D) inadmissible, because the police did not inform Tony of his constitutional rights

PART C. CHOOSING THE NARROWEST JUSTIFYING PRINCIPLE

DIRECTIONS: In this section you will be given several groups of imaginary law cases. Each question will present a set of facts and a fictitious court holding, which you are to presume to be valid. Following each case are four legal principles, lettered (A), (B), (C), and (D). You are to choose the narrowest (most precise) principle which explains the court decision given. However, this principle may not conflict with the holdings given in any of the preceding cases in the same group. The correct answer to the first case in any group will always be the most precise principle which correctly explains the legal decision made. From the second question until the end of each group, you are to select the narrowest principle which does not conflict with any of the previous holdings.

These questions do not presuppose any specific legal knowledge on your part. They are to be answered entirely by the ordinary processes of logical reasoning. Indicate your choice by blackening the appropriate space on the answer sheet.

Group One

29. Suzie did volunteer work for her congressman, Adam Smith, on his election campaign. On the basis of this work, she feels that she deserves a full-time paid position in his Washington office. When Congressman

Smith goes to Washington without Suzie, she decides to get even. She calls the local paper and tells a reporter that the campaign consisted of three months of sex and drug orgies. When the reporter presses her for more information, she describes several orgies in lurid detail. Unfortunately, these details, like everything else about Suzie's story, are completely fictitious. The paper prints the story attributed to "a highly reliable source" without checking with the Congressman. When he reads it, he is enraged. Smith sues the paper for defamation.

Held, for the paper.

The *narrowest principle* that reasonably explains this legal decision is:

(A) No one is liable for publishing false information which he believes to be true.

(B) A newspaper is not liable for negligently publishing false information about a public official.

(C) A newspaper is not liable for the publication of false information which it believes to be true.

(D) No one is liable for publishing false information about a public official.

30. Dusty, the publisher of the *Daily Tabloid,* decides to run a series of articles on organized crime. In keeping with the paper's reputation for publishing "The Whole Story," articles consist mainly of rumors, gossip, and innuendo. The paper reports that underworld informants have linked Father O'Brien, a popular local priest, to prostitution and blackmail rings. Neither Dusty nor any of his reporters interviewed the priest to verify the story. Father O'Brien sues the *Daily Tabloid* for defamation.

Held, for Father O'Brien.

The *narrowest principle* that reasonably explains this decision and is *not inconsistent* with the ruling given in the previous case is:

(A) A newspaper is liable for publishing false information about an individual which injures his reputation.

(B) One who publishes a falsehood which injures the reputation of another is liable unless he has a reasonable basis in fact for believing the truth of what he published.

(C) A newspaper is liable for what it reports if the matter published is untrue, and is published without a reasonable attempt to ascertain its truth or falsity.

(D) A newspaper is liable for publishing a false or defamatory story about one who is not a public official if it does not give the subject of those stories an opportunity to explain or to deny them.

31. During the mayoral election in Appleburg, the *Daily Applesause* newspaper publishes cartoons showing the mayor as a pig feeding at the public trough. The cartoons are accompanied by captions which accuse the mayor of taking bribes in exchange for certain contract awards. The mayor is not amused, especially when he loses the election and polls show that cartoons and accusations made a significant contribution to his defeat. The mayor sues the newspaper for defamation.

Held, for the mayor.

The *narrowest principle* which explains this decision and is *not inconsistent* with the rulings given in the preceding cases in this group is:

(A) A public official may recover damages from one who intentionally publishes a false accusation of specific criminal acts of official misconduct.

(B) The publisher of a statement which is likely to injure the reputation of a public official must exercise more than ordinary care to insure that the statement is true.

(C) One who maliciously publishes information which causes injury to the reputation of another is liable for that injury.

(D) One who publishes misinformation about another is strictly liable for the harm caused by such publication.

32. Davis owns a neighborhood grocery store and he distributes a weekly flyer advertising his specials. As a goodwill gesture, he includes announcements of community events, births, weddings, etc., which his customers submit to him. As a practical joke, John tells him that Paula has given birth to a lovely daughter. Davis prints the birth announcement. Unfortunately, Davis did not know that Paula had only been married a month and was not even pregnant. He immediately publishes a retraction, but Paula still sues him for defamation.

Held, for Paula.

The *narrowest principle* which reasonably explains this decision and is *not inconsistent* with the rulings given in the preceding cases in this group is:

(A) One who publishes a false statement about another is absolutely liable for any injury to the other's reputation caused by such publication.

(B) Retail merchants may not publish news items.

(C) A merchant may not publish information about a person for purposes of trade without that person's consent.

(D) No one may publish personal data about married women.

33. Jack, a 70-year-old grandfather, wrote a letter to the editor of his local paper criticizing an editorial which urged voters to defeat a proposed bond issue for senior citizen housing. The editor had held a grudge against Jack for years, so he printed the letter and a reply which said, in part, "Why should we or anyone else pay attention to the drivel spewed forth by a criminal like you?" When he was 16, Jack had been convicted of shoplifting and paid a fine, but he hadn't even received a parking ticket since then. Jack sues the paper for defamation.

Held, for the paper.

The *narrowest principle* which explains this decision and is *not inconsistent* with the rulings given in the preceding cases in this group is:

(A) A newspaper is liable for the injury caused by what it publishes about a private citizen only if the citizen can prove that the matter published is literally untrue.

(B) A newspaper is liable for what it reports only if it demonstrates a wanton disregard for the rights of the public.

(C) No one may recover damages for defamation for the publication of a true statement, regardless of the motive of the publisher.

(D) The constitutional guarantee of freedom of the press immunizes a newspaper from liability for what it publishes.

34. One night Donald suffers insomnia and starts brooding about the soft voices and girlish giggling coming from Phoebe's apartment next door. The voices are too quiet to distinguish words, but Donald's insomnia has made him hypersensitive. He gets up, types a petition to the landlord demanding that he evict Phoebe because she has loose morals and is maintaining a public nuisance, and then posts copies of the petition in the elevators and mailroom. As a result, Phoebe suffers great embarrassment. Her boyfriend refuses to visit her apartment and her parents disinherit her despite her protestations of innocence. To vindicate herself, Phoebe sues Donald for defamation.

Held, for Phoebe.

The *narrowest principle* which explains this decision and is *not inconsistent* with the rulings given in the preceding cases in this group is:

(A) The publisher of a defamatory statement will be liable to the person defamed regardless of extenuating circumstances.

(B) Malicious intent is a necessary element for liability for defamation.

(C) In order to find a defendant other than a newspaper publisher liable for defamation, the plaintiff must show that the defendant had actual knowledge of the falsity of the defamatory statement.

(D) If the defendant is not a newspaper publisher, the plaintiff need only prove the falsity of the defamatory statement and the fact of injury in order to recover for defamation.

Group Two

35. George and Sam were the drivers of two cars involved in a collision. Although neither of them was injured, both cars were totally destroyed. When George brings a civil action against Sam for his negligent driving, George offers evidence that Sam had received three tickets for reckless driving during the two months prior to the accident. Sam's attorney objects on the grounds that the evidence is irrelevant and, therefore, inadmissible.

    Held, the evidence is admissible.

    The *narrowest principle* which justifies this holding is

    (A) In automobile accident cases, irrelevant evidence is admissible.
    (B) In negligence cases involving only property damage, evidence about the defendant's conduct of a similar nature is irrelevant.
    (C) If the defendant's driving on a certain occasion is an issue in the litigation, then evidence about his driving at other times is relevant to the determination of that issue.
    (D) In automobile accident cases, the jury may not consider certain evidence, even if that evidence is relevant to the matters in issue, if the evidence is such that it may prejudice the jury adversely with respect to the defendant.

36. Harry and Mike got involved in an argument over the merits of their favorite football teams. The argument was abruptly terminated when Mike attacked Harry with a convenient beer bottle. At Mike's trial for criminal assault, the prosecution offers evidence that on several prior occasions Mike had gone into violent rages and had beaten his wife. Mike's attorney objects that the evidence is inadmissible because it is irrelevant.

    Held, the evidence is inadmissible.

    The *narrowest principle* which justifies this decision, and is *not inconsistent* with the holding in the preceding case is:

    (A) Evidence about the defendant's conduct on occasions which are similar, but unrelated, to the events which are the subject matter of the trial is not relevant to the case and must be excluded.
    (B) At a criminal trial, evidence which may be relevant must be excluded if there is a substantial chance that the jury may infer from such evidence conclusions detrimental to the defendant's interest about matters which are not in issue at the trial.
    (C) In cases involving personal injury, no evidence may be introduced about the defendant's character or prior conduct.
    (D) In a criminal trial, evidence will be excluded only if there is no possible inference to be drawn from it that would indicate that the defendant is guilty.

37. Mary and Jim start fighting in a crowded restaurant. Mary leaps up from the table and calls Jim a thief and a scoundrel. Jim brings a civil action against Mary for public defamation. At the trial, Mary offers evidence that Jim was convicted of shoplifting twenty years ago, when he was eighteen years old. Jim's attorney objects on the grounds that the evidence is irrelevant.

Held, the evidence is admissible.

The *narrowest principle* that reasonably explains this result, and is *not inconsistent* with the rulings in the preceding cases in this group is:

(A) If a party's character is brought directly into issue by the facts of the case, then evidence about character will be admissible even if it is possible that the jury may be prejudiced against that party by such evidence.

(B) If the plaintiff in an action asserts that the defendant has defamed him through a malicious falsehood, then the defendant may introduce evidence which tends to prove the truth of the alleged falsehood despite the probability that such evidence will prejudice the jury.

(C) Evidence about a party's conduct will not be admissible if that conduct occurred long before the present case.

(D) Although evidence about a party's prior criminal convictions is inadmissible to prove him guilty of the crime charged in the present prosecution, such evidence is admissible to impeach his testimony and to cause the jury to doubt the truth of his allegations.

38. John is charged with robbing Phil's Liquor Store. When he takes the witness stand to testify about his alibi, the prosecutor attempts to introduce evidence about a previous conviction for perjury. John's lawyer objects on grounds of relevance.

Held, the evidence about the prior conviction is admissible.

The *narrowest principle* that reasonably explains this result, and is *not inconsistent* with the decisions in the preceding cases in this group is:

(A) Convictions for prior crimes involving moral turpitude or perjury may be introduced to impeach the credibility of any witness.

(B) A defendant who takes the witness stand in his own behalf waives his right to exclude evidence about his prior misconduct.

(C) If the defendant in a criminal trial relies on an alibi defense, then evidence need not be relevant to the crime in question to be admissible.

(D) If a defendant in a criminal trial elects to testify in his own behalf, then the prosecution may introduce evidence which may tend to prejudice the jury if the primary purpose of introducing that evidence is to make the jury doubt the truth of the defendant's testimony.

39. Dick has been charged with perjury. At his trial the prosecution offers evidence that, three years previously, Dick had been convicted of perjury, bribery, and jury tampering. Dick's attorney objects that the evidence is irrelevant and, hence, inadmissible.

Held, the evidence is inadmissible.

The *narrowest principle* that justifies this decision, and is *not inconsistent* with the holdings of the preceding cases in this group is:

(A) In a criminal trial, evidence about the defendant's prior convictions is not relevant to the determination of whether or not he committed the crime of which he stands accused; and the risk that the jury will be prejudiced against him by such evidence is so great that it must always be excluded.

(B) Prior convictions for perjury may be introduced to impeach the credibility of any witness.

(C) Prior convictions, when offered as proof of the defendant's propensity, inclination, or disposition to commit the crime for which he is being tried, are not admissible as evidence unless the prior crime is the same as the one with which he is charged.

(D) The prosecution may introduce evidence of the defendant's prior convictions in a criminal trial only if the defendant testifies.

40. Lilith, an unmarried woman, discovers that she is pregnant. She brings a paternity action against Charlie, claiming that he is the father of her unborn child and that he should be compelled to support the tyke. Charlie offers evidence that Lilith had intimate relations with at least a dozen men during the three months before the baby was conceived. Lilith's attorney objects to the introduction of this evidence on the grounds of relevance.

Held, the evidence is admissible.

The *narrowest principle* that reasonably explains this legal decision, and is *not inconsistent* with the previous cases in this group is:

(A) When the plaintiff's conduct supports a reasonable inference that the defendant did not cause the plaintiff's injury, then evidence about that conduct will be admissible even though it is likely to unreasonably prejudice the jury against the plaintiff.

(B) If a party's character is brought directly into issue by the facts of the case, then evidence about character will be admissible even though it may be prejudicial.

(C) Prior actions which indicate a party's inclination to engage in the conduct which is the subject matter of a case are admissible.

(D) Only the defendant may object to the introduction of evidence about his character on the grounds of irrelevance.

END OF TEST

TEST III. PRACTICAL JUDGMENT

TIME: 20 Minutes. 20 Questions.

DIRECTIONS: In this test you will be presented with a detailed case study of a practical business situation. Read the study carefully. Then answer the two sets of questions based upon the reading. In the Data Evaluation questions, you will be asked to classify certain facts on the basis of their importance to the case presented. In the Data Application questions you will be asked to make judgments based upon your comprehension of the information.

Correct and explanatory answers are provided at the end of the exam. After you have completed the entire exam, read the explanations carefully. They'll reinforce your strengths and pinpoint your weaknesses so that you know just what to study to raise your score.

Business Situation. Tonsitol

Tonsitol, an antibacterial gargle, was introduced in 1962 by the Mycophil Company and proved to be one of the company's most successful products. By 1976, sales of the product represented a significant share of the mouthwash market in competition with the two leaders: Listerine and Lavoris. Heavy consumer advertising by these competitors, pressure from the company's sales force, and other influences led the Mycophil management to consider the advisability of advertising Tonsitol directly to consumers. Such action would represent a drastic change in policy. Mycophil and other ethical pharmaceutical manufacturers[1] traditionally confined their advertising to the medical, dental, and pharmaceutical professions, as appropriate for individual products. This was based upon the long established feeling that consumer advertising would cheapen the name of the company in the eyes of doctors and possibly even create ill will. Nevertheless, the Mycophil management did not want to neglect an opportunity. Ms. Yolanda Hauser, Vice President for Marketing, was assigned to study whether Tonsitol possessed characteristics which would warrant extensive consumer advertising and, if so, what should be the general nature of the advertising campaign.

The Mycophil Company had a sales volume in 1975 of more than $30 million. Sales of Tonsitol in that year amounted to slightly over $4 million and had been growing at a more rapid rate than the sales volume of any other Mycophil product. While the profit margin on Tonsitol was not as great as that for other Mycophil products, the company felt that this product had a better profit potential than some of the higher margin items.

As oral deodorants, mouthwashes sold throughout the country and around the calendar at a fairly even rate. However, as a gargle for sore throats there were wide variations seasonally and geographically. Since Mycophil

---

1. An ethical pharmaceutical house is one which does not advertise directly to consumers, because its products are available only by prescription.

promoted Tonsitol through the medical and dental professions and emphasized the medicinal value of its product, Tonsitol suffered from these fluctuations. Moreover, the frequency of purchase by loyal users was considerably below that of Listerine and Lavoris, which were used more commonly as oral deodorants.

Sales of Tonsitol were much stronger in the North than in the South and Far West. They were particularly strong in Washington, D.C., Detroit, Chicago, Cleveland, and Cincinnati. They tended to peak during the periods of heavy incidence of colds and sore throats. During the flu epidemic in the fall and winter of 1969, sales of Tonsitol increased almost 40 percent in contrast with a 10 percent increase in sales of competitive products.

In 1975, Tonsitol sales accounted for approximately 15 percent of the mouthwash market. Listerine, the leader, accounted for more than 50 percent, and Lavoris for about 20 percent. Both Listerine and Lavoris emphasized the oral deodorant theme, but also discussed protection against sore throats. In 1975, Mycophil spent $140,000 on trade and medical publication advertising of Tonsitol in addition to its distribution of samples, point of purchase displays, and other promotional material. Listerine spent about 8 percent of sales, or $1,100,000, on general magazine advertising alone. Total advertising of Listerine was estimated to amount to 20 percent of sales, in contrast to an estimated 16 percent for the industry.

Tonsitol was sold in 6-ounce and 1-pint bottles. It possessed several characteristics which gave it an advantage over its competitors. It was mildly alkaline, which helped reduce excessive oral acidity, odor producing bacteria, and tooth decay. Excess acidity irritates membranes of the mouth and throat, and the mild alkalinity of Tonsitol was said to neutralize and soothe inflamed tissues. The antibacterial action of Tonsitol was made more effective by the low surface tension of the solution, which was about one-half that of water. This permitted quick, deep penetration and detergent action. Tonsitol was lemon yellow in color, had a pleasant flavor, and a refreshing aftertaste. Retail prices for the leading mouthwashes varied somewhat because of bottle size and fair trade restrictions, but tended to be grouped at fifty cents for 6 ounces.

Patent protection on the basic process by which the principal ingredient of Tonsitol was made was due to expire in 1978, and it did not appear possible to gain further protection. The registered trademark, Tonsitol, would of course remain exclusively the property of the Mycophil Company.

The early success of Tonsitol indicated that a lozenge similar to a cough drop might have even greater market acceptance because of the convenience with which it could be carried and used. Therefore, in 1965, the company introduced such a lozenge and gave it the Tonsitol name. The effectiveness of the lozenge was comparable to that of the solution. In planning for the promotion of Tonsitol, Ms. Hauser decided the Tonsitol lozenges should be distributed and promoted in the same way as the mouthwash. Consequently, she had to design one marketing program to include both products.

Current marketing practices for Tonsitol were similar to those used by Mycophil to promote its ethical products, focusing on physicians and dentists who were visited by Mycophil representatives, informed of the advantages of the Tonsitol products, given samples of the products for distribution to patients, and urged to recommend them. In addition, drugstores and wholesale drug houses were informed more fully of the products and urged to stock them.

Ms. Hauser suggested two possible alternatives to this strategy. As one modification she recommended that several moves in the direction of more aggressive promotion of Tonsitol be taken short of a full scale, consumer-oriented advertising campaign. These tactics were focused on making an impact on the consumer at the point of sale.

The second alternative was a multimedia advertising program. Since Mycophil was primarily a manufacturer of ethical pharmaceuticals, the company had no experience in mass-market advertising. Ms. Hauser advised that if this option were chosen more study would be required to determine the most effective media. Although she proposed a budget based on the average expenditures in the industry, she indicated that the expenditures might be varied to increase when sales of Tonsitol decreased. She suggested that several advertising agencies be asked to prepare proposals for a campaign within the parameters established by her budget.

The management policy committee reviewed her memorandum (Exhibit "A"), but postponed making a decision until more was known about the effects of the programs on Mycophil's image and goodwill.

EXHIBIT A

MEMO TO: Management Policy Committee

FROM: Hauser, V.P. Marketing

SUBJECT: Marketing of Tonsitol

I. Background

Tonsitol antiseptic mouthwash is one of the few proprietary products this company makes. At the present time it accounts for 13% of our sales but only 10% of our profits. Our patent on the basic production process is due to expire in 1978, so we can expect imitations to appear shortly thereafter, although we will continue to have the exclusive use of the Tonsitol trademark. Because Tonsitol has been marketed as an antiseptic sore throat gargle rather than as a breath freshener, it has less brand loyalty and more seasonal and geographical variations in sales than either of the major competing brands: Lavoris and Listerine. Any marketing program which we undertake must be evaluated primarily in terms of its ability to increase the value of the trademark and secondarily in terms of its effectiveness in smoothing the sales curve both regionally and seasonally.

II.   Current Strategy

In keeping with the company's established policy, Tonsitol has been marketed like an ethical drug. The program has been directed at doctors, dentists, and pharmacists. The direct sales presentations have stressed Tonsitol's antiseptic qualities. Advertising, which has the same emphasis, has been limited to trade journals and has been allotted 45% of the total marketing budget. The only difference between the Tonsitol promotion and the normal ethical drug promotion is that the former includes the use of point of sale displays. These displays have a conservative appearance and have been designed primarily to insure that they do not detract from our corporate image as an ethical pharmaceutical house.

Tonsitol has been well received by retail pharmacists because it is sold only in drugstores whereas competing brands are also sold in supermarkets and discount houses. Secondly, it carries a margin for the retailer of 45% of the retail price against 35% for other mouthwashes. It also appears that druggists take professional pride in recommending a product associated with an ethical drug company.

III.   First Alternate Strategy

We have not determined the relative value of recommendations to consumers by the medical and dental professions as opposed to those by pharmacists; however, since minor sore throat pain rarely warrants a trip to the doctor, druggists have more occasion than physicians to give advice about antiseptic gargles. As indicated above, our relations with retail outlets are excellent and can be used to our advantage with, at most, a marginal increase in the marketing budget and at minimal risk to our corporate image.

First, the company can offer display allowances to retailers to encourage them to use counter displays. These displays should be made brighter and more colorful. Humor should be incorporated as an effective means of getting the consumer's attention. Tonsitol's characteristic ethical label and package can be redesigned to make them more attractive from a merchandising viewpoint. Since we lack experience in packaging consumer goods, we would require the services of an outside consultant to undertake this redesign.

Second, the distribution of free samples is a relatively inexpensive means of increasing consumer awareness. Initially, we can attach sample lozenges to bottles of Tonsitol liquid. Later we can attach sample bottles of liquid to packages of lozenges. Finally, samples of both the liquid and the lozenge may be distributed directly to consumers in selected high volume drug stores and at the opening of new drug stores.

To minimize the company's risk, we should initially test market in a limited number of areas. This test marketing should be done in one or two areas where Tonsitol sales are normally strong such as Washington, D.C., and in one or two areas where sales are weak such as Dallas.

Other than the initial $10,000 cost of redesigning the Tonsitol packages and point of sale displays, this program can be funded by reallocating funds from the existing promotional budget. I recommend that if this strategy be instituted, we plan for a six-month trial period from January through June. Our normal advertising costs during this period in the Washington and Dallas areas are about $15,000 and other promotional expenses are about $10,000. The cost of a six-month test campaign is estimated to be $20,000 exclusive of one time start-up expenses.

IV. Second Alternate Strategy

Both of the major competing brands rely heavily upon mass-media advertising. Mycophil, since it is primarily an ethical drug house, has had no experience in this form of promotion, but it would seem that consumer-oriented advertising is the most effective means of developing brand identification and brand loyalty. It is also the most costly means of achieving those ends. In order to reduce the company's risk and develop in-house expertise, we should test such a program in only two regions, Washington, D.C. and Dallas.

The cost of a six-month trial program of advertising in general circulation magazines, radio, and television in those two areas would be $70,000. The precise type of advertising and the most effective media mix are outside my field of competence, so I suggest that a local advertising agency be retained in each city to provide assistance in those areas. Such an advertising campaign should be supported by repackaging the Tonsitol products and redesigning the point of sale displays. This would add $10,000 to the total cost.

V. Recommendations and Conclusions

The great imponderable element in either strategy is whether a consumer-oriented marketing campaign will damage our reputation as an ethical drug company and, consequently, hurt the sales of our non-proprietary products. Those products do account for over 80% of our sales and profit, so the effect of a test program on the sales of our ethical drugs in the target areas must be watched carefully. In addition to the obvious cost savings of regional rather than national marketing campaigns, such localized programs will minimize the extent of any injury to our goodwill in the medical, dental, and pharmaceutical professions.

DATA EVALUATION

DIRECTIONS: Based on your analysis of the Situation, classify each of the following items in one of five categories. On your answer sheet blacken the space under:

(A) if the item is a MAJOR OBJECTIVE in making the decision; that is, one of the outcomes or results sought by the decision-maker.

(B) if the item is a MAJOR FACTOR in arriving at the decision; that is, a consideration explicitly mentioned in the passage that is basic in determining the decision.

(C) if the item is a MINOR FACTOR in making the decision; that is, a secondary consideration that affects the criteria tangentially, relating to a Major Factor rather than to an Objective.

(D) if the item is a MAJOR ASSUMPTION made in deliberating; that is, a supposition or projection made by the decision-maker before weighing the variables.

(E) if the item is an UNIMPORTANT ISSUE in getting to the point; that is, a factor that is insignificant or not immediately relevant to the situation.

1. Mycophil's total sales in 1975

2. Cost of redesigning the Tonsitol package

3. Enhancing the value of the Tonsitol trademark

4. Expiration of the basic patent for Tonsitol

5. Increase in Tonsitol's sales during the 1969 influenza epidemic

6. Relationship between retailer's attitudes and sales of Tonsitol

7. Mycophil's lack of experience in consumer advertising

8. Expansion of Tonsitol's market share

9. Mycophil's policy on consumer advertising

10. Tonsitol's reputation as a sore throat gargle

11. Competitors' use of consumer advertising

12. Reduction of seasonal and geographic variations in Tonsitol's sales

13. Retail price differential between Tonsitol and competing brands

14. Suitability of Washington, D.C. and Dallas for test marketing

DATA APPLICATION

DIRECTIONS: Based on your understanding of the Business Situation, answer the following questions testing your comprehension of the information supplied in the passage. For each question, select the choice which best answers the question or completes the statement.

15. Which of the following were *not* reasons given for Mycophil's consideration of direct advertising of Tonsitol?

    I. Advertising practices of competitors
   II. Mycophil's traditional advertising policy
  III. Expiration of the basic Tonsitol patent
  IV. Pressures from retail druggists
   V. Attitudes of Mycophil's sales force

    (A) I and II only   (D) I, III, and V only
    (B) II, III, and V only   (E) III and V only
    (C) II and IV only

16. It may be inferred that a reason for Ms. Hauser's selection of Dallas as a potential test market is that

    (A) Dallas' climate is not conducive to upper respiratory infections
    (B) Mycophil's sales people in the Southwest are not as motivated as those in the Northeast
    (C) Tonsitol's competitors advertise more heavily in the Southwest than in the Northeast
    (D) Tonsitol's competitors advertise less heavily in the Southwest than in the Northeast
    (E) Tonsitol had been increasing its share of the mouthwash market faster in Dallas than in other cities

17. About how much more would the average druggist net by selling a case of 144 6-ounce bottles of Tonsitol instead of a case of Lavoris?

    (A) 0   (D) $28.00
    (B) $7.00   (E) $72.00
    (C) $14.00

18. Assuming that the ratio of marketing expenses to sales was the same for Tonsitol as for Mycophil's other products, approximately how much did Mycophil spend on marketing in 1975?

    (A) $140,000   (D) $1,800,000
    (B) $300,000   (E) $2,300,000
    (C) $1,100,000

19. In 1975, total sales of Listerine were about

(A) $1,100,000
(B) $2,800,000
(C) $5,500,000
(D) $14,000,000
(E) $30,000,000

20. It is most reasonable to expect that the opinions of Mycophil's executives most differ from those of their competitors with regard to

(A) the potential mouthwash market in the Northeastern United States
(B) the importance of oral hygiene
(C) the effectiveness of consumer advertising in creating brand loyalty for mouthwashes
(D) the value of endorsements by retail pharmacists
(E) the relationship between influenza epidemics and the demand for antibacterial mouthwashes

END OF TEST

Go on to do the following Test in this Examination, just as you would be expected to do on the actual exam. You will find correct answers for the entire Examination following the last question. Check your answers carefully after you have completed the whole Examination.

TEST IV. QUANTITATIVE COMPARISON

TIME: 15 Minutes. 25 Questions.

DIRECTIONS: *For each of the following questions two quantities are given . . . one in Column A; and one in Column B. Compare the two quantities and mark your answer sheet with the correct, lettered conclusion. These are your options:*
  - A: *if the quantity in Column A is the greater;*
  - B: *if the quantity in Column B is the greater;*
  - C: *if the two quantities are equal;*
  - D: *if the relationship cannot be determined from the information given.*

COMMON INFORMATION: *In each question, information pertinent to one or both of the quantities to be compared is given in the Common Information column. A symbol that appears in any column represents that same thing in Column A as in Column B.*

NUMBERS: *All numbers used are real numbers.*

FIGURES: *Assume that the position of points, angles, regions, and so forth, are in the order shown.*

Assume that the lines shown as straight are indeed straight. Figures are assumed to lie in a plane unless otherwise indicated.

Figures accompanying questions are intended to provide information you can use in answering the questions. However, unless a note states that a figure is drawn to scale, you should solve the problems by using your knowledge of mathematics, and NOT by estimating sizes by sight or by measurement.

Correct and explanatory answers are provided at the end of the exam.

	Common Information	*Column A.*	*Column B.*
1.		$\dfrac{a(b + c)}{b}$	$\dfrac{b(a + c)}{b}$
	$a = 4 \quad b = 3 \quad c = 2$		
2.		$\dfrac{a}{b} \times c$	$\dfrac{a}{c} \times b$
3.		$3 \times 4 + 6$	30
4.		$\sqrt[3]{100}$	5

	Common Information	Column A.	Column B.
5.		Length $\overline{Aa}$	Length $\overline{Ba}$
6.		3 × Area △ aAb	Area △ ABC
7.		Length $\overline{AB}$	Length $\overline{BC}$
8.		2 × Area △ Bac	Area of parallelogram abCc
9.	ab ‖ BC	Perimeter of △ acB	Perimeter of △ Aba

	Common Information	Column A.	Column B.
10.		HHTT	HTTH
11.		HHHH	HHHT
12.	Consider tossing a coin. Probability of throwing	Both H and T in any order	H or T
13.		HHHHH	.03
14.		2H 2T, in any order	HHTT

	Column A.	Column B.
15.	$(2 \times 10^{-4})(5 \times 10^{2})$	$(5 \times 10^{-4})(2 \times 10^{2})$
16.	$\sqrt[3]{9 \times 10^{-6}}$	$\sqrt[2]{910 \times 10^{-6}}$
17.	$\dfrac{.025}{.6}$	$\dfrac{2.4}{6}$
18.	$\dfrac{5}{7} + \dfrac{6}{4}$	$\dfrac{6}{7} + \dfrac{5}{4}$
19.	$\sqrt[3]{0.001}$	$\sqrt{0.01}$
20.	$\dfrac{1/5 - 1/6}{1/6}$	$1/5$
21.	$\dfrac{1/7 - 1/8}{1/8}$	$8/7$

	Common Information	Column A.	Column B.
22.		$\dfrac{1}{y}$	$\dfrac{1}{x}$
23.	y > x > 0	y − 2	x − 2
24.		y − x	x − y
25.		−y	−x

TEST V. ERROR RECOGNITION

TIME: 20 Minutes. 35 Questions.

DIRECTIONS: This is a test of your ability to recognize standard written English. Some of the sentences presented are acceptable as written English. Others contain errors of diction, verbosity or grammar. No one sentence contains more than one kind of error. Read each sentence carefully, then classify each according to the categories that follow. Mark your answer sheet:

(A) if the sentence contains an error in DICTION; that is, the use of a word which is incorrect because its meaning does not fit the sentence, or because it is not acceptable in standard written English.

(B) if the sentence is VERBOSE; that is, wordy or repetitious without justification by the need for emphasis.

(C) if the sentence contains FAULTY GRAMMAR; that is, errors in parallelism, number, case, tense, etc.

(D) if the sentence contains none of these errors.

Correct and explanatory answers are provided at the end of the exam. After you have completed the entire exam, read the explanations carefully. They'll reinforce your strengths and pinpoint your weaknesses so that you know just what to study to raise your score.

1. He had to risk them being late.

2. Either pencil or pen are satisfactory.

3. Mr. Benson is the tallest of the two men.

4. Who do you wish to see?

5. He was too ingenious to suspect that he was being tricked.

6. In the province of Ontario alone, lots of informal schools have come into existence since 1967.

7. My roommate need never worry about finances.

8. It is a very questionable proposition that mankind has advanced forward in the course of the last two millennia.

9. Dr. Smith indicated that the new school would be built in the Bronx, since that borough's need for new facilities was so acute.

10. The President of Bilkmore Steel Corporation remarked that the steel industry cannot now afford to cut prices at the present time.

11. The theme of Langston Hughes' work has been the common man, more specifically the ordinary Negro and his pleasures and sorrows.

12. I was not attempting to belittle Dickens when I inferred that his novels are melodramatic.

13. He lost all hope of recovering his eyeglasses as they sank into the turgid waters.

14. The Senator insisted that the United States would always stick up for its allies.

15. A new diagnostic procedure for arthritis of the joints was reported today.

16. There seems to be several opinions about the matter.

17. Ten miles seem a very long distance when you have to walk it.

18. Some of the electrical equipment were removed owing to the threat of fire.

19. I was surprised at John being here.

20. Because of your neglectfulness and heedlesness, this business has lost its capital.

21. It has taken me several days to get the hang of driving.

22. I no longer pay any attention to his comings and goings.

23. The mayor announced that labor and management had a mutually acceptable arrangement satisfactory to both parties to the dispute.

24. The navy announced that a task force, including an aircraft carrier, two cruisers and transports loaded with marines, was steaming southward.

25. The union has given its top officers a substantial pay boost.

26. It was a hard but wholesome life, under which the people suffered many privations and enjoyed many advantages, without any clear realization of the existence of either one of them.

27. The two sections of the bridge will be joined together tomorrow afternoon.

28. Collecting Canadian paper money is a popular hobby.

29. The next step is to complete the arrangements for the swapping of war prisoners.

30. The coach languished praise on John for his running in last night's game.

31. His job done, he went home.

32. The news today are most encouraging.

33. When I go camping, I usually raise at daybreak to walk in the woods.

34. George and myself built Robert's new house, which is in New Jersey.

35. I believe that the judge handed down a fair, equitable decision.
END OF TEST

410 / Law School Admission Test

TEST VI. SENTENCE CORRECTION

TIME: 20 Minutes. 25 Questions.

DIRECTIONS: Some part of each of the following sentences is underlined. After each sentence are five ways of stating the underlined part. Choice A simply repeats the original sentence or phrase. If you think that the original sentence is more effective than any of the alternatives, pick Choice A. If you believe the underlined part is incorrect, select from the other choices (B, C, D, or E) the one you think is best and blacken the corresponding space on the answer sheet. In choosing the best alternative, consider grammar, sentence structure, punctuation and word usage. Do not choose an answer that changes the meaning of the original sentence.

Correct and explanatory answers are provided at the end of the exam. After you have completed the entire exam, read the explanations carefully. They'll reinforce your strengths and pinpoint your weaknesses so that you know just what to study to raise your score.

1. I caught sight of him buying a rifle.

    (A) him buying a rifle.
    (B) his buying a rifle.
    (C) he buying a rifle.
    (D) him, buying a rifle.
    (E) a rifle being bought by him.

2. Carter received orders to attack the Federal right wing, which he did immediately.

    (A) Carter received orders to attack the Federal right wing, which he did immediately.
    (B) Carter received orders to attack the Federal right wing, so he did.
    (C) Upon Carter's receiving orders to attack the Federal right wing, he did so immediately.
    (D) Once Carter had received orders to attack the Federal right wing, he immediately began the attack.
    (E) As soon as Carter received orders, he attacked the Federal right wing.

3. I am in search for a position as administrator.

    (A) I am in search for a position as administrator.
    (B) I am in search for a position of administrator.
    (C) I am in search of a position as administrator.
    (D) I am searching for a position of administrator.
    (E) I am in search of a position of administrator.

4. My shirt always wrinkles <u>when hurrying to the office.</u>

    (A) when hurrying to the office.   (D) hurrying to the office.
    (B) when I am hurrying to the office.   (E) at the office.
    (C) while hurrying to the office.

5. <u>Father sent me a check; to cover all my expenses for the first semester.</u>

    (A) Father sent me a check; to cover all my expenses for the first semester.
    (B) To cover all my expenses for the first semester, father sent me a check.
    (C) Covering all my expenses for the first semester, father sent me a check.
    (D) All my expenses for the first semester are covered in the check father sent me.
    (E) Father sent me a check to cover all my expenses in the first semester.

6. <u>Neither Racine nor the Elizabethans appeals to Clarence,</u> who dislikes everything exuberant.

    (A) Neither Racine nor the Elizabethans appeals to Clarence,
    (B) Neither Racine nor the Elizabethans has an appeal for Clarence,
    (C) Neither Racine nor the Elizabethans appeal to Clarence,
    (D) Neither Racine or the Elizabethans appeal to Clarence,
    (E) Neither Racine nor the Elizabethans appealing to Clarence,

7. Florence was just as surprised <u>by the gift I gave her as you gave her.</u>

    (A) by the gift I gave her as you gave her.
    (B) by my gift as by your gift.
    (C) by my gift and your gift.
    (D) by the gift I gave her and by the gift you gave her.
    (E) by both of our gifts.

8. These are the duties of the president of a literary society: to preside at regular meetings, <u>he calls special meetings, and the appointment of committees.</u>

    (A) he calls special meetings, and the appointment of committees.
    (B) he calls special meetings, and he appoints committees.
    (C) to call special meetings; he also appoints committees.
    (D) to call special meetings and appoint committees.
    (E) to call special meetings, and to appoint committees.

9. <u>All the sweaters are reversible.</u>

    (A) All the sweaters are reversible.
    (B) The foregoing types of sweater all have the property of reversibility.

(C) All these sweaters have the property of reversibility.
(D) These sweaters have reverse properties.
(E) The foregoing types of sweater are all reversible.

10. I read in the newspaper <u>that rubber is being made from a plant grown in this country</u>.

(A) that rubber is being made from a plant grown in this country.
(B) where rubber is being made in this country.
(C) where they are making rubber from a plant grown in this country.
(D) that a plant grown in this country is producing rubber.
(E) to the effect that rubber is being made from a plant grown in this country.

11. Farmers have always <u>rose</u> early.

(A) rose   (D) risen
(B) rised   (E) raisen
(C) raised

12. He thought the price was high, <u>since</u> he had so little to spend.

(A) since   (D) being that
(B) being as   (E) being as how
(C) seeing as how

13. They gave quarters to the youngest, <u>John and I</u>.

(A) John and I.   (D) to John and to me.
(B) John and me.   (E) namely John and I.
(C) John and myself.

14. I always liked engineers, <u>and I have chosen that as my profession</u>.

(A) and I have chosen that as my profession.
(B) and I have chosen this as my profession.
(C) and I have decided to become one.
(D) and I have decided to become an engineer myself.
(E) and I have opted for that as a career.

15. <u>Hitler had no hesitation to use force</u>.

(A) Hitler had no hesitation to use force.
(B) Hitler did not hesitate in using force.
(C) Hitler had no hesitation in the use of force.
(D) Hitler had no hesitation to the use of force.
(E) Hitler did not hesitate to use force.

16. In talking with Henry, I learned the news.

    (A) In talking with Henry, I learned the news.
    (B) In talking with Henry, I found out.
    (C) In talking with Henry, the news was told to me.
    (D) In talking with Henry, the news leaked out.
    (E) In talking with Henry, he told me the news.

17. A sober-dressing man who exhibited his vanity only in the dull perfection of his clothes and the wearing always of a corded edge to his waistcoat.

    (A) A sober-dressing man who exhibited his vanity only in the dull perfection of his clothes and the wearing always of a corded edge to his waistcoat.
    (B) He was a sober-dressing man who exhibited his vanity only in the dull perfection of his clothes and the wearing always of a corded edge to his waistcoat.
    (C) He was a sober-dressing man who exhibited his vanity only in the dull perfection of his clothes and wore always a corded edge to his waistcoat.
    (D) A sober-dressing man, exhibiting his vanity only in the dull perfection of his clothes and the wearing always of a corded edge to his waistcoat.
    (E) Exhibiting his vanity only in the dull perfection of his clothes and the wearing always of a corded edge to his waistcoat, sober-dressing was the way to describe him.

18. The home side struggled along with weak pitching, anemic fielding, and what hitting they did was lifeless.

    (A) and what hitting they did was lifeless.   (D) and their hitting was terrible.
    (B) and their hitting was lifeless.   (E) and lifeless hitting.
    (C) and a lifeless sort of hitting.

19. As the car skidded to the edge of the cliff, we thought we were doomed, and our seats were grabbed in fear.

    (A) and our seats were grabbed in fear.
    (B) and we grabbed fearfully at our seats
    (C) and we grabbed our seats in fear.
    (D) and fearfully we grabbed our seats.
    (E) and fear made us grab our seats.

20. The city is famous for its musicians, its science, and its architecture.

    (A) its musicians, its science, and its architecture.
    (B) music, its science, and architecture.
    (C) its musicians, science, and architecture.
    (D) its musicians and science, as well as its architecture.
    (E) its musicians, its scientists, and its architects.

21. Most teachers with whom I come into contact are high in respect of intelligence.

    (A) Most teachers with whom I come into contact are high in respect of intelligence.
    (B) Most teachers with whom I come into contact are highly intelligent.
    (C) Most teachers whom I meet are highly intelligent.
    (D) Most teachers whom I meet are high in respect of intelligence.
    (E) Most teachers with whom I come into contact are high in intelligence.

22. The reason I whistle is because I am happy.

    (A) The reason I whistle is because I am happy.
    (B) The reason I whistle is that I am happy.
    (C) Because I am happy is the reason I whistle.
    (D) That I am happy is the reason I whistle.
    (E) The reason I whistle is because of happiness.

23. After five minutes over the fire, the hamburger had shrinked to half its original size.

    (A) shrinked   (D) shrunk
    (B) shrank   (E) shrunked
    (C) shranked

24. She can neither hear nor see.

    (A) She can neither hear nor see.
    (B) She can either hear or see.
    (C) She can neither hear or see.
    (D) Neither can she hear nor can she see.
    (E) She neither can see nor hear.

25. The happiest people there were himself and his mother.

    (A) himself   (D) his own self
    (B) he   (E) his self
    (C) him

END OF TEST

Go on to do the following Test in this Examination, just as you would be expected to do on the actual exam. You will find correct answers for the entire Examination following the last question. Check your answers carefully after you have completed the whole Examination.

TEST VII. VALIDITY OF CONCLUSION

TIME: 30 Minutes. 50 Questions.

DIRECTIONS: This section consists of fact patterns or cases with the conclusion or ruling of the court for each case. Following the outcome of each case are additional statements which may affect the result. Read each statement carefully, then mark your Answer Sheet:

(A) if the statement proves the result;
(B) if the statement tends to affirm the result but does not prove it;
(C) if the statement disproves the result;
(D) if the statement tends to weaken the result but does not disprove it;
(E) if the statement is irrelevant to the result.

Correct and explanatory answers are provided at the end of the exam. After you have completed the entire exam, read the explanations carefully. They'll reinforce your strengths and pinpoint your weaknesses so that you know just what to study to raise your score.

Case One

Geologists, working for Tennessee Gulf Gold Corporation (TGG), recently discovered large silver deposits. The company kept the discovery secret until it could determine the magnitude of its find. However, certain TGG employees made large purchases of TGG stock during this period. When questioned by reporters at the time, TGG executives denied any significant silver discovery. Smith, who was not an employee of TGG, bought a large amount of the company stock during this period. When the news of the silver strike was finally released, the price of TGG stock tripled.

CONCLUSION: Smith was found guilty of dealing on inside information.

1.   Smith's best friend was a TGG executive.

2.   Smith was related to a TGG employee who also purchased stock during this period.

3.   Smith was a geologist.

4.   Smith overheard a TGG employee talking about the silver strike before he bought his stock.

5.   Smith was known to speculate in stocks.

6.   Many relatives of TGG executives bought the company's stock during this period.

7. Smith sold his stock before the news of the silver strike was made public.

8. Smith is an employee of one of TGG's creditors.

9. Smith sold the property, on which TGG found the silver, at a low price.

10. While working as a telephone repairman, Smith overheard a conversation between two TGG geologists concerning the best way to mine silver.

11. Smith observed increased activity by TGG truckers and heavy equipment handlers near the mining site.

12. Smith bought eight other large blocks of stock in different companies at the same time he bought the TGG stock.

13. The company was suffering a silver shortage and Smith knew that the price of silver was bound to rise.

Case Two

On September 15, 1976, a Chevy van owned and driven by George Susanna was stopped by the border patrol at a checkpoint near the California-Mexico border. Mr. Susanna's wife, Maria; their two children, ages 11 and 13; and two acquaintances, Billy and Bob Elders, were passengers in the van. A search of the van revealed several pounds of marijuana. Immediately after the discovery of the marijuana the four adults were placed under arrest and advised of their right to remain silent.

CONCLUSION: George Susanna is convicted of knowingly transporting narcotics across the border.

14. Mrs. Susanna stated, "We had no idea that the drugs were in the van." However, this statement contradicts an earlier statement made by Mrs. Susanna.

15. There is a tape recording of Mrs. Susanna's first statement admitting that she knew the Elders possessed drugs when they entered the van.

16. Billy Elders declines to testify at George's trial on 5th Amendment grounds despite a grant of immunity.

17. A letter is discovered from Billy to his brother Bob which says, "Don't worry, George owes me one more favor. He'll do it for us."

18. George Susanna was a minister in the First Church of God.

19. Billy Elders first brought the marijuana into the van and unsuccessfully attempted to conceal it from the others.

20. George Susanna was a heroin addict.

21. The Elders had used George's van to transport marijuana in the past.

22. The marijuana was concealed in a suitcase belonging to Billy Elders.

23. George's 13-year-old daughter knew the marijuana was in the van and was about to tell her father when they were stopped by the Border Patrol.

24. Marijuana has a very distinctive smell.

25. George did not know the Elders personally and it was they who had brought the marijuana into the van.

Case Three

The M.V. Titanic, an oil tanker owned by MVP, Inc., a Delaware corporation, but registered under the Liberian flag, ran aground on the shoals off Nantucket on October 19, 1976. Before the Titanic sank, it released eight million gallons of crude oil into the Atlantic, causing enormous damage to the Grand Banks Fishing Grounds and the Nantucket shoreline. Several crewman died in the resulting explosion.

At the hearing, counsel for the Federal Maritime Commission opened the proceedings by offering a commission report detailing the prior safety record of Captain Nemo and First Mate Tenetur, both of whom had been involved in at least three major oil spills in the past.

CONCLUSION: MVP, Inc. is found liable for the negligent operation of an unsafe vessel.

26. First Mate Tenetur has been convicted of drunken driving three times in the past.

27. MVP ships have an unfavorable accident record by industry standards.

28. Ships of Liberian registry have an unfavorable accident record by industry standards.

29. The *Nantucket Daily Whale,* a local newspaper, reported clear weather on the date of the accident.

30. The ship had been fully overhauled before this voyage.

31. The shoals upon which the Titanic ran aground were not clearly marked on any known navigation chart.

32. The nearsighted helmsman, McGoo, was on the bow watch during the time of the accident.

33. Captain Nemo had made many successful voyages through the ice packed Bering Strait during heavy fog in the past.

34. The engine room chief, before his death, had stated that the ship was in fine condition, but the crew was inexperienced.

35. The Captain testified that he was asleep at the time of the accident, and that Tenetur was at the helm.

36. An entry in the ship's log indicated that the Titanic was on the correct course and heading.

37. The automatic course recorder, which mechanically records course and speed, indicated that the Titanic was 180° off course and proceeding at a reckless speed. The recorder was in perfect working order.

38. Tests of the Navy's new electronic devices, in the Nantucket area, were playing havoc with ships' compasses.

Case Four

The Civil Rights Division of the Justice Department has, after an internal finding of probable cause, commenced an action for injunctive relief and punitive damages against Minerals, Chemicals, Petroleum, Inc. (MCP), and its President, Vice-President, and Personnel Director, for allegedly discriminating against women in hiring and promotion in violation of a Federal Statute which provides:

"No person or corporation shall willfully discriminate in hiring or promotion on the basis of sex."

CONCLUSION: MCP is found guilty of discrimination on the basis of sex.

39. A statistical abstract shows that MCP has never had a female executive in a policy making position.

40. One of MCP's major competitors has two females in policy making positions.

41. Most of MCP's competitors don't employ females in top decision making roles.

42. A statistical abstract shows that in the past year female clerical workers have only put in 20% as much overtime as male clerical workers.

43. The President, Vice-President, and Personnel Manager belong to the "Males First" club, which excludes women.

44. Although nine male clerical workers had been promoted to executive job status during the past five years, no female clerical worker has ever been similarly promoted.

45. MCP receives eight times as many job applications from males as it does from females.

46. Ten unsuccessful female job applicants had been questioned about their views on the women's movement.

47. The President of MCP once boasted, after several drinks, at an after hours cocktail party, that "No woman will ever take my job."

48. Most executives in MCP's industry are engineers and only 5% of all engineers are women.

49. MCP's chief recruitment officer had received instructions from management a number of years prior to the Justice Department's action to seek out more women employees for executive and clerical positions.

50. MCP's Board of Directors adopted a bylaw which states that no woman shall ever become President of MCP.

END OF TEST

TEST VIII. PRACTICAL JUDGMENT

TIME: 20 Minutes. 25 Questions.

DIRECTIONS: In this test you will be presented with a detailed case study of a practical business situation. Read the study carefully. Then answer the two sets of questions based upon the reading. In the Data Evaluation questions, you will be asked to classify certain facts on the basis of their importance to the case presented. In the Data Application questions you will be asked to make judgments based upon your comprehension of the information.

Correct and explanatory answers are provided at the end of the exam. After you have completed the entire exam, read the explanations carefully. They'll reinforce your strengths and pinpoint your weaknesses so that you know just what to study to raise your score.

Business Situation. Info-Data Corp.

In July, the directors of Info-Data Corp. were scheduled to meet to discuss some matters of great importance to the corporation. Among the issues on the agenda was the decision on how to raise $10 million needed to pay for a new computer system to be delivered in the fall of that year. The new system had been ordered in October of the previous year, and when the directors met in March, they agreed that at the July meeting each of them would be prepared to present and to defend his preferred method of raising the money.

Mr. James Eaton, financial vice-president of Info-Data, was assigned the task of supplying the directors with information they might need in making such a decision. Since the board was dominated by insiders, much of the communication had been verbal. The management group, which included the president and five vice-presidents, made up six of the eleven directors. Eaton had talked with the outside directors by telephone and had mailed them certain financial statements.

The new system would provide centralized processing and high speed input and output to replace 3 smaller computers that Info-Data had been using to provide time-sharing (direct access to a computer by means of a teletype and telephone cables) on a regional basis. In addition, the new installation would substantially reduce the cost of performing the consulting work that generated 40 percent of the firm's income.

It was estimated the change-over would require $10 million more than would be realized from the sale of the small computers which were being replaced. The board had agreed to acquire the needed funds for management's use, but, as late as March, was still unable to agree on how to raise the money. When the March meeting adjourned, Eaton stated that the decision would have to be made at the summer meeting to assure that cash would be available by early October.

In March, the directors had agreed only that the money should be raised by the sale of one of three kinds of securities: common stock, straight debentures, or convertible debentures. Several directors quickly expressed concern over the possible stock market reaction to such a sale, particularly since the assets to be purchased with the proceeds of the sale could not be expected to produce an increase in earnings for from six months to a year.

Info-Data had been founded 15 years earlier by Dr. Frank Norbert, the current president, Dr. Jack Newman, vice-president and director of research, and five graduates of a major midwestern business school, two of whom had since left the company. The corporation had prospered as a provider of a broad range of services related to information and data processing. Eight years ago, the firm had sold 30% of its common stock in a public offering. As the business expanded from off-site consulting into system design and time-sharing, the capital required was obtained from a sale of debentures and a second offering of common stock. Additional stock and debt securities were issued to purchase several companies which had technical and marketing capabilities which management felt would supplement those of Info-Data.

The management group, the six founders who were still active in the business, owned about 20 percent of the corporation's 2 million outstanding shares of stock; the outside board members held a nominal number of shares; and none of the 3,000 other stockholders owned more than 30,000 shares. Tax considerations made it unwise for any of the insiders to sell his stock, so the company was generally managed toward increasing earnings per share and, indirectly, increasing the price of the stock. Recently, the firm's stock had sold on the American Stock Exchange for between $26 and $28 per share. At its March meeting, the board of directors had authorized the payment of a 20 cent quarterly dividend to common stockholders which completed a total dividend payment of 80 cents for the 12 months ending in March, the highest annual dividend payment the corporation had ever made.

Over the past 6 years, the company's profits had been erratic. Although it was not unusual for similar businesses to experience fluctuating earnings, Mr. Eaton felt that the main reason for Info-Data's earnings pattern had been the need to integrate the equipment, software (computer programs), personnel, and debt of the firms that Info-Data had acquired into a unified operational structure. Dr. Newman projected earnings before taxes and interest would increase at an average annual rate of between 8 and 13 percent for the next five years. This belief was based on three factors: (1) obtaining greater efficiency by eliminating redundant computer capacity, (2) increasing the average billings per customer by providing greater time-sharing capability, and (3) expanding the number of customers by reducing the minimum cost of Info-Data's basic services. Currently, total earnings before interest and taxes were $8 million. Annual interest payments amounted to $2.4 million.

Some members of the management group favored a sale of straight debentures (debt securities whose owners are guaranteed payment of a face amount at maturity and interest periodically until maturity but who do not share in the firm's profits) because selling additional stock would dilute their proportionate ownership of the company and potentially reduce earnings per share. They believed that securities analysts would rate these new debentures "B" which would necessitate paying interest at the rate of 9 percent on securities with a 20-year maturity.

Eaton hoped that during the summer meeting it would be possible for the directors to take some positive steps that would influence the analysts to assign a credit rating higher than "B" to the firm's new debentures, thereby reducing the interest rate on the currently contemplated issue to about 8.6 percent. The resulting annual interest savings were estimated at approximately $40,000. Of course, it would be possible to sell securities with a shorter maturity. However, it was not clear what such an action would mean in terms of lower interest rates.

Three outside directors had suggested to Eaton that the $10 million be raised through the sale of convertible debentures. Convertible debentures had become popular in the financial markets during the 1960s, especially when issued by companies adequately covering interest charges and possessing acceptable characteristics of growth. Because the convertible debenture purchaser received the preferred, protected position of the creditor along with an opportunity to participate in the company's growth (by converting the debentures into common stock), many investors considered convertible debentures "perfect" investment instruments.

The directors favoring the sale of convertible debentures had suggested a conversion ratio of 30 shares of stock for each $1,000 debenture and a 20-year maturity. They had indicated that the market interest rates on convertible debentures were typically below the rates on straight debt issues. The differential depended on many factors including the life of the security. These directors anticipated that Info-Data's convertible debentures with a conversion ratio of 30 to 1 could be sold at an interest rate of 8 percent.

Eaton had discussed the possibility of selling common shares with several investment banking firms and concluded that a new issue of stock could be sold at a price of $25 per share. He learned also that regardless of the type of security the company sold, the total cost of the offering including commissions, legal fees, and other expenses would amount to almost $400,000.

DATA EVALUATION

DIRECTIONS: Based on your analysis of the Situation, classify each of the following items in one of five categories. On your answer sheet blacken the space under:

(A) *if the item is a MAJOR OBJECTIVE in making the decision; that is, one of the outcomes or results sought by the decision-maker.*

(B) *if the item is a MAJOR FACTOR in arriving at the decision; that is, a consideration explicitly mentioned in the passage that is basic in determining the decision.*

(C) *if the item is a MINOR FACTOR in making the decision; that is, a secondary consideration that affects the criteria tangentially, relating to a Major Factor rather than to an Objective.*

(D) *if the item is a MAJOR ASSUMPTION made in deliberating; that is, a supposition or projection made by the decision-maker before weighing the variables.*

(E) *if the item is an UNIMPORTANT ISSUE in getting to the point; that is, a factor that is insignificant or not immediately relevant to the situation.*

1. Total expenses involved in each type of security offering

2. Plausibility of 8% to 13% rate of growth in earnings for the next five years

3. Acquisition of capital to finance the purchase of new equipment

4. Effect of a sale of stock or convertible debentures on earnings per share

5. Amount of dividends paid by Info-Data during the past 12 months

6. Percentage of total outstanding shares held by "inside" directors

7. Relationship between convertibility of debentures and effective interest rate

8. Maturity date of the debentures

9. Increasing efficiency by elimination of redundant computing capacity

10. Maximization of earnings per share

11. Interest rates to be paid on debentures

12. Contribution of consulting contracts to Info-Data's total income

13. Profitability of the firms Info-Data has acquired

14. Difference between the cost of the new computer system and the resale value of the old ones

15. Conversion ratio of convertible debentures

16. Providing centralized processing for Info-Data's time-sharing operations

17. Rating given Info-Data debentures by securities analysts

18. Extent of investor interest in new Info-Data securities

DATA APPLICATION

DIRECTIONS: Based on your understanding of the Business Situation, answer the following questions testing your comprehension of the information supplied in the passage. For each question, select the choice which best answers the question or completes the statement.

19. If the board decides to raise capital by selling stock, then approximately what percent of the outstanding shares will be held by the insiders after the offering if they purchase no additional stock?

    (A) 8%   (B) 17%   (C) 20%   (D) 25%   (E) 50%

20. If Info-Data's earnings grow at the lowest rate predicted by Dr. Newman, then what will be the effect on next year's earnings before taxes, but after interest, if straight debentures rated "B" are used to finance the new system?

    (A) $40,000 decrease   (D) $300,000 decrease
    (B) $400,000 increase   (E) No change
    (C) $900,000 decrease

21. If Info-Data sold the convertible debentures as described in the passage, instead of stock, and all of them were converted, then the ratio of the number of shares of stock issued as a result of conversion to the number that would have to be issued initially to provide capital for the new system is approximately

    (A) 1/30   (B) 1/4   (C) 3/4   (D) 4/3   (E) 30/1

22. The directors who favored the sale of straight debentures would be most likely to change their views if

    (A) Dr. Newman reduced his estimate of increased profitability
    (B) interest rates on similarly rated debentures declined
    (C) Info-Data debentures were rated higher than "B"
    (D) the price of Info-Data stock dropped to $20.00 per share
    (E) the quarterly dividend payment was increased

23. If the ratio of profits (before interest and taxes) to Info-Data's stock remains constant, what is the earliest date that one can reasonably expect the holders of convertible debentures to be willing to convert to stock?

    (A)   Immediately
    (B)   Within 1 year of issue
    (C)   2 to 3 years after issue
    (D)   5 to 6 years after issue
    (E)   18 to 20 years after issue

24. Which of the following can be inferred about a sale of 20-year convertible debentures with a 20 to 1 conversion ratio rather than a 30 to 1 ratio?

    I. The interest rate would be less than 8%
    II. The interest rate would be more than 8%
    III. The insiders would be more opposed to the lower ratio
    IV. The insiders would be more opposed to the higher ratio
    V. Sales commissions and legal fees would be greater for the lower ratio
    VI. Sales commissions and legal fees would be greater for the higher ratio

    (A)   I and III only
    (B)   II only
    (C)   IV only
    (D)   II, IV, and VI only
    (E)   II and IV only

25. It can be inferred that the management group differs most from the outside directors in their

    (A)   perception of the reasons for Info-Data's erratic earnings behavior
    (B)   confidence in Dr. Newman's projections
    (C)   interest in increasing the firm's profits
    (D)   willingness to accept the risk of poor performance in exchange for the potential of excellent performance
    (E)   assessment of the importance of purchasing the new computer system

END OF EXAMINATION

Now that you have completed the last Test in this Examination, use your available time to make sure that you have written in your answers correctly on the Answer Sheet. Then, after your time is up, check your answers with the Correct Answers we have provided for you. Derive your scores for each Test Category and determine where you are weak so as to plan your study accordingly.

CORRECT ANSWERS FOR VERISIMILAR EXAMINATION V.

Now compare your answers with these Correct Key Answers. If your answers differ from these, go back and study the Practice Questions to see where and how you made your mistakes. In doing this, the following Explanatory Answers should prove helpful. They provide concise clarifications of the basic points behind the Key Answers. Even where your Key Answers are the same as ours, go over the explanations carefully because they may be quite useful in helping you pick up extra points on the exam.

TEST I. LOGICAL REASONING

1.C	3.C	5.D	7.A	9.B
2.A	4.B	6.E	8.E	10.C

TEST II. PRINCIPLES AND CASES

1.C	6.D	11.B	16.C	21.C	26.B	31.A	36.B
2.B	7.B	12.A	17.D	22.D	27.D	32.C	37.B
3.A	8.A	13.B	18.C	23.B	28.C	33.C	38.D
4.D	9.C	14.C	19.B	24.A	29.B	34.D	39.D
5.A	10.D	15.B	20.A	25.B	30.D	35.C	40.A

TEST III. PRACTICAL JUDGMENT

1.E	4.B	7.C	10.C	13.E	16.A	19.D
2.C	5.E	8.A	11.B	14.D	17.B	20.D
3.A	6.D	9.B	12.A	15.C	18.E	

TEST IV. QUANTITATIVE COMPARISON

1.A	5.C	9.C	13.A	17.B	21.B	25.B
2.B	6.B	10.C	14.A	18.A	22.B	
3.B	7.D	11.C	15.C	19.C	23.A	
4.B	8.C	12.B	16.B	20.C	24.A	

TEST V. ERROR RECOGNITION

1.C	6.A	11.D	16.C	21.A	26.D	31.D
2.C	7.D	12.A	17.C	22.D	27.B	32.C
3.C	8.B	13.A	18.C	23.B	28.D	33.C
4.C	9.D	14.A	19.C	24.D	29.A	34.C
5.A	10.B	15.A	20.B	25.A	30.A	35.B

TEST VI. SENTENCE CORRECTION

1.A	5.E	9.A	13.B	17.B	21.C	25.B
2.E	6.C	10.A	14.C	18.E	22.B	
3.C	7.B	11.D	15.E	19.C	23.D	
4.B	8.E	12.A	16.A	20.E	24.A	

TEST VII. VALIDITY OF CONCLUSION

1.B	8.E	15.B	22.D	29.B	36.D	43.E	50.A
2.B	9.D	16.E	23.E	30.D	37.A	44.B	
3.E	10.B	17.B	24.B	31.D	38.D	45.D	
4.A	11.B	18.D	25.D	32.A	39.B	46.B	
5.D	12.D	19.A	26.E	33.D	40.B	47.E	
6.E	13.E	20.E	27.B	34.B	41.D	48.D	
7.D	14.B	21.B	28.B	35.E	42.B	49.C	

TEST VIII. PRACTICAL JUDGMENT

1.E	5.E	9.A	13.E	17.C	21.C	25.D
2.D	6.C	10.A	14.B	18.D	22.A	
3.A	7.D	11.B	15.C	19.B	23.C	
4.B	8.C	12.E	16.A	20.D	24.E	

EXPLANATORY ANSWERS FOR VERISIMILAR EXAMINATION V.

Here you have the heart of the Question and Answer Method. . . .getting help when and where you need it. Where one of your Key Answers differs from ours you have a problem which can easily be remedied by reading the explanation. Then, if you have time, you might be able to pick up points on the exam by reading the other explanations, even where you wrote the Key Answers correctly. These explanations stress fundamental facts, ideas, and principles which just might pop up as questions on future exams.

TEST I. LOGICAL REASONING

1. **(C)** The use of foreign aid funds by the U.S. is the only choice directly mentioned in the passage. All other choices are merely hinted at.

2. **(A)** is correct because Mary's statement implies that her domestic spaghetti will not be pleasing to John. The other choices require the addition of facts not stated in the conversation.

3. **(C)** It is directly stated that Iran cannot afford the new steel mill, and the use of the phrase "wants to build" implies that it is still in the early stages of development. Also, there is no mention of any need for such a steel mill.

4. **(B)** Reading and writing, which the author claims results in "literary people," is mentioned as the specific bane of Nepal.

5. **(D)** The electrician is the only person speaking in his own area of expertise on a topic which does not arouse emotionally defensive reactions. All of the other respondents are either speaking on emotional topics or outside their own area of expertise.

6. **(E)** The implication of the passage is that Americans must do something to negate their greedy image, and altruistic programs would appear to be such a response. All of the other responses imply self interest which according to the author is bad for our image.

7. **(A)** The only important statement made is that it is the exhibitors being coerced and therefore by process of elimination the ten combining competitors must be distributors.

8. **(E)** Mary implies that she is disappointed, for John's sake, that they won't be near the sea on their vacation. Her disappointment could only be due to the fact that she interpreted John's remark as a desire to go crab fishing.

9. **(B)** The author lists several examples of contagious diseases and then says that where you find these diseases you will not find an ordered solution to national problems. This condition must imply that if there

were no such diseases you would find an ordered society. Therefore, the author's statement may be paraphrased, "Sick people mean sick societies," when the word 'sick' is used in sense of epidemic.

10. **(C)** The statement in the passage sets up a dichotomy, i.e., power is a necessary element of monopoly, however, monopoly power is not necessary for illegality but merely to fix prices even when the ability to do so is lacking. All of the other alternatives deal only with one side of the dichotomy or the other.

TEST II. PRINCIPLES AND CASES

1. **(C)** is correct because the principle makes the defendant's liability depend on the impossibility of any other person being the cause of the plaintiff's injury. (A) is incorrect because it omits the second condition upon which liability is founded. Choices (B) and (D) do not relate to the principle.

2. **(B)** is correct because it implies that Dr. Galen is not a full-time employee of the hospital so the hospital will not be liable for her misconduct. (A) raises the question of degree of care which is relevant only when applied to full-time employees. (C) begs the question and (D) confuses "agents" with "full-time employees."

3. **(A)** is correct because it establishes the grounds for the implied contract which the principle says will be enforced. (B) is incorrect because it does not refer to "common practices" but to duties. (C) ignores the effect of the principle. (D) is not supported by the facts.

4. **(D)** is correct because it concerns the issue of unequal bargaining power. Choices (A) and (B) are incorrect because they do not relate to the principle. (C) incorrectly limits "unequal bargaining power" to monopoly situations.

5. **(A)** is correct because it indicates the condition whose breach by Dr. Galen exempts Johnson from liability. (B) and (C) are incorrect because they are unrelated to the principle. (D) overlooks the first alternative remedy available to the non-breaching party.

6. **(D)** is correct because it indicates that Dr. Galen failed to meet even the minimum standard set forth in the principle. (A) avoids the issue of defining the standard against which she will be measured. (B) ignores the question of whether or not the particular mistake made by Galen is grounds for liability. (C) misreads the principle to imply that the acceptance of a lower standard of conduct is an admission of incompetence.

7. **(B)** is correct because it establishes the reasonableness of the fee which the principle requires. (A) does not deal with the principle. (C) imposes a condition which the principle specifically denies. (D) introduces an issue which is not relevant to this question.

8. **(A)** is correct because it states the essential element of the legal injury for which Johnson seeks to recover. **(B)** introduces the irrelevant issue of the broken collarbone. **(C)** overlooks the fact that the principle implies that to avoid liability, the plaintiff must have consented to the "manner" of the touching. **(D)** erroneously interprets the principle's reference to "ordinary social contact" to mean "typical contact for those in the same circumstances as the parties."

9. **(C)** is correct because the principle states that if there is a breach of the peace, the repossessing seller must return the goods seized. **(A)** is incorrect because the seller's duty to return the goods is not contingent on who causes the breach of the peace. Choices **(B)** and **(D)** are incorrect because neither the buyer's financial condition nor the opportunity given him to pay his debt are relevant to the principle.

10. **(D)** is correct because the principle puts two conditions on the reservation of title. The second condition was met when Puma told the BDC Salesman of Briar's interest, but the first was not fulfilled as is indicated by this choice. **(A)** is incorrect because it ignores the unsatisfied condition. Choices **(B)** and **(C)** introduce issues which are not relevant to this principle.

11. **(B)** is correct because it was reasonable to infer from Max's initial polite request for the keys to the toolshed and his taking only the drill bits that a legitimate dispute over the ownership of the pipe could have been resolved by discussion, if not with Max then with his superiors. **(A)** contradicts the facts of the case. **(C)** deals only with the reasonableness of Briar's belief in his ownership, not the equally important issue of the reasonableness of his actions. **(D)** correctly focuses on the issue of the reasonableness of Briar's actions, but since in light of all the circumstances no use of force was reasonable, the distinction created by this choice is irrelevant.

12. **(A)** is correct because it is a more supportable choice than **(B)**. The question of "good faith" is subjective while the question of "knowledge" is objective and can be resolved as in **(A)** on the basis of the facts presented in the case. **(C)** ignores these two elements of the principle and **(D)** does not relate to the principle.

13. **(B)** is correct because it gives Briar the victory on the basis of the exception created by the principle. **(A)** may be reasonably in accord with the spirit of the principle but ignores its terms. Choices **(C)** and **(D)** each refer to one element of the principle but fail to exclude the exception.

14. **(C)** is correct because it identifies the act which constituted the intentional adverse exercise of control. **(A)** is incorrect because the principle speaks of what the owner may receive. **(B)** is incorrect because the principle's requirement of intent describes the type of control, not the effect on the owner's rights. **(D)** merely restates the facts without justifying the result in view of the principle.

15. **(B)** is correct because even though Smith lacked actual authority to sell the policy, the company will be bound by Smith's acts which lie within the scope of his apparent authority. That scope is set forth in (B). None of the other choices resolves the question of apparent authority.

16. **(C)** is correct because Ankloff's action was not even apparently authorized according to the definition of apparent authority given in the principle. (A) and (D) are contrary to common sense. (B) misses the issue of the reasonableness of the third party's opinion.

17. **(D)** is correct because an agent need only be as careful with his principal's money as he is with his own. Choice (A) is contrary to the facts as given, (B) is unsupported by the principle, and (C) does not resolve the key issue of Andrew's negligence.

18. **(C)** is correct because an agent is not liable for authorized acts and Douglas did no more than he was authorized to do. Choices (A) and (D) imply that Douglas had some duty not specified in the principle. Choice (B) raises an irrelevant issue.

19. **(B)** is correct because the principle defines apparent authority as arising from the acts of the principal, not the agent. XYZ never gave Twilight any reason to believe that Adams had the authority to do what he did. (A) is inconsistent with the principle. (C) is unreasonable because XYZ had never done business with Twilight. Choice (D) misses the actual issue which is whether or not Adams had the authority, not whether a hypothetical purchasing agent has the authority.

20. **(A)** is correct because it supports Mike's claim of actual authority exempting him from personal liability. Choice (B) supports Sam's claim of apparent authority which would result in liability for Mike as well as for Fleet Trucking. (C) ignores the provision in the principle which permits actual authority to be based on implied as well as on expressed understandings. Choice (D) contradicts the facts as given.

21. **(C)** is correct because the principle states that a principal is bound by the authorized acts of his agent, which does not mean that a third party will not be bound by the contract he makes if the principal chooses to enforce it. The other choices erroneously apply the principle to the relationship between agent and third party where it actually refers to the relationship between agent and principal.

22. **(D)** is correct because the fact that the out-of-court statement is being used to prove the truth of what it asserts makes it hearsay. Since it does not fall within one of the exceptions, it is inadmissible. Choices (A) and (B) misinterpret the exceptions. (C) is only relevant once it has been ascertained that the statement is hearsay.

23. **(B)** is correct because the statement does not fall within the definition of hearsay given in the principle. Therefore, the question of whether it falls within one of the exceptions, indicated by choices (A) and (C), need not be reached. Choice (D) introduces the irrelevant issue of the speaker's knowledge.

24. **(A)** is correct because the words themselves are part of the illegal transaction with which Louie is charged. The statement is not being introduced to prove that "Snookers won the Eighth." Choice (B) is unsupported by the facts. Choice (C) does not apply since the statement is not hearsay. Choice (D) introduces the irrelevant issue of the speaker's intent.

25. **(B)** correctly identifies the exception that makes the drunk driving verdict admissible. Choice (A) creates a distinction without a difference since the guilty verdict is an assertion that John was both drunk and driving. Choice (C) erroneously introduces an irrelevant principle. (D) ignores the four exceptions given in the principle.

26. **(B)** is correct because the designation of Quincy as beneficiary on the application has independent legal significance. Whoever is named on the application as beneficiary is the beneficiary by virtue of being named. The application is self-proving. Choice (A) misinterprets the "dying statement" exception. Choices (C) and (D) overlook the fact that not all out-of-court statements are hearsay.

27. **(D)** is correct because it gives the basis for finding that Ebenezer's testimony is within the exception for statements against the speaker's interest. (A) correctly identifies the testimony as hearsay but fails to find the exception which makes it admissible. (B) introduces an extraneous rule of law. (C) misquotes the "spontaneous reaction" exception by omitting the key word "immediate."

28. **(C)** is correct because the relevant exception to the hearsay rule requires that the speaker be aware that his statement is damaging to his position. Choice (A) focuses on the same exception but is incorrect because it makes no reference to the speaker's awareness of the effects of his statement. (B) is incorrect because Tony's statement is being introduced to show by implication his involvement in the crime, so it is hearsay. Choice (D) introduces an irrelevant rule of law.

29. **(B)** is correct because it is the only choice which includes the three elements of publisher, victim, and falsity of the matter published. Choices (A) and (D) are broader because they are not restricted to newspapers. Choice (C) is too broad because it is not limited to public officials.

30. **(D)** is correct because it is the only choice which is consistent with question 29. Choices (B) and (C) explain this result but do not distinguish between this case and the previous one. Choice (A) is both inconsistent and too broad.

31. **(A)** is correct because it is the only choice which is limited by the content of the false statement. Choice (C) does not contain this limitation. Choices (B) and (D) are inconsistent with question 29.

32. **(C)** is correct because it is more reasonable and more specific than (B) or (D). Choice (A) is inconsistent with question 29.

33. **(C)** is correct because it is narrower than (B). Choices (A) and (D) are inconsistent with question 30.

34. **(D)** is correct because the other alternatives are inconsistent with prior questions. (A) conflicts with questions 29 and 33; (B) and (C) are inconsistent with question 32.

35. **(C)** is correct because it deals with the specific type of evidence mentioned in the case. (A) is not as narrow as (C). Choices (B) and (D) do not explain the result.

36. **(B)** is correct because choices (A) and (C) conflict with the previous question and (D) fails to explain the result.

37. **(B)** is the most reasonable explanation. It is narrower than choice (A) because it deals only with an action for defamation. Choice (D) raises the extraneous issue of impeaching the plaintiff's testimony.

38. **(D)** is narrower than the other three alternatives because it is limited to a specific type of trial.

39. **(D)** is the only alternative that correctly distinguishes this case from the previous one. Choice (A) is inconsistent with question 38. Choices (B) and (C) do not explain this result.

40. **(A)** is the narrowest consistent choice. Choices (B) and (C) are inconsistent with question 39. Choice (D) is much broader than (A).

TEST III. PRACTICAL JUDGMENT

DATA EVALUATION

(A) means that the Conclusion is a Major Objective;
(B) means that the Conclusion is a Major Factor;
(C) means that the Conclusion is a Minor Factor;
(D) means that the Conclusion is a Major Assumption;
(E) means that the Conclusion is an Unimportant Issue.

1. **(E)** Mycophil's total sales is not relevant to the specific problem of how to promote Tonsitol.

2. **(C)** This is one of several minor factors that the company will consider, but only if it makes the basic decision to undertake a consumer advertising program.

3. **(A)** This is one of the major objectives that Ms. Hauser specified in her memo.

4. **(B)** The expiration of the basic patent is a major factor which creates the need to maximize the value of the Tonsitol trademark.

5. **(E)** The market behavior of Tonsitol at a certain time in the past has no bearing on the issues confronting Mycophil at the present.

6. **(D)** This is a major assumption that Ms. Hauser makes.

7. **(C)** Mycophil's inexperience in consumer marketing is a minor factor that leads Ms. Hauser to advise caution when instituting the new program.

8. **(A)** This is a major objective which is implicit in all marketing decisions in a competitive economy.

9. **(B)** This is a major factor which weighs against Ms. Hauser's proposals.

10. **(C)** Tonsitol's reputation as an antiseptic gargle is a minor factor which is responsible for some of its sales fluctuations and, therefore, indirectly the cause of one of the problems which Ms. Hauser is attempting to solve.

11. **(B)** This is one of the major factors which led the Mycophil management to consider a consumer advertising program.

12. **(A)** This is one of the major objectives that Ms. Hauser sets forth in her memo.

13. **(E)** According to the passage, all three mouthwashes cost about $0.50 for a 6-ounce bottle, so the price differential can have no relevance to the decision.

14. **(D)** This is a major assumption Ms. Hauser makes which is not tested or referred to an outside expert for verification.

DATA APPLICATION

15. **(C)** Reasons (I) and (V) are given in the first paragraph of the passage, so (C), the only choice which correctly excludes both of them, must be the correct answer.

16. **(A)** Ms. Hauser recommends Dallas as a test market because Tonsitol's sales there are weak. The discussion of the variations in the sales of Tonsitol implies that sales are strong in those areas where and

at those times when there is a high incidence of sore throats. Conversely, since sales in Dallas are low, there must be a low incidence of colds and sore throats. Since the passage only deals with Tonsitol, no inference about the overall effectiveness of the sales force can be supported, so (B) is wrong. (C) and (D) must both be eliminated because the passage makes no mention of regional variations in competitors' behavior. Neither is there any support in the passage for choice (E).

17. **(B)** The retailer's margin for Tonsitol is 45% of the $0.50 retail price, or $0.225 per bottle, $32.40 per case. Listerine's margin is 35% of $0.50, $0.175 per bottle, $25.20 per case. The difference is: $32.40 − $25.20 = $7.20.

18. **(E)** In the memo, Ms. Hauser states that the $140,000 for trade and professional journal advertising is 45% of the marketing budget for Tonsitol. Hence that budget must be: $\frac{\$140,000}{0.45} = \$310,000$.

The question specifies the relationship:

$$\frac{\text{Total Marketing Expense}}{\text{Total Sales}} \quad \frac{\text{Tonsitol Marketing Expense}}{\text{Tonsitol Sales}}$$

$$= \frac{310,000}{4,000,000} \text{ or about 7.5\%}$$

Hence, Total Marketing Expense − 7.5% of $30 million (total sales) = $2.25 million.

19. **(D)** According to the passage, Listerine's advertising expense of $1,100,000 was 8% of its sales, so:

$$\text{Sales} = \frac{\$1,100,000}{.08}$$

An alternative approach comes from the ratio between market shares of Listerine and Tonsitol, $\frac{50}{15}$.

20. **(D)** Mycophil gives retailers a margin nearly 1/3 greater than that allowed by its competitors (45% as opposed to 35%).

TEST IV. QUANTITATIVE COMPARISON

1. **(A)** $\frac{20}{3} > 6$

2. **(B)** $8/3 < 6$

3. **(B)** When parentheses are omitted, multiplication is performed before addition: $18 < 30$.

4. **(B)** $5^3 = 125$, so $\sqrt[3]{100} < 5$.

5. **(C)** a is the midpoint of $\overline{AB}$, so $\overline{Aa} = \overline{Ba}$.

6. **(B)** Area of $\triangle$ aAb = area of $\triangle$ Bac = 1/2 area of parallelogram abCc = 1/4 area of $\triangle$ ABC.

7. **(D)** Not enough information about this is given.

8. **(C)** See 6.

9. **(C)** $\triangle$ acB is congruent to $\triangle$ Aba, therefore their perimeters are equal.

10. **(C)** The probability of throwing any specified series of H and T is the same as that of throwing any other specified series of the same length.

11. **(C)** See 10.

12. **(B)** Since there is some chance of throwing only heads, the probability of the event that includes this result is greater than the probability of one that does not.

13. **(A)** $(1/2)^5 = 1/32 > .03$

14. **(A)** There are more ways to throw 2 heads and 2 tails than HHTT.

15. **(C)** $.1 = .1$

16. **(B)** $.02 < .03$

17. **(B)** $.04 < .4$

18. **(A)** $\frac{62}{28} > \frac{59}{28}$

19. **(C)** $0.1 = 0.1$

20. **(C)** $1/5 = 1/5$

21. **(B)** $1/7 < 8/7$

22. **(B)** Since $y > x$, $1 > x/y$, $1/x > 1/y$

23. **(A)** If the same quantity is subtracted from both sides of an inequality, the direction of the inequality sign is unchanged.

24. **(A)** $y - x > 0 > x - y$

25. **(B)** Multiplying an inequality by -1 reverses the direction of the inequality sign.

TEST V. ERROR RECOGNITION

(A) means the sentence contains an error in DICTION;
(B) means the sentence is VERBOSE;
(C) means the sentence contains FAULTY GRAMMAR;
(D) means the sentence contains NO ERROR.

1. **(C)** "——*their* being late." In a sentence like "He had to risk———being late" the missing word must always be a possessive pronoun (my, her, their, etc.).

2. **(C)** "Either pencil or pen *is* satisfactory." When two nouns in the singular are joined by *or, nor, either . . . or, neither . . . nor,* the verb is normally singular.

3. **(C)** "——the *taller* of the two men." The comparative degree of comparison is used when comparing two items. The superlative degree of comparison is used when comparing three or more items. (Mr. Jones is the tallest of the three men.)

4. **(C)** "*Whom* do you wish to see?" The interrogative pronoun *who* has the form *whom* in the object position (Whom do you wish to see? To whom are you talking?), and *who* in the subject position (Who is the author of *Moby Dick*?).

5. **(A)** "———too *ingenuous* to suspect———" *Ingenious* means clever. *Ingenuous* means naive.

6. **(A)** "———*a great many* informal schools have come into existence———" *Lots of* is a colloquial expression meaning *a great many.*

7. **(D)** No errors.

8. **(B)** "———mankind has *advanced* in the course of the last two millennia." *Advance* means go *forward*.

9. **(D)** No errors.

10. **(B)** "———cannot now afford to cut prices." *Now* and *at the present time* are synonyms.

11. **(D)** No errors.

12. **(A)** "———when I *implied* that———" *To infer* is to deduce. *To imply* is to signify or to hint.

13. **(A)** "———into the *turbid* waters." *Turgid* means swollen, distended. *Turbid* means muddy, cloudy.

14. **(A)** "———would always *defend* its allies." *To stick up for* (*someone*) is a colloquialism.

15. **(A)** "———for arthritis was reported———" *Arthritis* is always *of the joints*.

16. **(C)** "There *seem* to be several opinions———" The true subject of the sentence is *opinions;* the word *there* is an expletive. The verb must agree with the true subject.

17. **(C)** "Ten miles *seems*———" A plural noun of extent, when considered as a unit, takes a singular verb.

18. **(C)** "Some of the electrical equipment *was* removed———" The indefinite pronoun *some* may take either singular or plural verbs, depending on the sense. In this sentence, since *equipment* is singular, the verb must be singular. The verb is plural in the sentence "Some of the radios were removed owing to the threat of fire." since *radios* is plural.

19. **(C)** "———at *John's* being here." The meaning of the sentence is not that I was surprised at John, but rather that I was surprised at his presence, at his being here. When a noun appears before a gerund (an --*ing* form of a verb, used as a noun) it takes the possessive case (*John's* being here).

20. **(B)** "Because of your neglectfulness, this business———" *Neglectfulness* and *heedlessness* are synonyms.

21. **(A)** "It has taken me several days *to get the knack of* driving." *To get the hang of* is a colloquial expression meaning *to get the knack of*.

22. **(D)** No errors.

23. **(B)** "————had found a mutually acceptable arrangement————" *Mutually acceptable* means *satisfactory to both parties*.

24. **(D)** No errors.

25. **(A)** "————a substantial pay *increase*." *Boost* used in this way is slang for *increase*.

26. **(D)** No errors.

27. **(B)** "————will be joined tomorrow afternoon." *Joined* means put or brought together.

28. **(D)** No errors.

29. **(A)** "————for the *exchange* of war prisoners." *To swap* is colloquial for *to exchange*.

30. **(A)** "The coach *lavished* praise————" *To languish* is to become weak or to pine. *To lavish* is to give generously or liberally.

31. **(D)** No errors.

32. **(C)** "The news today *is*————" Some nouns like news, measles, and summons, although plural in form, are singular in meaning and take singular verbs.

33. **(C)** "————I usually *rise* at daybreak————" *To rise* is an intransitive verb. (I *rise* at daybreak.) *To raise* is a transitive verb. (I *raise* hamsters.)

34. **(C)** "George and *I* built Robert's new house————" George built the house, and *I* (not myself) built the house. Therefore, George and I built the house. Compound personal pronouns (himself, myself, themselves, etc.) are used only reflexively (John hit himself) and emphatically (Mary made the blouse herself), never in place of personal pronouns.

35. **(B)** "————a *fair* decision." *Fair* and *equitable* are synonyms.

TEST VI. SENTENCE CORRECTION

1. **(A)** is correct. The emphasis in this sentence is on *him,* not on *buying* which is a participle modifying *him*. Therefore, *his* (B), the possessive form, which is used when the pronoun precedes a *gerund,* is wrong. (C) is wrong, because the object of a preposition (*of*) takes the objective case (*him*), not the nominative case (*he*). (D) suggests that *I* was buying the rifle. (E) changes the meaning of the original sentence.

2. **(E)** is correct. (A) and (B) put the principal statement in a subordinate clause. *So* is used colloquially in (B). (C) is awkward and (D) is wordy.

3. **(C)** is correct. The idioms are *in search of* and *a position as*.

4. **(B)** is correct. In (A), (C), and (D), the *shirt* hurries to the office. (E) changes the meaning of the original sentence.

5. **(E)** is correct. (A) contains a sentence fragment. (B) and (C) imply that *father*, not the *check*, is to cover the expenses. (D) shifts the focus of the sentence from *father* to *expenses*.

6. **(C)** is correct. In a *neither . . . nor* construction, the verb (*appeal*) agrees with the subject of *nor* (Elizabethans). (A) and (B) violate this rule. (D) uses the unacceptable *neither . . . or*. (E) is a run-on sentence.

7. **(B)** Florence was *just as* surprised by your gift *as* by my gift. Choices (C), (D), and (E) do not follow this idiom. The expression *as you gave her* (A) omits too much of the original thought to be clear.

8. **(E)** is correct. (A), (B), (C), and (D) all lack parallel structure. (C) also changes the meaning of the original sentence.

9. **(A)** is correct. It is unnecessary to use expressions like *the foregoing types* and *have the property of*, since the thought can be expressed quite simply as in (A). Choices (B), (C), and (E), then, are wordy. Choice (D) is meaningless.

10. **(A)** is correct. Not a *where* clause, but a *that* clause can be used as a predicate noun. Choices (B) and (C) are therefore wrong. According to (D) the plant itself is making the rubber. The expression *to the effect*, in Choice (E), is unnecessary and confusing.

11. **(D)** *Risen* is the past participle of the intransitive verb *to rise*, which means to move from a lower position to a higher; *rose* is the past tense form of the same verb. *Raised* is the past tense form of the transitive verb *to raise*, which means to make upright. (B) and (E) are not acceptable forms of either verb.

12. **(A)** is correct. *Being as, being that, being as how*, and *seeing as how* are illiterate expressions for *because, since*, or *seeing as*.

13. **(B)** is correct. A pronoun in apposition (*me*) takes the case of its antecedent (*youngest*). Since *youngest* is the object of the preposition *to*, the pronoun takes the objective case. Use of *myself* in this sentence would be colloquial. Choice (D) changes the meaning of the original sentence.

14. **(C)** is correct. Choices (A), (B), and (E) do not mention the *profession* or *career* to which they refer. Choice (D) is wordy.

15. **(E)** is correct. Choices (A) and (B) mix two idioms: Hitler *had no hesitation in using force* and Hitler *did not hesitate to use force.* (C) and (D) wrongly substitute *in* or *to the use of force* for *in using force.*

16. **(A)** is correct. The phrase *in talking with Henry* must modify *I.* Choices (C), (D), and (E) are wrong for this reason. (B) and (C) contain colloquialisms (*found out* and *leaked out*).

17. **(B)** is correct. (A) and (D) are sentence fragments. (C) changes the meaning of the original sentence: the fact that the man wore a corded edge to his waistcoat is one of the two ways in which he showed his vanity. In Choice (E), *sober dressing,* not he, seems to be *exhibiting vanity.*

18. **(E)** is correct. This sentence requires parallel construction, which is lacking in choices (A), (B), and (C). Choice (D) changes the meaning of the original sentence.

19. **(C)** is correct. Choices (A) and (D) are awkward. *Grabbing at* something, as in (B), is different from *grabbing* it. Choice (E) shifts the focus from *we* to *fear.*

20. **(E)** is correct. Choices (A), (C), and (D) combine classes which are not parallel (*musicians, science, architecture*). (B) lacks parallel structure.

21. **(C)** is correct. *With whom I come into contact* and *high in respect of intelligence* are roundabout expressions.

22. **(B)** is correct. A *because* clause is always adverbial, and cannot be used in place of a noun clause beginning with *that.* Therefore, (A), (C), and (E) are incorrect. (D) is awkward.

23. **(D)** The past participle of the verb *to shrink* is *shrunk. Shrink* is the present form, *shrank* the past form.

24. **(A)** The construction is *neither . . . nor.* Choice (C) wrongly uses *or.* Choice (B) changes the meaning of the original sentence. Choice (D) is wordy. Choice (E) is wrong because similar parts of speech do not follow *neither* and *nor* (*neither can, nor hear*).

25. **(B)** The predicate nominative of a sentence takes the nominative case (*he*). *Himself* is colloquial here, and *his own self* and *his self* are illiterate.

TEST VII. VALIDITY OF CONCLUSION

(A) the statement proves the result;
(B) the statement tends to affirm the result but does not prove it;
(C) the statement disproves the result;
(D) the statement tends to weaken the result but does not disprove it;
(E) the statement is irrelevant to the result.

1. **(B)** This statement reinforces the conclusion. It is true that Smith might not have spoken to his friend during this period, or even if he had, the friend might not have told him anything about the silver, but at least the possibility of getting inside information existed.

2. **(B)** As in question 1, we can at least make the inference that Smith had access to the information of the silver strike even though this inference may be rebuttable.

3. **(E)** The key question is, "Did Smith have access to TGG information concerning a silver strike?" The fact that he is a geologist does not imply that he had access to TGG's inside information.

4. **(A)** This statement proves that Smith knew of information not generally available to the public.

5. **(D)** Smith might have bought the stock by chance while having no inside information.

6. **(E)** The best response to this statement is, "So what," unless of course Smith was related to a TGG employee or knew one of the relatives. However, the statement doesn't give us these facts.

7. **(D)** If Smith had known of the silver strike, it is logical to assume that he would have held onto the stock. Nevertheless a guilty conscience might have caused Smith to sell the stock before the price went up, thus we cannot say that this statement definitely disproves the conclusion.

8. **(E)** Based on the facts given, we have no reason to believe that TGG's creditors knew of the silver strike.

9. **(D)** Smith might have been a poor trader, but knowing that there was silver on the land, he was wise enough to later buy TGG stock. However, this is only a remote possibility, and under most circumstances his action would weaken the conclusion.

10. **(B)** We have no way of knowing that the TGG geologists were referring to the silver strike in question, but since they might have been, this statement reinforces the conclusion.

11. **(B)** Smith might have become suspicious that there were good reasons for TGG to increase its mining activities.

12. **(D)** The possibility exists that Smith might have bought the TGG stock for reasons other than inside information.

13. **(E)** Just because silver prices might rise doesn't mean that Smith knew of TGG's silver strike.

14. **(B)** This statement reinforces the conclusion because it appears that Mrs. Susanna knew that she had something to hide.

15. **(B)** There is proof of Mrs. Susanna's contradictory statements and thus an inference, even if a weak one, that George knew of the drugs.

16. **(E)** Billy Elders is not tied to George by a marital bond and there is no reason, based on this statement alone, that George should have known of the marijuana.

17. **(B)** The statement tends to prove that Billy knew George and the ambiguous favor mentioned might have been related to drugs.

18. **(D)** George's profession, even if he is a minister, should not be used to discover the truth of the matter, but it at least weakens any assumption that he would knowingly transport drugs.

19. **(A)** Only if Billy unsuccessfully tried to hide the marijuana from the others might this mean that the others knew of the marijuana.

20. **(E)** This statement does not relate to the importance of transporting marijuana.

21. **(B)** If someone uses a vehicle, a reasonable man might assume that it is done with the owner's permission. And if the use was frequently to transport drugs, it may be reasonable to assume that the owner knew of this use.

22. **(D)** There appears to be an attempt to conceal the marijuana from the others by Billy Elders. Nevertheless, this by itself does not mean that George did not know of the marijuana's existence.

23. **(E)** George might have had independent knowledge of the marijuana and therefore it is irrelevant whether George's daughter knew of its existence.

24. **(B)** If George knew how marijuana smelled there might be reason to believe that George knew that he was transporting marijuana.

25. **(D)** It does not seem reasonable that someone would knowingly transport strangers, carrying drugs, across a border.

26. **(E)** There is no relation between Tenetur's drunken driving in the past and operating a ship negligently. After all, the Captain might have been operating the ship. Tenetur's drunken driving is too remote from the accident to be relevant.

27. **(B)** Statistical evidence might prove that MVP was lax in enforcing safety standards on its ships.

28. **(B)** As in 27, statistical evidence might also show certain laxities for a specific class of ships.

29. **(B)** If the weather was clear there seems little reason to assume other causes for the accident except carelessness. Nevertheless, the statement made by the *Nantucket Daily Whale* may be in error. The answer to this question would be (A) if we were told that, in fact, the weather was clear on the day of the accident.

30. **(D)** At least some care in maintenance has been evidenced by MVP.

31. **(D)** If the shoals were not clearly marked on any navigation chart, then it would be unreasonable to assume that Nemo or the crew should know of their existence. However, this does not mean that the ship wasn't operated negligently independent of their knowledge.

32. **(A)** Using a nearsighted crewman for bow watch is negligent in and of itself.

33. **(D)** Nemo's past careful conduct would seem to imply future careful conduct. The answer to this question is different from the answer to question 26 because the conduct in question is of a similar nature.

34. **(B)** If there is evidence that the crew was inexperienced, this might be construed to imply that they were also negligent.

35. **(E)** It is reasonable for senior officers to take turns at the helm while the others rest, and Tenetur might have been operating the ship carefully.

36. **(D)** There is evidence of careful operation of the ship in the ship's log. However, this information might not be accurate.

37. **(A)** Since the recorder was in perfect working order, there appears to be clear evidence of negligence in the ship's operation.

38. **(D)** The accident might have been caused by means other than negligence in maintenance of the ship or in the actions of the crew.

39. **(B)** The answer to this question is not (A) since we do not know whether or not any qualified females applied for the job. Nevertheless, this fact may provide some evidence of discrimination.

40. **(B)** We have independent reason to believe that certain females are qualified for executive positions in this industry.

41. **(D)** We have independent evidence to believe that there is some good reason for not employing females in top decision making positions in this industry.

42. **(B)** We have reason to believe that women clerical workers were discriminated against. However, the women might have requested that they not have to put in much overtime.

43. **(E)** The activities of these executives, unrelated to the corporation, do not mean that the corporation was discriminating.

44. **(B)** There is evidence of discriminatory promotion practices. However, we do not know whether or not nine workers is a statistically significant number.

45. **(D)** The reason for the lack of female executives in MCP may be that not enough qualified females have applied for the jobs.

46. **(B)** This does not seem to be an appropriate question to ask of a job applicant.

47. **(E)** This is an independent action performed by the President, not during working hours, and while under the influence of alcohol. The statement is also ambiguous and therefore potentially misleading.

48. **(D)** There appears to be a scarcity of female executive talent for MCP to call upon to fill its executive positions.

49. **(C)** This statement strongly implies that MCP was an equal opportunity employer.

50. **(A)** This bylaw is discriminatory in and of itself.

TEST VIII. PRACTICAL JUDGMENT

DATA EVALUATION

(A) means that the Conclusion is a Major Objective;
(B) means that the Conclusion is a Major Factor;
(C) means that the Conclusion is a Minor Factor;
(D) means that the Conclusion is a Major Assumption;
(E) means that the Conclusion is an Unimportant Issue.

1. **(E)** This is unimportant because it is the same for each of the alternatives.

2. **(D)** This is a major assumption on which the decision to make a $10 million investment is based. If earnings fail to increase, the company will be hurt by the increase in its indebtedness and the dilution of its earnings per share.

3. **(A)** This is a major objective which the board is attempting to achieve by selling stock or debentures.

4. **(B)** Since the members of the management group have much of their personal wealth invested in Info-Data stock, the effect of the offering on the value of that stock is a major factor in their decision.

5. **(E)** Last year's dividends have no bearing on how the company raises new capital.

6. **(C)** The amount of stock held by insiders affects the importance they attach to dilution of earnings per share, so it is a minor factor.

7. **(D)** This is a major assumption upon which the choice between the level of interest payments and the amount of dilution will be based.

8. **(C)** The term of the debentures is a minor factor which influences the interest rate.

9. **(A)** This is one of the objectives that the board wants to accomplish by acquiring the new computer.

10. **(A)** This is given as one of the basic goals of the company's management.

11. **(B)** This is the major factor that will be balanced against dilution in deciding among the alternatives.

12. **(E)** The sources of Info-Data's revenues are irrelevant to the decision on how to raise funds.

13. **(E)** This has no influence on the question of how to raise capital.

14. **(B)** This determines the amount of capital required which is a major factor in deciding how it should be raised.

15. **(C)** This is a minor factor which affects the major factor of the interest rate on the debentures.

16. **(A)** This is one of the results which management wants to achieve by replacing the computers.

17. **(C)** This is a minor factor which will affect the interest rate on the debentures.

18. **(D)** This is a major assumption made by the board before it considers the alternative means of raising capital.

DATA APPLICATION

19. **(B)** In order to raise $10 million, Info-Data must sell 400,000 new shares at $25 each. Before the offering, the insiders owned 20% of 2 million or 400,000 shares. After the offering, they would be holding 400,000 out of 2,400,000 shares or 17%.

20. **(D)** This year, earnings after interest are $8 million − $2.4 million in interest = $5.6 million. If earnings grow at 8%, the lowest predicted rate, then next year earnings will be $8.64 million, but interest payments will increase by $900,000 (9% of $10 million). Hence, earnings after interest will be $5.3 million, which is a decrease of $300,000.

21. **(C)** To raise $10 million, 10,000 convertible debentures must be issued, each of which would be converted to 30 common shares for a total of 300,000 shares, 3/4 of the 400,000 shares that the company must sell at $25 to raise the same amount.

22. **(A)** Since interest on the debentures must be paid regardless of Info-Data's earnings, the directors would be reluctant to undertake such an obligation if the earnings were not likely to increase by more than the interest payments. Choices (B) and (C) both imply a lower interest rate on the debentures, so the board would find debentures more attractive. Choice (D) makes the sale of stock less attractive and choice (E) is irrelevant.

23. **(C)** Holders of convertible debentures can be expected to exercise their conversion right when the price of Info-Data stock is higher than 1/30 of $1,000 or $33.33. The stock is now selling for between $26 and $28, so the conversion value of the debentures is about 25% higher than the current market price. Dr. Newman projected a maximum growth rate of 13%, so it will take at least 2 years for earnings and the stock price to increase by 25%.

24. **(E)** The lower conversion ratio is equivalent to a higher price for the stock. 20 shares for a $1,000 debenture means a conversion value of $50 per share. This higher conversion value makes it less likely that debenture owners will exercise their conversion right, hence they will demand more than the 8% interest rate that they would take if the ratio were 30 to 1, so (II) can be inferred. Similarly, the insiders who are concerned about dilution will prefer debentures which have less chance of being converted (IV). Therefore, (E) is correct.

25. **(D)** is correct because the insiders' preference for paying higher interest rather than offering convertible debentures means that they wish to assume the risk that the earnings growth will be less than the fixed interest charges, rather than sacrifice the opportunity for an increase in the stock price resulting from greater earnings spread over the same number of shares. There is nothing in the passage to support any of the other choices.